# POUDRE CANYON
## ROCK CLIMBING GUIDE
### 3RD EDITION

BY BENNETT SCOTT

Jason Tarry on the Poudre Falls testpiece **The Albatross**\*\*\*\* **14a**   Photo: Jesse Levine

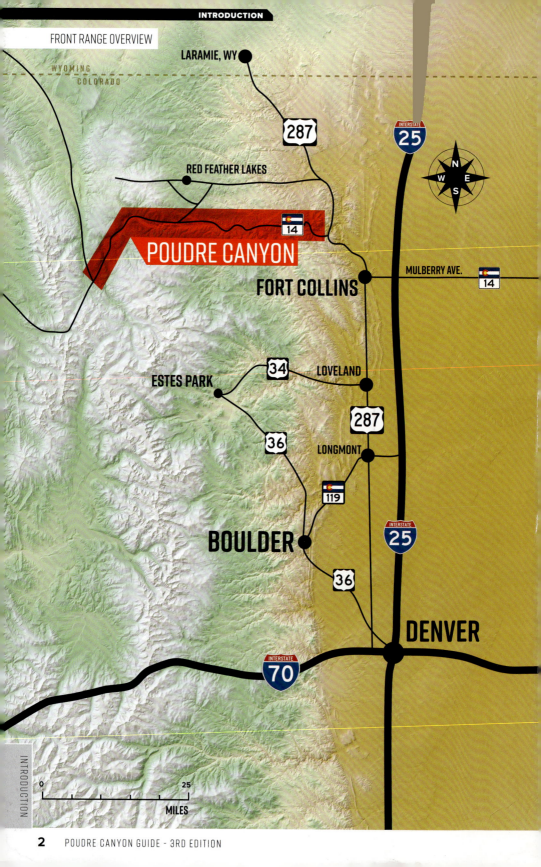

# INTRODUCTION

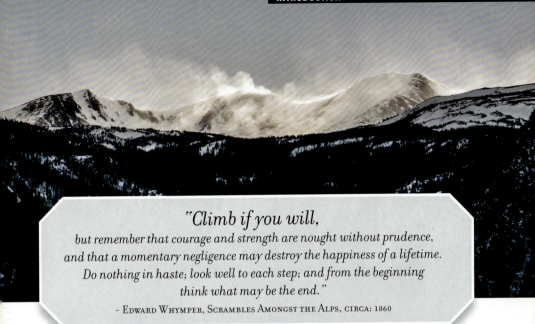

> *"Climb if you will,*
> *but remember that courage and strength are nought without prudence,*
> *and that a momentary negligence may destroy the happiness of a lifetime.*
> *Do nothing in haste; look well to each step; and from the beginning*
> *think what may be the end."*
>
> – Edward Whymper, Scrambles Amongst the Alps, circa 1860

**WARNING: Climbing is an inherently dangerous activity that may result in serious injury or death. Read this before you use this guide.**

The author and publisher cannot verify the accuracy of information presented in this guide including, but not limited to approach or descent routes, problem/route descriptions and/or ratings, maps, directions, access information, property boundaries, or management regulations.

This guide is a compilation of information from a variety of sources. Although the author painstakingly researched the information he provided, it is impossible for him to give first hand knowledge of all the routes presented. In addition, translating route descriptions can be difficult, so errors will occur. Always use your best judgment, and back off if a route seems overly dangerous.

Regardless of the rating, a climbing mishap can result in injury or death. We assume no responsibility for the safety of those who use this guidebook. If you are not an experienced and proficient climber, seek instruction before climbing.

Do not attempt climbing without proper equipment and training. In addition, this guide should not be used as an instructional manual. Information presented in this guide is based on opinions and should not be relied on for personal safety. The author and publisher assume no responsibility in the event of injury or death. Do not use this guidebook if you are unwilling to assume total responsibility for your safety.

THE AUTHOR AND PUBLISHER MAKE NO WARRANTY, WHETHER EXPRESSED OR IMPLIED, THAT THE INFORMATION PRESENTED HEREIN IS ACCURATE. FURTHERMORE, THERE ARE NO WARRANTIES OF MERCHANTABILITY OR FITNESS FOR A PARTICULAR PURPOSE. THE USER ASSUMES ALL RISKS ASSOCIATED WITH THE USE OF THIS GUIDE.

### COPYRIGHT NOTICE

"Poudre Canyon Rock Climbing Guide, Third Edition" by Bennett Scott
2018 © 2018 Fixed Pin Publishing, LLC. All rights reserved.
2018 © Bennett Scott. All rights reserved.

No part of this book may be reproduced in any form by any electronic or mechanical means (including photocopying, recording, or information storage and retrieval) without permission in writing from the author or Fixed Pin Publishing, except for reading and browsing those portions made available via the World Wide Web. No part of this book, in any physical or electronic medium, may be distributed or re-purposed without permission in writing from the author or Fixed Pin Publishing.

ISBN#: 978-0-9895156-9-6
Printed in China
Photos © Bennett Scott 2018, © Cameron Cross 2010 unless otherwise noted.

COVER PHOTO: Ian Dory on one of the crux moves of **Cradle of Liberty**\*\*\*\* **13c** at Boston Peak   Photo: Andy Cross

Craig DeMartino pulling hard on one of the best 5.12s in the canyon, **Tailspin\*\*\* 12b**  Photo: Cam Maier/Bearcam Media

# TABLE OF CONTENTS

## POUDRE CANYON
### ROCK CLIMBING GUIDE
#### 3RD EDITION

### INTRODUCTION                                      7
- About Fort Collins ......................................... 7
- About the Poudre Canyon............................ 9
- How to Climb Year Round ........................ 11
- Overview Map............................................. 12
- Climbing History......................................... 14
- What's in a Route Description? ............... 17
- Author's Note ............................................. 19
- Meet Some Locals...................................... 21

### LOWER CANYON                                    31
- Picnic Rock.................................................. 33
- French Arête / Mike's Roof....................... 35
- Happy Hour Crag ....................................... 39
- Poudre Practice Rock................................. 42
- Greyrock...................................................... 43
- Pine Vu Area ............................................... 47
- Brink's Rock ................................................ 51
- Triple Tier Areas......................................... 55
- Crystal Wall ................................................ 63
- Palace .......................................................... 69
- Stove Prairie Road ..................................... 82

### NARROWS                                              85
- Widowmakers / Electric Ocean ................ 87
- Colors Crag ................................................. 97
- The Keep ..................................................... 99
- Ra's Buttress Area.................................... 101
- Sheep Mountain ....................................... 105
- Narrows Blocs........................................... 135
- Ice Canyon ................................................ 145
- The Trough ............................................... 149
- Eden Area ................................................. 151
- Twilight Area ............................................ 153
- Snake Eyes Walls ..................................... 161
- Supercollider / Solar Panel ..................... 165
- The Beach / Last Turn Crag.................... 169
- Mountain Park Boulder ........................... 174
- Iceland ...................................................... 175
- Grandpa's Bridge ..................................... 179

### WEST OF RUSTIC                                 183
- Hatchery Boulder Area ............................ 185
- Pearl Area ................................................. 187
- Critical Mass Area .................................... 192
- Turtle Crag ............................................... 193
- Roaring Creek Boulder ............................ 197
- Bliss State Wildlife Area (S.W.A.) ........... 199
- Bog Area ................................................... 201
- Prione ....................................................... 211
- Vista Crag.................................................. 217
- 420 Boulders ............................................ 219
- Boston Peak.............................................. 233
- Black Boulder Area .................................. 239
- Merlin Boulder ......................................... 243
- Pearl Necklace Area................................. 245
- Gandalf Area ............................................ 247
- Poudre Falls ............................................. 257
- Bristlecone Castle .................................... 281

Andy Abalera on the final moves of **Big Black Moose**\*\*\* **12b**   Photo: Bennett Scott

# WELCOME TO
# FORT COLLINS

Fort Collins is a vibrant, friendly city of 164,000 tucked against the foothills of the Rocky Mountains in Northern Colorado. The city boasts a lively arts and cultural scene, shopping in historic Old Town, a strong economy, and is a haven for outdoor enthusiasts. Boasting a mild climate, thriving high-tech industry, and some of the best microbreweries in the world, it's no wonder Fort Collins annually ranks among the most livable small cities in the United States.

##  GYMS

Fort Collins is blessed with two excellent training facilities. Ascent Studio is the powerhouse in town, providing the only stand alone climbing gym in town. But Miramont/Genesis is a close second, if you're looking for a quieter environment with quality setting and other gym related activities.

**ASCENT STUDIO**
2150 Joseph Allen Dr ➤ (970) 999-5596

**MIRAMONT / GENESIS**
1800 Heath Pkwy ➤ (970) 221-5000

## GEAR

These are the best three locations to find quality climbing gear in town. Jax and Ascent are both local businesses so please support them first if possible.

**ASCENT STUDIO**
2150 Joseph Allen Dr ➤ (970) 999-5596

**JAX OUTDOOR GEAR**
1200 N College Ave ➤ (970) 221-0544

**R.E.I.**
4025 S College Ave ➤ (970) 223-0123

## CAMPING IN FORT COLLINS

Fort Collins is limited as far as camping options. Best bet is to find a couch to crash on or a place to park your sweet Sprinter van. Both of the KOA options are nice, but a bit far from town. Horsetooth Reservoir and Lory State Park also have camping options.

**LAKESIDE KOA**
1910 Lakeside Resort Ln ➤ (970) 484-9880

**POUDRE CANYON KOA**
6670 North US Highway 287 ➤ (970) 493-9758

## INTRODUCTION

## RESTAURANTS

There are a crazy amount of restaurants per capita in Fort Collins. Every style, genre and price point is represented across our little town. This is a list of a few of my favorite spots to get some good grub before or after a climbing day.

**CHOICE CITY BUTCHER & DELI**
104 W Olive St ➤ (970) 490-2489

**CREPERIE & FRENCH BAKERY OF FORT COLLINS**
2722 S College Ave ➤ (970) 224-2640

**LA LUZ - MEXICAN FARE**
200 Walnut Street ➤ (970) 493-1129

**MOE'S ORIGINAL BAR-B-QUE**
181 N College Ave ➤ (970) 482-7675

**NICK'S ITALIAN**
1100 S College Ave ➤ (970) 631-8301

**SNOOZE AN A.M. EATERY**
144 W Mountain Ave ➤ (970) 482-9253

**STAR OF INDIA**
2900 Harvard St ➤ (970) 225-1740

**SUSHI JEJU**
238 S College Ave ➤ (970) 416-7733

## BREWERIES

Beer and craft brewing are synonymous with Fort Collins. Starting in the late '80s, powerhouses of the craft brewing world were born here like Odell Brewing and New Belgium Brewing. The crystal clear water that pours out of the Poudre Canyon has long been associated with the high quality of the beer in Fort Collins. There are over 25 licensed breweries in town to choose from, but here are a few of my faves.

**EQUINOX BREWING**
133 Remington St ➤ (970) 484-1368

**HORSE & DRAGON BREWING**
124 Racquette Dr ➤ (970) 631-8038

**NEW BELGIUM BREWING**
500 Linden St ➤ (970) 221-0524

**ODELL BREWING COMPANY**
1800 E Lincoln Ave ➤ (970) 498-9070

**SNOWBANK BREWING**
225 N Lemay Ave Suite 1 ➤ (970) 999-5658

## OTHER CLIMBING AREAS

Fort Collins has a bunch of other climbing options beside the Poudre Canyon. Check out **nococlimbing.org** for more info.

**HORSETOOTH RESERVOIR • LORY STATE PARK • HORSETOOTH ROCK • CARTER LAKE • RED FEATHER LAKES**

# Archer's
## Poudre River Resort

**OPEN YEAR ROUND**
Located 33 Miles Up The Canyon From Ted's Place

Country Store for all your last minute climbing day needs!
Free Internet Connection • Beer, Wine & Spirits • Cabin Rentals
Tent Sites • Food, Snacks & Water • Poudre Canyon Grill

We love Rock Climbers!

**970.881.2139**
Toll Free: 888.822.0588
poudreriverresort.com

33021 Poudre Canyon Highway
Bellvue, Colorado 80512

Our resort offers you studio, one and two bedroom log cabins, full service R/V sites and tent sites. Premium Showers and Hot Tub with sites located right on the river.

Our Country Store carries food, snacks, water, camping equipment & Poudre Canyon Memorabilia. Grab a Burger and Frys during the warmer months at our Poudre Canyon Grill

## INTRODUCTION

### ALL THE BETA YOU NEED FOR THE
# POUDRE CANYON

### BY THE NUMBERS

**806 ROUTES** IN TOTAL

|  |  |
|---|---|
| 5.7 | 50 |
| 5.8 | 42 |
| 5.9 | 69 |
| 5.10 | 197 |
| 5.11 | 235 |
| 5.12 | 163 |
| 5.13 | 45 |
| 5.14 | 5 |

**434 BOULDER** PROBLEMS IN TOTAL

|  |  |
|---|---|
| v0-v2 | 53 |
| v3-v4 | 117 |
| v5-v6 | 91 |
| v7-v8 | 93 |
| v9-v10 | 59 |
| v11-Above | 21 |

Cache La Poudre Canyon runs for about 50 miles starting near Bellvue Colorado and runs all the way up to Cameron Pass. Initially settled by the Ute Indian Nation its name comes from French settlers using the canyon to "Stash their gun powder". It is one of the few rivers in the country with a Wild and Scenic designation from the Bureau of Land Management. Most of the canyon is within the Canyon Lakes Ranger District of the Roosevelt National Forest but some portions are also under Dept. of Wildlife (DOW) management. Below you will find everything else you need to know as a climber visiting the canyon.

## FOOD & SUPPLIES

There aren't a lot of options for food in the canyon, but enough to get you by.

**TED'S PLACE** ➤ 0.0 Miles
Basically just a gas station, bathrooms, meet-up spot

**MISHAWAKA AMPHITHEATRE** ➤ 13.7 Miles
World famous music venue, full menu, bar on the River

**GLEN ECHO RESORT** ➤ 31.4 Miles
Full menu including breakfast, full Bar, general Store

**ARCHER'S RESORT** ➤ 33.0 Miles
General store, liquor store, Canyon Grill in the summer

## CAMPING IN THE CANYON

There are many pay camping options throughout the canyon during the warmer months. Most of these sites are maintained by the Forest Service. You can find more info at Recreation.gov, look under the Arapaho & Roosevelt National Forests listings. Most sites cost in the $6-12 range and some even take online reservations. In addition there are several privately owned options scattered throughout the canyon. Archers Resort is easily one of the best and you can book your riverside camp spot at poudreriverresort.com.

Free Camping is becoming harder and harder to find as the population in Northern Colorado continues to rise. Best to befriend a local to get more details on those spots in the canyon, but the Pingree Park Road, Red Feather Lakes, and Laramie River Road are good places to start. Car camping is officially illegal in the canyon, but if you maintain a low profile, good things can happen.

## RIVER CROSSINGS

Many of the areas in the canyon require a river crossing. If you see this symbol, it means dealing with the river will be the first part of your climbing day. This can range from a pleasant ankle deep walk to a death defying experience. Assessing river depth and conditions is a learned skill, so if you are at all unsure about whether a crossing is safe or not, just change plans and go somewhere without one.

Tyroleans are not used in the canyon for a couple of reasons. There is a large boating community on the river and tyroleans can become a safety issue for them. Secondly, the river is not crossable for only 2-3 months out of the year and there are plenty of climbing area's that do not require a river crossing.

Consider investing in a pair of waders, they can be found at Jax Outdoor Gear or any other retailer who sells fishing equipment. If you don't have waders, then sandals or an old pair of tennis shoes work just fine. In the winter, the river is frozen most of the time making crossing a snap. Assessing the quality and thickness of the ice is another learned skill and should not be taken lightly. If you are concerned about the quality of the ice at all, just go somewhere without a river crossing for that climbing day.

Roy Quanstrom demonstrating the infamous "just go down to your undies" technique   Photo: B. Scott

POUDRE CANYON GUIDE - 3RD EDITION

## HIGH PARK FIRE

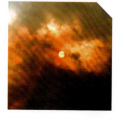

On June 9, 2012 a lightning strike started the High Park fire in a difficult to access area above the Buckhorn Road, west of Masonville, CO. The High Park fire burned over 87,284 acres (136.381 sq mi; 353.23 km²), becoming the second-largest fire in recorded Colorado history by area burned.

The fire struck a large portion of the Narrows and the Lower Poudre Canyon. Several climbing areas were hit directly but no damage to the routes has ever been found. It did create hazardous access and hiking conditions in several locations that the book describes individually.

**BEWARE OF BURNT AND UNSTABLE TREES!**
The forest is still recovering and renewing itself at many climbing areas. If it's a windy day, be on the look out for falling trees. In addition, the hillsides in the burn zones are generally unstable and have some rockfall potential, so be vigilante.

## BOLTING AND DEVELOPMENT

New routes and boulder problems continue to be found and developed in the canyon to this day. As the saying goes though, 1% of the climbing population does 99% of the work. Developing routes and boulder problems is a craft, years of experience leads to a better understanding of how to safely and ethically change the landscape for climbing. Finding a mentor or more experienced climber to show you the way is highly suggested.

Most of the hardware in the canyon is 3/8" SS wedge bolts, 1/2" SS wedge bolts or SS 5-piece bolts. Although we are in an extremely arid and dry climate, stainless is always preferred to increase the life-span of the bolt. **If you come across any bolts or anchors that are in need of replacement or repair, please contact the NCCC at nococlimbers@gmail.com.**

## FIXED CARABINERS
### FOR LOWERING OFF SPORT CLIMBS

Many of the climbs in the canyon are slowly becoming equipped with fixed carabiners at the anchor stations. If you come across fixed carabiners: **First do a quick check to make sure they are not overly worn and sharp. Second clip your rope directly into them and lower to the ground, no need to clean them.** Cleaning anchors is one of the most hazardous parts of roped climbing. Communication errors, simple mistakes and belayer error have ended in numerous accidents and deaths. The NCCC is committed to managing these carabiners as they become worn and will continue to update them. BUT if you find a worn carabiner, make the sacrifice and donate a fresh one of your own to the cause. Please use your own draws for top-roping and only lower off the fixed carabiners.

## 💩 WASTE DISPOSAL

More people, more poop as the saying goes. Disposing of your waste is a crucial part of being in the mountains. Keeping a sturdy garden trowel with you is a perfect way to dig a cat-hole and bury your waste. Wag Bags are another great option to bring your waste out of the woods. Don't go to the bathroom within 100 yards of a water source or a parking area. There are lots of public bathroom options in the canyon; when in doubt, get in the car and find one of those.

## DOGS

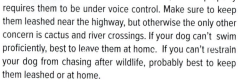

I am very biased when its comes to this subject. I have dogs, my friends have dogs, and our climbing crew is regularly outnumbered by dogs. Some folks don't like dogs at the crag, which is understandable...I guess. Seriously though, be aware of other folks at the crag that might not like dogs. If someone is uncomfortable, just leash them up or leave the dogs at home in the future. The canyon is a great place to go climbing with your pooch. Dogs are allowed anywhere on Forest Service land; DOW property requires them to be under voice control. Make sure to keep them leashed near the highway, but otherwise the only other concern is cactus and river crossings. If your dog can't swim proficiently, best to leave them at home. If you can't restrain your dog from chasing after wildlife, probably best to keep them leashed or at home.

## WILDLIFE

Northern Colorado is filled with a wide variety of wild life, I mean come on, it's the Rockies! In the canyon, you will frequently see bighorn sheep, mountain goats and moose. These animals will be on or near the highway so be aware and always yield to the animals. Moose are not worth messing with, take photos from a distance and give them a wide birth. Rattlesnakes are probably the only real threat to humans in the canyon. Look out for them in the Lower Canyon during the summer months. Yes, mountain lions, bears and lynx all live in the area, but consider yourself lucky if you see one, they generally have little or no interest in humans.

# HOW TO
# CLIMB YEAR ROUND
## IN THE POUDRE CANYON

The Poudre Canyon and Northern Colorado are year round climbing areas. That's a big reason why there are so many climbers on the Front Range in general. I have provided some tips and tricks for climbing everyday in every season.

USE THESE SUN/SHADE SYMBOLS IN THE BOOK TO STEER YOU TO WARM OR COOL CLIMBING CONDITIONS.

### SPRING - MARCH ➤ MAY

Winter is finally starting to pass but it's not all gone yet. Temperatures vary from the 30°s F to the mid 60°s F. The ice is all gone from the river, so you're back to wading to get across. Shaded crags are chilly but beginning to be doable again. This is generally the wettest time of year here, so you might need a rain jacket. But usually the rains only last for a short period of time. Find a dry overhang to have some lunch under; by the time you finish the rain will also have stopped and the rock will be drying back out.

**SPRING SUMMARY:** Don't run off at the first sign of rain… give it an hour or less, you will probably be back on the rock again soon.

### SUMMER - JUNE ➤ AUGUST

The river is raging and the heat has come back to town. This is about the only time of year where climbing in the Lower Canyon and the Narrows is pretty tough, depending on your heat tolerance. Most climbers stick to the West of Rustic areas during these months. Chasing shade is still a good idea. Bouldering can be rough for the harder grades, but higher altitude spots like Bristlecone Castle, Gandalf and Poudre Falls can be doable.

**SUMMER SUMMARY:** Chase shade and try to not climb in direct sunlight. Climb in the mornings and late afternoons. Chilling by the river during the middle of the day is probably more fun than trying to climb on the really hot days. Don't try to cross the river until late-July.

### FALL - SEPTEMBER ➤ NOVEMBER

SEND-tember and ROCK-tober have finally come. Largely considered the best time to climb anywhere in the northern hemisphere of planet Earth. Northern Colorado is no exception: sunny days with cool breezes, autumnal leaves exploding in color, and the time has come to send your project! September is usually hot so you're probably still chasing shade. October is sublime, climb every darn day you can. November is excellent too, but by the end of November we start getting occasional snow fall and that darn icy cold wind starts blowing again.

**FALL SUMMARY:** Embrace the most heavenly time of year for climbers. Play hookie, skip class, call in sick…whatever it takes … you should go climbing a lot.

### WINTER - DECEMBER ➤ FEBRUARY

Winter is one of the best times for climbing in the canyon. Most people can't fathom the idea of climbing in the colder months, but it's simply not cold if you know where to go. The river crossings are usually all ice, which makes crossing the river a snap.

Cold finger tips can be remedied using "Hot Rocks". A technique developed and perfected by Dan Yager, it involves a specially lined (plumber's tape) chalk bag and heating small round stones on a stove. This technique has allowed people to comfortably sport climb in sub-30°F weather.

Another trap people fall into is assuming the weather in Fort Collins is the same as in the canyon. This is easily the BIGGEST misconception. Folks in the know routinely drive out of a snowy frigid Fort Collins with temps at or below 20°F to find themselves climbing in t-shirts in the canyon later that day. A good indicator from town is looking at Greyrock: if it appears devoid of snow, than there's a 90% chance that the south-facing crags in the Lower Canyon are bone-dry and sunny. When in doubt, just follow your psyche and go see what it's like up there.

**WINTER SUMMARY:** Don't assume the weather is the same in town as in the canyon. When in doubt just head up there and see. If all hope is lost, you can at least go on a hike and get some fresh air.

# POUDRE CANYON - OVERVIEW

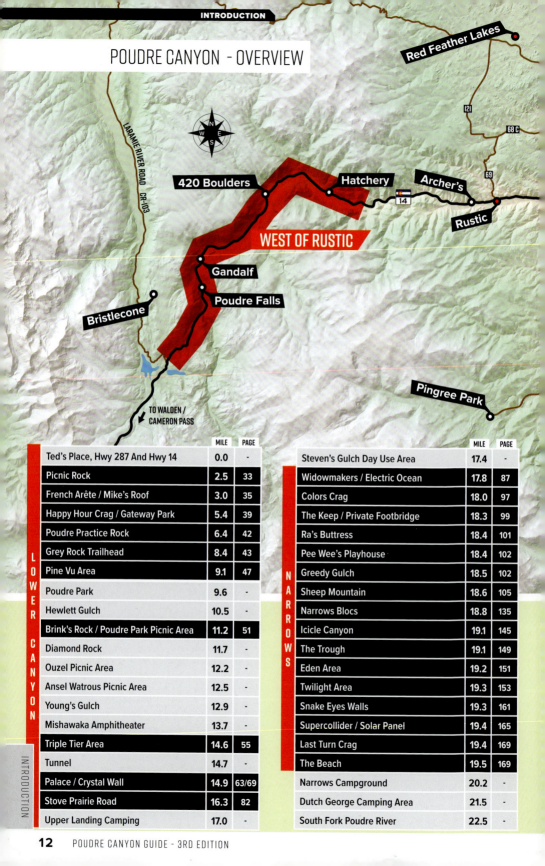

| | MILE | PAGE |
|---|---|---|
| Ted's Place, Hwy 287 And Hwy 14 | 0.0 | - |
| Picnic Rock | 2.5 | 33 |
| French Arête / Mike's Roof | 3.0 | 35 |
| Happy Hour Crag / Gateway Park | 5.4 | 39 |
| Poudre Practice Rock | 6.4 | 42 |
| Grey Rock Trailhead | 8.4 | 43 |
| Pine Vu Area | 9.1 | 47 |
| Poudre Park | 9.6 | - |
| Hewlett Gulch | 10.5 | - |
| Brink's Rock / Poudre Park Picnic Area | 11.2 | 51 |
| Diamond Rock | 11.7 | - |
| Ouzel Picnic Area | 12.2 | - |
| Ansel Watrous Picnic Area | 12.5 | - |
| Young's Gulch | 12.9 | - |
| Mishawaka Amphitheater | 13.7 | - |
| Triple Tier Area | 14.6 | 55 |
| Tunnel | 14.7 | - |
| Palace / Crystal Wall | 14.9 | 63/69 |
| Stove Prairie Road | 16.3 | 82 |
| Upper Landing Camping | 17.0 | - |

| | MILE | PAGE |
|---|---|---|
| Steven's Gulch Day Use Area | 17.4 | - |
| Widowmakers / Electric Ocean | 17.8 | 87 |
| Colors Crag | 18.0 | 97 |
| The Keep / Private Footbridge | 18.3 | 99 |
| Ra's Buttress | 18.4 | 101 |
| Pee Wee's Playhouse | 18.4 | 102 |
| Greedy Gulch | 18.5 | 102 |
| Sheep Mountain | 18.6 | 105 |
| Narrows Blocs | 18.8 | 135 |
| Icicle Canyon | 19.1 | 145 |
| The Trough | 19.1 | 149 |
| Eden Area | 19.2 | 151 |
| Twilight Area | 19.3 | 153 |
| Snake Eyes Walls | 19.3 | 161 |
| Supercollider / Solar Panel | 19.4 | 165 |
| Last Turn Crag | 19.4 | 169 |
| The Beach | 19.5 | 169 |
| Narrows Campground | 20.2 | - |
| Dutch George Camping Area | 21.5 | - |
| South Fork Poudre River | 22.5 | - |

# INTRODUCTION

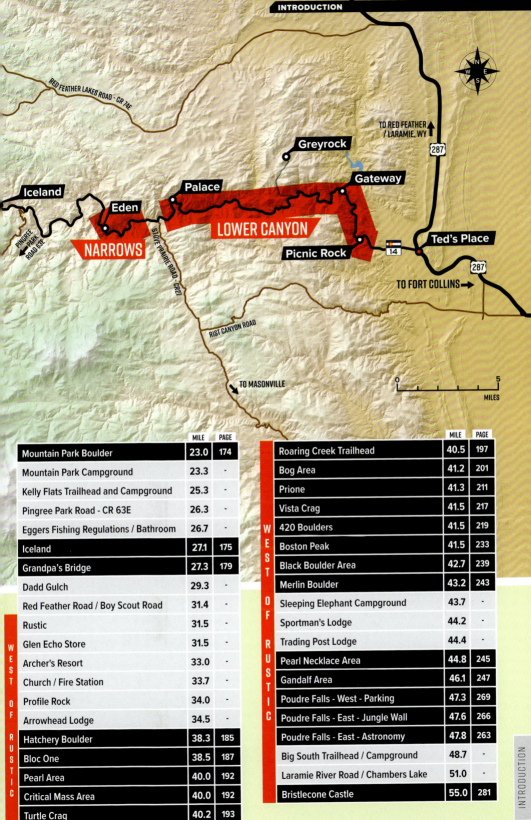

| | MILE | PAGE |
|---|---|---|
| Mountain Park Boulder | 23.0 | 174 |
| Mountain Park Campground | 23.3 | - |
| Kelly Flats Trailhead and Campground | 25.3 | - |
| Pingree Park Road - CR 63E | 26.3 | - |
| Eggers Fishing Regulations / Bathroom | 26.7 | - |
| Iceland | 27.1 | 175 |
| Grandpa's Bridge | 27.3 | 179 |
| Dadd Gulch | 29.3 | - |
| Red Feather Road / Boy Scout Road | 31.4 | - |
| Rustic | 31.5 | - |
| Glen Echo Store | 31.5 | - |
| Archer's Resort | 33.0 | - |
| Church / Fire Station | 33.7 | - |
| Profile Rock | 34.0 | - |
| Arrowhead Lodge | 34.5 | - |
| Hatchery Boulder | 38.3 | 185 |
| Bloc One | 38.5 | 187 |
| Pearl Area | 40.0 | 192 |
| Critical Mass Area | 40.0 | 192 |
| Turtle Crag | 40.2 | 193 |

| | MILE | PAGE |
|---|---|---|
| Roaring Creek Trailhead | 40.5 | 197 |
| Bog Area | 41.2 | 201 |
| Prione | 41.3 | 211 |
| Vista Crag | 41.5 | 217 |
| 420 Boulders | 41.5 | 219 |
| Boston Peak | 41.5 | 233 |
| Black Boulder Area | 42.7 | 239 |
| Merlin Boulder | 43.2 | 243 |
| Sleeping Elephant Campground | 43.7 | - |
| Sportman's Lodge | 44.2 | - |
| Trading Post Lodge | 44.4 | - |
| Pearl Necklace Area | 44.8 | 245 |
| Gandalf Area | 46.1 | 247 |
| Poudre Falls - West - Parking | 47.3 | 269 |
| Poudre Falls - East - Jungle Wall | 47.6 | 266 |
| Poudre Falls - East - Astronomy | 47.8 | 263 |
| Big South Trailhead / Campground | 48.7 | - |
| Laramie River Road / Chambers Lake | 51.0 | - |
| Bristlecone Castle | 55.0 | 281 |

# INTRODUCTION

Boston Peak

# CLIMBING HISTORY
## OF THE POUDRE CANYON

*Author's Note: Most of this history was compiled and researched by Cameron Cross for the Poudre Canyon Rock Climbing Guide Second Edition (2010).*

The Climbing History for the Poudre Canyon is long and extensive. Overshadowed by the climbing mecca of Boulder, CO, the canyon was often considered un-worthy or a waste of time. A lot of the early climbers in the canyon assumed no one would ever repeat their climbs and that everything in the canyon was obscure. Because of this, generations of climbers began to overlap each other with no knowledge of anyone coming before them. Areas like the Palace and Greyrock have been re-written time and time again so it can be hard to nail down who was actually the first. This book does not attempt to capture all of that history 100%, but rather reference everything by its contemporary name and the most accepted history of the canyon.

The earliest climbers in the canyon were the Arapahoe, Ute and Cheyenne Indian tribes. These nomadic tribes considered the canyon a sacred place and tried to stake a reservation there to protect it from white settlers. Unfortunately, they were overruled and most were forced to move to the Wind River Reservation in central Wyoming by the 1870s.

The Poudre River was originally called the Cache La Poudre. According to legend, a group of French fur trappers were traveling north and camped along the banks near present day Laporte in the early 1800s. A snow storm hit them that night and the next day they decided to lighten their loads to make traveling in the snow easier. They decided to hide (cache) their gunpowder (la poudre) on the banks of the river and the name Cache la Poudre (hide the powder) was born.

While climbing likely began in the Poudre as early as the 1950s, the first documented ascents appeared in the late '60s and early '70s. By most accounts, ROTC Rock (now known as Picnic Rock) and Greyrock were the first areas to see climbing activity. The routes developed during this time period (primarily by Steve Allen & Rodney Ley) were climbed in ground-up style, and often focused on ascending interesting formations and features. Given that active protection (camming devices) hadn't been invented yet, pitons were a common form of protection and can still be found at various crags in the canyon as a reminder of these historic ascents.

The next wave of development stretched from the early '80s to mid '90s and was focused on Greyrock and the Narrows areas. At Greyrock in the early '80s, climbers such as Jeff Bassett, Don Braddy, Pat McGrane, Jim Brink and others began to establish bold, ground-up "Bachar" style face routes where groundfall potential was nearly always a concern and climbers were forced to be competent mentally, physically, and technically. By the mid '80s, Greyrock attracted locals including Craig Luebben, Ken Gibson, Sari Schmetterer, Steve Drake and others who began to develop more difficult, but generally better protected lines. In addition, the first bolted lines in the Psilocybin Canyon (Palace), Crystal Wall, and the Narrows began to appear in the early '90s, with Craig Luebben, Lizz Grenard, Rob Poutre, Ron Ambrose, Steve McCorkel, Vance White, Casey Rosenbach and others doing the majority of the development.

From the late '90s to the late 2000s, a third wave of development was taking over the canyon. Shifting from the bold, ground-up style of the '80s to a focus on establishing physically demanding but safely bolted routes, developers such as Derek Peavey, Tim Wilhelmi, Steve McCorkel, Judson Doyle, Ken Gibson, Sam Shannon, Bryan Beavers, Greg Martin, Paul Heyliger, Greg Hand, and others have established the majority of the popular sport climbing crags, including the Palace, Crystal Wall, Triple Tier Area, Electric Ocean, and Sheep Mountain. This group of climbers changed the game in the canyon and helped transform the area into a modern bolt protected climbing area.

A view through the Tunnel at the Triple Tier Area when the Tunnel was first constructed

# INTRODUCTION

The Narrows when the road was first built, Eve's Cave on the right and Last Turn Crag is visible in the upper left-hand corner

Previous guidebooks to the Poudre Canyon

Simultaneously there was another wave of climbing development hitting the canyon....Bouldering. The explosion of Bouldering's popularity in the United States began to hit in the early 2000s. Suddenly, bouldering was less about training for routes and more of its own pursuit and climbing style. Guys like Hank Jones, Pat Goodman, Jeremy Bisher, Ryan Anglemeyer, Tom Blackford, Francis Sanzaro, Will Lemaire, Mike Mangino, Mike Auldridge, Herm Feissner, Jay Shambo and the author began exploring the boulders West of Rustic. Iconic climbers like Mark Wilford and Scott Blunk had played on these boulders too in the decades prior but nothing like the year 2000's wave of development. Areas like the 420 Boulders, the Bog, Pearl Area and Gandalf came to light and showed the potential for bouldering the canyon had to offer.

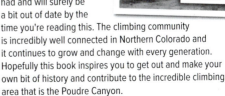

The author on the F.A. of **Swarm**\*\*\*\* v7
Circa: 2001   Photo. Pat Goodman

In 2010, Cameron Cross and myself set out to write a proper guidebook for the canyon. Spurred by some egregious errors in a certain Falcon Publishing guidebook, we had already released a digital version to refute the mistakes in the Falcon book. Then Cam was approached by Fixed Pin Publishing and an anonymous donor to create the Poudre Canyon Rock Climbing Guide Second Edition in print. This book was a non-profit venture dedicated to preserving the memory and legacy of Craig Luebben. Craig had always intended to write a Poudre Canyon guide but unfortunately passed away in a climbing accident before he could complete it. Fixed Pin Publishing and every retailer that carried the book donated their profits from the sale of the book to Giulia's (Craig's daughter) college fund. Another amazing example of the climbing community reaching out to help a fallen brother and his family.

Fast forward nearly a decade and the canyon has been anything but quiet. New routes and new boulder problems are established on a weekly basis. Entirely new climbing areas have been developed like Poudre Falls, Boston Peak, Bristlecone Castle, Narrows Blocs, Widowmakers and many many more. This book has over double the amount of routes the second edition had and will surely be a bit out of date by the time you're reading this. The climbing community is incredibly well connected in Northern Colorado and it continues to grow and change with every generation. Hopefully this book inspires you to get out and make your own bit of history and contribute to the incredible climbing area that is the Poudre Canyon.

Profile Rock

## INTRODUCTION

# THANK YOU

Creating a rock climbing guidebook is a serious labor of love. Drawing a line on a rock and sticking a name to it is probably the easiest part. Hiking the miles, asking all the right questions, knowing all the key players, stacking the cairns, swinging the pick axe, scrubbing the lichen, hanging in a harness for hours at a time, this is what makes or breaks a good guidebook. To say I could do all of this alone is ridiculous. It takes an army of people committed to a dream of telling the right story about a place close to many people's hearts. There's no way I can thank all of you, but to all of you who helped along the way, I am forever indebted.

To my two favorite people on earth, **Sue and Sam**. Thank you for understanding me when I leave to go climbing all the time. I am lucky to have you in my life and you make me a better and more well rounded human every day. This book would never have happened without my two special people supporting my passion project.
I love you!

To **Mom and Dad**, my biggest climbing sponsors since 1996! You have helped me and my family in so many ways, we are forever indebted to you. You have taught me to be a good person, a hard worker and to enjoy our limited time on this planet. I thought about you often while writing this book and I hope it is something you are proud of too.

To **Cameron Cross**, my friend and co-author of the second edition. Cam's tireless efforts researching the history of the canyon are unsurpassed. Thanks for laying the groundwork for me to build upon buddy.

EDITOR - **Elizabeth Carroll** is one of my oldest friends. She is incredibly meticulous and detail oriented. There was no question in my mind who I NEEDED to help me edit this book. Her tireless efforts made this book as polished as it is. Thanks for everything Beth... next 100 beers are on me!

PUBLISHER - **Ben Schneider and Jason Haas** were both my gurus of "guidebooking." A sea of knowledge, they helped steer this book to the format it is in today. Not only publishers, I consider both of these guys to be my brothers in the tribe of climbing.

MAPS - **Mike Boruta** did an incredible job creating custom graphics for land shading and topography on the maps.

PHOTOGRAPHERS - **Tom Bol, Rob Baker, Andy Cross, Jesse Levine, Cameron Maier, Gustavo Moser & Eric Page.** I do not consider myself a photographer, my photos are documentary with a touch of Photoshop...at best. These folks on the other hand are experts at their craft and this book would not be nearly as rad without their donations. Thanks for letting me put my awesome photos next to my "ok" ones!

*My two goof balls, Sue and Sam vacationing in Rappallo ITA*

*My Dad and I after climbing his first 14'er, Longs Peak via Keyhole*

*My Mom taking a hike at a snowy Arthur's Rock*

# INTRODUCTION

# WHAT'S IN A ROUTE DESCRIPTION?

### STAR SCALE
✹ = ★
The star scale is a way of ranking climbs by overall quality from 0 stars to 4 stars being the best climbs around. Rock quality, movement, setting, landing/base area, ease of access, safety, etc...all go into play when it comes to determining the star scale.

### GRADING SCALE
This guide uses the Yosemite Decimal System for roped rock climbs and the John "Verm" Sherman V-Scale for all the boulder problems.

**The Yosemite Decimal System (YDS)** is a three-part system used for rating the difficulty of walks, hikes, and climbs. The Class 5 portion of the scale is primarily a rock climbing classification system. The grade scale ranges from 5.0-5.15 at time of writing.

**The "V" scale,** devised by John "Vermin" Sherman at Hueco Tanks, Texas in the 1990s, is the most widely used system in North America for Bouldering. Although open-ended, the "V" system covers a range from V0 to V16.

### COLOR SYSTEM
A color coded system has been adopted in the 3rd Edition to help identify the grades you are looking for quickly. See chart at bottom of page for more details.

### ROUTE NAME
This is where most climbers unleash heaping amounts of pent up creativity. Sometimes vulgar, sometimes sweet but always telling.

### # NUMBER
This corresponds with the topo to tell you which route is which.

**38. ● Route Name** ** **12a** (# Bolts)
The description of the climb involves, rock quality, movement, hold types, where the crux is, and possibly some history about the origin of the route or boulder problem.
FA: Jane Doe

### FIRST ASCENT (F.A.)
F.A. describes the person or group of people who made the first redpoint of the climb. Someone else may have bolted the route or cleaned the boulder problem. The author has spent a painstaking amount of time to verify all of this info but it can be hard data to keep track of.

### GEAR / BOLTS / SAFETY DESCRIPTION
This portion of the description describes what equipment you will need to safely ascend the rock climb.

**BOLTS**
Sport climbs are described by the number of bolts it takes to get to an anchor. Anchors are not described in the bolt count so bring a couple extra draws as a rule.

**GEAR**
If the climb requires traditional protection it will say (GEAR). Standard rack to 3 inches is mandatory. Unusual size gear is in the description.

**ROPES**
70 Meter ropes are considered standard in the canyon. If you climb on anything less, make sure to knot the ends of your rope.

**PADS**
If the climb is a Boulder Problem it will say (Pads). If it is unusually tall or risky, it will say (4-5 Pads). But with all bouldering, use your own discretion and bring more pads if needed.

### ROUTE LINES
The topo lines in the book correspond to the line of travel the route or boulder problem takes.

**ROUTES**
Circle indicates anchor location or end of pitch

**BOULDERS**
Circle indicates approx. starting hand holds. Dashed lines indicate start and end of dyno problems.

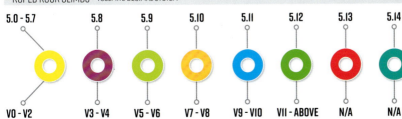

**ROPED ROCK CLIMBS** - YOSEMITE DECIMAL SYSTEM

| 5.0 - 5.7 | 5.8 | 5.9 | 5.10 | 5.11 | 5.12 | 5.13 | 5.14 | PROJECT ROUTE |
|---|---|---|---|---|---|---|---|---|
| V0 - V2 | V3 - V4 | V5 - V6 | V7 - V8 | V9 - V10 | V11 - ABOVE | N/A | N/A | PROJECT BOULDER |

**BOULDER PROBLEMS** - JOHN SHERMAN V-SCALE

The author working moves on a striking arête project at Boston Peak   Photo: A. Cross

## INTRODUCTION

## AUTHOR'S NOTE

» **BENNETT SCOTT** «

DATE OF BIRTH: **November 1979**   IDEAL CLIMBING WEIGHT: **155 lbs**
HEIGHT: **6'0"**   APE INDEX: **+4"**

The Author on **Ode To Failure** at Arthur's Rock Around 1999  Photo: Brad Jackson

I dream of huge boulders and grand cliffs that seem to be shaped by a sculptor. Endless landscapes of canyons and dense forests filled with secrets only climbers understand. I wander these places in my subconscious looking at all the possibilities. I never climb in these dreams but just wander around exploring a world that does not exist. Sometimes, it's a lush alpine tundra of flowers and waterfalls dotted with massive gray and white granite boulders. Other times, it's an endless canyon of towering walls, streaked black and white with aesthetic features hanging over me in every direction. It always feels like the same place though, a home away from home that I relish to have in the back of my mind. The dream of endless possibilities to climb and explore in a truly wondrous landscape is what I've always been hopelessly obsessed and focused on in my life.

In 1998 I moved to Fort Collins, Colorado from Bath, Ohio to start a degree in rock climbing at Colorado State University. I had been climbing for a few years by then but I was still as green as any Ohio climber. Upon arriving in Colorado, I assumed that everything had been climbed and the chances of finding new rock were pretty slim. A poor understanding of the sheer size of the Rocky Mountains coupled with an infantile understanding of the Colorado climbing community led to this failed assumption.

Those first few years in Northern Colorado were overall pretty life changing for me. Climbers like Pat Goodman, Hank Jones, Francis Sanzaro, Will Lemaire, Brad Jackson and Herm Feissner took me under their wing and showed me how to be a better climber and the potential for new routes and boulder problems that seemed to be hiding around every corner. Walking through undeveloped areas like the 420 Boulders, The Bog, Gandalf, Arthur's Rock and Red Feather Lakes are some of my fondest memories from those early years.

Fast forward 20 years and I'm still here, just as psyched as ever with a seemingly never-ending list of projects to throw myself at or develop from a blank canvas. The climbing community has changed and evolved just like they all do, but there are a lot of locals like me who never left and never intend to.

My goal for this book is to document the development the canyon has had over the last eight years and to show what the current climbing community is motivated on. Not to shed the past though, all climbers stand on the shoulders of those who preceded them. We have built upon the foundations our local legends put in place and brought the canyon to a higher level of quality and difficulty that was never dreamed of before.

I am not much of a social media person, something about sharing things all the time bothers me. But here I am, sharing and spraying the Poudre encyclopedia in my head from the last 20 years. Guidebooks are a time-stamp, a stopping point. As the author, you make a subjective decision about what's relevant and what isn't. This is my interpretation of that, take it or leave it, good or bad.

I hope you enjoy this book and it motivates you to explore the canyon and push your own limits as a climber. Chances are, we will run into each other and I hope you will be having as much fun as I always do.

## TOP 5 - BOULDERS
FAVORITE OR MOST MEMORABLE IN THE POUDRE CANYON

- » **Gandalf**** v6** > GANDALF AREA
- » **Small Axe**** v8** > PEARL AREA
- » **Indian Ladder**** v5** > BOG AREA
- » **Eye of Samara*** v10** > PEARL AREA
- » **Sharma Lunge*** v10** > 420 BOULDERS

## TOP 5 - ROUTES
FAVORITE OR MOST MEMORABLE IN THE POUDRE CANYON

- » **Albatross**** 14a** > POUDRE FALLS
- » **Paul Revere**** 13d** > BOSTON PEAK
- » **Chocolate Stout*** 14a** > THE BEACH
- » **Rustic Wilderness**** 13c** > WILD WALL
- » **Straw Into Gold**** 13d** > VISTA CRAG

*Climber Spotlight:*
Ken Klein is as synonymous with Fort Collins as anyone. A dedicated Board Member for the NCCC and a Poudre Canyon aficionado. Originally a farm kid from Iowa who left the great plains for Fort Collins and never looked back. A climber since 2003, Ken has been dedicated and in love with climbing for a long time. As a youth coach, he continues to inspire the next generation of climbing addicts.

Ken Klein on the incredible stone and steep angles of **Harder They Come**\*\*\* v9   Photo: Gustavo Moser

# INTRODUCTION

Zach Robbins, Cam Shubb, Ryan Nelson, Dede Humphrey, Ken Duncan, Andy Cross And Jim Brink climbing together on a sunny day at Sheep Mountain  Photo: B. Scott

## MEET SOME
# LOCALS

We are lucky to have so many incredible climbers and all around good people in the Fort Collins climbing community. Most folks are genuinely dedicated to protecting and preserving the amazing climbing resources we have out our back door. The following is a collection of bios from some of the most legendary and beloved characters in our little world of Northern Colorado rock climbing. This could easily be my favorite part of the entire guidebook...Enjoy!

## » CRAIG DEMARTINO «

DATE OF BIRTH: **September 1965**   IDEAL CLIMBING WEIGHT: **140 lbs**
HEIGHT: **5'11"**   APE INDEX: **+2"**

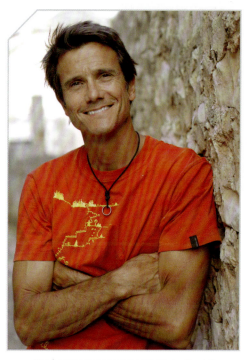

I've been climbing most of my life, 30 years total, spread to areas all around the world. Choosing to live in Colorado was one of the best things I did some 20 years ago and the canyon was one of the first places I saw when I was deciding where to live. I drove in from the Western Slope on my way east after a Yosemite trip, and drove down the canyon. I thought if I could live near it, it would be an amazing place to call home.

Flash forward 20 years and its a place I've climbed, raised a family, and become a part of in every sense. I love climbing at Upper Echelon with my wife Cyndy, crossing the river to the Palace, and getting smacked down at the Beach. Out of all the areas, I still think the Crystal Wall is one of my favorites. The routes have such a fun, powerful feeling and I never tire of the view from the front side looking out over the river. It's also where I pulled a loose block off Tool Man, caught it on my chest, pushed it off, and kept climbing to the anchor. It was one of the only times I've pulled something big off, and the memory stays with me because it was so surprising, it was comical. Plus, no one got hurt, and the route's a little cleaner now!

The Tunnel in the Lower Canyon  Photo: B. Scott

The canyon has so much to offer to any level of climber, from all day missions to an afternoon cragging at a roadside cliff. Thats one of the things that makes it an easy place to love.

## TOP 5
FAVORITE OR MOST MEMORABLE CLIMBS IN THE POUDRE CANYON
» **The General Lee** ** **12b** > CRYSTAL WALL
» **O.D.K.** **** **12a** > UPPER ECHELON
» **Tailspin** **** **12b** > UPPER ECHELON
» **Tool Man** ** **11c** > CRYSTAL WALL
» **Ballet Of The Bulge** *** **11b** > CRYSTAL WALL

POUDRE CANYON GUIDE - 3RD EDITION   **21**

# INTRODUCTION

## » KEN DUNCAN «

DATE OF BIRTH: **June 1957**   IDEAL CLIMBING WEIGHT: **145 lbs**
HEIGHT: **5'10"**   APE INDEX: **+0"**

From the time I was a little kid growing up in Missouri, I've always had a passion for the outdoors. Early on it was hunting and fishing, later it became canoeing, studying natural history and backpacking. During high school, I discovered climbing and suddenly all my previous passions ceased to exist.

After high school, I came to CSU, ostensibly to study wildlife biology, but in truth to climb. At that time, the bouldering around Fort Collins was great but longer routes were lacking. For roped climbing, we generally headed to Boulder, Lumpy or Vedauwoo. This was the mid '70s long before sport climbing existed and other than Greyrock, the Poudre didn't really lend itself to trad climbing. However two obscure Poudre trad routes from that era are still memorable. The first was the east ridge of Crystal Wall. Starting at the river we climbed over the tunnel, and continued to the summit in multiple pitches. The ridge has spectacular position and the climbing was easy and fun. However the volume of loose rock, combined with the line of cars below, make this a route that should never be repeated. After summiting, we returned to the base and headed to the major weakness on the north face. Forty-odd years later I still remember climbing up into the unknown, with only the occasional stopper or hex for protection, before topping out a second time. Now known as Thursday Afternoon Hooky, this remains a seldom climbed and heady route.

Times have changed and with the advent of bolting the Poudre has been developed into a great climbing area with far more routes than I ever imagined possible. It's become my go to area when I need a climbing fix.

## TOP 5
FAVORITE OR MOST MEMORABLE CLIMBS IN THE POUDRE CANYON

- » **Fish & Whistle**\*\*\*\* **11b** > EDEN AREA, NARROWS
- » **Forbidden Fruit**\*\* **12a** > EDEN AREA, NARROWS
- » **Sporting Green**\*\*\* **12a** > PALACE
- » **Intergalactic**\*\*\* **12c** > POUDRE FALLS
- » **The General Lee**\*\* **12b** > CRYSTAL WALL

## » PAUL HEYLIGER «

DATE OF BIRTH: **1958**   IDEAL CLIMBING WEIGHT: **148 lbs**
HEIGHT: **5'10"**   APE INDEX: **+0"**

To my eternal gratitude, my dad sacrificed precious weekends to take a climbing class with me and fellow 14-year old Brian Parsons. The years that followed now seem so anachronistic. There were car rides begged from parents, a molasses-paced crawl through the grades, terror-filled adventures where the gear didn't always hold, and the biggest miracle of all - we stayed alive. Halfway up the Bastille Crack, we watched a team on Werk Supp and thought: if we could ever climb that route, we would be so happy. And we did. And we were.

Decades later, the profound rewards associated with specific routes are undiminished. But memories of the Poudre having to do with friendship, teamwork, and selflessness are even more indissoluble: Jon Dory, hunched in a protective cave and belaying for four hours as a massive flake gets cleaned off; Tod Anderson, stonemasoning belay platforms before the drill-dust has settled; John Durkin, hauling hardware to God-knows-where, pragmatically asking "You think people will ever come here?"; Brian, spending all day prepping another new line and proposing that we save the send for a friend; Greg Hand, laughing maniacally in gale-force winds because the ropes extend 100 feet horizontally and he can't tie on the brushes; Jim Brink, boldly suggesting to me that he can trad up quivering choss-rot to summit a new wall while I desperately wonder how I'm going to carry his body back across the river; and my wife, Janette, answering the front door where the UPS guy dumps boxes at her feet as she turns toward me, incredulous, and asks: "Bolts? Again?!?"

Years pass. Priorities shift. But obsessions endure, and I think: if I can keep heading up this magical canyon with friends, family, or alone, I will be so happy. And I do. And ... I am.

## TOP 5
FAVORITE OR MOST MEMORABLE CLIMBS IN THE POUDRE CANYON

- » **Vindicated**\*\* **9** > SHEEP MOUNTAIN
- » **Luck of the Irish**\*\*\* **10c** > UPPER SNAKE EYES
- » **Balaam**\* **11c** > CRYSTAL WALL
- » **Bostock From Little Bird**\*\*\* **11b** > SHEEP MOUNTAIN
- » **White as Snow**\*\*\* **12a** > SHEEP MOUNTAIN

Ethan Pringle casually onsighting the uber-classic **Callan's Crack**\*\*\*\* **12a**  Photo: B. Scott

## INTRODUCTION

Gandalf, Small Axe, and Twilight were not as well traveled but would slowly build in popularity throughout the years. My motivation has always been spurred on by climbing the highest quality of lines, regardless of grade, so I made it a priority to search out and climb the best lines the canyon has to offer. The ones that required a little extra effort and sense of adventure only added to the overall experience. I quickly found out that the best boulders are spread throughout the entire canyon, often hidden by dense trees, tucked away in narrow gullies, or protected by a dicey river crossing.

These seemingly negative characteristics have not been discouraging but rather ignited my passion for the canyon, as it has done for so many others. It seems to promote a natural sense of adventure and a desire to uncover the next amazing line. I am lucky to have been involved in the development of several memorable lines but even luckier to have shared the experiences with many great friends. After a short stint in southern Colorado, I am happy to be back north and look forward to once again having the Poudre at my fingertips.

## » COLLIN HORVAT «

DATE OF BIRTH: **October 1983**    IDEAL CLIMBING WEIGHT: **150 lbs**
HEIGHT: **5'10"**    APE INDEX: **+0"**

I started climbing in the canyon during the fall of 2007 after moving to Fort Collins for graduate school at CSU. Although I am well aware of the quality of the sport climbing in the Poudre, my primary focus has always been the bouldering. With the combination of rock quality and the lure of area test-pieces, the 420s were the main attraction for me and the majority of boulderers visiting the canyon at the time. However, in the quiet background there were a number of established gems and amazing new lines going up in obscure areas throughout the canyon. Lines such as

## TOP 5
FAVORITE OR MOST MEMORABLE CLIMBS IN THE POUDRE CANYON

- » **Gandalf**\*\*\*\* **v6** > GANDALF AREA
- » **Small Axe**\*\*\*\* **v8** > PEARL AREA
- » **Fire on the Mountain**\*\*\* **v11** > WIDOWMAKERS
- » **Graveyard Machine**\*\*\* **v8** > PRIONE
- » **Canopener**\*\*\* **v11** > 420 BOULDERS

---

## » DEDE HUMPHREY «

DATE OF BIRTH: **February 1971**    IDEAL CLIMBING WEIGHT: **120 lbs**
HEIGHT: **5'3"**    APE INDEX: **+0"**

I was born in 1971 in the very flat state of Florida. Grew up outdoors, splitting my time between exploring the woods, walking the beach or swimming in the many natural springs of the state. It wasn't until college that I discovered the allure of kayaking, backpacking and climbing. Unfortunately, none of these pursuits were actually IN Florida. After several years and countless hours of driving up to Chattanooga -without A/C or power steering - I made the decision to move west.

Best decision ever! I met my husband, Guy - married 20 years this year. Now instead of driving eight hours to the nearest climbing - we drive one hour (but whine about the traffic and crowds for the other seven hours). One of the things we love best about the Poudre Canyon is the vibe: better drive, fun people and some ever-changing rock. Talk to Poudre developers and you will hear some epic trundling stories. My partner, Ken and I have had some crazy ones: including slicing a virgin 70m rope into two beautiful 35m gym ropes. Doh! Try explaining that one to your husband.

I've been climbing for 25+ years now. I've watched the sport evolve, get bolts (lose bolts) and go main-stream (mixed feelings on that one). But I love that you see more women outside. You see kids warming up on your projects now too. My best relationships have grown out of climbing. I've been blessed with some great partners and life-long friends. I wouldn't trade it for the world.

## TOP 5
FAVORITE OR MOST MEMORABLE CLIMBS IN THE POUDRE CANYON

- » **Iron Maiden**\*\*\* **11c** > BRISTLECONE CASTLE
- » **Intergalactic**\*\*\* **12c** > POUDRE FALLS
- » **Nova**\*\*\* **11b** > POUDRE FALLS
- » **Silver Salute**\*\*\* **11c** > POUDRE FALLS
- » **Icarus**\*\*\* **11b** > NARROWS

# INTRODUCTION

## » STEVE MCCORKEL «

DATE OF BIRTH: **November 1968**   IDEAL CLIMBING WEIGHT: **175 lbs**
HEIGHT: **5'11"**   APE INDEX: **+0"**

My wife Becky and I were married in 1992, and we moved to Fort Collins in '93. With a copy of Craig Luebben's Poudre Canyon article in Rock and Ice, we headed up the canyon for our first time. Craig inspired me to seek out some projects of my own and we soon made The Sunday Buttress (Lion's Den) a favorite hang. Some of the climbs I did there were named after my family. Few people were climbing in the canyon at that time, and it was difficult to find willing partners. The canyon was not yet well received by many climbers. Then, entered bouldering. Everybody did it! Which kept the crags secluded. Our son Noah (and later our daughter Autumn) accompanied us constantly. I remember many times, exploring and setting up or scoping a route, only to later coerce them into joining the adventure. I found places like the Wild Wall and Boston Peak to be outrageous! Close friends finally joined in some exploration: friends like Kurt Strobel, who can take responsibility for a few route names, as well as the idea to explore Boston Peak. Matt Flach provoked some further establishment of a couple of high quality crack routes, and was game for many climbing days. My son too, who grew quickly with enthusiasm for the canyon, and the desire to dabble in some exploration. Climbing with him has only been second best to my wife, whom to this day, encourages me. Without these great people and others, the Poudre Canyon would be a rustic and lonely place. I've had many solitary adventures in the canyon, but to be sure, sharing these experiences has kept me coming back. The Poudre Canyon is a place worthy of a lifetime of wild experiences.

## TOP 5
FAVORITE OR MOST MEMORABLE CLIMBS IN THE POUDRE CANYON

» **Stanley's Steamer 11c** > PALACE
» **Pura Aventura*** 11** > BOSTON PEAK
» **Sunday's Child*** 12c** > PALACE
» **Foreplay/Longtime**** 13a** > BOSTON PEAK
» **Golden Harvest*** 11c** > PALACE

## » SAM ROTHSTEIN «

DATE OF BIRTH: **January 1995**   IDEAL CLIMBING WEIGHT: **140 lbs**
HEIGHT: **5'8"**   APE INDEX: **+2"**

Originally from a suburb near Boston, I moved to Fort Collins in the fall of 2013 to attend Colorado State University and spend more time in the mountains. Having been drawn to the outdoors from an early age, when I found climbing in 2011 it was an obvious fit. As a kid, my main entertainment was romping around the woods with friends. Fifteen years later, I find myself doing the same things, but in a 40 mile playground known as the Poudre Canyon.

The main bouldering areas had countless impeccable problems, but the canyon was overflowing with rock. I knew there had to be more climbing. I started taking days off just to stomp up brushy hillsides and chossy gullies in hopes of finding something new. When I first stumbled upon some climbs barely worthy of chalk, I was immediately hooked on first ascents. Privileged with some guidance from the old guard, I was taught where to find the best unclimbed rock and the techniques needed to develop it.

Thankfully, my friends shared a similar passion for developing and were willing to help build landings and scrub lichen. With the support of Brett Hoffman, Jake Atkinson, Nick Perl, Beau Elliott, and Kepler Worobec, new problems were put up all over the canyon. Climbs were added to the Widowmakers, the Narrows Blocs, Gandalf, Bristlecone and random spots in between. As my search for new rock continued, I realized that climbing in the canyon is essentially infinite. So to anyone who feels this book won't provide a lifetime of frustration, fulfillment and bliss, I encourage you to explore for yourself.

## TOP 5
FAVORITE OR MOST MEMORABLE CLIMBS IN THE POUDRE CANYON

» **Divergence SDS*** v10** > 420 BOULDERS
» **The Fable**** v3** > NARROWS BLOCS
» **Hippo Hoedown*** v7** > NARROWS BLOCS
» **Flight Syndrome*** v9** > GANDALF AREA
» **Rude Beauty**** v8** > POUDRE FALLS

*Climber Spotlight:*
How hard do you really try? How psyched can you possibly be about rock climbing? Ryan Nelson is the definition of pure psych. Ryan's out finding new boulders, bolting new routes and working on his projects all the time. His tireless dedication to Northern Colorado rock climbing includes being a NCCC board member and a constant steward to these climbing areas. If you need a burst of climbing motivation, Ryan is the best guy for the job.

Ryan Nelson giving 110% on the pumpy finish to the **Reckoning**\*\*\* **12d**  Photo: B. Scott

# INTRODUCTION

Levi Van Weddingen on the amazing stone of **Simple*** v6**  Photo: B. Scott

Bryan Beavers traversing around on the **Poudre Pig,** located between the Palace and Stove Prairie Road  Photo: B. Scott

## INTRODUCTION

In 1972 my junior high school teacher, Carl, took a few of us kids up the Poudre to learn how to rock climb. We didn't go far up, just to the Picnic Rock formation. Carl set up an anchor on top of one of the cliffs. From a ledge on top of the cliff he would belay us up the 40ft wall. We were excited at the challenge and exposure. We had simple gear. Hiking boots for footwear and a 1 inch nylon diaper sling for a harness. When it was my turn to climb I clipped in and worked my way up the cliff. It was quite steep but had good holds. At the top I was psyched, Carl told me to clip into the anchor and then untie from the rope. I clipped into a carabiner and then dropped the rope to the next climber below. As my friend started up the climb I yelled down words of encouragement. I wanted to watch him climb so I leaned out as far as I could to watch him. As I leaned out, excited to watch my friend, I felt a sudden jerk at my waist. My teacher had looked over at me and realized that the carabiner I had clipped into was merely clipped to a belt loop on my jeans. He instantly grabbed my waist and pulled me in. I had been fully loading the Levis belt loop while looking down at a 40 footer straight to the deck. It was nearly my first and last day of climbing.

## » MARK WILFORD «

DATE OF BIRTH: **January 1959**    IDEAL CLIMBING WEIGHT: **170 lbs**
HEIGHT: **5'11"**    APE INDEX: **+0"**

I've been climbing for over forty years now. Climbing has taken me around the world to all seven continents. I've run the gamut, from bouldering and free climbing to waterfall ice and Karakorum big walls. I've had plenty of adventures and close calls over the years as well. I've taken 50ft whippers on trad climbs and endured open bivouacs at 6,000 meters. I have more ankle sprains from high bouldering than I can count and have scared the crap out of myself solo on the north face of Mt. Alberta. But one of my closest calls over the years was right at the beginning.

## TOP 5
FAVORITE OR MOST MEMORABLE CLIMBS IN THE POUDRE CANYON

» **Group Therapy**\*\*\*\* **WI6, M5** > NARROWS
» **East Of Eden**\*\*\*\* **9** > NARROWS
» **High As I Wanna Be**\* **12a** > NARROWS
» **Dear Slabby**\*\*\* **11b** > PALACE
» **Better Than Watching Television**\*\*\* **11c** > CRYSTAL WALL

## » JASON TARRY «

DATE OF BIRTH: **April 1977**    IDEAL CLIMBING WEIGHT: **170 lbs**
HEIGHT: **5'10"**    APE INDEX: **+2"**

There is a point near the mouth of the canyon where my worn, tangled thoughts of work, family and car maintenance shift to fresh-faced curiosity and enthusiasm. Colorado Highway 14 west of Ted's Place meanders through the mountains with its constant river partner representing directionless access to unending firsts. Each twist and turn of the pavement is nearly memorized from the countless outings; however, each bend still reveals a landscape full of wonder and potential.

I moved to Colorado from Ohio fifteen years ago in search of a place that would accommodate my endless motivation to climb and explore. Living in Fort Collins with the Poudre Canyon in my backyard was ideal. I've recognized that my motivation for climbing initially came from a determination to find, develop and send that "perfect line." Over the years, my focus on climbing and finding the perfect piece of stone has had to share time with work, friendship and a family. I've learned that I might never find perfection, but my experiences in the Poudre Canyon climbing around on flawed rock with great friends is far superior. This lesson may have skewed my vision, so if you see me stumble out of the woods with a fuzzy faced dog and lichen in my eyebrows saying, "I found a great new line just up the hill," the rock is likely choss and it's way the hell up the hill.

## TOP 5
FAVORITE OR MOST MEMORABLE CLIMBS IN THE POUDRE CANYON

» **Water Rights**\*\*\* **12b** > POUDRE FALLS
» **Harmonic Resonance**\*\*\* **13c** > NARROWS
» **The Albatross**\*\*\*\* **14a** > POUDRE FALLS
» **Gandalf**\*\*\*\* **v6** > GANDALF AREA
» **Eukie Extension**\*\*\* **13a** > VISTA CRAG

**0 - 17.4 MILES** FROM TED'S PLACE

# LOWER CANYON

Inception of the infamous Tunnel in the heart of the Lower Canyon   Photo: B. Scott

**208 ROUTES** IN TOTAL

GRADE DISTRIBUTION

**21 BOULDER** PROBLEMS IN TOTAL

**TYPE(S): SPORT, TRAD, & BOULDERING**
**DIFFICULTY RANGE: 5.8 - 5.13B, V1-V11**
**APPROACH TIME: 5 SEC - 45 MIN**
**SEASON: YEAR ROUND**

## CLIMBING OVERVIEW

The Lower Canyon is the oldest and consequently most trafficked portion of the canyon. The most popular roped climbing areas lie here, areas like Greyrock, the Palace, Crystal Wall and Upper Echelon dominate the Lower Canyon. The newer areas described in this book are also worth a visit for any rock climber including Happy Hour Crag and Brink's Rock which hold quality new routes. Bouldering in the Lower Canyon was typically not well known besides Greyrock. But Mike's Roof, French Arête and Pine Vu are all worthy after work spots for any bouldering enthusiast.

The climbing history is deep here as well. Spanning several generations starting most prominently with the adventures of **Rodney Ley and Steve Allen**, next would be the massive wave of development in the 90s to early 2000s that resulted in development or re-writing of the major areas. **Tim Wilhelmi, Steve McCorkel, Paul Heyliger, Derek Peavey, Judson Doyle, Sam Shannon, Ken Gibson, Bryan Beavers** and many others sunk the bolts that built the most popular route climbing areas in the canyon.

## GETTING THERE

The Lower Canyon is considered the stretch of highway between Ted's Place and Stove Prairie Road; the closest portion of the canyon to Fort Collins. If you only have enough time for a half-day of climbing, this is where you will be.

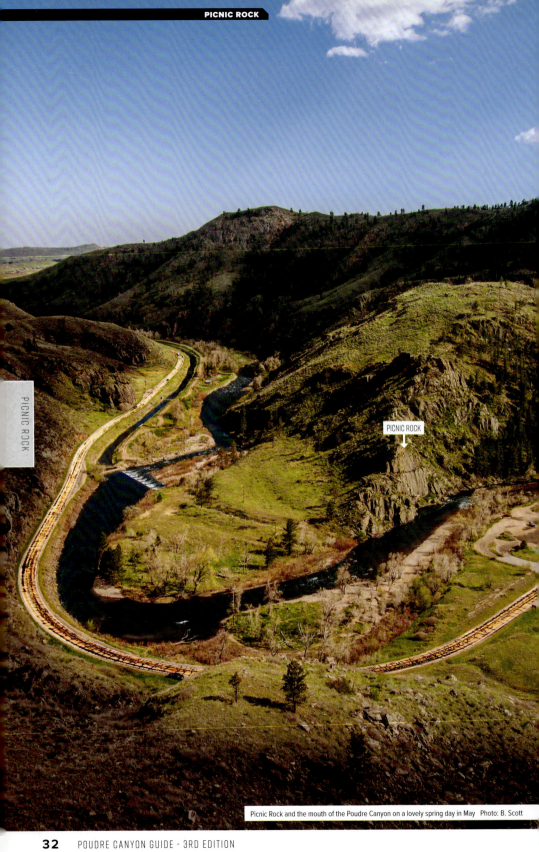
Picnic Rock and the mouth of the Poudre Canyon on a lovely spring day in May   Photo: B. Scott

**2.5 MILES** FROM TED'S PLACE

# PICNIC ROCK

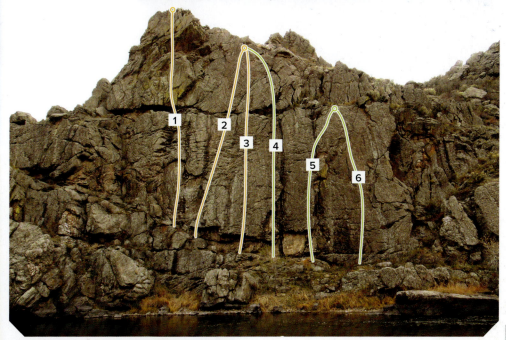

TYPE(S): **SPORT & TRAD**
DIFFICULTY RANGE: **5.9 - 5.10**
APPROACH TIME: **2 MIN**
SEASON: **SPRING, SUMMER & FALL**

## CLIMBING OVERVIEW

Picnic Rock, a.k.a. ROTC Rock is a very popular stop in the canyon. People have come here for generations to swim, fish and relax at this scenic day use area. According to Rodney Ley and Steve Allen's guide to the canyon, people have been climbing here since the 1950s. It was also a practice ground for ROTC students from CSU to learn rappelling. But in contemporary times, Picnic Rock was largely ignored by climbers. That all changed in 2017 when Ken Duncan and Dede Humphrey realized the potential for the area and re-established the majority of the routes with modern hardware. Weekends could be hectic during the summer months, but otherwise this is a great small crag with several fun and convenient routes.

## GETTING THERE

**GPS: 40°40'16.17"N 105°13'47.91"W**

From Ted's Place, drive approx. 2.5 miles up the canyon to the large parking area and facilities on your left. There is no overnight camping allowed.

**1. ○ Skinny Dipping* 10d (14 Bolts)**
Skinny Dipping is a nice, long, sustained, face pitch. Techy climbing on small positive edges leads up a steep, smooth face past an overhang. Continue up easier but sustained terrain passing a tough move off the first ledge.
FA: K. Duncan, D. Humphrey

**2. ○ Less Lichen, More Lovin'*** 10a (8 Bolts + GEAR)**
Start in the dihedral, and follow a line of bolts with intermittent gear to the shared anchor.
FA: K. Duncan, D. Humphrey

**3. ○ Picnic Blank It** 10b (9 Bolts + GEAR)**
This has a roof crux followed by some thin slabbing. Turn the roof, and follow a line of bolts with intermittent gear to the shared anchor at the top of the wall.
FA: K. Duncan, D. Humphrey

**4. ○ Chips and Beer** 9 (9 Bolts + GEAR)**
Chips and Beer has fun movement in the dihedral. Turn the roof to get into the hanging dihedral, then follow bolts and gear to the shared anchors.
FA: K. Duncan, D. Humphrey

**5. ○ Uninvited Guest* 9 (GEAR)**
A Buzzworm sat at the top of the route. Climb the right-facing dihedral and crack to a shared anchor.
FA: K. Duncan, D. Humphrey

**6. ○ Adults Only Picnic** 9 (GEAR)**
This is a heady trad route that will keep your attention. Climb a series of intermittent cracks to a shared anchor. Continue straight up at the top where the crack veers right.
FA: K. Duncan, D. Humphrey

Matt Robbins on the classic **Mike's Roof*** **v5**  Photo: B. Scott

**3.0 MILES** FROM TED'S PLACE

# FRENCH ARÊTE / MIKE'S ROOF

TYPE(S): **BOULDERING**
DIFFICULTY RANGE: **V1 - V8**
APPROACH TIME: **10 MIN - 30 MIN**
SEASON: **FALL, WINTER & SPRING**

**RIVER CROSSING REQUIRED**

## FRENCH ARÊTE

This small but excellent boulder can provide a nice after work session, especially when paired with Mike's Roof. Its is fairly obvious from Hwy 14, located on a small bench above the river with several other smaller boulders.

**1. French Arête** v7 (Pads)
The name sake boulder problem starts on the arête in a SDS. Slap up the double arête feature to reach the horizontal slopey jug. Continue moving left hand up the arête and compress to reach the true finish of the problem. Escaping out right at the slopey jug is much harder than it looks and not nearly as much fun.
FA: Cory French

**2. Unknown Slab 1** v1 (Pads)
A decent three move problem to get your fingers warmed up.
FA: Unknown

**3. Unknown Slab 2** v1 (Pads)
Another easy face climb with nice rock and good edges.
FA: Unknown

## CLIMBING OVERVIEW

A decent collection of bouldering that is close to town and of surprising quality. The French Arête and its surrounding boulders have been climbed on for years with the one main sticking being the French Arête itself. Mike's Roof is a newly discovered boulder by Mike Englestad and later developed by Jason Nadeau, Matt Robbins and Brian Camp.

## GETTING THERE

**GPS: 40°40'22.39"N 105°14'20.42"W**
From Ted's Place, drive approx. three miles up the canyon passing Picnic Rock to a set of three different parking options. After crossing the river, locate the French Arête about 50yards from the river's edge on a small bench above the river. Mike's Roof is a short 20min walk up the gulley to the south of French Arête. There is a decently cairned trail which follows the stream, switching sides at a few points.

## SNAKEPIT BOULDER

This large boulder/cliff is located about 50 yards uphill from the French Arête Boulder. Good rock and tall climbs makes this worth a visit.

**4. Snakeskin** v8 (4-5 Pads)
Aesthetic and committing, this new-school highball will test your endurance and your head space.
FA: Beau Elliot

**5. Snakepit** v7 (4-5 Pads)
A nice tall face on good stone with lots of interesting pinches and crimpers.
FA: S. Rothstein

POUDRE CANYON GUIDE - 3RD EDITION

# MIKE'S ROOF

This stand alone boulder hovering over a bubbling brook is a great "close to town" excursion. The rock quality is fairly unusual for the canyon, featuring a fine textured rock that is a mix of granite and gneiss, creating excellent sloping holds and bighter edges. From French Arête, locate the valley to the south and follow the cairned path as it follows the stream all the way to the boulder.

### 6. ○ Crack in a Ship** v2 (Pads)
Located on a small boulder right before the Mike's Roof boulder. This deceptively tricky boulder problem involves pulling off two holds in a seam to an awesome sloper followed by a classic mantle. Great for kids and fun for adults wearing approach shoes to increase the difficulty just a bit.
**FA: Sam Scott**

### 7. ○ The Scorpion and the Bobcat** v6 (Pads)
SDS on some rocks in the middle of the stream on a nice left-hand undercling and the arête. Tension move into the big jug and perform some taxing moves heading left on thin edges. The topout up the slab and arête is easy but not trivial.
**FA: Matt Robbins**

### 8. ○ The Landscaper** v5 (Pads)
SDS the same as The Scorpion but after the first move, mantle up and right into the scoop feature to reach the arête. Less awkward than The Scorpion but both are worth doing.
**FA: Jason Nadeau**

Sam Scott (age 5) working hard towards the send of **Crack In A Ship** v2  Photo: B. Scott

**FRENCH ARÊTE / MIKE'S ROOF**

## MIKE'S ROOF - WEST SIDE

**9. Mike's Roof*** v5** (Pads)
The namesake of the area climbs nice rock on interesting holds right over the stream. SDS on two underclings and do a big move to the amazing slopey rail feature. Keep tension to slap the edges at the lip before a classy mantle onto the slab to reach the arête.
FA: J. Nadeau

**10. Unnamed** v6** (Pads)
SDS the same as Mike's Roof and climb the problem to the lip of the roof. Here, traverse right about three moves and do a slightly more technical mantle with slopey hands but a good foot. The slab is thought provoking but not very hard.
FA: M. Robbins

**11. Black Beard's Traverse** v7** (Pads)
The final variation worth doing at Mike's Roof. After doing the SDS moves to the lip, begin a long section of resistance climbing on interesting edges and slopers. The feet are just bad enough to make the last few easy moves pumpy.
FA: J. Nadeau

Fatty Throbbins takes another lap on **Mike's Roof*** v5   Photo: B. Scott

***Climber Spotlight:***
Bryan Beavers is pretty much a Fort Collins landmark. He and his family run the famous Beavers Market in Old Town Fort Collins and Bryan has been climbing here his entire life. A constant developer, Bryan has spent enormous amounts of time and money to bolt new routes in the canyon. Some of the best 5.10s and 5.11s in the canyon were bolted by Bryan and his hard routes like Twinkletoes*** 13a are sought after by all the hard climbers.

Bryan Beavers on the thought provoking edges of **Jame-O-Slab**\*\*\* **10c**  Photo: B. Scott

**5.4 MILES** FROM TED'S PLACE

# HAPPY HOUR CRAG

GRADE DISTRIBUTION

**TYPE(S): SPORT**
**DIFFICULTY RANGE: 5.8 - 5.12C**
**APPROACH TIME: 20 MIN**
**SEASON: FALL, WINTER & SPRING**

## CLIMBING OVERVIEW

Happy Hour is a great convenience crag bolted and developed primarily by Bryan and Kathy Beavers over the winter of 2011. It features lots of sunny moderates on decent to excellent stone. This is a fantastic winter crag and after work spot. A great crag for beginner lead climbers with routes like Three Flakes to the Wind and Sun Deck Specials.

## GETTING THERE

**GPS:** 40°42'0.59"N 105°15'3.82"W
From Ted's Place, drive approx. 5.4 miles up the canyon to a large pullout on the east side of the road right at the entrance to Gateway Park. Park here and walk upstream about 50 yds until you can find a place to safely cross. Do not go near any of the damn structures downstream of the parking.

**1.** ○ **The Eluebbenator*** **11b** (GEAR)
Romp up the unprotected slab that might be 5.4. Launch into the right angling hand and fist crack to the Cab Ride anchor. Gear to 4 inches.
FA: B. Beavers

**2.** ○ **Cab Ride**** **10c** (6 Bolts)
Romp up some of the best 5.5 climbing around to the horizontal break. A reachy move back right gets you over the bulge with more easy but fun climbing to the anchor.
FA: B. Beavers, K. Beavers

**3.** ○ **Liquor Jugs**** **10a** (10 Bolts)
Ramble up the fun grey slab, then continue past the ledge on surprisingly juggy holds out the left side of the tan overhang.
FA: B. Beavers, K. Beavers

**4.** ○ **Three Flakes to the Wind**** **8** (12 Bolts)
A beautiful slab of shiny grey schist leads to some cool pocket features. A move onto the slab is followed by a long section of fun 5.6 climbing to the anchor.
FA: B. Beavers, K. Beavers

**5.** ○ **Sun Deck Specials**** **7** (12 Bolts)
A fun mega-moderate that seems to go on forever.
FA: B. Beavers, K. Beavers

POUDRE CANYON GUIDE - 3RD EDITION    **39**

Casey Martin cruising up the fun headwall of **Cab Ride*** **10c**   Photo: B. Scott

### 6. Balcony Railbumper** 12c (10 Bolts)
The hardest route at the crag starts with some steep arête climbing on big holds to the ledge. Carefully step right to the next arête and engage a hard steep boulder problem to reach the chains.
FA: B. Beavers

### 7. Balcony Direct Project (9 Bolts)
A harder steeper version of Balcony Railbumper.
Bolted by B. Scott

### 8. If Not for the Pigeons** 10a (9 Bolts)
This excellent climb has some exquisite rock on it. Climb cool slopey holds until you can chicken wing your way up the wide crack before stepping right to the anchor.
FA: B. Beavers, K. Beavers

### 9. Pigeon Hole Bouncer** 11b (9 Bolts)
Ramble up some ledgy terrain on absolutely stellar rock to a tricky boulder problem on sidepulls at Bolt 4.
FA: B. Beavers, K. Beavers

### 10. Tanked** 10b (13 Bolts)
This route climbs the undulating arête feature. Thought provoking climbing stays right of the bolt line.
FA: B. Beavers, K. Beavers

### 11. Jame-O-Slab*** 10c (10 Bolts)
The best route at the area tackles a long slab of excellent schist rock. Be prepared for lots of highsteps, slopey edges and full value bolt spacing.
FA: B. Beavers, K. Beavers

### 12. Yet Another 9 (GEAR)
Climb the obvious crack feature to the shared anchor.
FA: B. Beavers

### 13. Car Bomb* 11b (9 Bolts)
The steep gray face on good but friable edges.
FA: B. Beavers

### 14. Hangover 9 (GEAR)
Climb the gear protected face to a series of right-facing flakes.
FA: B. Beavers

### 15. Tequila Worm 11a (7 Bolts)
Loose rock and strange climbing, climb this one after you've climbed all the others here.
FA: B. Beavers

### 16. Going Green* 9 (GEAR)
Climb the interesting crack feature near the arête.
FA: B. Beavers

### 17. Booze Tube** 10b (8 Bolts)
The lowest route on the hill climbs a fun arête feature on great rock. Lots of sidepulls and fun crimps.
FA: B. Beavers

**6.7 MILES** FROM TED'S PLACE

# POUDRE PRACTICE ROCK

TYPE(S): **BOULDERING, SPORT CLIMBING**
DIFFICULTY RANGE: **V0 - V3, 5.10B - 5.11D**
APPROACH TIME: **1 SEC**
SEASON: **YEAR ROUND**

## CLIMBING OVERVIEW

Poudre Practice Rock is located on City of Fort Collins property. People have been climbing here for decades due to its proximity to the road and short drive from the mouth of the canyon. Mostly used as a bouldering and top-roping area in years past. In the Ley/Allen Guidebook it is first described as: "...this rock is virgin, that is a compliment to the rock, not a reflection on the sexuality of Poudre Climbers." Not sure what that means exactly, but this cliff is a nice roadside crag with enough climbing for a half day of fun.

In years past, top-rope anchors were set-up using trees back from the lip of the cliff. In 2018, the author installed bolted anchors to prevent further erosion of the cliff top from the long ropes or webbing needed to anchor off the trees.

## GETTING THERE

**GPS: 40°41'33.39"N 105°15'40.98"W**
From Ted's Place, drive approx. 6.7 miles up the canyon to a large pullout directly in front of the crag on the south side of the road.

### 1. ○ Bouldering Traverse* v2 (Pads)
This fun little romp can be climbed in either direction but most folks start on the left and traverse right. Slippery feet and polished hands may make this feel pumpy for the grade.
FA: Unknown

### 2. ○ A-Frame Roof** 11d (5 Bolts)
On the left side of the wall is an obvious A-shaped roof. Jugs take you into the roof which ends with the crux pulling over the roof off underclings. Easy climbing leads to the anchor.
FA: Unknown, Bolted by B. Scott '18

### 3. ○ Tan Panel** 11c (6 Bolts)
Start at the left end of the bouldering traverse. Climb steep terrain to a tricky move getting into the big undercling. Technical face climbing with another crux takes you up the vertical face to the anchor. Easily top-roped.
FA: Unknown, Bolted by B. Scott '18

### 4. ○ Bisecting Fist Crack** 10b (GEAR)
Start in one of two ways: either up the strenuous but easier-to-protect angling crack, or climb the left leaning series of blocky face holds which is hard to protect. When the two starts connect, there's one tricky move getting over a bulge/shelf, then easy climbing up the left-facing corner to the bolted anchor. Easily set up as a top-rope.
FA: Unknown

### 5. ○ White Panel** 11c (6 Bolts)
This route has been top-roped for years but no name has ever stuck. It is now a nice bolted lead climb that can also be easily top-roped. Start off with a tricky boulder problem to reach the break past Bolt 1. Perform a hard crux moving left above Bolt 2 or traverse way left to avoid it. One more reachy crux awaits above the mid-way ledge.
FA: Unknown, Bolted by B. Scott '18

# GREYROCK

**8.4 MILES** FROM TED'S PLACE

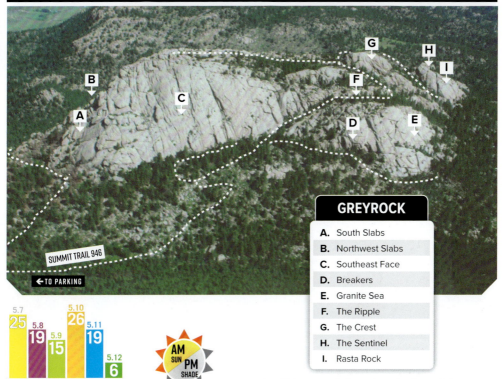

**GREYROCK**

- A. South Slabs
- B. Northwest Slabs
- C. Southeast Face
- D. Breakers
- E. Granite Sea
- F. The Ripple
- G. The Crest
- H. The Sentinel
- I. Rasta Rock

**GRADE DISTRIBUTION**
*(Not all of these routes are listed in this Edition)*

**TYPE(S): TRAD, SPORT, BOULDERING**
**DIFFICULTY RANGE: 5.4 - 5.12; V0 - V10**
**APPROACH TIME: 1 - 1.5 HR**
**SEASON: MAR - JUNE; AUG - NOV**

*Author's Note: Most of the information for this section was written and compiled by Cameron Cross for the Second Edition of the Poudre Canyon Rock Climbing Guide (2010).*

## CLIMBING OVERVIEW

Greyrock is an iconic landmark for Fort Collins and the Poudre Canyon. At an elevation of 7,613 feet (2,320 m), it is easily visible from Fort Collins and has beckoned to hikers and climbers for generations. Greyrock is the best place in the Fort Collins area to find cracks and multi-pitch routes. Greyrock's Southeast Face routes ascend up to 500 feet.

Much of Greyrock's climbing history is unrecorded. Climbers were likely active by the 1950s, and probably much earlier. **Steve Allen** began exploring Greyrock in 1969, and estimates that most of the moderate cracks were climbed by the mid-70s. The majority of routes listed were established in the 1980s. The most active first ascentionists during this period were **Pat McGrane, Jeff Bassett, Don Braddy, Ken Gibson, Kent Wheeler, Chuck Grossman, Sari Schmetterer and Craig Luebben.**

In addition to a plethora of cracks, Greyrock hosts many bolted and mixed protection lines. Many routes require traditional protection to supplement runouts between bolts. Stoppers, small cams such as TCUs or C3s, Tricams, and Loweballs are the most useful; the standard rack also includes brass nuts and cams to three inches.

This guidebook contains only a brief description of the climbing at Greyrock. For more detailed information, please consult "Poudre Canyon Rock Climbing Second Edition" (2010) which contains a comprehensive guide to the area.

## GETTING THERE

**GPS: 40°42'54.39"N 105°17'29.14"W**
From Ted's Place, take Hwy 14 west approx. 8.55 miles to the well-marked parking area. In addition to the parking lot on the south side of the road, there is overflow parking on both sides of the highway.

Follow a well-established trail for half a mile to a junction between the Summit Trail and the Meadows Trail. The Summit Trail provides quicker access to almost all of the climbing at Greyrock. After two miles, the Summit Trail enters the upper meadow where a dramatic view of the South Slabs and the Southeast Face appears. There is a wooden bench where the Summit and Meadows Trails reconnect. Stay on the Summit Trail for another 15min until you can branch off on a climber trail to the base of the Southeast Face.

# GREYROCK

SOUTHEAST FACE

## C - SOUTHEAST FACE

The Southeast Face provides the longest routes on Greyrock - up to five pitches in length. Usually the angle eases as you get higher. Many cracks not listed are 5.5 to 5.8.

From the Meadow intersection, follow the Summit Trail northeast toward Greyrock. Shortly after passing the first "Summit Trail 946" wooden post, you will find a cairn. Veer left here, following a faint climber's trail toward the wall and beginning of Southeast Face routes. The triple crack system of the "Chipmunk Routes" is the best landmark to get oriented.

### 1. ○ Go Spuds Go*** 12a (GEAR)
This lone route sits by itself on the lowest point of rock between the South Slabs and the Southeast Face presenting an ominous 15 foot, 5-to-8 inch roof/crack. Handstacks, kneelocks and chicken wings may get one to the top.
**FA:** C. Luebben '88

### 2. ○ Alvin* 6 (GEAR)
This climb is the left-most of the triple "Chipmunk Cracks". Scamper up the wide crack to a ledge and belay. Follow Theodore to top. Bring a couple of wide pieces.
**FA:** Unknown

### 3. ○ Theodore** 6 (GEAR)
The middle of the three hand cracks.
**P1:** Nice hand jamming to the ledge. Belay at a tree, almost a full 200 feet up.
**P2:** Move left around a giant roof and follow a left-facing corner system to a face section and belay in a gulley at the top of the roof.
**P3:** Follow groove to belay at bushy ledge.
**P4:** Choose your own adventure to the top, either continuing up the groove, or traversing right out onto the slab.
**FA:** Unknown

### 4. ○ Simon** 8 (GEAR)
The right-most of the "Chipmunk Cracks" is the most challenging with good stone and splitter cracks.
**P1:** Good hand jams lead up the slightly awkward first pitch. Follow a grassy but pleasant crack.
**P2:** Pass the large overhang on the right side via a hand/fist crack or lightning bolt finger crack.
**P3:** Join Theodore or move right onto a sparsely protected slab and finish near Dog Face.
**FA:** Unknown

### 5. ○ Dog Face* 10a (2 Bolts)
For homely climbers. Immediately left of Mr. Gone lies an exciting face with two bolts, runout as hell.
**FA:** J. Brink, P. McGrane '88

### 6. ⊙ Mr. Gone*** 10a (3 Bolts + GEAR)
The blank lower face was originally climbed without bolts by Moderson and McGrane in 1982. Bolts were added later that year by Bassett and Braddy and the route was completed. This is one of the best routes on Greyrock.
**P1:** Clip three bolts en route to the classic finger crack, being careful of the runout to Bolt 3. Rappel or continue.
**P2:** Go up and right with slim protection to the prow. Climb the center of this steep feature past a bolt, move right and follow easier cracks, or finish straight up (10a R).
**FA: J. Bassett, D. Braddy '82**

### 7. ⊙ Jetstream Deluxe** 9 (GEAR)
Just right of Mr. Gone lies a crack in a shallow corner. There is a tree in the crack. Fire up the easy crack which gets thinner and more flared, make an awkward step left and face climb to a nice finger crack and belay ledge. Follow this and other discontinuous cracks up and rightward to the top of Greyrock.
**FA: Unknown**

### 8. ⊙ The Greatest Route at Greyrock*** 8 (GEAR)
This is, without a doubt, Greyrock's best 5.8 climb. Start 80 feet to the right of Jetstream Deluxe in a very short left-facing dihedral with a capped roof at 15 feet.
**P1:** Climb the short corner and step right to avoid the roof, or layback an exciting crack to the right of the corner. Veer back left and meander up incipient cracks set in perfect stone (5.8). Belay at a small stance in a prominent horizontal slash.
**P2:** Follow the shallow corner up and left on excellent rock to the base of the large roof. Grab the hero jug and enjoy the view, then jam a steep hand crack 5.8+ through the roof and set a belay.
**P3:** Follow the face/crack 5.6 to a comfy belay near the summit. From here, it is easy 5th class to the top.
**FA: Unknown**

### 9. ⊙ Forward Never Straight** 9 (GEAR)
20 feet right of The Greatest Route at Greyrock lies a short right-facing corner capped by a roof with hand jams. Cracks and a slightly runout face lead to a hanging belay at the horizontal crack. Climb the face to another crack, belay near the roof and finish on The Greatest Route at Greyrock.
**FA: Laurie Parcell, C. Luebben, S. Schmetterer, Sally Moser**

### 10. ⊙ Rites of Passage* 8 (GEAR)
This very prominent left-facing corner offers hand jamming, off-width size crack and face climbing to a tree belay. Move up and left across the face to a belay near the Greatest Route at Greyrock roof. Continue for two pitches, passing a large dead tree.
**FA: P. McGrane**

### 11. ⊙ Barfy's Favorite** 7 (GEAR)
A fun climb and classic when linked with Judy's Jaunt.
**P1:** Start atop a boulder and surmount the bulge. Follow the superb hand-crack to a tree belay.
**P2:** Lichenous cracks lead to a second tree.
**P3:** Continue up to a nice hand/finger crack, then move left to a large belay ledge. Several variations exist for this pitch, but they all end at the large belay ledge.
**P4:** Continue up a right-facing dihedral, pull the short roof, and cruise to the top.
**FA: Unknown**

*Craig Luebben on the classic* **Jaminy Crackit** ** 11d *Photo: C. Luebben*

### 12. ⊙ Judy's Jaunt Variation*** 7 (GEAR)
Start on Barfy's Favorite. At the second large tree, move up right and belay high. Continue up the slightly runout face and right over a small roof to discontinuous cracks. Continue on Barfy's Favorite up the roof/corner.
**FA: Unknown**

### 13. ⊙ Misty Mountain Hop* 7 (GEAR)
Ascend the face right of Barfy's Favorite, using horizontal cracks for pro. Continue past a large, mostly detached flake. Near the top, follow a ramp leftward to the Rites Of Passage belay. Rappel or finish up on Judy's Jaunt.
**FA: Unknown**

### 14. ⊙ Central Chimney* 4 (GEAR)
This decent beginners route follows the obvious fissure to the top of Greyrock.
**FA: Unknown**

### 15. ⊙ Dancing Ladies* 7 (GEAR)
Start up the Central Chimney and waltz right to a large ledge with a tree. Follow discontinuous cracks to the top.
**FA: P. McGrane, Vicki McGrane**

### 16. ⊙ What Is And What Should Never Be 9 (GEAR)
Climb up and over a roof with a left-facing dihedral above and to the right of the Central Chimney. Scour the face in search of pro. Rappel from a tree atop the long pitch.
**FA: Unknown**

### 17. ⊙ The Inner Mounting Flame** 11c (GEAR)
Hot thin edging and friction moves lead to a ramp. Traverse right and rappel Black Dog, or climb straight up easier rock for three more pitches.
**FA: C. Luebben, S. Schmetterer**

### 18. ⊙ Black Dog* 8 (GEAR)
Ascend a large flake leaning against the lower wall and climb cracks past two small roofs. Continue up or rappel.
**FA: Unknown**

### 19. ⊙ Keep the River Free** 10a (GEAR)
Easy terrain leads to the apex of the roof. Dance over the crux roof and up to a belay. Ramble up discontinuous cracks to the top (easier but may be runout in spots).
**FA: Unknown**

Sam Rothstein grabbing horrendous holds on **Diamond in the Rough**** v11  Photo: B. Scott

**9.1 MILES** FROM TED'S PLACE

# PINE VU AREA

A young Mark Wilford climbing **The Odyssey*** 12b  Photo: C. Luebben

TYPE(S): **SPORT & BOULDERING**
DIFFICULTY RANGE: **5.6 - 5.12B, V0-VII**
APPROACH TIME: **1 MIN - 10 MIN**
SEASON: **YEAR ROUND**

**RIVER CROSSING REQUIRED**

## CLIMBING OVERVIEW

Pine Vu is actually a very old climbing zone that has long been forgotten and neglected. The Ley/Allen guidebook describes this area by the "Pine-Vu Lodge". Commenting that this lodge was a "hippy haven" and run by a bunch of "freaks". Those wild times have long gone but the boulders and cliffs still remain. The few sport climbs are of average quality and generally not suggested since they are basically right on the road and the status of the hardware is unknown. The bouldering on the other hand is close to town, on good stone, and has a variety of grades to keep any climber intrigued for an afternoon.

AM SUN / PM SHADE

ODYSSEY WALL

## GETTING THERE

GPS: 40°41'22.50"N 105°17'35.04"W
From Ted's Place, drive approx. 9.1 miles up the canyon to a massive pullout on the north side of the road. Cross the river here to reach the boulders or walk up the road 50yds to reach the routes.

## ODYSSEY WALL

**1.** ○ **Old Project** (8 Bolts)
A elegant and steep line supposedly in the 5.13 range but never completed.
**Bolted by Craig Luebben**

**2.** ● **The Odyssey*** 12b (7 Bolts)
This infamous route from Craig probably hasn't been climbed in over 20 years. The proximity to the road and the questionable nature of the old hardware has forced this route into obscurity.
**FA: C. Luebben**

**3.** ○ **Don't Damn It*** 7 (6 Bolts)
This route is a bit farther off the road but climbers still need to be aware of cars and dropping loose rock onto the highway. A good route for beginner leaders.
**FA: C. Luebben**

**4.** ○ **Rusty Chains and Yellow Tat*** 6 (7 Bolts)
This is another good route for beginner lead climbers. Decent stone filled with jugs and knobs on an undulating slab.
**FA: C. Luebben**

PINE VU AREA

Kepler Worobec on the exposed highball **Chromosphere**\*\*\* **v8**   Photo: B. Scott

LOW WATER ARÊTE

## LOW WATER ARÊTE

A small boulder on perfect polished rock in a lovely setting.

### 5. ○ Low Water Arête** v8 (Pads)
Start crouched squeezing the arête. Lip traverse and slap your way up horrible slopers to the easy mantle.
**FA:** Unknown

RIVER MECHANICS

## RIVER MECHANICS BOULDER

This boulder sits on the roadside of the river and does not require a crossing to get to.

### 6. ○ River Mechanics** v4 (Pads)
From the large rock platform, pull onto the lowest rail on the face above the river. A few crimpy moves and a potentially mossy topout will keep you dry.
**FA:** Unknown

### 7. ○ Hydrology* v2 (Pads)
Start on the other side of the boulder and climb out the crimp seam to the easy topout.
**FA:** Unknown

TIERED

## TIERED BOULDER

This large riverside bloc has potential for lots of moderates, or better yet has tons of moderates whose history has been lost to time.

### 8. ○ Blocky Arête* v2 (Pads)
Start on some nice jugs and move up and right until you can gain a short dihedral to the topout.
**FA:** Unknown

John Shireman on his namesake problem sometime in the early 1990s
This image appeared in Colorado Front Range Bouldering: Fort Collins Area
by Bob Horan © 1995   Photo: J. Latendresse

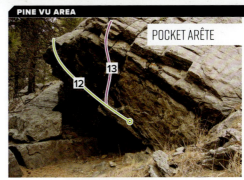

PINE VU AREA

POCKET ARÊTE

KLEIN ROOF

DIAMOND

## KLEIN ROOF

Named after the plaque and the lost adventurer it describes, that is located on an adjacent boulder (Mark Klein 1970-1993), this rock also has a lot of climbing history. In the old Bob Horan guide "Fort Collins Area Bouldering", there are two photos for the Poudre Canyon/Red Feather Lakes section. One photo is of John Shireman climbing the layback edges on the left side of this boulder. Names for the boulders and the first ascentionists have been lost to time, but these boulders have been climbed on for generations, that part is for sure.

**9.** ○ **Shireman Problem\*\* v4** (Pads)
Start on an obvious edge and angle up and right following the line of holds with bad feet to a tricky mantle.
**FA:** John Shireman

**10.** ○ **Easy Sit\* v2** (Pads)
In the center of the roof is a nice jug with an obvious two move problem on good rock to a slopey mantle.
**FA:** Unknown

**11.** ○ **Butt Dragger Traverse\* v4** (Pads)
From the start of Easy Sit, traverse right on small edges in a seam with bad feet on polished stone.
**FA:** Unknown

## POCKET ARÊTE BOULDER

A fantastic small boulder with very unusual rock. From the Low-Water Arête boulder, navigate your way directly uphill for about 50 yds to this nice overhanging boulder.

**12.** ○ **Pocket Arête\*\*\* v6** (Pads)
Amazing granite/gneiss pockets make this climb a must do for any local. SDS on some nice opposing edges and move up the arête through the two awesome pockets to incuts at the lip.
**FA:** Unknown

**13.** ○ **Easy Exit\* v4** (Pads)
Start the same as the previous problem but exit right on bigger holds rather than climbing through the pockets.
**FA:** Unknown

## DIAMOND BOULDER

A huge boulder that has been largely ignored by the climbing community. Good rock and a few nice lines that are painfully close to town.

**14.** ○ **Chromosphere\*\*\* v8** (4-5 Pads)
A fun highball that starts hard but finishes on easier yet committing terrain. Start on a jug and do big moves around the arête until you can gain the mid-way jugs. Move up and left on big holds with committing exposure.
**FA:** Kepler Worobec

**15.** ○ **Super Chrome\*\*\* v10** (4-5 Pads)
The mega-link-up is all endurance. Start as for Unwilling and move left using a tricky heel-toe cam into the start of Chromosphere. Rest up and keep it together through the airy finish of Chromosphere.
**FA:** N. Perl, B. Scott

**16.** ○ **Unwilling\*\*\* v6** (Pads)
Start in the back of the roof and follow the seam/crack up and out the steep roof. A deceptively tricky crux guards the end of the roof followed by committing moves to gain the lip and exit slab.
**FA:** Jake Atkinson, S. Rothstein

**17.** ○ **Diamond in the Rough\*\* v11** (Pads)
Unusual pocketed rock that will do nothing to help you succeed on this one. SDS on a pocket and campus out miserable holds to the break and easy topout.
**FA:** S. Rothstein

Levi Van Weddingen on the photogenic crux of **Red Rocket**\*\*\* **13b**  Photo: B. Scott

**11.2 MILES** FROM TED'S PLACE

# BRINK'S ROCK

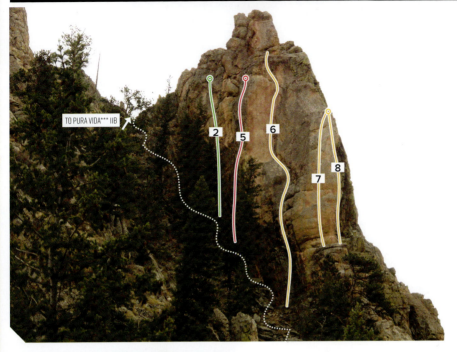

TYPE(S): **SPORT & TRAD**
DIFFICULTY RANGE: **5.10 - 5.13B**
APPROACH TIME: **20 MIN**
SEASON: **SPRING, SUMMER & FALL**

RIVER CROSSING REQUIRED

MOSTLY SUNNY ALL DAY

## CLIMBING OVERVIEW

Brink's Rock is named after iconic Fort Collins climber Mr. Jim Brink. Jim and Keith Schepflin were the first people to climb on this formation back in the early 1980s. At some point, the two face climbs and the trad route **Steamliner**\*\* **11b** were established. Around 2009, the author and friends began developing the sport routes in the corridor and the infamous pillar of **Pura Vida**\*\*\* **11b**.

## GETTING THERE

**GPS: 40°41'27.68"N 105°19'27.66"W**

From Ted's Place, drive approx. 11.2 miles up the canyon to Poudre Park Picnic area on the north side of Hwy 14. This is just past the turn for Hewlett Gulch. From the parking area, you can cross the river just downstream or alternatively, there is another pullout farther upstream which works as well. In the summer months when wading is impossible, you can park at the Hewlett Gulch Trailhead and walk upstream along the edge of the river to reach the crag.

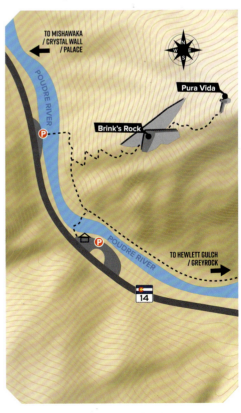

POUDRE CANYON GUIDE - 3RD EDITION

CORRIDOR WALL

## BRINK'S ROCK

To reach most of the climbing at Brink's Rock you want to head towards the corridor on the north side of the formation. In winter you can cross the frozen river right at the Picnic Area. In early spring and fall, the best crossing is upstream from the Picnic Area closer to the pullout. In summer, park at the Hewlett Gulch Trailhead and walk upstream on the edge of the river. All of these ways get you to the base of the gulley which takes you up to the prominent corridor on the north side of Brink's Rock.

### 1. ● Jersey Snake Bite* 12a (10 Bolts)
Named after a certain rattlesnake encounter involving a frightened New Jersey native. At the highest part of the corridor lies a short bulge. Carefully climb past some rotten rock to Bolt 2. Steep moves on incut holds leads to the anchor on better stone.
**FA:** B. Scott

### 2. ● Feather Tree** 12c (10 Bolts)
This versatile route climbs another section of nice brown rock. Start with easy edge climbing to a thuggy two move crux at Bolt 4. More thought provoking climbing on knobs and crimps gets you to the chains.
**FA:** B. Scott

### 3. ● Steamliner** 11b (GEAR)
At one point there was an Indian Creek style plaque below this climb with the name "Steamliner 5.11" written on it. No other info is known except that it is a nice crack with excellent gear placements.
**FA:** Unknown

### 4. ● Fake News** 12a (11 Bolts)
Start with some excellent edge climbing on bullet rock past a cruxy section at Bolt 2. Continue on some slabby terrain to the overhanging prow right of the wide crack. Slap and compress your way up the prow to the anchor.
**FA:** Connor Jeffress, Levi Van Weddingen

### 5. ● Red Rocket*** 13b (12 Bolts)
Start up easy terrain before engaging some powerful crimp moves. A juggy rail gets you back right to the arête and a tricky mantle move is required to gain the big rest. From the rest, a height dependent series of moves gets you into position on the knobs and the last few hard moves moving left to a crack and finally the anchor.
**FA:** B. Scott

### 6. ● Brink's Corner** 10 (GEAR)
The original route on the wall climbs the obvious pink left facing corner. Start with either of the hand and fist cracks to gain the ramp that leads left to the prominent corner.
**FA:** Jim Brink, Keith Schepflin

### 7. ● Unknown Face Climb 1* 10c (8 Bolts + GEAR)
A tricky 5th class scramble up the west face of Brink's Rock will deposit you on the ledge below this and the next climb. Climb the arête with some sketchy looking gear placements. Move onto the face and arête, up crumbly rock to the anchor.
**FA:** Unknown

### 8. ● Unknown Face Climb 2* 11a (8 Bolts + GEAR)
Start the same as the previous route but after the inital gear protected arête, traverse out left onto the face to another line of bolts.
**FA:** Unknown

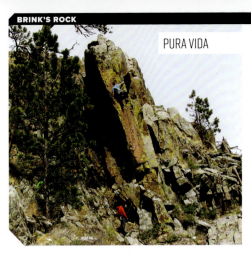

BRINK'S ROCK

PURA VIDA

Jason Tarry getting to use his favorite heel on **Pura Vida*** **11b**  Photo: B. Scott

### 9. ◉ Pura Vida*** 11b (6 Bolts)
This unusual pillar feature is worth the extra hike for its amazing rock quality and atypical movement. Cross the river and follow the description to the corridor on the north side of Brink's Rock. From here, continue walking up the corridor until it ends. Then traverse the hillside in the downstream direction for 100 yds to the base of this cool little pillar. Compression climbing leads to a final move at the last bolt.
FA: C. Tirrell, Andreas, B. Scott

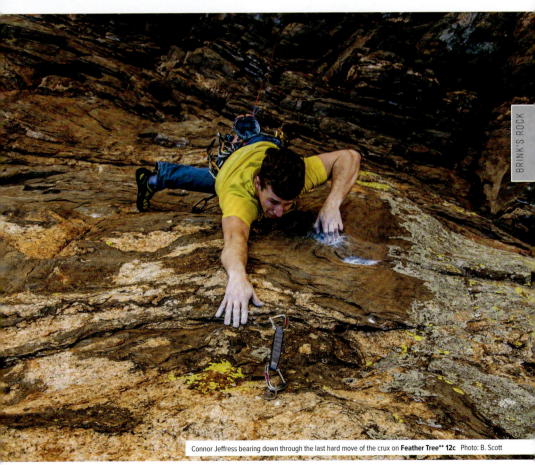

Connor Jeffress bearing down through the last hard move of the crux on **Feather Tree** **12c**  Photo: B. Scott

The author on the F.A. of **Dark Pony**\*\*\* 13b  Photo: C. Cross

**18.0 MILES** FROM TED'S PLACE

# TRIPLE TIER AREAS

Craig DeMartino bearing down on **O.D.K.**\*\*\*\* **12a**  Photo: C. Maier

**TYPE(S): TRAD, SPORT**
**DIFFICULTY RANGE: 5.9 - 5.13C**
**APPROACH TIME: 10 - 20 MIN**
**SEASON: YEAR ROUND**

*Author's Note: Most of the information for this section was written and compiled by Cameron Cross for the Second Edition of the Poudre Canyon Rock Climbing Guide (2010).*

## CLIMBING OVERVIEW

The Triple Tier Area offers some of the best sport routes in the canyon. Early ascents in the area were more focused on the lower-angled climbing on the south side of the Triple Tier ridge, but also included an ascent of the Laughing Man, a small, sketchy tower on the southwest edge of the Upper Echelon. In the late 1990s, **Don Braddy, Jeff Bassett** and others aided up various lines at the Upper Echelon, but no info was recorded and only a random smattering of manky fixed gear marks the ascents. Around 2005, development of the various tiers began with **Paul Heyliger, Greg Hand** and others working on the Chimney Sweep Wall, while **Bryan Beavers, Derek Peavey, Matt Samet and Ken Gibson** developed most of the Middle Class Wall and Upper Echelon.

## GETTING THERE

**GPS: 40°41'29.47"N 105°22'25.84"W**
To reach the Chimney Sweep Wall, Middle Class Wall, Upper Echelon, Laughing Man and Sail formation, park in the long pullout on the west side of the road immediately before the tunnel. The Sail, Chimney Sweep Wall, Middle Class Wall, Upper Echelon, and Laughing Man are all reached via the Triple Tier Trail, which is found 100 yards downstream from the parking pullout. Details about approach beta to the Fist and Undertall Wall can be found in their individual sections.

POUDRE CANYON GUIDE - 3RD EDITION  **55**

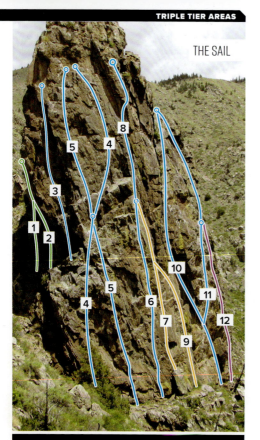

## THE SAIL

To reach the Sail, park and hike up the Triple Tier Trail. Hike to the Upper Echelon, then continue through the narrow saddle on the wall's right side passing below the Laughing Man. From the saddle, follow a faint path south to the backside of the Sail, which will be visible. Routes are listed from left to right as you approach from the backside.

### 1. ◯ Keelhaul*** 12c (10 Bolts)
Begin on the sharp downhill SW arête of the Sail, then traverse left after clipping Bolt 3. Climb into a powerful shallow dihedral feature, then up to shared anchors with the next route.
FA: Ted Lanzano, Matt Samet

### 2. ◯ Half-Mast*** 12b (10 Bolts)
Begin as for previous route, but make fun moves up, then step right back to the arête and keep it together for a short crimping crux up higher. Excellent position.
FA: M. Samet, Kristin Bjornsen '09

### 3. ◯ Guard Your Dingy** 11a (7 Bolts)
A small overhang and mantle gains the face. From there, work up and slightly left to the arête and enjoy the great exposure. Finish with some stem moves in a dihedral and topout on a large ledge where the chains await.
FA: Dan Yager, Spencer Anderson '10

### 4. ◯ Plate Tectonics 11a (11 Bolts)
**P1:** Climb the face to the right of the uphill arête, belaying at the bolted station.
**P2:** Follow a flake system to the right, climbing the right line past 5 bolts. It's possible to link these two pitches.
FA: Bryan Beavers '08

### 5. ◯ Mish Mast 11d (12 Bolts)
**P1:** Begin just left of the left-facing corner system. Move into the corner, then finish up the green lichen stripe with a slightly awkward crux at the top. Belay as for Plate Tectonics.
**P2:** Follow the far left bolt line past 5 more bolts. Linking the first two pitches of both routes is possible, as is lowering with a 60 meter rope from the top anchors.
FA: B. Beavers

### 6. ◯ Anchor Thief* 11c (9 Bolts)
Located about five feet to the left of the big flake block at the base of the wall, head straight up the wall passing a short undercling crux and cool compression moves up the final headwall. Avoid stepping right at the top for the full pump value.
FA: B. Beavers

### 7. ◯ Velvet Brown** 10c (8 Bolts)
Make crux moves off the large flake block, then continue up the thoughtful and excellent brown streak and upper dihedral.
FA: B. Beavers

TRIPLE TIER AREAS

THE FIST

## THE FIST

To reach the Fist, park as for the Triple Tier Areas, walk downstream 300 yards, then find a suitable wading spot to get to the tower's base.

**13.** ○ **Abbey Ale 10b** (2 Bolts + GEAR)
Begin as for Legos, but step left around the corner just below the roof. As Craig Luebben pulled onto the summit on the first ascent, he was pleasantly surprised to find a cold bottle of his favorite New Belgium brew, Abbey Ale, waiting for him. A couple of his friends had scrambled to the top and stashed it there prior to his ascent as a summit bonus.
FA: C. Luebben

**14.** ○ **Legos 11** (2 Bolts + GEAR)
Start off of the ledge on the south face of the freestanding portion of the Fist by either climbing a short, but ledgy and bushy pitch out of the river, or bushwack up the gulley. From the ledge, clip a couple of bolts, then pull a short roof to easier terrain and the summit.
FA: B. Beavers, L. Schultz '04

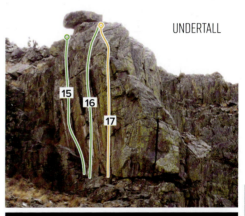

UNDERTALL

## UNDERTALL WALL

Park at the Triple Tier Parking and walk downstream until you find a good place to cross. Climb the hillside via the left side of the talus, then traverse back right to the crag.

**8.** ○ **Choss Dodger 11b** (14 Bolts)
Continue past the anchors of Velvet Brown for another six bolts of climbing.
FA: B. Beavers '10

**9.** ○ **Velvet Tan 10c** (8 Bolts)
Begin in the middle of the large flake, head up easy climbing to connect with the crux of Velvet Brown.
FA: B. Beavers '09

**10.** ○ **Magneto\* 11** (GEAR)
Begin as for Wolverine, but continue following the crack system left around the corner and out a short roof up high. A pin protects the upper roof, but the pro is tricky in spots, so be careful.
FA: Unknown FFA: B. Beavers '10

**11.** ○ **Wolverine\*\* 11** (GEAR)
Follow a left-angling crack that splits the lower half of the wall. Move right midway up the crack after clipping a fixed pin, but before it turns into a corner feature, finishing on an easier but sparsely protected slab to anchors in a pegmatite depression feature.
FA: B. Beavers '08

**12.** ○ **Bandito's Bat Roost 8** (GEAR)
Choose your own adventure up the east face of the Sail, ending on the anchors of Wolverine, or continuing another pitch to the summit. This was likely the first route developed on the formation and the exact location of the line is somewhat vague. Random pins and other historic memorabilia can be found scattered on the face.
FA: Steve Allen, Jim Peyrouse '71

**15.** ○ **Booty Prize\* 12a** (4 Bolts)
Scramble up ledges to Bolt 1, climb edgy terrain to a hard crux at the last bolt on some of the best rock in the Lower Canyon.
FA: B. Scott

**16.** ○ **Frozen Echo\*\* 12c** (4 Bolts + GEAR)
Boulder up beautiful rock past edges and slots to a rest before the black headwall. Place two small pieces through the pumpy headwall crack to the anchors.
FA: B. Scott

**17.** ○ **Undertall\* 10a** (GEAR)
Climb the perfect, laser-cut hand-crack on the right side of the overhanging wall. Beware of loose rock in the upper half of the route.
FA: Bryan Beavers, Lance Schultz '04

**TRIPLE TIER AREAS**

Matt Robbins on the exposed but wonderfully juggy finish to **Streaky Stylee**\*\*\* **11d**   Photo: B. Scott

## CHIMNEY SWEEP WALL

From the Triple Tier parking near the tunnel, walk downstream 100 yards, turning onto the Triple Tier Trail, a small cairned path found shortly after the road sign. Follow the trail through the scree field and up the narrowing gulley (be careful not to knock rocks onto the road). Traverse left along a narrow ledge about 100 yards up the trail to reach the Chimney Sweep Wall.

**18.** ◯ **Git Wood**\* **11c** (4 Bolts)
"Until I was 12, I thought my name was git wood" – Don Maynard. This route climbs a tan streak on the far left side of the wall, starting just right of a black streak with a large moss patch down low. Bring a long sling for a bomber horn at the break.
**FA: P. Heyliger**

**19.** ◯ **The Flue**\*\* **10c** (5 Bolts)
Make easy layback moves up the flake/ledge system, following black hangers.
**FA: P. Heyliger**

**20.** ◯ **Soot**\*\* **12a** (4 Bolts + GEAR)
Head up the short layback flake past two bolts to a shallow left-facing dihedral before moving past two more bolts to the anchors. Watch for the yellowjacket nest at the top! Finger-sized pieces protect the runout in the middle.
**FA: P. Heyliger**

**21.** ◯ **Elijah**\*\* **12b** (3 Bolts + GEAR)
Climb the flake system left of the orange lichen spots. Small cams and stoppers protect the beginning, while a #0.5 Camalot is useful for protecting the finish.
**FA: P. Heyliger**

**22.** ◯ **Bert**\* **10b** (4 Bolts)
Follow the right-angling ramp/corner system.

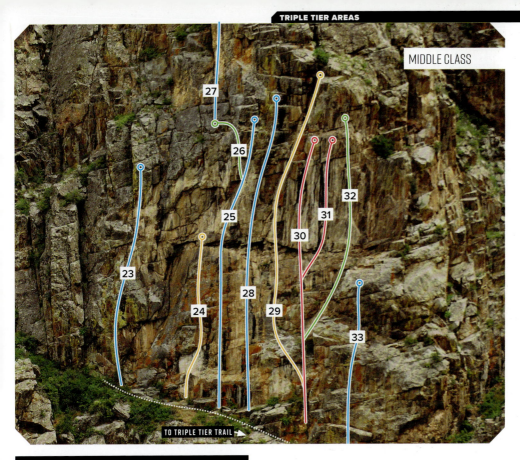

## MIDDLE CLASS WALL

Located directly above the Chimney Sweep Wall and about another 40 yards up the trail is the Middle Class Wall. From the Triple Tier Trail, make a short scramble move to attain the ledge system that leads left to the base of the main portion of the Middle Class Wall.

### 23. ○ Blue Collar Baby** 11b (10 Bolts)
Begin 10 yards left of Streaky Stylee, just below an obvious layback feature. Move up and left into a technical stemming crux, then follow the clean rock up to a steeper finish.
FA: B. Beavers '09

### 24. ○ Middle Management** 10c (5 Bolts)
On the far left side of the smiley face, undercling/layback out a small roof then continue up to the ledge in the middle of the wall. A bit spicy at the end, but the upper slabby crux is well protected.
FA: B. Beavers, Walz '10

### 25. ○ Streaky Stylee*** 11d (11 Bolts)
Scramble up a ledge to a right angling crack that is technical and a little heady. Engage the techy brown face on perfect stone to the ledge. From here, a tricky start off underclings leads to a right angling slab/dihedral. Take a deep breath and superhero your way up huge jugs to an awkward mantle at the anchor.
FA: B. Beavers '08

### 26. ○ Overtime** 12b (10 Bolts)
Climb the first eight bolts of Streaky Stylee then move left for a short, bouldery bulge finish and anchors at the base of the Upper Middle Class Wall.
FA: B. Beavers '10

### 27. ○ Black Eye in the Sky** 11d (6 Bolts)
This short pitch offers excellent position on the clean cut Upper Middle Class Wall, but is difficult to reach. From the anchors of Overtime, climb up, then move right onto the exposed streaked prow above. Descend by returning to Overtime anchors or by making a double rope rappel 175 ft to the ground.

**Variation: Black Eye in Overtime** 12b (19 Bolts)
A link-up can be done by climbing Overtime into Black Eye In The Sky with the use of long draws.
FA: B. Beavers '10

### 28. ○ Goin' Streakin'** 11d (11 Bolts)
From the right side of the smiley face, head up the black streak on the slab, eventually pulling the roof of the crack route, then traversing back left to climb the headwall by staying just right of the angling prow on Streaky Stylee.
FA: B. Beavers '09

### 29. Middle Class Cracker** 10b (GEAR)
This fun route follows the crack system that starts just right of the smiley face. Climb the short dihedral, undercling out the roof, surmount the slab crux, then enjoy the right angling crack that splits the right side of the headwall. Be wary of loose blocks on the middle ledge.
**FA: B. Beavers '09**

### 30. Twinkletoes*** 13a (11 Bolts)
One of the best lines from Mr. Beavers. Ramble up the shared ledgy start to the bolt-on boulder at the base of the headwall. A hard crux off the ledge leads to continuous climbing on underclings and sidepulls with a huck to the finish.
**FA: B. Beavers '09**

### 31. Gulf Stream** 13b (10 Bolts)
The central line on the overhanging headwall. Climb the start of Twinkletoes or Mass Appeal to reach the ledge. Amazing rock and very technical movement will get you to the last crux right before the anchor.
**FA: Derek Peavey '10**

### 32. Mass Appeal** 12b (11 Bolts)
Climb the streak on the far right side of the Middle Class Wall. The upper part is a beautiful overhanging wall, but there is a bit of slab climbing to get there.
**FA: D. Peavey, B. Beavers '09**

### 33. Lichenback 11b (7 Bolts)
Begin 10 feet right of Mass Appeal, then climb through a series of layback moves to easier terrain above.
**FA: B. Beavers, Kathy Beavers '10**

## UPPER ECHELON

The "creme de la creme" for hard sport climbing in the Lower Canyon. Pioneered primarily by **Derek Peavey and Ken Gibson**, this crag hosts a dense collection of quality sport climbs on some of the best rock around. True pump-fests exist here as compared to the bouldery nature of a lot of the canyon's sport climbing. Hike past the Middle Class Wall, taking care on the loose scree trail leading up the gulley.

### 34. Pinklepile 11b (10 Bolts)
Climb blocky/chossy ground to an obvious ledge feature. Continue towards a steep prow and the crux right before the anchor. Seldom climbed.
**FA: Matt Samet, Kristen Bjornsen '09**

### 35. Tamed Donkeys* 11d (7 Bolts)
Start as for Moose Knuckles, but move left along the flake system to a low crux and fun mantle at the top. Bolt 1 is high, but the climbing is easy and can be protected with a finger-sized piece of gear.
**FA: D. Peavey, K. Gibson '08**

### 36. Moose Knuckles*** 12b (GEAR)
Another traditional testpiece from Steve. Those who have done it rave about its quality. Climb the obvious splitter crack on the left side of the upper tier. The crux comes down low at the short roof section, but be sure to bring a large piece or two for the upper part. A #5 Camalot works best.
**FA: Steve McCorkel '08**

# TRIPLE TIER AREAS

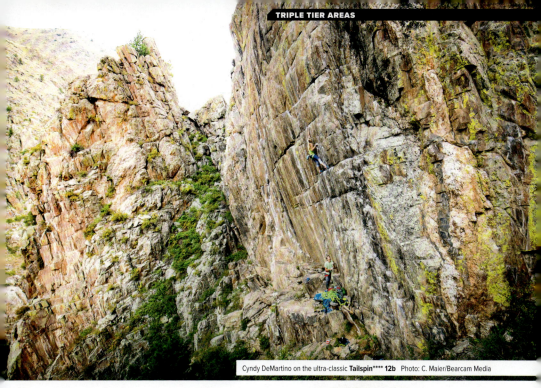

Cyndy DeMartino on the ultra-classic **Tailspin**\*\*\*\* **12b**  Photo: C. Maier/Bearcam Media

### 37. O.D.K.\*\*\*\* 12a (10 Bolts)
Old Dirty Ken is hands down one of the most famous rock climbs in the entire canyon. Climbing a stunning swath of white and orange granite, this route will test your technical skills and your ability to recover. A corner stone for anyone trying to break into 5.12. Climb a hard boulder problem at Bolt 2 on sidepulls. Then the infamous second crux climbing up a seam to a ledge at Bolt 5. This leads to a never ending section of pumpy 5.11 climbing to the anchor.
FA: D. Peavey, K. Gibson '06

### 38. The Pinklebear\*\* 12c (12 Bolts)
Similar in nature to O.D.K., climb big moves on nice edges to a rest on a ledge. From here, crimping is the name of the game on sharp and small two and three finger crimps. Finish on the Dream of Poudre slab.
FA: M. Samet, D. Peavey '09

### 39. Dream of Poudre\*\*\*\* 13a (10 Bolts)
This stunning route from Mr. Peavey climbs an incredible black streak on some of the best holds around. A corner stone for breaking into the grade of 5.13, this route should not be missed. The direct start at Bolt 2 can be skipped by traversing left into Pinklebear and then back right to avoid the big move, this variation gets (12d).
FA: D. Peavey, Adam Peters '08

### 40. Dark Pony\*\*\* 13b (10 Bolts)
Climb the crux of Dream of Poudre, then move right after clipping Bolt 3. Head up through short boulder problems until you reach a technical dyno crux to a glory jug just before pulling onto the slab. Finish at the anchors of Dream of Poudre or Folsom Flute.
FA: Ben Scott '09

### 41. Dark Horse Project\*\*\* (11 Bolts)
The hardest line at the crag and the initial jug broke making it even harder. A cheater stone gives you access to the first holds on a long v10/11 boulder problem culminating in a fierce deadpoint move to the first hold on Dark Pony.
Bolted by B. Scott

### 42. Folsom Flute\*\*\* 13c (10 Bolts)
Seldom done due to the brutal and low-percentage nature of the first two moves. If you survive that, a beautiful series of 5.12 cruxes broken by big rests leads to a final crimpy boulder before the headwall slab. The direct start can be skipped by starting on Tailspin and traversing into Folsom Flute at Bolt 1 (12c). An excellent, three-star variation.
FA: B. Scott, D. Peavey '09

### 43. Tailspin\*\*\*\* 12b (10 Bolts)
The other iconic 5.12 route on this wall. Different in nature than O.D.K., being much more thuggy and bouldery with big moves on slopey holds and jugs. If you enjoy climbing 5.12, this route should be very high on your tick list.
FA: D. Peavey, K. Gibson '06

### 44. Shoulda Coulda\* 11a (7 Bolts)
Hated by many, loved by few, this route sees the most traffic for being the only "decent" warm-up for the harder routes. A lot of climbers get pulled into the gulley/chimney to the right of the arête and have a hard time getting back. It is best climbed as an arête.
FA: D. Peavey, K. Gibson '09

### 45. Girl Problems\* 9 (5 Bolts)
Start with a crux down low, then move through increasingly easier terrain on nice big blocky holds and ledges reminiscent of the Crystal Wall.
FA: B. Scott

**CRYSTAL WALL**

**Climber Spotlight:**
Andy Cross is an awesome photographer and a great climber. He went above and beyond to help me get the shots I needed for this guidebook. Without his skills and help, this guidebook would not be nearly as rad. When he shot the photo of Ian Dory for the cover, I think he was hanging in his harness for nearly two hours in freezing wind and shade. We were all worried he was getting hypothermia but Andy didn't come down until he got the shot.

Andy Cross on the classic final crux to **Silver Girl**** **10c** Photo: B. Scott

# CRYSTAL WALL

**18.0 MILES** FROM TED'S PLACE

**GRADE DISTRIBUTION**

**TYPE(S): SPORT & TRAD**
**DIFFICULTY RANGE: 5.8 - 5.12D**
**APPROACH TIME: 10-20 MIN**
**SEASON: SPRING, SUMMER & FALL**

*Author's Note: Most of the information for this section was written and compiled by Cameron Cross for the Second Edition of the Poudre Canyon Rock Climbing Guide (2010).*

## CLIMBING OVERVIEW

This wall, which lies above the Crystal Rapids on the Poudre River, received sporadic exploration by climbers like **Craig Luebben, Vance White, Casey Rosenbach,** and **Lizz Grenard** until the late '90s when the crag was briefly forgotten. As development slowed at the nearby Palace in 2004, locals **Bryan Beavers, Derek Peavey, Ken Gibson, Paul Heyliger** and others began establishing many excellent routes. Today, the Crystal Wall offers several of the area's finest lines of all grades.

With north and west aspects, the Crystal Wall stays shaded until late afternoon during the summer. In addition, no river crossing is required, making the wall a popular summer destination when many of the other crags in the canyon are either inaccessible or too hot. The approach isn't super dog friendly, nor is the scree field that runs the length of the west face. Be very careful about rockfall, as the entire wall is directly above the road.

## GETTING THERE

**GPS: 40°41'36.78"N 105°22'35.58"W**
The Crystal Wall and Palace share the same parking pullout, which can be found 15.2 miles from Ted's Place. Alternatively, there is another pullout on the west side of the Tunnel.

Walk downstream 200 yards on the riverside of the road, past a road sign, then carefully cross the road. The trail scrambles up a steep ramp through the roadcut, passing a small tree and fixed rope. From here, follow the obvious cairned trail to the northwest corner of the Crystal Wall. The first climb you will come to is **Clean Up On Aisle 9**. Branching off to the left takes you to the north face routes, while heading right leads up the steep scree gulley to the West Face and the County Line Wall.

Nearly all the routes have bolted belay stations, where making one or two 60 meter rappels will bring you back to the ground. Descend from the few traditional lines with natural anchors by locating the nearest bolted rappel station. Walking off to the southwest is possible, but not recommended.

## NORTH FACE - LEFT SIDE

## NORTH FACE - CRYSTAL WALL

### 1. Down on the Pharm** 8 (10 Bolts)
Hidden on the far left side of the Crystal Wall, this route starts 50 feet left of BlackWave. Head up good rock on a slab before stepping right over a corner and continuing to a ledge and belay.
**FA:** Sam Shannon

### 2. Black Wave** 12c (11 Bolts)
An excellent face and slab climb on cool undulating stone. Technical resistance climbing with a final crux out the last bit of the wave feature.
**FA:** D. Peavey

### 3. Orange Crimpsicle** 12d (11 Bolts)
From the far left edge of the large ledge system, move up a green and orange streak on very thin holds.
**FA:** D. Peavey '04

### 4. Mood for a Day 10a / 11a (GEAR)
Begin in the shallow corner system just right of Orange Crimpsicle.
**P1:** Follow the seldom traveled crack system up the dihedral to belay on the obvious ledge just above the anchor of Fahrenheit 5.11.
**P2:** Step back left and continue up the dihedral, moving right at the top to anchors of Fahrenheit 5.11.
**FA:** Unknown

### 5. Bananarête** 9 (9 Bolts)
One of the finer and more traveled 9s at Crystal Wall. Fun and steep climbing through some long, juggy pulls leads to a few technical moves before the chains.
**FA:** P. Heyliger, J. Durkin

### 6. Bolt Dependence* 11b (8 Bolts)
Start to the right of a licheny crack system on a nice yellow panel. Climb flat edges and cool laybacks to the ledge.
**FA:** D. Peavey '10

### 7. Fahrenheit 5.11** 10b / 12b (9 Bolts)
**P1:** Climb up the black streak to the right of Bolt Dependence.
**P2:** Continue up a wavy slab on thin crimps.
**FA:** D. Peavey, Tim Wilhelmi, J. Doyle '04

### 8. Fantastic Planet** 9 / 11c (4 Bolts + GEAR)
This was one of the first routes to be developed on the wall.
**P1:** Climb fractured rock in the tan streak past three bolts to a large flake, then continue past one more bolt up a wavy slab to chains of previous route.
**P2:** Climb the sparsely bolted face to the right of Fahrenheit 5.11, using gear to supplement the runouts. It is possible to move right at the crux and make the climb significantly easier.
**FA:** C. Luebben

### 9. The O-Face** 11d (14 Bolts)
Climb up dirty rock just left of Thursday Afternoon Hooky. Continue up the ramp until you can step right onto the orange face. A hard reachy crux gets you to the "o" feature and the easy romp to the finish.
**FA:** D. Peavey

### 10. Thursday Afternoon Hooky 10b R (GEAR)
This is the obvious crack line splitting the Crystal Wall.
**P1:** Climb the crack right of Fantastic Planet. Set up a belay before the pro runs out in the dihedral or step right to the anchors of Tool Man.
**P2:** Continue up the corner as it eventually turns into a stem box and the protection becomes difficult.
**FA:** Unknown

### NORTH FACE - CENTER

**11.** ⭕ **Tool Man**\*\* **11c** (9 Bolts)
Begin just right of Thursday Afternoon Hooky, moving past several bolts of fun moderate climbing before reaching a crimpy boulder problem at the last bolt. Two grey-spackled hangers mark the beginning of this route.
FA: B. Beavers

**12.** ⭕ **Tour De Poudre**\*\*\*\* **10b / 12b** (7 Bolts)
With the first pitch going at 10b, this route is one of the finest in the canyon, and an absolute must-do for anyone visiting.
**P1:** Climb past seven bolts to a series of right-facing gastons before heading up the final headwall with big moves between good holds (10b).
**P2:** Make difficult moves up thin crimps before the angle eventually eases (12b).
FA: D. Peavey, T. Wilhelmi, J. Doyle '04

**13.** ⭕ **Silver Girl**\*\* **10c** (11 Bolts)
Head up past the blocky section of climbing to a shallow pegmatite groove, making cruxy moves at the last bolt before clipping the Fixe sport anchor.
FA: T. Wilhelmi, D. Peavey, Ceceli Wilhelmi '04

**14.** ⭕ **Crystal Method**\* **11+ R** (4 Bolts + GEAR)
Begin just right of Silver Girl, following the intermittent crack system to a bolt with a red painted hanger, then make delicate moves above crux, until gear reappears and the climbing eases up slightly. Continue climbing straight up, staying to the left of the second pitch of Fantastic Planet. Descend as for Fantastic Planet.
FA: B. Beavers '05

**15.** ⭕ **Balaam**\* **11c** (9 Bolts)
Easy climbing to a hole at Bolt 3 leads to a short layback section and crimpy crux near the top. Easily top-roped by leading Fantastic Planet.
FA: Unknown

**16.** ⭕ **Better Than Watching Television**\*\*\* **11c** (7 Bolts)
**P1:** Begin at two old cold shuts, meander right, then back left again before clipping Metolius rap bolts. This pitch originally only had three bolts but has since been retrobolted, making it far more popular, even though it is still spicier than most other routes of its grade on the wall (10a).
**P2:** Climb thin crimps with a low crux and easing difficulty up the long slab (11c).
FA: Vance White, Casey Rosenback '94/'95

## NORTH FACE - RIGHT SIDE

This is the first set of routes you will come to on your hike in. This right side of the north face offers an excellent collection of moderate sport climbs that are frequently busy in good weather months.

### 17. Better Than the Internet** 11b (18 Bolts + GEAR)
**P1:** Climb the long grey streak on typically awesome Crystal Wall Rock. (13 Bolts)
**P2:** The second pitch requires a light rack and some choss/pigeon navigation to get to the really nice bolted finish. On the F.A. the route was climbed in one long pitch.
FA: B. Beavers

### 18. Gates of Crystal** 8 (5 Bolts)
Just to the right of two trees on the Crystal Wall's western edge that follows the left line of bolts up blocky edges.
FA: Unknown

### 19. Lunch Bucket Crack** 8 (4 Bolts)
Follow the bolted crack feature. A hand-sized piece of gear can supplement the runout between Bolts 2-3 and another hand-sized cam for the run to the anchors.
FA: Unknown

### 20. Clean-Up on Aisle 9** 9 (6 Bolts)
Another excellent moderate on great blocky edges. A must-do for any aspiring beginner lead climber.
FA: Unknown

### 21. Dr. Food** 10b (7 Bolts)
A more recent addition to this wall of moderates featuring more fun climbing on big blocky holds and edges.
FA: Unknown

### 22. Saline Lock** 9 (7 Bolts)
More blocky jugs up a nice panel of stone. Long and sustained for the grade.
FA: Unknown

## WEST FACE - CRYSTAL WALL

Approach by taking the right fork in the trail as you near the northwest corner of the main buttress.

### 23. Sea of Lichen 8 (5 Bolts)
Make easy, but unprotected moves up to the bottom of the steep, green lichen covered pegmatite band, then step left onto the slabby, but lichen-covered face.
FA: B. Beavers '05

### 24. Pet Cemetary 11c (5 Bolts)
Climb the hand/finger crack to the ledge, then step slightly left and clip bolts as you squeeze your way up the prow. A bit contrived, but fun. Named for the plethora of dead animals that were found inside the Nancy crack and at the base during the time of the F.A.
FA: B. Beavers, Steve Reed '03

### 25. Nancy 8 (GEAR)
Abundant edges lead through this nasty, rotten, overhanging off-width/chimney on the west face of Crystal Wall. The first ascent leader named this after his sister - what a tribute! Bring extra wide gear, although it is possible to clip several bolts from nearby sport lines if you desire.
FA: C. Luebben, J. Brink

### 26. Pumpin' Puff Muffins* 10 (GEAR)
Great hand, fist and off-width jamming leads up the steep west face of the Crystal Wall. Bring extra large hand pieces as well as Big Bros.
FA: C. Luebben, J. Brink

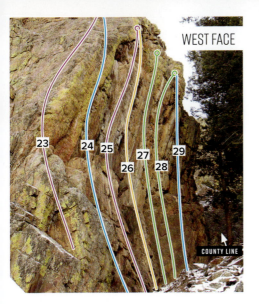

**27. Good Ol' Boys* 12b** (5 Bolts)
Climb the face to the right of Pumpin' Puff Muffins, moving to the prow/off-width at the last bolt. Bailing left earlier makes it easier.
FA: B. Beavers '05

**28. The General Lee** 12b** (8 Bolts)
Start as for Good Ol' Boys, but head up and right through the fractured face after Bolt 2. Fun movement and the rock is better than it looks.
FA: B. Beavers '03

**29. Bosch Hog 11d** (5 Bolts)
Squeeze up the steep, broken prow just left of the off-width on the right side of the wall, finishing on the anchors of The General Lee.
FA: B. Beavers '03

## COUNTY LINE WALL

The County Line Wall, a.k.a. Southwest Alcove is accessed by walking past the wall that holds The General Lee for another 50yds up the gulley.

**30. County Line*** 8** (7 Bolts)
Climb the southwest arête of the Crystal wall. Excellent stone and movement.
FA: Laura Girard '05

**31. Inyerbuttkwa** 10c** (6 Bolts)
Climb the steep arête in the corridor, finishing with a technical move just before the anchors. Name derives from the French expression, "Il n'y a pas de quoi" which means "you're welcome".
FA: B. Beavers, S. Reed '03

**32. Ballet of the Bulge*** 11b** (5 Bolts)
Follow thin crimps on excellent rock up the right side of the corridor face, ending at the chains of Inyerbuttkwa.
FA: B. Beavers, Kathy Beavers '03

**33. She's A Daisy* 9** (12 Bolts)
This route is found 40 yards uphill from County Line. Follow the broken, blunt prow to the top of the only semi-solid section of the upper west wall. This route can be identified by its red painted hangers.
FA: B. Beavers, L. Schultz '04

**34. Britney's Spear** 11c** (5 Bolts)
Ascend the north face of the steep prow feature at the top of the Crystal Wall formation. An approach pitch climbs the gulley from the east side of the County Line corridor.
FA: B. Beavers, Lance Schultz, Jack Reed '04

*The next two routes are located on a suspended pillar at the top of the Crystal Wall formation. From County Line, continue walking all the way up the gulley until you can gain the ridge and walk back left to the prow feature. Look at the Crystal Wall overview map to get a better understanding.*

**35. Open Project** (6 Bolts)
Climb the left arête on the prow.
Bolted by: D. Peavey

**36. Eye in the Sky*** 12d** (6 Bolts)
Climb the right arête of the pillar, staying primarily on the south face.
FA: D. Peavey, K. Gibson '09

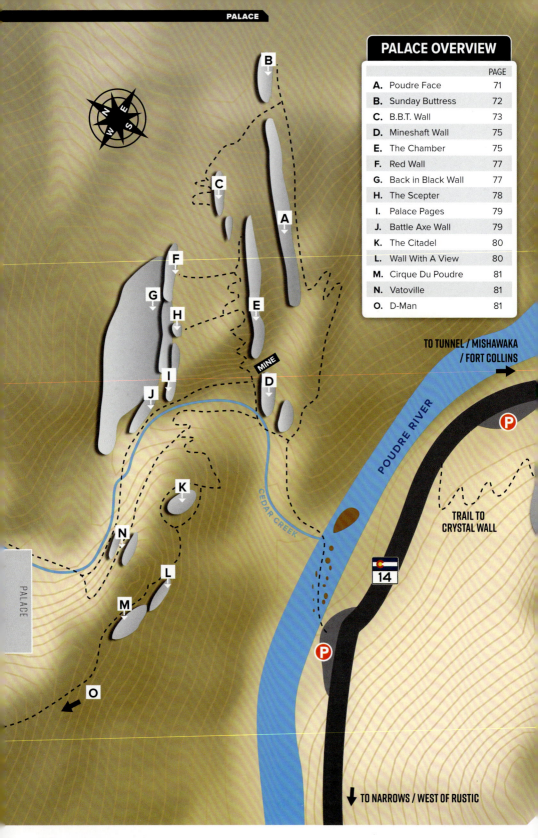

**14.9 MILES** FROM TED'S PLACE

# PALACE

**TYPE(S): TRAD, SPORT**
**DIFFICULTY RANGE: 5.7 - 5.13A**
**APPROACH TIME: 10 - 20 MIN**
**SEASON: YEAR ROUND**

*Author's Note: Most of the information for this section was written and compiled by Cameron Cross for the Second Edition of the Poudre Canyon Rock Climbing Guide (2010).*

## CLIMBING OVERVIEW

The Palace is an impressive assortment of spires and thin rock fins just upstream from the Crystal Rapids and Baldwin Tunnel. Carved in half by Cedar Creek, the Palace was once the site of a prospector homestead in the late 1800s (the ruins can still be found 400 yards past Vatoville) and an unproductive mine which was quickly abandoned. Although the Palace was never a source of valuable minerals, the area has long been a rich resource for climbers.

The earliest climbing exploration of the area is largely a mystery. Climbers had summited the main pinnacles and walls by the early '70s, although no info is available about specific ascents. In 1972, the area was dubbed Psilocybin Canyon and many of the crack lines received early ascents. However, it wasn't until the early '90s that the area began to see significant development. **Rob Poutre, Ron Ambrose** and others bolted routes on the Tommyknocker Wall (now Mineshaft Wall) and the Citadel. Shortly thereafter, **Steve McCorkel** and others established several routes on Sunday Buttress, a.k.a. Lion's Den. Beginning in 1998, **Tim Wilhelmi, Derek Peavey, Judson Doyle, Sam Shannon, Ken Gibson** and others became very active in establishing sport lines, and by 2006, the majority of routes had been bolted. Now commonly known as the Palace, the area is the most popular sport climbing destination near Fort Collins, and offers over 100 routes of all grades.

Given the geology of the area, the Palace has a wide variety of aspects, making it climbable for much of the year, even well into winter. Spring runoff generally makes the river impassible from May through late July. Tyrolean traverses are discouraged given the width of the river and number of rafters and boaters that pass by during high water. The rock quality is varied and can be bullet hard or crystally and flaky. Despite lots of traffic, rockfall can be common and wearing a helmet is a good idea. The Palace is maze-like and many walls are directly above other routes or access trails, so please be extremely careful to avoid knocking rocks down on other climbers.

# PALACE

Dogs are allowed, but please keep them on a leash to respect other climbers and for their safety. Bears and mountain lions have been seen at the Palace, and rattlesnakes are common in the summer.

## GETTING THERE

**GPS: 40°41'38.37"N 105°22'43.90"W**
Park in the large pullout on the north side of the road 14.9 miles from Ted's Place.

Wade across the river, then find the main access trail that follows Cedar Creek upstream toward the Palace. The shallowest path across the river is found by angling from the parking lot, downstream toward the line of rocks and island. Just before reaching the island, cross the final channel. Wading straight across is possible at lower water, but a deep channel exists just before the far bank. A wading staff, trekking poles, waders and a dry set of clothes are recommended. The crossing becomes dangerous and impassable when the river reaches 1.75 ft or higher. If the crossing looks dubious, it's best to find a different crag for the day like Sheep Mountain or Solar Panel.

*Climber Spotlight:*
Mark Wilford is a legend in the climbing community at large, not just Fort Collins. Mark is known for being talented in all the disciplines of climbing and for bold F.A.s in places like Pakistan, Greenland, India and the Canadian Rockies. When we hiked up to the Citadel to shoot this photo, Mark made a casual comment that he first climbed the pinnacle when he was 13 years old in the sweet summer of 1974. The Poudre Canyon is a place even the best climbers can enjoy for a lifetime.

Mark Wilford taking a cruise on **Let Down Your Hair** ** **10b** on the citadel   Photo: B. Scott

POUDRE FACE

## A - POUDRE FACE

Visible from the parking lot, the Poudre Face is the obvious long wall that guards the entrance into the Palace. In general, the rock tends to be a bit crystally, but there are a number of moderate routes and the wall gets early morning sun, making it a popular destination in the winter. Be wary of snakes in the summer.

To reach the Poudre Face, cross the river and follow the trail leading up the Cedar Creek. Upon reaching Drawbridge, a short bolted route which marks the beginning of climbing at the Palace, take the right fork of the trail and continue hiking another couple of minutes.

**1. Where's the Beef?*** 12c (5 Bolts)
Make thin, technical moves up the pegmatite face speckled with green lichen. Located about 40 yards below where the trail switchbacks and first touches the Poudre Face, this is the lowest route on the wall.
FA: Derek Peavey, Judson Doyle, Tim Wilhelmi '05

**2. Check Your Head*** 10c (10 Bolts)
This was the first bolted line to be developed on the Poudre Face. Follow the juggy right leaning crack, moving slightly left to the anchors at the top. First climbed by Steve McCorkel on gear prior to being bolted.
FA: S. McCorkel

**3. Check Your Six** 11b (9 Bolts)
This is a direct start to Check Your Head. Make thin slab moves up to easier climbing.
FA: S. Shannon, T. Wilhelmi '04

**4. Cheerleaders Gone Hippie* 9 (8 Bolts)
Climb the crack feature right of Check Your Head to a crux in the water runnel. Bolt 1 is a glue-in.
FA: S. Shannon, T. Wilhelmi '03

**5. Rocks for Jocks 8 R (4 Bolts)
Grovel up the chimney, clipping a couple of random bolts, then step left onto the face, pull a short bulge and finish with Cheerleaders Gone Hippie. Bizarre and not recommended.
FA: S. Shannon '04

**6. Crossbow 10b (8 Bolts)
Meander up the broken face, clipping red painted hangers.
FA: S. Shannon '04

**7. Flail* 11a (7 Bolts)
Found ten yards uphill from Crossbow, this route ascends the green arête just left of the bushy gulley with a thoughtful squeezing crux up high. Surprisingly more solid than it looks.
FA: S. Shannon, T. Wilhelmi '04

**8. Cal Trop 9 (4 Bolts)
The bolts follow the obvious clean rock, but the climbing pulls you to the juggy arête to the left.
FA: S. Shannon '03

**9. Creepy* 10b (8 Bolts)
Climb the green lichen streak with a bulge midway up. This route is much better since a large loose block has been removed.
FA: S. Shannon, T. Wilhelmi '03

**10. B.A.H. 9 (5 Bolts)
Big jugs lead out bulges. The acronym stands for Big Assed Holds, although if you say it fast, it takes on another meaning.
FA: S. Shannon solo

**11. Palace Guard 10b (3 Bolts + GEAR)
Make bouldery crux moves past two bolts, then climb the enjoyable finger crack, finishing with one more bolt at the top. Finger-sized gear and stoppers protect the crack.
FA: S. Shannon solo

**PALACE**

SUNDAY BUTTRESS

**12.** ○ **Loyalist 9** (5 Bolts)
Climb the flake layback left of the bushy water runnel.
FA: S. Shannon '03

**13.** ○ **River Rats 7** (5 Bolts)
Follow jugs up the bulbous arête.
FA: S. Shannon '05

**14.** ○ **Turtle Head 7** (4 Bolts)
Located 15 yards uphill from River Rats is this moderate which climbs big moves on good holds up the face to the left of the orange and black streak.
FA: S. Shannon '05

**15.** ○ **Orange You Glad 7** (9 Bolts)
Climb the orange lichen covered groove to the pillar finish.
FA: S. Shannon '05

## B - SUNDAY BUTTRESS

Just uphill from the Poudre Face is a tall, clean wall with several routes on it. The rock quality is exceptional on several of the lines and the cracks are the best the Palace has to offer.

To reach the Sunday Buttress (a.k.a. Lions Den) hike past the Poudre Face, continuing uphill on a faint trail, then traverse right along a ledge system to the base of the crag. A line of cairns leading to the B.B.T. Wall branches off to the left just after the end of the Poudre Face.

**16.** ○ **Scrapin' and Scrubbin' 10a** (GEAR)
Climb the far left crack line on the Sunday Buttress. This route is super bushy and still has a bit of lichen adventure. Shares anchors with Pug's Den.
FA: B. Beavers, Jeff Waltz '10

**17.** ○ **Pug's Den* 11c** (10 Bolts)
Begin just left of Big As a House, following a line of bolts up, then out left to the prow to finish. Nice rock. Use a long draw on Bolt 5 to lessen rope drag.
FA: B. & Kathy Beavers, J. Waltz '10

**18.** ○ **Big as a House 10b** (GEAR)
Climb the broken crack feature to the left of Sunday's Child. Follow the crack feature to the right before reaching the V-slot to reach the chain anchors of Sunday's Child.
FA: S. McCorkel, Joe Vallone '93

**19.** ○ **Sunday's Child*** 12c** (6 Bolts + GEAR)
Start in the obvious flake seam with superb rock, moving slightly left, then over a short roof at the top. Bring a #0.5 Camalot to supplement the bolts.
FA: S. McCorkel, Becky McCorkel '95

**20.** ○ **Harvest Moon*** 11d** (GEAR)
Crux comes right off the ground on this one, the F.A. placed a nut via stick-clip to protect it. Continue up the obvious crack to a ledge, step right and up another crack to shared anchors with Golden Harvest.
FA: S. McCorkel, Kurt Stroble, Matt Flach

**21.** ○ **Golden Harvest**** 11c** (GEAR)
Easily the best traditional route at the Palace. Start up the A-shaped alcove to a tricky section moving into the left-facing corner. Easier terrain up the nice crack leads to the anchor.
FA: M. Flach, S. McCorkel

**22.** ○ **Stanley's Steamer 11c** (6 Bolts + GEAR)
From the right side of the small roof, follow the blunt layback feature to the lower angle gulley, then step right onto the face and a line of bolts.
FA: S. McCorkel, Joe Carpenter '92

**23.** ○ **Shit, Piss, Spit Up & Drool** 12b** (8 Bolts + GEAR)
Do a short boulder problem past two bolts, then climb a short crack section before stepping left to the bolt line finish of Stanley's Steamer.
FA: S. McCorkel, B. McCorkel '95

**24.** ○ **Rabble Rouser* 10b** (2 Bolts + GEAR)
Ten yards right of the main Sunday Buttress face, you will find this climb, which starts in a short finger crack, then moves past two bolts and finishes with a thin crack. Bring extra thin gear and a #3 Camalot for above Bolt 2.
FA: S. Shannon, T. Wilhelmi '05

B.B.T. WALL

## PALACE
# C - B.B.T. WALL

The B.B.T. (a.k.a. Big Beaver Tail) is a small fin that sits directly above the Upper Chamber Wall. Despite being a part of the Upper Chamber Wall, a short section of cliff band makes accessing the B.B.T. Wall from the Upper Chamber Wall impossible. The B.B.T. Wall offers a couple of nice routes and is worth a visit if you are chasing shade or looking for excellent views of the rest of the Palace.

To reach the B.B.T. Wall, hike toward the Sunday Buttress and turn left onto a faint cairned path just after passing the end of the Poudre Face. The path leads up and over the ridge, dropping you into the corridor with the B.B.T. on your left.

**27.** ○ **Lichen It\*\* 12a** (6 Bolts)
Flat edges on the wall's left arête lead to harder climbing the higher you get. Nice rock, but don't blow the 3rd clip.
FA: B. Beavers '03

**28.** ○ **Steep and Cheap\*\* 11d** (7 Bolts)
From the obvious crack feature up the center of the wall, climb left to finish on Lichen It.
FA: B. Beavers '03

**25.** ○ **Bodies Like Sheep 10c** (4 Bolts + GEAR)
Wrangle your way up to the giant bulb and Bolt 1, then cruise past three more bolts and an easier finish.
FA: S. Shannon, T. Wilhelmi '05

**29.** ○ **Gangsta Man in a Cadillac\* 11a** (7 Bolts)
Climb the first three bolts of Steep & Cheap, then veer right up the white streak.
FA: B. Beavers, K. Beavers '03

**26.** ○ **The 13th Step\* 10a** (GEAR)
Just to the right of the previous route, you will find a nice, right-leaning finger crack. Jam the crack and squeeze the arête to the top of this nice route. The crack takes gear to two inches and can be a bit tricky to protect.
FA: Chris Donharl, S. Shannon '05

**30.** ○ **Breakin' Trail 10c** (7 Bolts)
Nice climbing up the right crack leads to a crumbly looking face up higher.
FA: B. Beavers, Steve Reed, Jack Reed '03

**31.** ○ **Forest Fire 11b** (7 Bolts)
Pull over a short roof at the bottom, then pick your way through the fractured face and more solid rounded prow finish. Clip the belayer into the bolt at the bottom.
FA: B. Beavers, S. Reed, J. Reed '03

**32.** ○ **Cross Mojonation! 11a** (7 Bolts)
From around the right arête, climb on dubious rock until you can cross back over onto the corridor face and finish on the last two bolts of Forest Fire. Clip the belayer into the bolt at the bottom.
FA: B. Beavers '03

Mike Botkin on the send of **Small Fry\*\* 12b**  Photo: M. Botkin

# D - MINESHAFT WALL

In general, the rock quality is excellent, the access is easy and the routes are fun, making the Mineshaft Wall one of the most popular walls at the Palace.

To reach the Mineshaft Wall, cross the Poudre and follow the trail up the Cedar Creek. You will pass a short three bolt route, Drawbridge and a five bolt route, It Is What It Is, just before reaching the main section of the Mineshaft Wall.

### 33. Cannon Ball** 12c (5 Bolts)
From the top of the mineshaft, make crimpy reaches to connect with Rapid Fire for the final two bolts.
FA: D. Peavey '06

### 34. Rapid Fire** 12d (8 Bolts)
Begin just right of the mine shaft. Climb the orange streak, making crux moves between Bolt 3 and Bolt 4, before heading up and left past four more bolts to a cold shut and quicklink anchor. Moving onto the jugs of Monstrosity is easy at a few points, but avoid them for the full value.
FA: D. Peavey, T. Wilhelmi, Rob Kennedy

### 35. Monstrosity*** 10b (9 Bolts)
The most famous route of its grade at the Palace. An excellent climb that is centrally located and has nice rock. The route meanders quite a bit around the bolt line but the good holds and stances are all right where you want them to be.
FA: T. Wilhelmi, Jim Bowes, Ceceli Wilhelmi

### 36. Armor Plated* 11c (8 Bolts)
Do a short boulder problem to Bolt 1, or traverse in from left before cruising up the slab and figuring out the long undercling crux at Bolt 6.
FA: R. Poutre, R. Ambrose '91-93

### 37. Strictly Business** 10c (4 Bolts)
Climb the blocky crack past Bolt 1, then continue straight up the face on good rock with slopey edges.
FA: R. Poutre, R. Ambrose '91-93

### 38. Death and Disfiguration* 11c (6 Bolts)
Follow left-angling crack on slopey edges and sidepulls to an easier bulge. There used to be a very large and very detached arch that was the route's namesake, but now it rests in pieces on the ground.
FA: D. Peavey, T. Wilhelmi, S. Shannon '04

### 39. PowerPoint 10d (5 Bolts)
Climb right arête to Bolt 4, then move left through blocky sidepulls to a jug on the face.
FA: D. Peavey, T. Wilhelmi '05

### 40. It Is What It Is* 11a (5 Bolts)
Climb the narrow face on the far right side of the Mineshaft Wall. Similar to Drawbridge, but harder.
FA: D. Peavey, J. Doyle '04

# E - THE CHAMBER

This extensive wall stretches upward from the Mineshaft Wall and offers a number of long routes. The wall is roughly divided into two parts – the Lower Chamber and Upper Chamber, which are separated by a chossy section of rock with no routes. The rock quality can vary significantly, but in general, the lines are sustained and can be devious. The trail for the Chamber also serves to access the Scepter and Red Wall.

## LOWER CHAMBER

### 41. The Brown Chossum Special 10d (9 Bolts)
Begin on a green-streaked arête about 15 yards uphill from the previous route. Climb the loose and broken face right of the shallow depression.
FA: B. Beavers '05

### 42. Last in Show 11b (13 Bolts)
Start at the switchback in the trail, following broken seams to the right of the right-angling groove, finishing on the green lichen covered bulge finish.
FA: T. Wilhelmi, D. Peavey '06

### 43. Road to Redemption*** 11b (12 Bolts)
Begin in the brown streak, climbing through short cruxes between good rests.
FA: D. Peavey, T. Wilhelmi, K. Gibson '05

### 44. Sanctus* 10d (6 Bolts)
Follow the faint black streak. Climbing directly up the bolt line increases the difficulty, but the path of least resistance wanders slightly.
FA: T. Wilhelmi, K. Gibson, J. Bowes

### 45. Drawn and Quartered 11a (5 Bolts)
Climb the short route uphill from the third switchback.
FA: T. Wilhelmi, J. Bowes, S. Shannon

### 46. Cruiser 9 (5 Bolts)
This is a good, short, but slightly devious moderate. While there are lots of holds, it takes a bit of groping to find the best ones.
FA: D. Peavey, J. Doyle, T. Wilhelmi '04

### 47. Love It or Hate It* 11b (15 Bolts)
Long route up broken features with crux up high.
FA: D. Peavey, T. Wilhelmi '05

### 48. The Rack* 10d (8 Bolts)
Begin right of the broken chimney feature, climbing sidepulls and edges up the orange streak, with a crux at the top.
FA: T. Wilhelmi, J. Bowes, C. Wilhelmi

### 49. In Between the Sheets 11b (6 Bolts)
Climb blocky holds left of Jester.
FA: D. Peavey, J. Doyle, K. Gibson '06

### 50. Jester*** 10b (10 Bolts)
Another excellent route for the grade. Don't let its appearance turn you away, technical climbing on blocky holds that goes on for ever and ever.
FA: T. Wilhelmi, J. Bowes

### 51. ○ Rusty Shackleford 11b (8 Bolts)
Right above the trail, this route goes up the overhanging face of the same color; be mindful of the loose block up higher.
FA: D. Peavey, J. Doyle '04

### 52. ○ Churchill Rejects*** 9 (8 Bolts)
Easily the most popular route of its grade at the Palace. Centrally located right next to the Mineshaft Wall, it is rare for this route to not have a party of climbers on it. Start with a crack up a short face which turns into a long series of corners to a blocky finish right of the anchor.
FA: S. Shannon

## UPPER CHAMBER

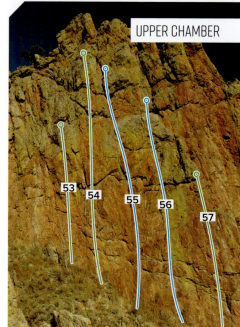

### 53. ○ Poudre Pie** 12a (6 Bolts)
Start in front of the dead tree. Climb to the green lichen-covered blunt prow.
FA: D. Peavey, J. Doyle, T. Wilhelmi '05

### 54. ○ Big Mac*** 12c (13 Bolts)
It's in your face and all over the place right from the get go.
FA: D. Peavey, T. Wilhelmi, J. Doyle '04

### 55. ○ Over the Ramparts 11c (10 Bolts)
You quickly dispatch with the crux on this one but it isn't over until you clip the chains.
FA: S. Shannon, T. Wilhelmi

### 56. ○ Green Lantern* 11d (8 Bolts)
A continuous route across good, green rock.
FA: T. Wilhelmi, K. Gibson, J. Bowes

### 57. ○ Small Fry*** 12a/b (7 Bolts)
Big, steep moves on big holds lead to a super thin crux.
FA: D. Peavey, T. Wilhelmi, K. Gibson '04

RED WALL

RAP STATION TO BACK ON BLACK WALL

## F - RED WALL

Located directly across from the Upper Chamber Wall, the Red Wall offers several longer slab routes and is a popular winter destination on cold days due to it's southern aspect.

To reach the crag, hike up the Chamber Wall Trail and veer left just before reaching Small Fry and the Upper Chamber.

### 58. Natty's 3.2 Light Slab 9 (5 Bolts)
Begin on the far left side of the detached wall to the left of the Red Wall. This route ascends a narrow pillar directly above the rap station to reach the Back on Black Wall, which is in the hidden corridor around the corner. For the time being, finish at the anchor of H.R. Puf 'N Stuff, although an extension will likely be bolted soon.
FA: D. Peavey, K. Gibson '08

### 59. H.R. Puf 'N Stuff* 9 (5 Bolts)
Squeeze your way up the broken pillar that is detached from the left side of the Red Wall.
FA: D. Peavey, J. Doyle '04

### 60. Uneedaluebben** 11a (12 Bolts)
P1: Begin right of the bushy crack, climbing over the bulge, streaked wall and belay at the pigeon roost (11a).
P2: Dubbed Don't Peav the Beav, this short pitch steps left onto face above roof, then continues up prow (11b).
FA: D. Peavey, T. Wilhelmi, K. Gibson '04, Don't Peav The Beav D. Peavey, B. Beavers '04

### 61. Lenora*** 11c (10 Bolts)
Two different types of classic; one is a woman in green pants, the other is a route at the Palace.
P1: Ascend the obvious crack feature, then step left into the depression and continue to chains (10c).
P2: Climb slab to top of Red Wall (11c).
FA: D. Peavey, T. Wilhelmi, K. Gibson '04

### 62. Red Hot Space Suit*** 12b (12 Bolts)
P1: Follow two parallel vertical seams before moving right into the crack feature, then move left as it peters out (12b).
P2: Climb directly up and over the bulge for a short pitch known as Moon Boots (11c).
FA: T. Wilhelmi, K. Gibson, J. Bowes, Moon Boots D. Peavey

### 63. Red Planet** 12a (11 Bolts)
Climb the face just left of the right-facing dihedral system, stepping left under the roof and up the slab. Two cruxes. It is also possible to climb Moon Boots as a second pitch.
FA: T. Wilhelmi, K. Gibson, J. Bowes

### 64. Blue Steel* 12a (8 Bolts)
You will find this route that climbs over two small roofs, then steps left to anchors on the far right side of the Red Wall.
FA: D. Peavey, J. Doyle '05

## G - BACK ON BLACK WALL

To reach this wall, approach as for the Red Wall, then walk to H.R. Puf 'N Stuff and rappel into the hidden corridor on the backside. There are three routes hiding in the corridor. Exit the corridor by ascending the fixed rope back to H.R. Puf 'N Stuff.

### 65. Back on Black** 12a (12 Bolts)
This is the right route of the three. Be sure to use a 70m rope; it is a long pitch.
FA: D. Peavey, J. Doyle, T. Wilhelmi '04

### 66. Boys Are Back in Town** 12a (13 Bolts)
Climb the tan face left of a long, dark streak. Long and sustained on some of the best rock at the Palace.
FA: D. Peavey, J. Doyle, T. Wilhelmi '04

### 67. No Respect** 11d (13 Bolts)
From a short crack feature, move onto the thin face before eventually pulling a short roof at the top, taking care not to bail right as there is a large flake that could rip off.
FA: D. Peavey, K. Gibson '06

## H - THE SCEPTER

The Scepter is a small, detached pillar between the Red Wall and Palace Pages. Although the climbing isn't as quality as other places in the canyon, the view and position are outstanding.

To reach the Scepter, hike up the Chamber Trail and branch off left before ascending to the Upper Chamber.

### 68. ○ The Scepter*** 10a (8 Bolts)
Climb up this outstanding feature using all of the holds you can. Be sure to mantle onto the summit in order to get the maximum value out of this route.
FA: T. Wilhelmi, C. Wilhelmi

### 69. ○ Hantavirus 10d (5 Bolts + GEAR)
Begin as for the Scepter, but step right at Bolt 2 then follow the northeast arête to the top. Supplementing the three bolts with a piece or two of small gear.
FA: S. McCorkel, Jim Green '96

Joel Wallin doing the victory stand on **The Scepter** ** 10a   Photo: Rob Baker

PALACE PAGES

## I - PALACE PAGES

The Palace Pages are narrow fins of rock that stretch from just below the Scepter down to the banks of Cedar Creek, offering some of the best lines in the area, including Dear Slabby and Sporting Green.

**70.** ⊙ **Sunday Paper* 9** (11 Bolts)
On the opposite side of the gulley, across from Obituary, this route goes up steep rock to a ledge and then climbs the attractive arête/column. Many fun variations up higher.
FA: Ian Barrett, S. Shannon

**71.** ⊙ **Obituary** 13a** (7 Bolts)
Powerful laybacking and a technical headwall define this route on the far left side of the wall. The hardest route at the Palace.
FA: D. Peavey '04

**72.** ⊙ **Sporting Green*** 12a** (7 Bolts)
Climb up the center of the overhanging wall, following the obvious crack system. Good jamming technique makes this route easier. Be wary of the loose block in the crack at Bolt 2. Belay at the small stance below Bolt 1.
FA: T. Wilhelmi, S. Shannon

*Variation:* Climb Dear Slabby into Sporting Green with the aid of one placed bolt for the traverse. A fun outing that's about 12c. Better than doing the chimney grovel up to the start of Sporting Green. FA: D. Peavey

**73.** ⊙ **Dear Slabby*** 11b** (10 Bolts)
One of the best routes at the Palace. An excellent series of seams on good rock take you to the top of the formation.
FA: T. Wilhelmi, S. Shannon, C Wlhelmi

**74.** ⊙ **Gossip Column 11a** (6 Bolts)
This highly visible route ascends the stair-stepped column that rises out of Cedar Creek about 40 yards upstream from the Mineshaft Wall. Bolt 1 is higher than normal, and be careful not to deck onto the upper ledge before reaching Bolt 5.
FA: T. Wilhelmi, C. Wilhelmi, R. Kennedy

## J - BATTLE AXE WALL

**75.** ⊙ **Ogre* 10a** (5 Bolts)
Not as scary as its namesake. Subtle footwork will see you to the top of this beast.
FA: T. Wilhelmi, S. Shannon, J. Bowes

**76.** ⊙ **Battle Axe* 9** (5 Bolts)
Take a swing at this one. Nearly every hold is a jug of one sort or another!
FA: T. Wilhelmi, S. Shannon, J. Bowes

**77.** ⊙ **DC Corner 6 X** (GEAR)
(a.k.a. Death Valley Queen)
This seldom-traveled trad line is the obvious corner directly above Battle Axe at the top of the cliff.
FA: R. Poutre, Lee Smith '91-93

**78.** ⊙ **Peeps* 9** (7 Bolts)
Located next to DC Corner, this short route is a bit tough to get to, but offers great views of the Palace.
FA: D. Peavey, T. Wilhelmi, J. Doyle

CITADEL

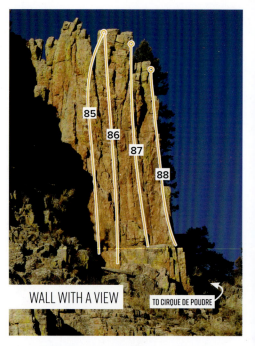

WALL WITH A VIEW — TO CIRQUE DE POUDRE

## K - THE CITADEL

Situated on the ridge next to Wall With A View, a lone tower stands watch over the Palace. There are several fun routes up the Citadel's southeast face as well as a handful of long, difficult lines up the steep back face. The views are spectacular from the top and the Citadel is an excellent all-year crag. Be wary of snakes in the summer.

To reach the Citadel, hike to the Palace Pages, then branch left southwest onto the main approach trail that leads up the rock ridge and onto the slope below the tower. This is also the access trail for Wall With A View and Cirque Du Poudre.

### 79. O Rapunzel, Rapunzel** 10a (11 Bolts)
Lots of great big holds, although some of them are hidden. If you can find the holds as well as work out the jams, you'll be cruising to the top.
FA: R. Poutre, R. Ambrose '91-93

### 80. O Let Down Your Hair** 10b (8 Bolts)
On the right side of the face that overlooks the river. A bit of a crack finish.
FA: R. Poutre, R. Ambrose '91-93

*The following routes are located on the back north side of the Citadel. They are listed from left to right as you approach from the main Citadel trail.*

### 81. O All in a Daze Work** 11c/d (12 Bolts)
Follow the blunt prow on the left side of the Citadel's north face. Thin at the top.
FA: R. Poutre, R. Ambrose '91-93

### 82. O Citadel** 11b (13 Bolts)
Begin in front of the juniper tree. Long and sustained.
FA: T. Wilhelmi, D. Peavey

### 83. O Wake of the Red Witch** 12c (14 Bolts)
Crimp your way up the fractured section to the thin and technical green streak.
FA: D. Peavey, T. Wilhelmi, K. Gibson '04

### 84. O Roll the Bonez* 12b (14 Bolts)
Stick-clip the high Bolt 1, then follow layback/sidepull features up the brown face.
FA: D. Peavey, T. Wilhelmi, J. Doyle '04

## L - WALL WITH A VIEW

Vying with the Citadel for the Palace's southern ridgeline, this prominent wall hosts a few quality routes. The established climbing, found on the right shoulder and backside, is certainly worth visiting. To reach Wall With A View, hike up the Citadel trail, branching left at the top. The short but excellent route Not Enough can be found on the backside of the formation.

### 85. O Spot of Bother 10d (8 Bolts)
Do a short boulder problem start before reaching the groove with big holds.
FA: T. Wilhelmi, S. Shannon, J. Bowes

### 86. O Route with a View** 10b (8 Bolts)
Climb the center crack feature, stepping right at the top to chains. This route was likely led on gear around '93.
FA: T. Wilhelmi, K. Gibson, J. Bowes

### 87. O Party Mixer 10c (4 Bolts + GEAR)
Use Bolt 1 as an anchor for the belayer. Begin up the bolt line and then finish with the finger crack on top.
FA: T. Wilhelmi, S. Shannon

# CIRQUE DU POUDRE

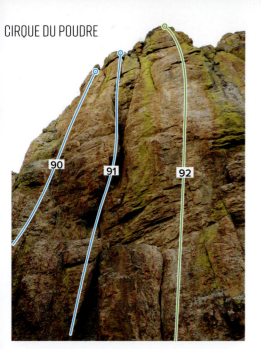

**88.** ⦿ **Speak Easy 10b** (8 Bolts)
Similar to Gossip Column, climb the narrow NE face of the pillar. The crux is down low and may be avoided by mantling onto the shelf above Bolt 2. Anchor the belayer into the bolt at the base on the right side of the ledge.
FA: T. Wilhelmi, S. Shannon

**89.** ⦿ **Not Enough**\*\* **9** (4 Bolts)
Found on the backside of the Wall With A View, this short but fun route starts in a finger crack, then moves slightly right onto bulbous edges up excellent stone.
FA: T. Wilhelmi, S. Shannon

## M - CIRQUE DU POUDRE

Tucked away on the backside of Wall With A View, is the Cirque Du Poudre. The cliff is a little tricky to get to, but offers some very nice, sustained lines that stay shaded for much of the day.

To reach Cirque Du Poudre, hike to the backside of the Wall With A View. Roughly five yards after passing Not Enough, look to the right for a slightly hidden 4th class downclimb. Carefully pick your way through the short cliff band, then continue left toward the obvious wall.

**90.** ⦿ **High Speed Digger**\* **11c** (9 Bolts)
The left-most route. Climb up to a decent ledge before launching off into the crux above. Hidden holds and good route finding ability really make a difference. Named after a late night bicycle accident.
FA: S. Shannon, T. Wilhelmi

**91.** ⦿ **Side Show**\*\* **11c** (8 Bolts)
The middle route. Interesting moves take you up this shallow chimney-like feature. Don't worry, the crux on this one is right at the end.
FA: T. Wilhelmi, K. Gibson, S. Shannon, J. Bowes

**92.** ⦿ **Cirque Du Poudre**\*\*\* **12c** (12 Bolts)
The right-hand route. A classic route on good stone and good edges. Originally contrived by staying on the face in the last panel of rock. Give yourself 13a if you leave the arête/crack out right off.
FA: T. Wilhelmi, S. Shannon, J. Bowes

## N - VATOVILLE

To reach Vatoville, hike past the Palace Pages and continue following the Cedar Creek streambed. The main cliff is found 40 yards past Battle Axe on the left at stream level. Escalera is found on a terrace above Ghost of Cedar Creek and may be approached by walking to the Bat Cave and traversing left or by veering right off the Citadel approach trail shortly after leaving the creek bed.

**93.** ⦿ **Ghost of Cedar Creek**\*\* **11a** (5 Bolts)
Climb the thin tan streak on positive edges.
FA: D. Peavey, K. Gibson, T. Wilhelmi '03

**94.** ⦿ **Melkor**\* **10d** (5 Bolts)
Tiptoe your way up the delicate black water groove. The center route.
FA: D. Peavey, J. Doyle '04

**95.** ⦿ **Arda**\*\* **10b** (5 Bolts)
Make thin and technical moves up the polished black face with tan splotches to a broken crack and easier climbing above. The right route.
FA: D. Peavey, J. Doyle '04

**96.** ⦿ **Escalera 8** (8 Bolts)
Spanish for "ladder". This fun route has something for everyone, from underclings to handjams. Move up and right into the dihedral/chimney and use everything you can find.
FA: S. Shannon, Steve Rodriguez

## O - D-MAN

This remote cliff hides in the back of the Palace, but offers a couple of routes.

To reach D-Man, follow a faint trail leading west from Cirque Du Poudre to the ridge. After traversing the ridge for 50yds, veer right on another faint trail leading to the top of the D-Man buttress.

**97.** ⦿ **D-Man**\*\* **11c** (4 Bolts)
Clip the belayer into a bolt and grab some huge holds, make some big moves, then pull the crux at the last bolt.
FA: T. Wilhelmi, R. Kennedy

**98.** ⦿ **A-Lady**\* **11a** (5 Bolts)
To the right of D-Man.
FA: D. Peavey, J. Doyle '05

**16.3 MILES** FROM TED'S PLACE

# STOVE PRAIRIE ROAD

### STOVE PRAIRIE CRACKS

TYPE(S): **TRAD, SPORT**
DIFFICULTY RANGE: **5.6 - 5.11A**
APPROACH TIME: **10 MIN - 45 MIN**
SEASON: **FALL, WINTER & SPRING**

**RIVER CROSSING REQUIRED**

## CLIMBING OVERVIEW

The Stove Prairie Road area is a group of crags that offer sunny south-facing climbing. Stove Prairie Cracks offer adventurous trad climbs while the Cactus Garden is more of a modern sport cliff.

**MOSTLY SUNNY ALL DAY**

## STOVE PRAIRIE CRACKS

The Stove Prairie Cracks area offers a variety of pillars and fins, but the routes featured are some of the better lines. Although none of the rock in this area should be trusted 100%. Be sure to wear a helmet and don't trust any antiquated fixed gear. Good swimming can be found downstream of the cracks in the summer.

## GETTING THERE

**GPS: 40°41'7.48"N 105°23'18.54"W**
To reach the Stove Prairie Cracks, drive 16.3 miles from Ted's Place and park in a pullout on the right. The cracks are visible across the river (which is usually wade-able below 1.0 ft). All routes have walk-off descents. Be careful of poison ivy.

**1.**  **Pegmatite Crack\* 7 (GEAR)**
This fun finger to hand-crack meanders up the pegmatite face about 75 yards uphill from the previous climbs. If it weren't for the hollow block in the middle and loose block at the top, it would be a fun moderate.
**FA: Unknown**

**2.** **Hollow Flake Face 7 (3 Bolts + GEAR)**
Climb the short finger crack, then solo on initially hollow flakes past three useless bolts. Clipping the bolts will keep you on route, but that's about it. Finishing on the short hand-crack is fun. Walk off to the left.
**FA: Unknown**

**3.** **Crack Dihedral\* 6 (GEAR)**
This fun corner, reminiscent of Devil's Tower, starts as a finger crack and eventually opens to perfect hands. If the rock quality wasn't mediocre, it would be an excellent line. Be careful of the loose block near the single bolt (manky) anchor. Bring extra hand sized pieces. Walk off as for the Finger Crack.
**FA: Unknown**

**4.** **Splitter Finger Crack 7 (GEAR)**
Begin in the thin finger crack, climb to the ledge, then make fun face moves to an easy finish. Bring extra thin gear and be wary. The lower portion of the route is a 6" plate that is completely detached from the wall with a packrat living behind it. Walk off to the right (north).
**FA: Unknown**

## CACTUS GARDEN

Cactus Garden is the large, south-facing wall at the head of the valley north of the Stove Prairie / Hwy 14 intersection (on the south face of Red Mountain). The wall is fairly sheltered and is warm on chilly days. A newer area developed by the ever active Ken Duncan and Dede Humphrey.

## GETTING THERE

**GPS: 40°41'22.39"N 105°23'33.49"W**

Park at the Stove Prairie / Hwy 14 intersection, cross the highway, and head downstream along the Poudre for about 100 yards to the first shallow crossing area. Cross the river, and head uphill to the ridgeline. Follow the ridge almost to its top. Cut left under the last big pine tree, and follow cairns that contour across the hillside passing behind a couple other trees to reach the cliff. Once at the cliff, scramble up a ramp which connects to the ledge crossing the face. The approach takes about 45min from the river.

**5. ○ Palo Verde** ** 11a** (9 Bolts)
The excellent green face starts by angling up and right through somewhat friable rock to an overlap then straight up on juggy holds to the anchors shared with Ocatillo.
FA: K. Duncan, D. Humphrey

**6. ○ Ocatillo*** 10c** (10 Bolts)
Thoughtful face climbing on the lower half leads to a juggy face to the anchors. Head up on a tricky face to a seam. Follow the seam to an overlap, then finish up another juggy face to the anchor.
FA: K. Duncan, D. Humphrey

**7. ○ Prickly Pair Left** ** 11a** (9 Bolts)
This has nice face climbing. Head straight up, and angle a bit left then back right under an overlap to anchors shared with Prickly Pair Right.
FA: K. Duncan, D. Humphrey

**8. ○ Prickly Pair Right** ** 11a** (9 Bolts)
This has thoughtful climbing on positive holds. Follow bolts angling up and right along an arête passing several small roofs.
FA: K. Duncan, D. Humphrey

**9. ○ Detachment Disorder** ** 11a** (9 Bolts)
Start in a large corner capped with a roof, step right around the roof, then move up and right to the crux tiered overhang which has some friable rock. Turn the overhang, and continue up passing a couple thin sections to the anchors.
FA: K. Duncan, D. Humphrey

# NARROWS

**17.4 - 20.0 MILES** FROM TED'S PLACE

The Poudre River churning through the heart of the Narrows  Photo: B. Scott

**361 ROUTES** IN TOTAL

- 5.7: 18
- 5.8: 8
- 5.9: 26
- 5.10: 98
- 5.11: 117
- 5.12: 74
- 5.13: 18
- 5.14: 2

GRADE DISTRIBUTION

**104 BOULDER** PROBLEMS IN TOTAL

- v0-v2: 16
- v3-v4: 21
- v5-v6: 25
- v7-v8: 22
- v9-v10: 17
- v11-Above: 3

**TYPE(S): SPORT, TRAD, & BOULDERING**
**DIFFICULTY RANGE: 5.8 - 5.14A, VI-VII**
**APPROACH TIME: 5 MIN-45 MIN**
**SEASON: YEAR ROUND**

## CLIMBING OVERVIEW

The Narrows is one of the most majestic and inspiring areas of the canyon for a rock climber. Large granite walls come right down to the roadside, streams bubble down from mysterious side canyons, and massive boulders peek out of the trees if you know where to look.

The Narrows has a long history of rock climbing going back to the early '70s. Many climbers have contributed routes to the area including **Rodney Ley, Craig Luebben, Mark Wilford, Paul Heyliger, Steve Allen, Rodney Ley, Greg Martin, Mike Duncan, Steve McCorkel,** and **Gregg Purnell** to name a few. Many of the routes were done in ground up style, but Crossing Over (F.A. early '90s) in the Middle Narrows was the first route bolted on rappel and signaled a shift toward a new ethic of route establishment.

After about 2000 or so, another wave of climbers began developing The Narrows in a purely sport climbing style. Climbers like **Paul Heyliger, Derek Peavey, Ken Gibson, Bryan Beavers, Ken Duncan, Dede Humphrey, Noah Kaufman, Jason Tarry, R.D. Pascoe** and **the author** continue to be active in this section of the canyon. On top of all that work, in 2015 the Narrows Blocs bouldering began being developed due to the tireless efforts of local climbers **Sam Rothstein, Brett Hoffman, Nick Perl** and many others.

## GETTING THERE

The Narrows is generally considered the section of the canyon between Stove Prairie Road / Steven's Gulch and the Narrows Campground. A four mile long section of the canyon comprising 25 different climbing areas.

POUDRE CANYON GUIDE - 3RD EDITION    85

Mike Englestad on the burly final knobs of **The Squeeze Box**** v6   Photo: B. Scott

**17.8 MILES** FROM TED'S PLACE

# WIDOWMAKERS / ELECTRIC OCEAN

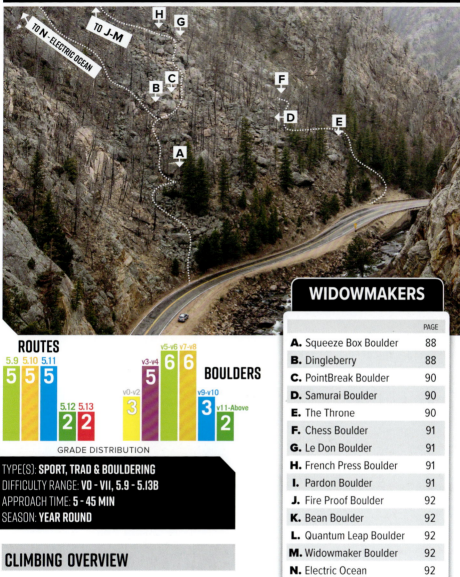

## ROUTES

Grade Distribution:
- 5.9: 5
- 5.10: 5
- 5.11: 5
- 5.12: 2
- 5.13: 2

## BOULDERS
- v0-v2: 3
- v3-v4: 5
- v5-v6: 6
- v7-v8: 6
- v9-v10: 3
- v11-Above: 2

**TYPE(S): SPORT, TRAD & BOULDERING**
**DIFFICULTY RANGE: V0 - VII, 5.9 – 5.13B**
**APPROACH TIME: 5 - 45 MIN**
**SEASON: YEAR ROUND**

### WIDOWMAKERS

| | | PAGE |
|---|---|---|
| A. | Squeeze Box Boulder | 88 |
| B. | Dingleberry | 88 |
| C. | PointBreak Boulder | 90 |
| D. | Samurai Boulder | 90 |
| E. | The Throne | 90 |
| F. | Chess Boulder | 91 |
| G. | Le Don Boulder | 91 |
| H. | French Press Boulder | 91 |
| I. | Pardon Boulder | 91 |
| J. | Fire Proof Boulder | 92 |
| K. | Bean Boulder | 92 |
| L. | Quantum Leap Boulder | 92 |
| M. | Widowmaker Boulder | 92 |
| N. | Electric Ocean | 92 |

## CLIMBING OVERVIEW

AM SHADE / PM SUN

This area was originally only known as the Electric Ocean. A small sport crag that was developed in the mid-'90s by **Greg Martin**, **Mike Duncan**, and **Rich Purnell**. The routes saw some traffic back in 2009 when **Cameron Cross** pulled off the first ascent of Prometheus Rising**** 13b. After that, the area began being explored by **Mike Englestad**, **Kirk Lauterbach** and **Paul Nadler** for its bouldering potential. Later, **Sam Rothstein** and **Brett Hoffman** added their own wave of development. Now the area is mostly referred to as the Widowmakers and the boulders see far more traffic than the routes ever did.

## GETTING THERE

**GPS: 40°40'38.58"N 105°24'43.33"W**

From Ted's Place drive 17.8 miles up the canyon to a massive pullout on the north side of the road just before a bridge and the Colors Crag parking. This pullout is also popular with boaters during the summer months; use Colors Crag parking as back-up.

Sam Rothstein on the brutal crimps of **Samurai**\*\* v12   Photo: B. Scott

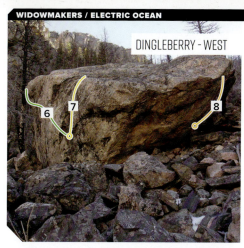

## A - SQUEEZE BOX BOULDER

One of the original and most obvious boulders in the area. Climbing on knobs similar to Arthur's Rock or the Black Hills of South Dakota. This is the first boulder you come to on your way up from the road; all the problems are on the downhill side of the boulder

### 1. ○ Moss King v4 (4-5 Pads)
Start 10 feet left of The Squeeze Box and climb sharp crimps angling up and right to bigger knobs that lead to the topout.
FA: S. Rothstein

### 2. ○ The Squeeze Box** v6 (4-5 Pads)
Not the best looking rock, but the climbing is well worth it. Start crouched on a match hold at the lip of the roof. Do a few big moves to gain incuts in the middle of the face. Take on two small and sharp crystals that lead to the holds at the lip and the easy topout.
FA: John Tolefsruder

### 3. ○ Fang* v6 (4-5 Pads)
A variation to Squeeze Box, start on the big jug near the arête and climb straight up the face. This route has an easier finish opposed to the heady Squeeze Box finish.
FA: S. Rothstein

### 4. ○ Black Widow* v7 (Pads)
Start crouched on the same holds as Squeeze Box, but move up and right to the jug then continue moving right around the arête with the adjacent boulder behind you at points.
FA: S. Rothstein

### 5. ○ Around the World** v3 (Pads)
On the boulder to the right of Squeeze Box is a decent little warm-up. Start low matched on the sidepull sloper, trend left to the large sidepull jug, then head back right though a crimp rail at the lip.
FA: S. Rothstein

## B - DINGLEBERRY BOULDER

Dingleberry boulder is just uphill from Squeeze Box. A mostly white boulder with a steep overhang on the right when looking uphill at it.

### 6. ○ Dingleberry Traverse* v5 (Pads)
Start on Dingleberry but traverse left on crimps and incuts. Pumpy and sustained with a scary landing in the middle.
FA: M. Englestad

### 7. ○ Dingleberry* v1 (Pads)
SDS on some nice black colored layback jugs and climb easy holds to the chill topout.
FA: M. Englestad

### 8. ○ Slice and Dice* v7 (Pads)
SDS on the obvious jug and do a big move left, followed by a foot-hand match with an even bigger move to a jug.
FA: Brett Hoffman

### 9. ○ Devil Wears Lace* v8 (Pads)
SDS the same as for Slice and Dice but move right to bighter crimps and the easy topout.
FA: S. Rothstein

**WIDOWMAKERS / ELECTRIC OCEAN**

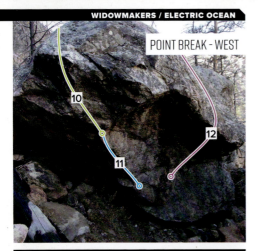
POINT BREAK - WEST

THRONE

## C - POINT BREAK BOULDER

The Point Break Boulder sits right next to the Dingleberry Boulder. Good rock with a nice collection of problems.

**10. ◯ Point Break\* v6** (Pads)
Start on a terrible left-hand crimp and a decent right-hand undercling at chest height. Bump through slopers, grab another undercling, and then hit the lip.
FA: S. Rothstein

**11. ◯ Pink Panther\* v9** (Pads)
A tougher SDS variation to Point Break.
FA: S. Rothstein

**12. ◯ The Mushroom\* v4** (Pads)
SDS on a slopey rail and move through a crimp and undercling to reach the lip. Move back left a bit to the easy mantle.
FA: B. Hoffman

**13. ◯ Blake's Dyno\*\* v8** (Pads)
On the west side of the Point Break boulder is this slightly overhung face with a band of rock sticking out underneath. Start matched on a flat edge and dyno to the lip, using the band of rock underneath for feet.
FA: Skyler Bol

POINT BREAK - EAST

## D - THRONE BOULDER

This boulder is almost roadside and can be approached two ways. The best way to walk is upstream from the parking area to the other side of the bridge. Locate a faint trail that heads directly up to the boulder. Alternatively you can traverse to hikers right from the Squeeze Box boulder to reach The Throne.

**14. ◯ The Throne\*\*\* v3** (4-5 Pads)
An epic slab problem that should not be underestimated. The perfect platform landing is only so wide and if you unfortunately miss it, consequences could be dire. Good rock and interesting movement make it worthwhile.
FA: B. Hoffman, B. Scott

SAMURAI

## E - SAMURAI BOULDER

Located uphill from the Throne Boulder. Nice rock, small edges and an imposing downhill face make this a good place to test your fingers.

**15. ◯ Samurai\*\* v12** (Pads)
Start on underclings and move into a bighter black crimp at head height, perform a brutal cross over to another crimp followed by a huge deadpoint to the jug hold at the lip.
FA: S. Rothstein

**16. ◯ Bone Tomahawk\*\* v10** (Pads)
Grab edges just above a slopey ledge/rail feature. Execute some hard moves on edges to the lip and an easy mantle.
FA: S. Rothstein

WIDOWMAKERS / ELECTRIC OCEAN

Peter Hurtgen taking a fitness lap on the classic **Le Don**\*\*\* v8   Photo: B. Scott

## F - CHESS BOULDER

This massive boulder sits just above the Throne in a little subtle depression.

**17.** **Chess**\*\* v2 (Pads)
Stand start on the middle of the slab, and climb straight up using crimps and sidepulls to reach the crux at the top.
FA: B. Hoffman, S. Rothstein

## G - LE DON BOULDER

**18.** **Le Don**\*\*\* v8 (Pads)
Easily one of the best, if not the best boulders in the area. This left leaning arête has excellent tight grain granite and fun sustained movement. Not to be missed.
FA: Paul Nadler

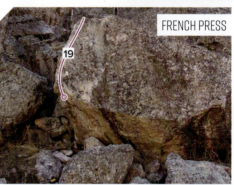

## H - FRENCH PRESS BOULDER

**19.** **French Press** v4 (Pads)
Located right next to Le Don, start on the jug undercling, and move through crimps to a tough and unusual mantle move near the top.
FA: M. Englestad

## I - PARDON BOULDER

**20.** **Pardon My French** v6 (Pads)
Located right above Le Don, start on two big jugs at head height, and angle your way up and right without dabbing on the boulder to the left.
FA: K. Lauterbach

## J - FIRE-PROOF BOULDER

This massive house-sized boulder sits in the middle of the talus field between Le Don and the Bean Boulder.

### 21. Fire-Proof*** v10 (Pads)
SDS on an obvious angled crimp rail. Make a series of long moves on good but pumpy edges. A crucial highstep leads to a tricky topout that should probably be cleaned on a rope to check the holds since a fall from the top could be bad.
FA: P. Nadler

## K - BEAN BOULDER

### 22. Scarbanzo** v7 (Pads)
This line may be overshadowed by Fire on the Mountain, but it is not to be missed. Start crouched on an obvious edge and climb technical and fingery terrain up and left on good rock and interesting edges.
FA: M. Englestad

### 23. Fire on the Mountain*** v11 (Pads)
This stunning prow feature is probably the main reason you walked this far up the hill. A compression testpiece, SDS on a flat edge and a sidepull, then pull into a strenuous toe-hook. Slap and squeeze your way up stellar rock to the surprisingly easy mantle. The stand start goes at a high quality v9 or so.
FA: Colin Horvat

## L - QUANTUM LEAP BOULDER

This small boulder sits just above Bean Boulder with a vertical downhill face.

### 24. Quantum Leap** v6 (Pads)
This fun little jump line is a fun challenge. Start on two small edges with low feet and perform a cool dyno/campus move to the lip hold.
FA: P. Nadler

## M - WIDOWMAKER BOULDER

This monster boulder sits perched at the very top of the talus field. An arduous 45 min approach will deposit you at the base of this stunning arête.

### 25. A Double-Edged Sword*** v2 (Pads)
This fun sharp arête sits directly to the left and a bit uphill from the Widowmaker. Excellent edge rails help you squeeze your way up this fun problem on great rock...but it's 45min up the hill.
FA: Lucas Johnson

### 26. The Widowmaker*** 13a (4 Bolts)
Originally done as a top-rope, bolts were later added and now it's a lead climb. Start at the horizontal break and pull the initial roof to a hard crux passing Bolt 2. The angle eases off from here but the last few moves are no gimmie.
TR FA: M. Englestad, Lead FA: S. Bol

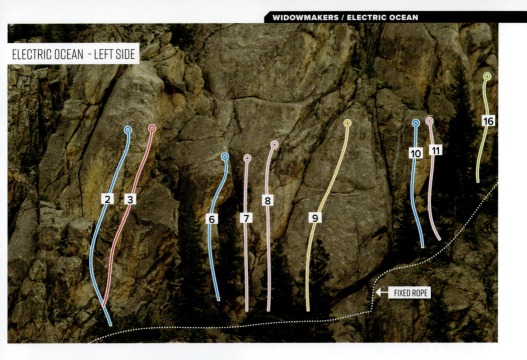

ELECTRIC OCEAN - LEFT SIDE

## N - ELECTRIC OCEAN

To reach the main crag of the Electric Ocean, follow the same cairned trail from the road but branch left after about 500yds up the hill. There will be cairns here that will lead you up through a series of ledges and gullies depositing you below the massive prow that holds Prometheus Rising. Approx. 45mins to 1 hour hiking time.

### 1. ○ Frogs* 9 (5 Bolts)
As the approach gulley narrows, you will reach a nice moderate climb on the right wall. Follow a left angling seam for two bolts, then move up into a shallow groove and over a bulge to anchors.
FA: G. Martin '95

### 2. ○ Mother Hibiscus Discordia 5.11 A1 (GEAR)
Begin in an obvious chimney. Climb up and into a black streaked crack just left of the blunt prow.
FA: G. Martin '96

### 3. ○ Prometheus Rising**** 13b (GEAR)
This route is one of the most striking & aesthetic lines in the Poudre Canyon and is well worth a trip up to the Electric Ocean. Start in the short off-width crack, pull a small roof boulder problem crux and keep it together up the long headwall. Placing gear can be a bit tricky, especially through the crux, so be careful. Bring extra thin gear and a #5 Camalot for the off-width.
FA: C. Cross '09

### 4. ○ Unknown Project (? Bolts)
Futuristic hanging dihedral with rap anchors at top.
Bolted by G. Martin

### 5. ○ Mr. Squigglie 10d (GEAR)
Begin on the off-width of Prometheus Rising, then continue to traverse right as the crack jogs right. An anchor was never added to the finish, making getting down a bit tricky, although it is possible to bushwhack up the gulley on the right and rappel from the anchors of Prometheus Rising.
FA: Rich Purnell '97

### 6. ○ Illusions** 11c (5 Bolts)
Begin on the right side of the large pegmatite pillar. Climb up the slab, then make fun, big moves over bulbous features to the anchor.
FA: G. Martin '95

### 7. ○ Temple of the Dog Project (6 Bolts)
Begin at the bottom left of the X, then follow insipient layback features past six bolts.
Bolted by M. Duncan

### 8. ○ Tangerine Project (8 Bolts)
This wavy face climb starts just left of a lichen-covered chimney. The route gets progressively thinner as you get higher, although easier climbing seems to try to pull you right of the bolt line.
Bolted by G. Martin

### 9. ○ The Iluminatia** 10b (7 Bolts + GEAR)
Visible from the parking lot, this low angle slab has a fun and slightly spicy climb on it. Make bouldery moves to get started, then weave your way up the slab to a crux at the final bolt. A hand or finger-sized piece is useful to protect a long runout in the middle.
FA: G. Martin '95

## ELECTRIC OCEAN - RIGHT SIDE

To reach the next routes, scramble across a ledge and up a steep corner. A fixed rope is often present for the corner moves, otherwise make easy 5th class scramble moves to gain the upper ledge system. The climbing isn't too hard, but you wouldn't want to fall.

**10. One Night Stand** 11b (6 Bolts)**
Ascend a short sloping ramp, then reach from underclings onto the right side of a multicolor face. Staying just left of the hanging arête, four bolts bring you to the finish of this short, but excellent route.
FA: Unknown '95

**11. Firewoman Project (4 Bolts)**
Make hard, bouldery moves past four bolts and onto a short slab before reaching painted rap bolts.
Bolted by M. Duncan

**12. Inside the Outside Whole 10d (GEAR)**
A short, wide crack is found just right of previous route. Start in a chimney and wiggle over a roof into the hand-crack above. Big Bros are useful.
FA: M. Duncan

**13. Rage Against the Machine 9 (GEAR)**
Flaky Death Chimney. Climb flaky, scabby choss without killing your belayer and you will be one of the few proud ascents. Standard rack + PhD in choss climbing.
FA: G. Martin '96

**14. Anahata 12a (7 Bolts)**
Step off a block to Bolt 1, then climb over bulbous, somewhat mediocre looking climbing to the chains.
FA: G. Martin '95

**15. Cosmic Trigger 9 (1 Bolt + GEAR)**
Climb the obvious arching crack system that splits the face. Wiggling into and out of the pod is likely the crux and most entertaining part for any nearby sport climbers. Move left at top to clip last bolt and anchors of previous route. One bolt, standard rack + big gear.
FA: G. Martin '95

**16. Vishokkuxxud-pokkuxxda*** 12a (7 Bolts)**
This excellent route follows superb rock up a shallow corner system. A bouldery crux leads to cool moves on big holds. Moving left at the end is the easiest, but going straight up will give you full value and added difficulty.
FA: M. Duncan '95

**17. Jibbin' 9 (5 Bolts)**
Start right of arête in black streak. Questionable rock quality. Just left of tree.
FA: G. Martin '95

**18. Spoon Woman 11a (1 Bolt + GEAR)**
A continuation of Jibbin' that climbs up and out the sharply pointed roof at the top of the crag. Gear plus one bolt high on hanging arête. May have bolted anchors, but no chains.
FA: G. Martin '96

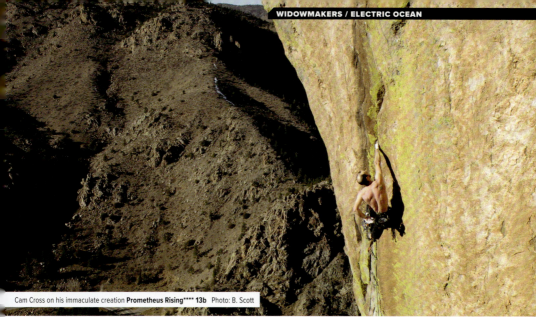
Cam Cross on his immaculate creation **Prometheus Rising**\*\*\*\* **13b**   Photo: B. Scott

### 19. Cyberpunk Project (11 Bolts)
Climb three bolts of slab, then two over large roof. Bolting seems incomplete on prow.
**Bolted by G. Martin '95**

### 20. Atlas Shrugged Project (7 Bolts + GEAR)
Climb to the top of the sharkstooth to clip Bolt 1. Head up the slab and into the obvious crack. Ascend the corner, reaching left to clip a bolt, then commit to moving onto the pegmatite face and up the bulging face.
**Bolted by G. Martin '95**

### 21. Ajna Sanctuary 10b (GEAR)
This short, but excellent trad line begins off the ledge above the previous routes. Climb the right leaning crack up the steep headwall.
**FA: G. Martin, R. Purnell '97**

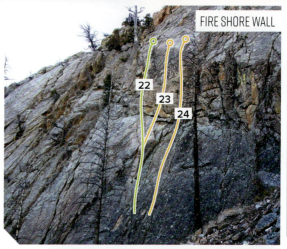

## FIRE SHORE WALL

Fire Shore is a section of clean, west-facing, featured rock that was barely spared during the High Park fire and is up and right of the main collection of routes. These routes are all almost exactly 100 feet long and would be popular with a shorter approach, but maybe somebody will do them.

### 22. For Shore* 9 (11 Bolts)
Climb the left side of the wall on nice rock.
**FA: P. Heyliger, Jon Dory**

### 23. Shore Enough* 10a (11 Bolts)
The middle route. Pleasant.
**FA: P. Heyliger, J. Dory**

### 24. Shore Footed** 10b/c (10 Bolts)
The right-hand route is the best on the wall with the crux at the bulge.
**FA: P. Heyliger, J. Dory**

Erin Robinson working on the **If 6 Was 9 Project**  Photo: A. Cross

**18.0 MILES** FROM TED'S PLACE

# COLORS CRAG

GRADE DISTRIBUTION

**TYPE(S): SPORT**
**DIFFICULTY RANGE: 5.10 - 5.12B**
**APPROACH TIME: 20 MIN**
**SEASON: SPRING, SUMMER & FALL**

## CLIMBING OVERVIEW

Colors Crag is a more recently developed crag seeing its first bolts circa 2009. It has a nice collection of routes that stay in shade most of the day. The rock quality varies from pegmatite choss to really compact granite in most places. The routes have cleaned up nicely but wearing a helmet is always a good call at Colors Crag.

## GETTING THERE

**GPS: 40°40'46.23"N 105°24'44.41"W**

From Ted's Place, drive approx. 18 miles up the canyon, passing Steven's Gulch Campground. Next Hwy 14 will cross over the Poudre River on a large bridge and then find a huge pullout parking area on the north side of the road.

From here, find the obvious trail that leads up the steep hillside to the northeast. Once you reach the top of the hill, the trail will turn downhill and across to the right placing you at the base of the crag.

POUDRE CANYON GUIDE - 3RD EDITION

# COLORS CRAG

**1.** ⬤ **Are You Experienced?** ** 10b** (9 Bolts)
The infamous bolted hand-crack, and yes it has been done on gear several times if you like. Start with some dirty ledgy terrain to reach the base of the crack. Climb the beautiful 50 foot hand and fist crack.
**FA: R.D. Pascoe**

**2.** ⬤ **Watchtower*** ** 11a** (7 Bolts)
Excellent climbing on pretty black and white streaked rock. Layback up a big flake to Bolt 2. Continuous climbing on big fun holds takes you to the top of the watchtower and a final slab to the anchor.
**FA: B. Scott**

**3.** ⬤ **Crosstown** ** 12a** (9 Bolts)
A series of layback jugs takes you to crimpy terrain past Bolt 3. A punchy move gets you through the overhang and up to the big ledge. A final layback section with technical footwork takes you up the final headwall to the chains.
**FA: R.D. Pascoe**

**4.** ⬤ **Castle Magic*** ** 12b** (8 Bolts)
Originally a mixed route, this route is now fully bolted by the F.A. Start with some juggy laybacks up a dihedral feature past 5 bolts. After the corner ends, enter the intimidating tan headwall past three more bolts. Pinches, knobs, crimps and excellent rock take you through a lot of committing 5.12 climbing to reach the chains.
**FA: C. Tirrell, B. Scott**

**5.** ⬤ **Magic Machine** ** 12b** (11 Bolts)
This is a fun link-up that adds a little more pump to Castle Magic. Start by climbing most of Machine Gun to Bolt 8 and a rest in a groove. Step left here, and clip Bolt 5 on Castle Magic before engaging the first of several excellent cruxes up the headwall.
**FA: B. Scott**

**6.** ⬤ **Machine Gun*** ** 11c** (11 Bolts)
Climb a left-facing corner feature past some pinches and layback features (beware of choss). Pumpy terrain leads over a short bulge to a stance in a groove. Move up and right over the last bulge through some sweet finger-locks to the chains. Great route only marred by bad rock at the start.
**FA: C. Tirrell, B. Scott**

**7.** ⬤ **If 6 was 9 Project** (8 Bolts)
Another infamous route at the crag, one of the first lines bolted and still a project. Start up the easy crack before launching into a sea of small edges to a final crux bulge.
**Bolted by B. Scott**

**8.** ⬤ **Fertile Crescent** ** 10b** (2 Bolts + GEAR)
Climb the right-arching crack past 2 bolts at the start. A high crux guards the chains on the redpoint.
**FA: D. McKee**

**9.** ⬤ **Izabella** ** 10c** (8 Bolts)
The easiest bolted route at the crag is a decent warm-up. Ramble up the unprotected slab to a series of tricky moves on big blocks to get established on the wall. More interesting laybacking up cracks leads to a final tricky move to clip the anchor chains.
**FA: R.D. Pascoe, B. Scott**

**19.0 MILES** FROM TED'S PLACE

# THE KEEP

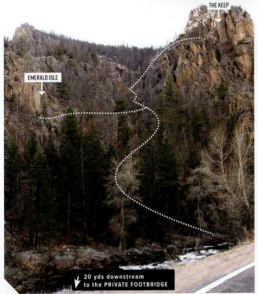

TYPE(S): **SPORT**
DIFFICULTY RANGE: **5.11B - 5.12C**
APPROACH TIME: **30 MIN**
SEASON: **SPRING, FALL & WINTER**

## CLIMBING OVERVIEW

Another newly developed sport crag that was discovered in 2016. The first route was **Date Night**\*\* **11c** opened by Owen Murphy. This area hosts a really nice collection of 5.12 climbs on varied rock types. Some of the rock is similar to the Palace while others seem similar to Upper Echelon or the Crystal Wall. The routes have been cleaned and bolted well but beware of some occasional loose rock due to lack of traffic.

## GETTING THERE

**GPS: 40°40'24.67"N 105°25'12.50"W**
From Ted's Place, drive approx. 19 miles up the canyon until you come to an obvious private foot bridge that crosses the river to some private cabins. There are two convenient pullouts near the footbridge you can use for parking. The best places to cross the river are up-stream from the footbridge. After crossing the river, find a subtle gulley feature that leads towards the crag. There are cairns but not much of a trail. Continue up the gulley until the cairns take you up the right side of the hill and wraps around to the base of the crag.

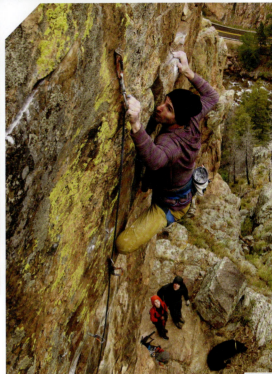

Ryan Nelson above the first crux of the **Reckoning**\*\*\* **12d**  Photo: B. Scott

This route is located on a mini-cliff on the way up to The Keep. After the waterfall/cliff in the gulley, cross to the left side of the gulley, and traverse across to reach the base of the climb. Some easy 5th class takes you from a tree to the base which is equipped with a belay bolt on the mossy ledge.

**1.** ● **Emerald Isle**\*\*\* **12b** (5 Bolts)
Emerald Isle ascends an awesome green arête that is quite visible from the highway. Start with a tricky sequence to gain the arête before clipping Bolt 2. From here, the climbing is sustained compression arête climbing on excellent stone for the next three bolts. Once you reach the crack, climb up and left along the crack to reach the anchor.
**FA: B. Scott**

POUDRE CANYON GUIDE - 3RD EDITION  **99**

# THE KEEP

## THE KEEP

### 2. Reckoning*** 12d (6 Bolts)
Reckoning is a great line up a nice swell of dark granite littered with just enough flat Poudre edges. Easy terrain leads into a crux jump move off a slopey sidepull to a monster, flat jug. More taxing pulls on small but friendly holds leads to the anchor.
**FA: B. Scott**

### 3. Radu** 12a (8 Bolts)
Named after the demonic entity named Radu Molasar. Start with a very tricky arête crux at Bolt 2. Easier climbing leads up the dihedral to a final tricky finish back on the arête with less-than-perfect rock.
**FA: B. Scott**

### 4. Glaeken** 12c (8 Bolts)
Glaeken is a fun route with a very technical crux at Bolt 4. From here, the climb gets a lot easier but equally fun on sculpted jugs leading up the broken crack feature.
**FA: B. Scott**

### 5. Taker* 11b (6 Bolts)
Taker has a nice line of holds that is a decent but pumpy warm-up. Start just left of Date Night, and climb jugs to a tricky clip at Bolt 3. Sustained edges and pinches leads to a final reachy move and a mantle to the anchor on Date Night.
**FA: B. Scott**

### 6. Date Night** 11c (5 Bolts)
This was the first line put up at The Keep, and it comes with some cool exposure. The route rides the face and arête of the pillar-like formation on the right. Move left near the top and make several exciting moves to the finish.
**FA: O. Murphy**

### 7. Silver Leaner** 12c (6 Bolts)
This angling crack feature is surprisingly pumpy and has great stone until the last 15 feet or so, despite how it looks from the ground. A direct start without using the ramp would send this route into the 5.13 level.
**FA: B. Scott**

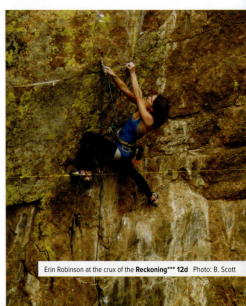

Erin Robinson at the crux of the **Reckoning*** 12d  Photo: B. Scott

**18.4 MILES** FROM TED'S PLACE

# RA'S BUTTRESS AREA

YPE(S): **SPORT & TRAD**
DIFFICULTY RANGE: **5.7 - 5.12B**
APPROACH TIME: **1 - 5 MIN**
SEASON: **YEAR ROUND**

## CLIMBING OVERVIEW

The Ra's Buttress Area is composed of a number of roadside crags looming over Hwy 14. Ra's Buttress is the most prominent feature and has the longest history of climbing, dating back to the early '70s with routes established by **Steve Allen** and **Rodney Ley**. The majority of the other crags in the area were developed in the '90s or later by **Craig Luebben, Paul Heyliger, Greg Hand** and others. Many of the routes were done in ground up style, but Crossing Over (F.A. early '90s) in Greedy Gulch was the first route bolted on rappel and signaled a shift toward a new ethic of route establishment.

**ROCKFALL DANGER - DO NOT CLIMB HERE**
The Author suggests avoiding this climbing area altogether. Any and all loose rock has a high probability of falling directly onto Hwy 14. There is no "climbing ban," but there are plenty of other areas where you don't have to worry about causing a major accident or death.

## GETTING THERE

**GPS: 40°40'30.90"N 105°25'6.45"W**
From Ted's Place, drive approx. 18.4 miles up the canyon to a small pullout either across from the foot bridge or there is a second pullout across from The River Why.

Unknown climber on Ra's Buttress   Photo: C. Luebben

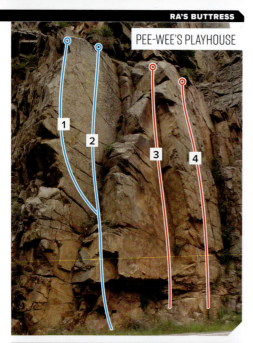

## PEE-WEE'S PLAYHOUSE

This clean, 60 foot tall face offers quality edging almost reminiscent of the sandstone at Horsetooth Reservoir. Per Forest Service regulations, the first two routes have been closed because they are within ten feet off the road.

Pee-Wee's Playhouse is found just upstream from Ra's Buttress, however, it's best to park just after Yankee Doodle Slab, then walk back down to the crag, being mindful of oncoming traffic.

**1. ○ The Pee-wee Erect** ** 11a (2 Bolts + GEAR)**
A single, tricky move may require contemplation near the top of this face/arête.
FA: C. Luebben et al

**2. ○ Pee-wee's Pretty Pumped!** *** 11d (2 Bolts + GEAR)**
Continuous 5.10 edging leads to a dicey lunge or thin finger traverse.
FA: C. Luebben et al

**3. ○ Pee-wee's Big Stem CLOSED**
Crack climb just left of Made You Look!
FA: C. Luebben et al

**4. ● Made You Look! CLOSED**
Although a quality climb, the hanger from Bolt 2 has been removed to keep climbers from getting hit by gawking tourists in RVs.
FA: C. Luebben et al

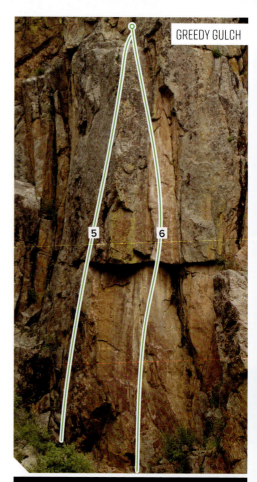

## GREEDY GULCH

Greedy Gulch is a hidden gulley on the north side of the highway, about 30 yards downstream from Yankee Doodle Slab. These seldom traveled 5.12s are excellent and worth adding to your tick-list. Both routes were recently re-bolted with modern SS hardware by Micah Wright in 2016.

**5. ○ Crossing Over*** 12b (7 Bolts)**
Powerful, technical and sustained - what more can one say? This line is also notable because it was the first rap bolted route in the canyon.
FA: C. Luebben et al

**6. ○ Someday Never Comes*** 12b (6 Bolts)**
An excellent, but often over-looked classic from Craig. Some really cool pinch features between parallel seams on this one. Strenuous, tenuous barndoor liebacking leads up the steep face and over the roof.
FA: C. Luebben et al.

RIVER WHY WALL

## THE RIVER WHY

This pretty little riverside wall has been noticed by climbers for years. Located across from Pee-Wee's Playhouse, it has a convenient parking pullout right in front of it. Cross 50 yds upstream from the wall to a pleasant little sandbar when the water is low.

### 7. ◯ The River Why** 10a (5 Bolts)
This line follows the prominent, yellowish arête through some fun, unfractured, river-polished stone. The route is actually slightly overhanging in sections making the slopey ledges a bit more exciting than they might seem. There are some critical little holds and sidepulls to look for near the top. Do not climb into the gulley full of lichen on the left.
FA: O. Murphy '17

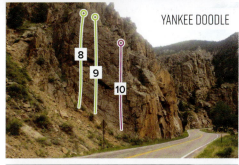

YANKEE DOODLE

## YANKEE DOODLE SLAB

This west-facing slab is found about 150 yards upstream from Ra's Buttress and offers three fun moderates. Parking is available at a pullout directly upstream from the wall on the right north side of the road. Please use caution when approaching the routes; the talus is loose and unconsolidated.

### 8. ◯ Sousa* 9 (7 Bolts)
Follow a pegmatite band over a small roof, then head past a few more bolts of nice slab climbing to the chains.
FA: Unknown

### 9. ◯ Bit of a Dandy** 9 (7 Bolts)
Fun moves over a small bulge lead to a pleasant headwall. The best of the three routes on the wall.
FA: Unknown

### 10. ◯ Yankee Doodle* 8 (3 Bolts + GEAR)
A small cam placed in a horizontal crack protects the crux at the bottom, followed by decent climbing up the right side of the wall.
FA: C. Luebben et al.

# SHEEP MOUNTAIN OVERVIEW

## SHEEP MOUNTAIN

| | | PG |
|---|---|---|
| A. | Main Area LEFT | 109 |
| B. | Main Area CENTER | 111 |
| C. | Main Area RIGHT | 113 |
| D. | Dihedrals Wall | 115 |
| E. | Tier 2 RIGHT | 118 |
| F. | Tier 2 LEFT | 118 |
| G. | Candyland | 119 |
| H. | White as Snow | 119 |
| I. | Once Upon a Time RIGHT | 120 |
| J. | Once Upon a Time LEFT | 121 |
| K. | Iron Curtain | 123 |
| L. | LOWER Daylight | 124 |
| M. | UPPER Daylight | 125 |
| N. | The Skeptic | 126 |
| O. | Narcissists Wall | 127 |
| P. | The Crypt | 128 |
| Q. | Shofar | 129 |
| R. | Taco Wall | 129 |
| S. | Skyline Boulders | 130 |

# SHEEP MOUNTAIN

**18.6 MILES FROM TED'S PLACE**

**173 ROUTES IN TOTAL**

GRADE DISTRIBUTION:
- 5.7: 11
- 5.8: 6
- 5.9: 17
- 5.10: 57
- 5.11: 54
- 5.12: 27
- 5.13: 1

**MOSTLY SUNNY ALL DAY**

**TYPE(S): SPORT, TRAD & BOULDERING**
**DIFFICULTY RANGE: 5.5-5.13**
**APPROACH TIME: 5 MIN - 1 HOUR**
**SEASON: YEAR ROUND**

## CLIMBING OVERVIEW

One can be forgiven for being a bit skeptical of the appearance of Sheep Mountain as seen from the road. For climbers used to the visual impact of the cliffs at Lumpy or Vedauwoo, it may take either persuasion or faith to believe that routes on its walls are worth a visit. But they are. There is no river crossing, winter temperatures are often ideal, the setting above the river can be wonderful, and there are a wide variety of fun routes from 5.5 to 5.13.

As is common in the Poudre, **Steve McCorkel** visited early and characteristically established a few of the best-looking lines on the wall. Since that initial development, a group of loyal climbers have spent a huge amount of time and effort to try to make this an enjoyable crag. This group included Tod Anderson, Bennett Austin, Jim Brink, Richard Burrows,

Jon Dory, Ken Duncan, John Durkin, Cam Heyliger, Luke Heyliger, Dede Humphrey, Brian Parsons, and **Thomas Wilson.** Within this dedicated crew stands one colossus. **Greg Hand** hiked up the hill dozens of times and has spent hundreds of hours sweating, freezing, cleaning, prying, brushing, belaying, and even climbing. Greg had a role in the vast majority of climbs here and Sheep Mountain in its current form would not exist without his efforts.

*Since most of the routes at Sheep Mountain were developed by this group of climbers, F.A. info is only listed when the first ascentionist was outside of this core group.*

Climbers have visited Sheep Mountain every month of the year. The approach sheds snow quickly in the winter and the Dihedrals Zone can have shade and cool temperatures even in early mid-summer mornings. The months of November-April probably offer the most reliable day-long conditions. Regardless of timing or initial skepticism, it may take only a single visit to share the opinion of some of us who love the Poudre and love this place; Sheep Mountain is a big crag with a big heart.

## GETTING THERE

**GPS: 40°40'44.38"N 105°25'24.82"W**

From Ted's Place drive approx. 18.6 miles up the canyon to a large pullout on the north side of the highway below a small scree field. Locate the cairned trail on the upstream side of this pullout. The trail switchbacks up some initial ledges until opening up into a switchbacked trail up the gentle hillside. The trail will deposit you at the middle of the Main Wall after about 20min.

Chynna Shipp on the varnished crack of **Mountain Standard** 10a  Photo: B. Scott

# TWO-MINUTE WALL

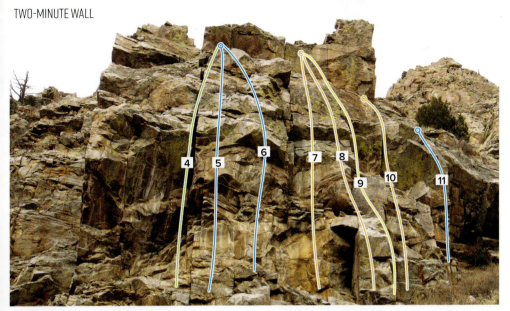

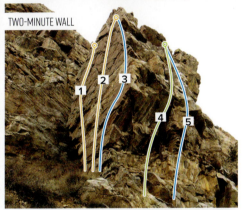

## TWO-MINUTE WALL

This small chunk of rock combines an extremely short approach with sections of relatively good rock. Some routes are climbable when the approach to Sheep is snow-clogged. Park in the next big pullout on the right past the main parking lot and follow the faint path that diagonals up and right to the roadside wall.

**1.** ○ **Unnamed 10b** (8 Bolts)
Deceptively awkward but generally good holds.

**2.** ○ **Mountain Standard*** **10a** (8 Bolts)
A nice line with good rock.

**3.** ○ **Six Seconds to Live*** **11a** (7 Bolts)
Cool moves and position for a short route.

**4.** ○ **Dr. Kelman I Presume*** **9** (3 Bolts + GEAR)
Named for our friend who we once watched take RP-ripping lead falls trying to ground-up a new 5.10 at Vedauwoo - at age 82. The gaping maw is just his size. Bolts low to 6 inch crack, take a few shoulder slings to clip bolts on the right on the easy 5th class finish.

**5.** ○ **Half Life*** **11b** (8 Bolts)
The grade might drop if you leave the bolt line.

**6.** ○ **Ticking Clock 12a** (8 Bolts)
Steep climbing to the technical bulge.

**7.** ○ **Two Minutes Hate 10b** (8 Bolts)
Take the cool orange wall past the rotten ledge to better stone up high.

**8.** ○ **A Desperate Man*** **10c** (9 Bolts)
When we first pointed out this wall, Rob Dory said "You're desperate." A perplexing start leads to pretty good arête climbing to the finish.

**9.** ○ **Unnamed*** **7** (7 Bolts)

**10.** ○ **Unnamed*** **10b** (3 Bolts + GEAR)

**11.** ○ **Unnamed 11c** (6 Bolts)
The left side of the gently overhanging arête finishes right to shared chains.

**12.** ○ **Unnamed*** **11a** (6 Bolts)
The steep featured arête is short and pretty sweet.

*Cut up the slope right then back left to access two short routes on good stone with shared chains:*

**13.** ○ **Left Unnamed 10c** (5 Bolts)

**14.** ○ **Right Unnamed 10c** (5 Bolts)

Ken Duncan approaching the cruxy roof system of **Rambo Peep**\*\*\* **11b**  Photo: B. Scott

MAIN AREA - LEFT SIDE

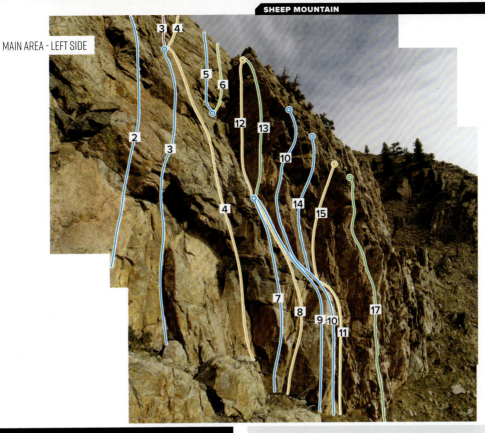

## A - MAIN AREA - LEFT SIDE

This area comprises the massive wall you reach once you get to the top of the trail from the parking lot. A densely packed zone of mostly sport routes that covers a wide range of grades and movements. Don't let the blocky appearance dissuade you, the rock is generally good and the routes are long and pumpy.

**1.** ○ **Snub Nose*** **6** (7 Bolts)
When you reach the the Main Wall on the trail, there is a small buttress on your left right below the Main Wall. Snub Nose climbs a nice slab with lots of holds.(not pictured)

**2.** ○ **Priceless**** **11a** (12 Bolts)
Take the pumpy right-face flake crux to the roof (5.10c) then up and right with an excellent (5.9) finish over the big roof.

**3.** ○ **Dirty Work*** **11c** (12 Bolts)
**P1:** The big left-facing corner leads to the excellent crux over the roof then up, right, and over a second and much easier 9+ roof to chains.
**P2:** The mellow second pitch goes right up the groove 5.8 with a few pieces of gear. (#2 Camalot to supplement the bolts)

**4.** ○ **Steel Wool**** **10b** (11 Bolts + GEAR)
The nice huge corner (gear to 3 inches) heads past a bolt to the left-leaning corner up and over a roof. The second pitch goes up the closely bolted headwall (5.10b) to an easier slab.

The upper headwall right of the second pitch of Steel Wool and left of the huge corner contains two worthwhile routes. The easiest approach is The Conclave 5.7 past chains and a few more connecting bolts up easy rock to a chained anchor at the base of this headwall.

**5.** ○ **Luke*** **11a** (11 Bolts)
The left-hand line above the chains is fully bolted past a tricky start, a puzzling crux, and a wonderful 5.9 finish.

**6.** ○ **I Am Your Father*** **9** (7 Bolts + GEAR)
Stem a move or two up the gulley, then follow a line of excellent gear placements and bomber incuts to a ledge, then up and right up the final slab.

**7.** ○ **I Shall Not Want*** **11b** (6 Bolts + GEAR)
Two boulder problems on great rock are separated by a hands-off rest, then fun climbing up the V-groove above. A #1 Camalot between Bolts 3 and 4 is useful.

**8.** ○ **Green Pastures*** **10a** (3 Bolts + GEAR)
Take the obvious V-corner with annual bushes. Finger-sized cams to a pull past a bolt, then a good crack big fingers/small hands past two roofs and two more bolts.

**9.** ○ **Bitter Clinger*** **11c** (8 Bolts)
The arête has good rock and moves but is short lived passing 5 bolts then head up wherever you want past a few more bolts to chains on the left.

MAIN AREA - LEFT SIDE

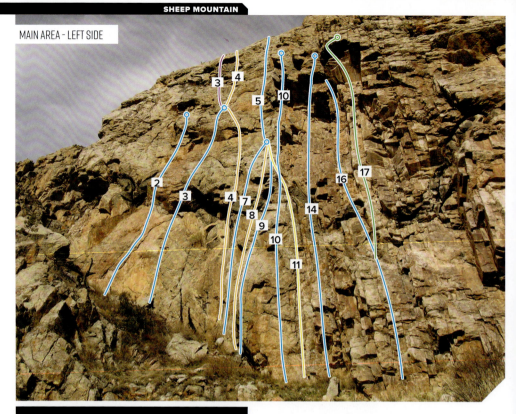

## A - MAIN AREA - LEFT SIDE

### 10. Rambo Peep*** 11b (12 Bolts)
This wild line takes the closely bolted wall left of the huge corner (5.10b) to easier rock, then up the steep orange corner to the monster roof feature. Clip a fixed chain draw and do a big move to a horn followed by another huge move to a jug at the arête. An easy romp up the arête gets you to the anchor.

### 11. The Conclave 7 (8 Bolts)
This total pile was mostly cleaned of garbage and given eight bolts to be used as an approach pitch for some of the routes up higher. Ends at common chains below The Burro.

*There is a small flatiron of stellar rock on the upper right side of the huge corner. These can be climbed as second pitches or link-ups of other climbs.*

### 12. The Pony** 10a (6 Bolts)
Named after the joke about the kid digging through manure because there had to be a pony in there somewhere. The left-hand route is superb climbing in excellent position on perfect rock and solid door-jam edges.

### 13. The Burro** 12a (5 Bolts)
Just like The Pony but with a bigger kick at the start.

### 14. Days Between Us** 11c (15 Bolts)
Dedicated to the visionary pioneer who made it past 30 feet of death blocks, banged in a few pins, and rapped off clothesline. Take the line of bolts just right of the corner past the relic pins on good stone to a crux sequence up and right over the roof. Equipped with a couple chain draws to help lowering on the descent.

### 15. Never Troubles the Wolf* 10b (11 Bolts)
Start at a low point and head up an arête then over a black bulge to the dihedral left of the rotten crack and up and right to the crux headwall.

### 16. Gaga at the Go-Go* 11b (10 Bolts)
Start up The Shearing and share its first four bolts but ease left and up the corner (#2 and #3 Camalots) then it steepens to a superb roof crux.

### 17. The Shearing** 12a (15 Bolts)
Takes the corner line on increasingly good rock 15 feet left of Three Bags Full 10b to a no-hands stance below the imposing roof. From here, big holds lead you to the left side of the roof and a very tricky lip encounter crux with small holds and awkward feet.

## B - MAIN AREA - CENTER

### 18. Three Bags Full** 10a (11 Bolts)
One of the best warm-ups at the entire area. So many different holds and jugs, you will probably never climb it the same way twice. If it feels strenuous, just stop and look around for a hidden jug.

### 19. Baadlands* 10a (7 Bolts + GEAR)
The prominent left-facing corner has good holds and steep climbing, with a few medium cams protecting the run to Bolt 2.

### 20. Smashing Young Ram* 12a/b (12 Bolts)
A closely bolted boulder-problem crux off the deck leads to fun climbing on good holds, then finish over a second roof and up to the anchor.

### 21. Wooly Bully* 9 (7 Bolts + GEAR)
Start about 15 feet right of Baadlands aiming for a crack about 10 feet up. Climb the crack to nice face climbing, then head over the upper roof, then up to chains. Optional #2 or #3 Camalot in crack at the start.

### 22. Haggis* 10a (8 Bolts + GEAR)
This mixed line just right of Wooly Bully is mostly 5.6-5.7 with one harder pull over the gear-protected crux. Bring a small rack up to a #2 Camalot including finger-sized cams for the crux.

### 23. Woolite** 9 (10 Bolts)
Head up a faint trail up and right, then back left to start this fine warm-up. Take the left route off the ledge, over a crux roof and up to an excellent arête finish.

### 24. Wooly Mammoth* 10a / 12b (10 Bolts)
Wandering but good climbing. To the right of Woolite is a faint seam in a shield leading to a ledge and bulge. Clip the high bolt and then either desperately crimp 12b or move back down and right, up the crack, then back left and up the final shield staying on the bolt line.

Dede Humphrey on the juggy roof of **Wooly Bully** 9  Photo: B. Scott

MAIN AREA - RIGHT

## C - MAIN AREA - RIGHT SIDE

### 25. ○ Even the Sheep are Bored 9 (8 Bolts)
The route on the far left is not worth it except the last 15 feet hand-traversing right at the break.

### 26. ○ Good to the Last Dip* 10c (8 Bolts)
Begin in the obvious right-facing corner and follow the bolt line over a cool roof move (10a), then an easy corner to the excellent final crux.

### 27. ○ Ewe Man Group* 10b (8 Bolts)
This surprisingly good jug-haul up steep rock takes the line over the bulge between the two cracks. The difficulty plummets after the last bolt, head up an easy crack to chains.

### 28. ○ Captain Awesome* 10c (3 Bolts + GEAR)
Follow 3 bolts up the panel to the superb 30-foot crack through splitter Poudre stone. Standard rack to 2 inches; a #4 Camalot fits but is not critical.

### 29. ○ Bighorns* 11a (8 Bolts)
The right-facing corner leads to steep climbing on creaking jugs up and right to the crux up to and past the overlap, then right on the contrived panel to chains.

### 30. ○ I Still Can't Sleep* 12b (9 Bolts)
Climb up and right to the obvious left-facing corner crux to a ledge and much easier finish.

### 31. ○ The Inner Light* 11d (7 Bolts)
Named for the classic Star Trek NG episode, a steep line of good holds takes the bulge just right of the black streak, ending with a victory cruise to chains.

### 32. ○ Ram Strong* 11d (3 Bolts + GEAR)
Big moves up and over the bulge past bolts leads to good gear. Followed by a fun finish past two more bolts in the right-facing corner to chains.

### 33. ○ One of These Days* 12a (6 Bolts)
The overhang with a left-angling flake-crack has several hard moves getting over the bulge to a fun and much easier finish on nice rock.

### 34. ○ Oh the Ewemanity!* 7 (5 Bolts + GEAR)
The overhanging flake goes on huge holds to a couple of gear placements in the easy corner. Two more bolts leads to a balancy clip of the chains. Named in honor of the earthshaking choss pitched in this area.

### 35. ○ The Omega 9 (5 Bolts)
Just before the cliff deteriorates, a line of 5 bolts heads up to and over a roof. No chains on these anchors, as the walk-off is trivial and obvious.

Jim Brink climbing on **Three Bags Full** 10a  Photo: A. Cross

DIHEDRALS

## D - DIHEDRALS WALL

This excellent panel of stone is the most obvious wall from Hwy 14. A dense series of dihedrals and arêtes characterize this wall. It is also surprisingly big, ranging from 100-200 feet in size. To reach this wall, follow the Sheep Mountain Trail to the Main Wall, then walk left or west towards the central gulley feature.

**1. Rumble in the Poudre\* 11a (13 Bolts)**
Just before the wedged roof boulder, on the far left side of the wall, climb up loose but easy rock to a shelf. A boulder-problem move (11a) is easily avoided on the left, then a bullet headwall (10d) leads to a superb roof (11a).

**2. Fractured Memories\* 10b (7 Bolts + GEAR)**
Clip a low bolt then move left and up the obvious crack (medium gear) to the base of a thin crack with a bolt at the bottom. Tackle this nice crux section (bomber wires) then up over two roofs.

**3. Tearing at All Their Dreams\*\* 11c (10 Bolts)**
Climb the shield of excellent rock on good incuts to the crux (11c). Move to a ledge, then a fun corner finish. Stepping off right to the arête at the crux lowers the grade to about 10b.

**4. To the Slaughter\* 11d (7 Bolts)**
Climb questionable rock below the prow with a crux bulge past a wedged flake and better stone up the arête, then step right to chains. The climb is easier than it looks.

**5. Sheepdog\* 11a (6 Bolts)**
This corner is taking a while to finish exfoliating.

**6. Work That Lovetron, Moses\* 10b (7 Bolts)**
The left wall of the dihedral has a friable start but transitions to much better rock.

**7. Werks Ewe Up\* 10d (5 Bolts + GEAR)**
The first corner left of the main dihedral on the left side provides a fine mixed route. Climb past slightly friable rock to a main corner containing excellent stone (5.8+) to a final crux sequence over the roof.

**8. Fear No Evil \*\* 11d (13 Bolts)**
Just right of Werks Ewe Up is another friable start to an undercling crux right and up, then continue up the left side of the arête on great rock.

**9. Roll the Stone Away\*\* 10b (12 Bolts)**
Left of the huge dihedral is this line up the right side of the arête with mostly excellent rock. One can bail at the first set of chains for a nice 5.9.

**10. Infernal Medicine\* 10a (4 Bolts + GEAR)**
Start up Book of Sheep but then follow the crack line on the left wall, then past a final bolted bulge.

**11. Book of Sheep\*\* 7 (4 Bolts + GEAR)**
The huge corner. There are not many 5.7 pitches like this in the Poudre, with good gear, good stances, and excellent rock; it's a great route for a beginner trad lead.

DIHEDRALS WALL

### 12. ○ The Upseizing* 10c (11 Bolts + GEAR)
"I'm starting to seize up," Greg Hand. This improbable line takes the wall just right of the corner (10a on sketchy rock that gets progressively better) to ten feet of excellent finger crack (crux) then over a roof to a final slanted wall (10a).

### 13. ○ Powder Her Face* 11a (11 Bolts + GEAR)
Just a bit harder than its brother to the left, take the steep wall with hidden incuts (second route right of Book) to the crack in the corner (gear, crux), then the imposing headwall above to chains.

### 14. ○ Till We Have Faces** 12a (15 Bolts)
Same start as Powder but when you hit the gear corner, move up and right to where the wall steepens on thin edges.

### 15. ○ Bostock From Little Bird*** 11b (15 Bolts)
A common F.A. reward. The third route right of the corner takes flaky rock to a crux over the bulge on excellent stone, then head up and right staying just left of the killer block to the superb arête finish on the right side of the upper flatiron.

### 16. ○ Hoof in the Grave* 10d (12 Bolts)
Climb the left wall of the huge corner, stepping off the killer block if you dare then up the wall above.

### 17. ○ Devo** 10b (5 Bolts + GEAR)
A steep bolt-protected start (crux) leads to an excellent gear corner with a tricky move near the top. Gear to #2 Camalot, emphasis on small cams.
FA: S. McCorkel

### 18. ○ Face the Change*** 11d (8 Bolts + GEAR)
This excellent route tackles the imposing face right of Devo. Start up Devo until you can commit to the bolt line and stunning headwall.
FA: S. McCorkel

### 19. ○ Laconia** 12b (11 Bolts)
Climb up a wide finger crack on a loose pillar to a line of bolts up a corner with continuous steep moves to a no-hands rest, then a final technical corner.

### 20. ○ Entropy*** 11a (10 Bolts)
The stunning right-facing corner is not to be missed. Technical climbing with hidden incuts everywhere.
FA: S. McCorkel

### 21. ○ Dumping K* 11a (8 Bolts + GEAR)
This exciting mixed route takes the line just left of the big corner, finishing on the seam.

### 22. ○ Rack of Lamb* 10a (3 Bolts + GEAR)
Good climbing up the main corner.

### 23. ○ Crack of Lamb** 11a (5 Bolts + GEAR)
The obvious roof crack.

### 24. ○ We are the Wooled* 11a (7 Bolts + GEAR)
Go up flaky-looking rock that angles up and right to a technical crux headwall and the gear-protected corner finish.

SHEEP MOUNTAIN

DIHEDRALS WALL

### 25. Between the Sheeps*** 10d (9 Bolts)
Just left of the prow, climb a corner to the obvious right-facing flakes (crux) to the photogenic arête.

### 26. Blood of the Lamb** 11b (11 Bolts)
The open corner behind the huge boulder has a friable face leading up to a steep roof with big holds. There is a second pitch that is surprisingly only 5.7 and all gear (wires to #3 Camalot) to a second set of chains.

### 27. Nanny State* 10b (8 Bolts + GEAR)
The obvious large corner is followed by a crux headwall to much easier climbing up a corner/crack (gear) to chains.

### 28. Never Forgotten** 10a (5 Bolts + GEAR)
P1: Take the right-slanting roof/corner just right of Nanny State, with a low crux followed by a short but superb panel of rock just over the roof. Easier but still fun climbing follows the obvious crack and leads to the chains on Nanny State.
P2: A green Camalot protects the cool (5.8) move to a bolt, then romp to the upper chains, with #1-3 Camalots protecting the easy runouts.

### 29. Vindicated** 9 (10 Bolts)
P1: Start a bit right of Never Forgotten and diagonal up and right over a roof (crux) then up and around the arête.
P2: The astonishing second pitch (5.7, 7 bolts) takes steep rock on big holds over a bulge past a slab (a few small cams in horizontals) to chains.

Levi Van Weddingen on the exposed finish of **Laconia** ** 12b  Photo: B. Scott

## E - TIER 2 - RIGHT SIDE

A short panel of good rock that has surprisingly fun movement. From the Main Wall, walk all the way to the right to reach an old dead tree and a gulley. Walk up the gulley 30 yds until you can traverse left to reach the right side of Tier 2.

**1. ○ Waiting in Wool 10a (3 Bolts)**
The short line up and left is for omnivores only.

**2. ○ Feed My Sheep* 11c (5 Bolts)**
The small corner and wall above. Every move is good.

**3. ○ Ghost in the Machine** 12d (5 Bolts)**
This bouldery face climb ascends a nice panel of brownish stone following a thin seam. The crux is at Bolt 2 with a wicked highstep move followed by a barn door reach to a jug. Rest up here as moving past Bolt 4 can easily spit you off.
FA: B. Scott

**4. ○ Toplob* 11a (6 Bolts)**
This acronymically named route takes the steep corner on good holds. Move left at the top to the anchor.

## F - TIER 2 - LEFT SIDE

A nice collection of corners and arêtes in a scenic location. From the Main Area, walk all the way to the right to reach an old dead tree and a gulley. Walk up the gulley 30 yds until you can traverse left to reach the right side of Tier 2. Continue walking left across the angled terrace to reach the left side routes.

**5. ○ They Call Me Mr. Stumpy* 10c (5 Bolts)**
This face climb is too uneven to be a great warm-up, with an awkward crux at the bulge, but has excellent rock and fun moves to chains.

**6. ○ Aries Arête* 11b (9 Bolts)**
Take the superb arête left of the corner on excellent rock to a thrilling 10b finish up a shallow groove.

**7. ○ Maundy Thursday* 10b (5 Bolts + GEAR)**
The open corner has a crux at the base, then fun climbing up the cracks. Bring #1-2 BD Camalot to reach the upper chains.

**8. ○ Wolf in Sheep's Clothing* 11b (7 Bolts)**
The right route in a small alcove takes the arête on good holds to a crux sequence above a small roof.

**9. ○ Got the Horse Right Here** 10a (9 Bolts)**
Good climbing up the grooved arête and headwall.

**10. ○ Dittos* 9 (4 Bolts + GEAR)**
Power up the layback gear to a sloping ledge and bolt, then traverse right and up the fun arête.

**11. ○ Megadittos* 12b (6 Bolts)**
The blunt arête eases at the break.

*The following route is not pictured and is located in the middle of the terrace of Tier 2.*

**12. ○ Back in the Saddle* 10b (GEAR)**
The F.A. of this obvious crack was done onsight by a guy in his 60s, who is missing a bunch of fingers, wearing a giant old-guy parka...in a snowstorm.

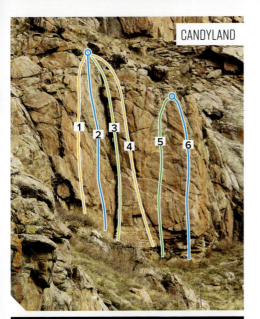

CANDYLAND

WHITE AS SNOW

## G - CANDYLAND

Although too short to be recommended, these routes are secluded and on largely excellent stone.

To reach Candyland, walk up the main trail to the Main Area and walk right to the obvious gulley. Walk up the gulley past Tier 2 and take the turn for White as Snow Wall. Traverse right across the hillside to reach Candyland.

### 1. Sweet Tooth 10c (5 Bolts)
A hard pull over a roof is followed by excellent 5.10 climbing trending up and right.

### 2. Toffee 11d (5 Bolts)
A few 11- moves down low lead to a tough crux up high.

### 3. Fat Ram 9 (GEAR)
Sweet short route at the style and grade, a few big cams to 6 inches takes you up the obvious crack.

### 4. Cracker Jack 10b (GEAR)
Climb a moderate open crack to a shelf, place a bunch of wires and cams, and punch up the nice crux.

### 5. Always Almonds 12a (4 Bolts)
Sequentially more difficult boulder problems with rests in between on good stone.

### 6. Cacao 11c (4 Bolts)
Make a hard move over the roof to excellent 5.10 climbing above on the clean face.

## H - WHITE AS SNOW WALL

A fun wall of 5.12s that has nice stone and moves even though the routes are a bit short.

To reach the White as Snow Wall, walk up the main trail to the Main Area and walk right to the obvious gulley. Walk up the gulley past the Tier 2 until you can traverse back left on grassy ledges and slabs.

### 1. Crimson Stain** 12b (6 Bolts + GEAR)
Power up a difficult move in the left-facing corner under the roof, then hand traverse right past the lip and then up the crack (gear) to easy slabs. The difficulty plummets when you hit the jams.

### 2. Cappuccino** 12c (7 Bolts)
A direct start to White as Snow that adds a powerful steep boulder problem on nice incut crimps.
FA: B. Scott, M. Tschohl

### 3. White as Snow*** 12a (6 Bolts)
The excellent wall up the left-leaning seams leads to lower-angled rock past a final bolt to chains.

### 4. Little Lamb 2 (GEAR)
Not sure who would make the hike to do trad 5.2 but this is a nice little line up the obvious corner. Small-medium gear.

### 5. Paschal Lamb* 10b (GEAR)
A bolt down low leads to the left-angling crack. Gear to 3 inches, including several small finger cams to a gear anchor up top. Walk off right.

# SHEEP MOUNTAIN

Ryan Nelson on the crux crimp of **Skin Deep\*** **11b** and some unusual checkerboard patina on the same route  Photo: B. Scott

ONCE UPON A TIME - RIGHT

## I - ONCE UPON A TIME - RIGHT

To reach the Once Upon A Time sector from the Main Area walk to the right end and up the subtle gulley past Tier 2. Traverse left above Tier 2, heading for White as Snow Wall. Right before you get there, look for a steep cairned gulley/corridor that takes you above the White as Snow Wall and leads directly to the right side of Once Upon A Time sector.

### 1. ○ They All Losers* 10a (4 Bolts + GEAR)
To the left of Comped at the Omni is a blunt arête that leads to a short dihedral feature. The arête is technical and the corner takes lots of gear.

### 2. ○ Comped at the Omni* 8 (5 Bolts)
A fairly even route left of the left-most groove.

### 3. ○ Captain Galapagos* 8 (5 Bolts)
A pull over the initial roof leads to an easier second roof and much easier finish to the same chains as Comped at the Omni.

### 4. ○ We'll Always Have Broomfield* 10c (6 Bolts)
A tough move or two past some quartz leads to the crux step left and up the arête to a trivial finish.

### 5. ○ Blue-Footed Boobie* 8 (5 Bolts)
Located to the right of We'll Always Have Broomfield, this crystalline roof and groove down low leads to a nice face finish on good rock.

ONCE UPON A TIME - LEFT

## J - ONCE UPON A TIME - LEFT

To reach the Once Upon A Time sector from the Main Area, walk to the right end and up the subtle gulley past Tier 2. Traverse left above Tier 2, heading for White as Snow Wall. Right before you get there, look for a steep cairned gulley/corridor that takes you above the White as Snow Wall and leads directly to the right side of Once Upon A Time sector. The left side lies about 50 yds farther uphill.

**1. ⦿ Mad Hatter 9** (7 Bolts)
Start behind a boulder on the left side and foot-traverse left then up.

**2. ⦿ Red Queen* 11c** (6 Bolts)
Start below two closely-spaced bolts and make a weird arête move to a jug, then up easier and fun climbing to chains.

**3. ⦿ Ever After* 12a** (6 Bolts)
Climb the obvious left leaning flake on gritty rock.

**4. ⦿ Once Upon a Time* 10d** (7 Bolts)
The undercling flake is better than it looks and leads to a tough move off the ledge. A final delicate move to clip the chains remains.

**5. ⦿ Skin Deep* 11b** (6 Bolts)
This route has some of the best rock in the entire area, unfortunately the checkerboard patina is only about 10 feet long. Still a worthy outing with a technical crimpy crux right at Bolt 2.

**6. ⦿ Little Things* 11a** (5 Bolts)
The left-facing corner (crux) leads to a fun mantle over a roof to chains.

**7. ⦿ Off with Their Heads 9** (4 Bolts + GEAR)
Make a pull past a low roof, then hit the easy crack (mid-sized cams) to the cool roof crux.

**8. ⦿ You're Not That Charming 8** (5 Bolts)
Take the somewhat contrived face to a pretty decent slot finish up the wide crack.

**9. ⦿ Sit Among the Ashes 9** (5 Bolts + GEAR)
Start right of the diagonal and take the roof past a second bolt, then up the crack to the wild flake crux at the top.

**10. ⦿ Fairy Godmother 5** (5 Bolts)
For a tiny bolted moderate, this route isn't bad. Follow some cool rails and fluted features to the open corner.

Ken Duncan working the crux of **Das Leben Der Anderen** *12c*  Photo: B. Scott

IRON CURTAIN

# K - IRON CURTAIN

To reach the Iron Curtain from the Main Wall, traverse hikers left past the Dihedrals Wall to the Central Gulley. Switchback up the Central Gulley until you can safely traverse back right to the base of the wall.

**1. Tear Down This Wall\* 12a (5 Bolts)**
We tried. Steep moves on big holds lead to a stance above the lip with the crux looming just above.

**2. Das Leben der Anderen\* 12c (5 Bolts)**
Head up and over fractured rock and the lip via a powerful sequence that slowly eases past the horizontals.

**3. Berlin Airlift 10a (6 Bolts)**
Trend up and left over the roof.

**4. Checkpoint Charlie\* 9 (3 Bolts + GEAR)**
Three bolts lead to a mellow crack.

**5. Iron Lady\* 10d (7 Bolts)**
Hard pulls on small edges down low are followed by nice face climbing over the roof.

**6. Change the Wind to Silence\*\* 9 / 10c (12 Bolts)**
A common plea up here. The first pitch up the rib is a fine warm-up but the crux second pitch puts you in one of the most spectacular positions on the mountain.

**7. Blood Runs Frozen\*\* 10c (9 Bolts)**
Face holds and stemming up the red corner are followed by fun arête moves up high.

**8. Harvest of Sorrow\* 11c (8 Bolts)**
Technical moves to the roof are followed by powerful pulls on better holds and an easier finish.

**9. Bridge Engineer\* 11c (9 Bolts)**
Perplexing stemming past a crux roof leads to easier climbing and a worthy finish.

**10. Mother Russia\* 12a (9 Bolts)**
Excellent moves up and over the roof are followed by an easier finish.

**11. Dash to Freedom\* 11b (9 Bolts)**
Take the crumbling hand traverse above the two belay bolts then up to much better rock and a superb sequence over the roof and the wall above on solid edges.

*There are no good belay options for the next three routes. The best choice might be to tie off the chains up and right and have the belayer clip into Bolt 1 of each route.*

**12. Tear in the Curtain\* 11d (7 Bolts)**
Big holds on questionable rock lead to the jamming crux through the roof on excellent stone.

**13. Be Not Afraid\* 12c (7 Bolts)**
Crunchy rock gives way to much better stone and desperate undercling/lieback moves past the roof crux.

**14. Empire of Crumbs 10b (6 Bolts)**
This used to be 5.9 but several holds have snapped off down low and it's gotten harder.

# SHEEP MOUNTAIN

## LOWER DAYLIGHT BUTTRESS

## L - LOWER DAYLIGHT BUTTRESS

For this sector, we paraphrase George Costanza: "If you were to take the best moves on all of these climbs and combine them into a single 40-foot route, it looks decent." This sector is defined by short routes - too short for any stars - at a wide variety of grades and a wide variety of rock quality.

To reach the Lower Daylight Buttress from the Main Area, traverse hikers left past the Dihedrals Wall to the Central Gulley. Switchback up the Central Gulley until you can safely traverse left out of the gulley to reach the Lower Daylight Buttress.

**1.** ◯ **Daylight Donuts 6** (6 Bolts)
Not shown, 20 feet left of De Dios.

**2.** ◯ **De Dios 11a** (6 Bolts)
Steep dihedral to crux bulge.

**3.** ◯ **Edge of Daylight 11a** (5 Bolts)
Grunge corner to cool arête with surprising jugs. This and the next two routes are actually worth a visit. Chains over the lip up high.

**4.** ◯ **Cleaning Day 11d** (4 Bolts)
There is clean and then there is "eat-off-the-rock Tod-clean." Sweet flake and face moves up great rock.

**5.** ◯ **Perfect Day 12a** (4 Bolts)
Big holds lead to a powerful lieback crux.

**6.** ◯ **Go Ahead Punk 11c** (4 Bolts)
Crux down low then powerful undercling finish. Stay right at the top to chains.

**7.** ◯ **Make My Day 12a** (4 Bolts)
Technical thin edges lead to a ledge, big move finish.

*The next three routes are located between Make My Day and Laugh and Play.*

**8.** ◯ **Just Another Day 10b** (6 Bolts)

**9.** ◯ **My Day Off 10c** (6 Bolts)

**10.** ◯ **You Call This Payday? 12a** (6 Bolts)
All three share chains 20 feet past the lip.

**11.** ◯ **Laugh and Play 7** (6 Bolts)
Start below two closely-spaced bolts and make a weird arête move to a jug, then up easier and fun climbing to chains.

**12.** ◯ **Mary 10b** (6 Bolts)
The arête is on good rock and almost worthy of a star.

**13.** ◯ **I Have No Crook 10c** (6 Bolts)
The non-descript start leads to a pumpy finish.

**14.** ◯ **Short Shank 9** (6 Bolts)
Climb the undulating slab on good stone.

**15.** ◯ **Sure to Go 6** (6 Bolts)
Just ten feet right, the featured groove is the first route you hit on the approach.

## M - UPPER DAYLIGHT BUTTRESS

To reach the Upper Daylight Buttress from the Main Wall, traverse hikers left past the Dihedrals Wall to the Central Gulley. Switchback up the Central Gulley until you can safely traverse left out ouf of the gulley to reach the Lower Daylight Buttress. Continue following ledges up and left to reach the Upper Daylight Buttress. These routes are all longer and star worthy compared to the Lower Daylight Buttress.

**16. Not My Day\* 9 (6 Bolts)**
Two technical cruxes make this demanding at the grade. Avoid the flake at the top.

**17. Freeze the Moon at Dawn\* 12b (7 Bolts)**
An easy start leads to a steep and beautiful finish.

**18. Unfinished\* 12a (6 Bolts)**
A nice line on good rock that still awaits a proper ascent.

The Poudre River beaming through the fog  Photo: B. Scott

THE SKEPTIC

## N - THE SKEPTIC

To reach The Skeptic, follow directions to Main Wall and head left past the Dihedrals. Scramble up the Central Gulley until you get to a large dead tree directly across from the Iron Curtain, but below the Narcissists Wall.

**1. Is the Rope Long Enough?*** 8 (14 Bolts)
Climb the wandering adventure sport route on the far left, bring long draws for Bolts 4 and 11.

**2. The Goats That Haunt Me*** 11c (15 Bolts)
Head up right of the corner to a single crux move near the break, then work up much steeper rock with a wild sequence on good stone finishing left.

**3. I Told You So*** 10d (11 Bolts)
The next line to the right, tough at the bulge.

**4. Two Righteous Hands*** 10d (8 Bolts)
The central line on the wall.

**5. Don't Doubt Me*** 11a (5 Bolts + GEAR)
The mixed route right of center, crux at the roof.

**6. The Skeptic**** 11c (8 Bolts)
When local climber John Durkin first came about this wall he declared: "These look like two bolt 5.8's!" The center route up good rock ends with a weird knob move at the roof.

**7. The Cynic*** 10c (7 Bolts)
The right seam. Nice edges on good rock.

Dede Humphrey on **Change The Wind To Silence**** 9 / 10c  Photo: A. Cross

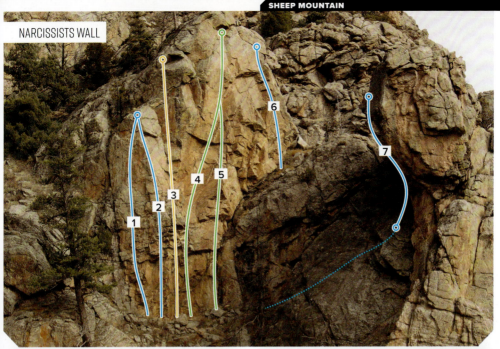

NARCISSISTS WALL

## 0 - NARCISSISTS WALL

Despite some variable rock quality, these lines all have good sections and are worthwhile. The best approach is to scramble up the gulley above The Skeptic, then traverse right past the tree in the lower left of the photo.

**1. ◉ I'm the One* 11a** (7 Bolts)
Nice climbing with the crux at the top.

**2. ◉ Wonderful Wonderful Me* 11a** (8 Bolts)
Fractured down low but excellent rock up high.

**3. ◉ Behold My Creation* 10a** (2 Bolts + GEAR)
Nice mixed line, small rack to #1 Camalot.

**4. ◉ So Long Self** 12a** (10 Bolts)
Start below the tomahawk flake, then up the wide open corner past several cruxes.

**5. ◉ Mirrors* 12a** (10 Bolts)
At present an alternate start to So Long Self with a hard sequence at the square-cut arête halfway up.

**6. ◉ Unnamed 11d** (8 Bolts)
More suspect rock at the start to clear the bulge, then better stone to the top.

**7. ◉ I Can't Look Away** 12a** (4 Bolts)
This route is actually on the Iron Curtain formation, but you access from Narcissists Wall so it is listed here. Easy 4th-class up the slab to a big ledge with two bolts (no chains to belay). Take the steep wall above on great rock and nice incuts. Tremendous position for a cool route.

## P - THE CRYPT

To reach The Crypt, approach as for The Skeptic but continue up the steep gulley to its right, then trend left up the ramp. The left wall has the best rock, sees very little sun, and is one of the first sectors to be in complete shade regardless of season.

### 1. Golgotha* 12a (8 bolts)
A leaning crux on the low wall is followed by more delicate moves up the arête up high.

### 2. Place of the Skull* 8 (8 bolts)
This route takes the obvious weaknesses all the way up.

### 3. Palm Sunday* 10b (8 bolts)
The first of three similar routes on the bald slab. Good rock and nice climbing.

### 4. The Spirit is Willing* 10c (6 bolts)
Slightly more difficult than its neighbors.

### 5. The Flesh is Weak* 10b (6 bolts)
The right margin also climbs well.

*The next set of routes are located up the Crypt gulley on the upper right side. These lines are characterized by poor, grainy rock down low that transitions into great stone up high.*

### 6. All Roads Lead to Capuchin 10a (8 bolts)
Climb quite a ways up the gulley past a few bolts on the left wall then swing up and right to a worthwhile finish.

### 7. The Way to Dusty Death* 12a (8 bolts)
Start just a few feet left of the huge corner and take a grainy 5.11 slab to the overlap, then up and right to an excellent finish on the mildly overhanging headwall.

### 8. Bone Book* 10b (8 bolts)
The massive corner is crumbly down low but gets better as you move up. Chains just over the lip.

### 9. Knochenmann 12b (8 bolts)
Start up Bone Book, then ease right up the grainy popcorn seam that gets better just as things get hard.

### 10. Not Dead Yet* 12a (10 bolts)
The awkward seam/crack down low leads to a pumpy finish on better rock.

LOWER SHOFAR

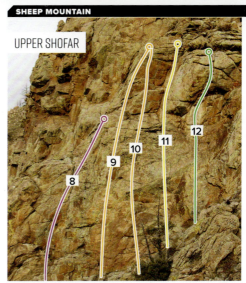

SHEEP MOUNTAIN

UPPER SHOFAR

## Q - SHOFAR

If the name is any indication, this crag requires some effort to get to. The best and safest way is to head to the Central Gulley just past the Dihedrals Wall. Head up and out of the gulley passing the Lower and Upper Daylight Buttresses. Move around the left side of the Upper Daylight Buttress and up a 5th class gulley with some large boulders. Go around the left side of the Taco Wall heading uphill to the base of Lower Shofar.

1. **The Debt*** 11b (8 bolts)
Corner to cool traverse left, then right and up.

2. **Visiting Privileges*** 11c (8 bolts)
Get past the undercling/wall crux to the sweet panel above.

3. **Walk Softly and Carry a Big Horn*** 10c (9 bolts)

4. **Blast a Blessing*** 10b (9 bolts)
The technical corner is followed by big holds on a steep wall.

5. **The Oboe**** 7 (8 bolts)
Nice climbing on big holds.

6. **Shofar Away*** 9 (8 bolts)
These two routes have nice climbing on good rock.

7. **Shofar So Good*** 9 (8 bolts)

8. **Unnamed 8** (5 bolts)

9. **Better Call Maynard*** 10c (10 bolts)
The best route on the face.

10. **Unnamed*** 10a (8 bolts)
Very even climbing with the crux at the top.

11. **Unnamed** 7 (7 Bolts)
Mellow the whole way up.

12. **Fourth Floor Walk-Up** 12a (7 bolts)
Easy slab to hard bulge on friable rock.

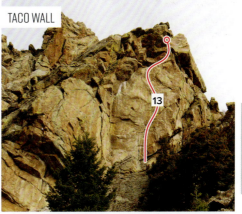

TACO WALL

## R - TACO WALL

This obscure little wall is at the farthest reaches of Sheep Mountain. The best way to get here is to follow directions to the Upper Daylight Buttress. From there, find the easiest way to walk around the left side of Upper Daylight and head up a short 5th class gulley choked with big boulders. This gulley should deposit you right in front of the Taco Wall.

13. **Taco Bell*** 13a (7 Bolts)
Named after Matt Tschohl's beloved dog Taco Bell, who was in fact named after the fast-food chain. The hardest sport route on the mountain will challenge all your finger strength and footwork skills up the spider web of seams. A steep start leads to a cruxy barn door move before the easy crack heading back right to the chains.
FA: B. Scott, M. Tschohl

## SHEEP MOUNTAIN

**SKYLINE BOULDERS OVERVIEW**

**SKYLINE BOULDERS**
- T  Man Dime Boulder
- U  Dudley Boulder
- V  Ghost Train Boulder
- W  Rapture Boulder
- X  Crunchy Boulder
- Y  Clams Boulder
- Z  Prometheus Boulder
- AA Crown Boulder

## S - SKYLINE BOULDERS

This small bouldering area was partially developed back in the winter/spring of 2011. A cluster of several huge boulders strangely perched at the very top of Sheep Mountain itself. Rock quality is generally excellent and there are lots of problems not listed in this guide.

## GETTING THERE

**GPS: 40°40'49.40"N 105°25'30.89"W**
To reach this area is no small feat, requiring one hour of steep hiking. Follow the main Sheep Mountain trail to the Main Area. Walk to the far right side and start up the shallow gulley. Pass the Tier Two Wall and head for the White as Snow Wall. Locate the hidden gulley trail that takes you above White As Snow Wall to the Once Upon a Time Wall-Left. Find a short gulley on the right side of the Once Upon a Time Wall-Left that leads to flat terrain where you can traverse back north to the Skyline Boulders.

MAN DIME

## T - MAN DIME BOULDER

Set apart from the main cluster, about 50 yds downhill.

**1.** ⬤ **Project Man Dime*** v3 (Pads)
Stand start on the green arête and head straight up utilizing the arête and crimps on left. Impeccable rock quality.
FA: Paul Dusatko, J. Tarry

DUDLEY

## U - DUDLEY BOULDER

A nice boulder to warm-up on with more of that perfect stone. Right below the Ghost Train Boulder.

**2.** ⬤ **Ben's Face*** v2 (Pads)
Climb middle slab via large sloping hold.
FA: B. Scott

**3.** ⬤ **Dudley's Arête*** v2 (Pads)
Use the right arête and left face crimps to climb a technical bottom to easy topout.
FA: Emily Dudley

Jason Tarry on **Project Man Dime**** v3  Photo: B. Scott

## V - GHOST TRAIN BOULDER

This amazing boulder seems out of place perched at the top of Sheep Mountain. More akin to something West of Rustic, this boulder is worth the long hike up the hill.

**4.** ○ **Slip and Slide**** v3** (Pads)
A nice warm-up that is surprisingly steep. SDS on a big undercling and move up and left through pinches and slopers.
FA: P. Dusatko, B. Scott

**5.** ○ **Ground Up Arête**** v2** (Pads)
An excellent warm-up following an interesting featured crack. Some cool sculpted holds on this one.
FA: P. Dusatko, B. Scott

**6.** ○ **Ghost Train****** v6** (Pads)
Most of the time when you decide to walk all the way up a mountain looking for boulders, you end up empty handed. But for some reason this awesome problem is up there. Good rock, aesthetic line, interesting movement that is no gimme, and a full value topout make this a classic.
FA: B. Scott

**7.** ○ **Phantom Menace****** v9** (Pads)
Paul and I heard a train drive down the canyon, it was probably a redneck with a train whistle on his HEMI diesel rig, but still, it was eerie and strange at the time. A 45° wall on bomber granite dotted with a line of bighter incut crimps. If you climb this grade, I'm not sure what else you could want.
FA: B. Scott

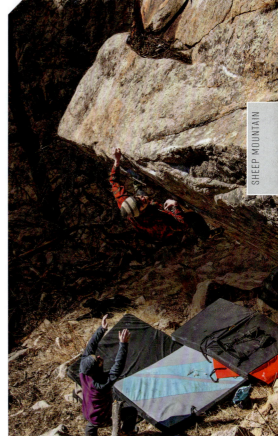

Ben Jurenka at the final crux of **Phantom Menace**** v9**   Photo: B. Scott

SHEEP MOUNTAIN

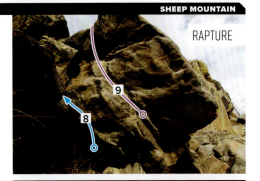
RAPTURE

CRUNCHY

## W - RAPTURE BOULDER

From the Ghost Train boulder, walk 30 yards to hikers left across the hillside. This boulder faces the Crunchy Boulder.

### 8. ○ Last Day on Earth* v9 (Pads)
Start crouched on a chossy undercling. Two very powerful moves get you into some decent incuts which lead up and left past a crack to a series of jugs out to the lip.
FA: S. Rothstein

### 9. ○ The Rapture*** v4 (Pads)
Established on the day of The Rapture (05/21/11), this steep long problem is more like a mini-sport route. Start on the big horn jug at head height and make continuous big moves on good holds over the tiered landing to the easy topout.
FA: B. Scott, C. Tirrell, J. Tarry

## X - CRUNCHY BOULDER

A majestic boulder sitting at the edge of the super steep hillside. Another incredible boulder that seems completely out of place.

### 10. ○ Smoke Dragon*** v7 (Pads)
One of the best roof climbs in the canyon, even if it is a drop-off problem. Start in the back of the cave, underclinging the beginning of the flake feature. Climb out the flake with feet on the kick wall until you're forced into the big move to the drop off jug.
FA: B. Scott, N. Perl

### 11. ○ Crunchy Grooves*** v7 (4-5 Pads)
Stand start on an obvious big, orange jug and perform a big move out right to a gaston which allows you to get established on the arête. Romp up the scary arête on all kinds of jugs and pinches. An amazing unfinished project would climb Smoke Dragon into Crunchy Grooves.
FA: B. Scott

## Y - CLAMS BOULDER

A worthy boulder that hides above two behemoth boulders. From the Rapture Boulder, scramble up the ledges left of Last Day on Earth to reach the Clams Boulder perched above.

### 12. ○ Mantle Mussel* v6 (Pads)
SDS on the obvious starting rail and climb directly out the steep crack with some tricky body English. Which is followed by an equally deceiving mantle.
FA: N. Perl

### 13. ○ Clams Casino*** v7 (Pads)
An excellent line out the short, but steep overhang. SDS on the obvious crescent-shaped hold and perform several compression moves to reach the easier but technical mantle.
FA: B. Scott

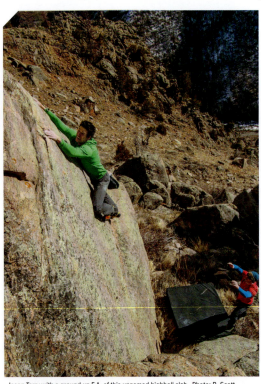
Jason Tarry with a ground up F.A. of this unnamed highball slab   Photo: B. Scott

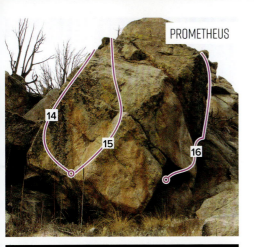

## Z - PROMETHEUS BOULDER

A nice boulder with several moderates to get the blood flowing for the harder stuff.

**14.** ⊙ **Arête-O-Matic*** v3 (Pads)
SDS on a nice edge and move up and left to the arête.
FA: B. Scott

**15.** ⊙ **Ledge-O-Matic*** v3 (Pads)
Same start as Arête-O-Matic but head up and right to a seam and a long but easy topout.
FA: J. Nadeau

**16.** ⊙ **Prometheus Dabbing**** v4 (Pads)
Start sitting in low cave and unlock a cryptic sequence to escape the cave to the right. Gain a large ledge, then head up on the right headwall. Finish with a juggy mantle off the huge ledge. Long and pumpy!
FA: P. Dusatko

## AA - CROWN BOULDER

About 20 yards uphill from the Prometheus Boulder lies this diamond-shaped block leaning on a slab. Named after the Skyline Boulders being a crown of boulders at the peak of Sheep Mountain.

**17.** ⊙ **The Crown**** v7 (4-5 Pads)
Excellent compression climbing on pinches and slopers to a spicy finish over the slab. Stand start on a jug on the right face and a pinch with the left. Slap and squeeze your way to the angled jug with three committing moves left to go.
FA: B. Scott

**18.** ⊙ **Crown Low**** v9 (4-5 Pads)
SDS on an obvious jug edge and add a few moves of power into the classic stand start.
FA: B. Scott

**19.** ⊙ **Party in the Back**** v2 (Pads)
Walk into the cave to find a unique series of sculpted jugs and pinches to a chimney style topout. If this doesn't make you smile, you should probably give up bouldering.
FA: D. Ludders, J. Tarry

Nick Perl getting the giggles on **Smoke Dragon**** v7   Photo: B. Scott

**18.8 MILES FROM TED'S PLACE**

# NARROWS BLOCS

Nick Perl on **Hot Fire**\*\*\* v8   Photo: B. Scott

**GRADE DISTRIBUTION**
- v0-v2: 7
- v3-v4: 6
- v5-v6: 12
- v7-v8: 11
- v9-v10: 8

**MOSTLY SHADE ALL DAY**

**TYPE(S): BOULDERING**
**DIFFICULTY RANGE: V0 - V10**
**APPROACH TIME: 15 MIN - 1 HOUR**
**SEASON: FALL, WINTER, & SPRING**

**RIVER CROSSING REQUIRED**

## CLIMBING OVERVIEW

The Narrows Blocs is a more recently developed bouldering area although it has been visited and walked through by climbers since the early 2000s. This massive field of boulders was once hidden under a dense forest until it was destroyed by the High Park Fire in 2012. After the fire, the boulders became much more obvious from the road and the area began being explored again. Climbers like **Brett Hoffman, Sam Rothstein, Jake Atkinson** and **Nick Perl** began an all out attack on the area, putting up many of the classic problems during the fall/winter of 2016/17. Massive amounts of work has been done to create landing areas at the base of most of the boulders using natural materials and elbow grease. The area has great potential and lots of problems left to develop if you're willing to put in the work.

## GETTING THERE

**GPS: 40°40'29.05"N 105°25'33.35"W**

From Ted's Place, drive approx. 18.8 miles into the heart of the Narrows to a massive pullout on the right, just after the Sheep Mountain parking. If you get to Icicle Canyon or East of Eden, you have gone to far. Depending on river levels, the easiest place to wade across is about 50 yards upstream from the parking area. After navigating the crossing, continue moving upstream until you reach a small talus field that comes right down to the river. Look for a cairned path heading up the talus to reach the first boulder, Promised Lands.

In general, there is a faint cairned trail to navigate to the main boulders but otherwise the area involves bushwhacking and route finding. It is a burn area from the 2012 High Park Fire, so be prepared for loose rocks, burnt/un-stable trees, and thorny bushes.

NARROWS BLOCS

PROMISED LANDS

## A - PROMISED LANDS BOULDER

This is the first boulder you come to on your way up the hill. Located at the top of the short talus field.

**1. ○ Promised Lands* v10** (Pads)
A pumpy traverse starting on the right side of the boulder and finishing as a drop off on the left side. A crucial jug has broken in the middle which made it much harder.
FA: B. Camp, Z. Lerner

**2. ○ Dihedral Project** (4-5 Pads)
A jaw-dropping project that has seen little or no attempts.

BLACK SLAB

## B - BLACK SLAB BOULDER

Nice sized boulder with several moderates that make decent warm-ups. Interesting texture on this boulder with even the occasional pocket feature.

**3. ○ Unnamed* v2** (Pads)
Stand start on an obvious edge and climb a couple moves up and right to a topout.
FA: Unknown

**4. ○ Unnamed Arête* v2** (Pads)
Getting on the arête maybe the hardest part, then easy moves on crystals and crimps to the top.
FA: Unknown

**5. ○ Pocket Slab*** v5** (Pads)
Excellent face and slab climbing that will test your foot work. Tricky to get established on the crystal undercling followed by a strenuous deadpoint to the lip.
FA: B. Scott

Chris Hofer snags the lip on **Pocket Slab*** v5   Photo: B. Scott

**6. ○ Layback Variation** v6** (Pads)
Start on a nice layback edge and move left into Pocket Slab.
FA: B. Scott

**7. ○ Unnamed Crimps* v5** (Pads)
Grab two nice incuts at chest height; the right one is a bit hollow. Do two hard moves to another set of crimps before the easy topout.
FA: Unknown

CORNERSHOP

TO ICE CANYON

## C - CORNERSHOP BOULDER

This boulder is directly above the Black Slab boulder. It's another decent warm-up in the lower part of the field.

**8. ○ Working the Corner*** v4** (Pads)
Techy dihedral climbing on smeary feet and small crimps. The topout is easy but it's a bit spicy if you mess up.
FA: J. Atkinson

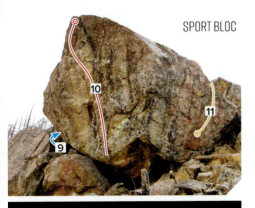

## D - SPORT BLOC

This impressive boulder is probably the most obvious one from Hwy 14. The boulder is about half the size of a house with three overhanging sides and excellent rock quality. From the Black Slab boulder, walk up and left onto the ridge and follow the cairns up to the Sport Bloc.

**9. Scalp Collector** v10 (Pads)
Start in the cave on two crimps and perform a big campus move to a sloper followed by a very tricky topout.
FA: S. Rothstein

**10. Sin of Man*** 13b (3 Bolts)
A bolted boulder problem due to the dismal and terrifying landing. Excellent rock and moves on incut sidepulls leads to a long reach at Bolt 2 and a redpoint crux getting to the arête just before the anchors. For full points the smaller boulder on the left at the start is considered "off."
FA: B. Scott

**11. Miss Rose** v8 (Pads)
Start low and follow crimps and edges up the cool seam features to an easy mantle.
FA: S. Rothstein

## E - PHOENIX BOULDER

Right above the Sport Bloc is this brightly colored boulder with rail features on the left side.

**12. Phoenix*** v7 (Pads)
Grab a juggy edge at head-height and move left to a crimp followed by a strenuous high-heel to reach a sidepull. This is followed by a perfect jug before the topout.
FA: B. Scott

**13. Pigeon* v2 (Pads)
Same start as the Phoenix but move right to a big flake feature and an easy mantle.
FA: B. Scott

## F - BLACK SEAM BOULDER

A very aesthetic looking boulder with an obvious project on its east side. Nothing else has been attempted or completed on this boulder to date.

The author on the last few moves of **Sin Of Man** 13b   Photo: Andy Cross

## G - HOT FIRE BOULDER

This is easily one of the best boulders in the area with a nice flat landing for most of the problems, including some epic highballs. The stone is very good and the climbing varies in style and movement across all of the problems. From the Black Seam Boulder, walk right across the hillside to a small ridge which takes you directly up to Hot Fire.

### 14. ◯ Backburner* v9 (Pads)
Located on the opposite side of the main face in a small corridor next to a short, white dihedral. SDS on opposing crimps and do a hard first move before continuing up the arête to an easy topout.
FA: S. Rothstein

### 15. ◯ Stone Cold*** v8 (4-5 Pads)
Climb the awesome overhanging prow/roof feature. Stand start on a good left crimp and a small pinch. The first move to the right-hand gaston is powerful, followed by pumpy climbing to a tenuous move getting hands over the lip. Topout is easy but not trivial.
FA: B. Scott

### 16. ◯ Hot Fire*** v8 (4-5 Pads)
The aesthetic red and green face up the center of the boulder. Stand start on a small edge in a seam and an obvious right-hand sidepull. The first move to another right-hand sidepull is hard, followed by an awesome toss to a perfect jug. Stay composed as you execute another 8-10 moves of sequential but only v3-ish climbing in the "I'd rather not fall zone."
FA: B. Scott

### 17. ◯ Charlie Chaplin* v4 (Pads)
This problem's landing is not the best looking but it's quite manageable and the problem is worth doing. Start on two slopey crimps and do a hard highstep pull-on-mantle to a nice pinch. Another big move gets you to a great jug at the lip and a classic mantle.
FA: B. Scott

### 18. ◯ Narrow Control*** v9 (Pads)
This problem is surprisingly good regardless of its short stature. SDS on the obvious edge and figure out how to get on the left-hand pinch. Tension is the key to reach the easy mantle from here.
FA: S. Rothstein

## NARROWS BLOCS

CRACKS

CRESCENT

## J - CRACKS BOULDER

Another massive boulder with a nice downhill face. From the Black Seam Boulder walk directly uphill about 20-30 yards. This boulder has several un-done lines waiting for ascents.

**22.** ◯ **Straight and Narrow**** v1** (Pads)
Climb the nice right-leaning crack feature on big holds and feet. An easy highball / solo, falling off the top half is probably a bad idea.
FA: Dylan Demyanek

## H - CRESCENT BOULDER

Another massive boulder that has several overhanging aspects to it. From the Hot Fire Boulder, walk uphill about 30 yds until a corridor between two boulders is found, this is where Moonrise is. Walk down the corridor and around to the right to find the Crescent.

**19.** ◯ **The Crescent*** v9** (Pads)
Stand start on two small crimps. Do a big move to the crescent-shaped rail before building feet and going big to the lip using a final sidepull.
FA: S. Rothstein, B. Scott

**20.** ◯ **Moonrise**** v6** (Pads)
Stand start and climb slopey crimps up the subtle groove/dihedral feature. The last few moves before the mantle are probably the hardest.
FA: S. Rothstein

CROSS WITH CARE

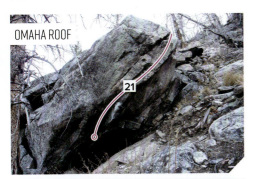

OMAHA ROOF

## K - CROSS WITH CARE

A nice cleaved boulder with an obvious arête and a decent landing. Located up and left of the Cracks Boulder.

**23.** ◯ **Cross with Care**** v5** (Pads)
Named after a certain climber's infamous river crossing accident that resulted in a smashed cheekbone, so yeah be careful crossing the river. Start in a crouched position compressing the two arêtes. Then layback up the main feature on big hands but techy feet.
FA: J. Atkinson

## I - OMAHA ROOF

A fun, short overhang with one obvious problem. Located next to the Crescent Boulder, but closer to the corridor that holds the problem Moonrise.

**21.** ◯ **Omaha Roof* v4** (Pads)
SDS on an obvious jug and do a big move to the blocky layback feature. Continue following the seam up and right following the line of nice flat holds.
FA: Sean Field, S. Rothstein

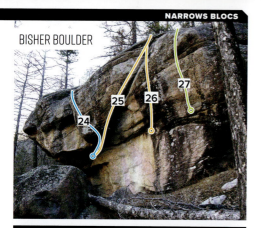

BISHER BOULDER

## L - BISHER BOULDER

One of the oldest established boulders in the area. A nice medium-sized boulder with flat landings and a nice variety of movement. From the Cracks Boulder, head left across the hillside past several other boulders to reach this bloc on the far left side of the main cluster.

### 24. ◉ Dead Hand*** v9 (Pads)
Originally attempted around 2004, this line took 12 years to actually get completed. Begin with some jugs in a seam at the back of the roof. Move through underclings on horrible smears for feet to a big incut. Move back left into the mini left-facing corner, and perform a series of bumps off a kneebar to a tricky lip encounter.
**FA: B. Scott**

### 25. ◉ Lock and Key** v8 (Pads)
Start the same as Dead Hand but climb the entire crack feature up and right. Very pumpy resistance climbing with a tricky move right at the end. If you start at the mid-way jug, it is about v6.
**FA: S. Rothstein**

### 26. ◉ Hippie Jump** v7 (Pads)
Start on some small edges and do a big move to some cool slopey edges. Move left into the finger-lock and topout of Lock and Key.
**FA: S. Rothstein**

### 27. ◉ Hippie Mafia*** v5 (Pads)
Obvious start holds in a seam at chest height. Move up to another horizontal seam before tackling some desperate slopers to reach a crucial pinch feature.
**FA: B. Scott**

Luis Bellido trying The Ledge Project near The Cobra Bloc  Photo: B. Scott

FEATHER

## M - FEATHER BOULDER

An excellent boulder on perfect rock that can be a bit tricky to find. Located about 100 yds downstream and a little uphill from the Bisher Boulder on the side of a subtle gulley feature. There are several other massive boulders here with development on-going to date.

### 28. ◉ Blue Feather*** v6 (Pads)
Start on a great jug in a dihedral feature. Big moves on good holds sends you up and left to the glory jug rail and the easy topout. Worth looking for this random gem.
**FA: N. Perl, S. Rothstein**

Jason Tarry on **Life Of Pie**** v8**, when it was still a project  Photo: B. Scott

## N - LOG RAFT BOULDER

Another massive boulder hidden in the remnants of the old forest. From the Hot Fire Boulder, head downhill and slightly upstream for about 30 yards to find this bloc.

### 29. Life of Pie*** v8 (Pads)
Start on the big jug rail and do two big and hard moves on crimps before you can gain the right arête and topout the same as Pi. Initially tried with a direct topout, it is unfortunately a bit contrived in the end.
FA: S. Rothstein

### 30. Pi** v6 (Pads)
Start on a cool pinch and sidepull and do a big move up the arête/jug. Lip traverse up the arête a few more moves until you can mantle out to the right on the easy slab.
FA: K. Worobec

## O - COBRA BLOC

This buried boulder is so big it's mostly a cliff line but its hard to tell since it's in the midst of a huge pile of blocs. From the Hot Fire Boulder or Crescent Boulder, walk uphill 20 yds and traverse right or upstream across the bottom of the cliff/boulders to reach the base of the Cobra.

### 31. Treebeard* v2 (Pads)
Located on the far left side of the boulder on an elevated platform of sorts. Climb the left arête near the massive burnt log and try not to dab on it.
FA: S. Field, S. Rothstein

### 32. Orange-Faced Devil*** v6 (4-5 Pads)
The intimidating dihedral feature on impeccable granite. Stem your way up until you can get on the edge on the right face. A massive move to another rail gives you access to an easy but heady topout.
FA: B. Scott

### 33. Strike** v6 (Pads)
Obvious jug edge to start, grab a finicky crystal pinch and a hard move to the subtle arête. Continue up the arête to a hard and big move to a hidden edge. Hard for the grade.
FA: B. Scott

### 34. Slither*** v2 (Pads)
An excellent moderate on perfect gray stone. Figure out how to layback up the initial layback feature to reach a crimp up and right. Then topout and downclimb the slab/chimney to the right.
FA: B. Scott

NARROWS BLOCS

HIPPO BOULDER

Ryan Nelson compressing up **Hippo Hoedown**\*\*\* v7   Photo: B. Scott

## P - THE LOFT

This guidebook covers only a small portion of this zone inside the Narrows Blocs. A stunning view looking down into the heart of the Narrows is an added bonus to these problems. To reach The Loft, walk uphill from Omaha Roof on some exposed rock until you reach the crest. Walk upstream from here along the edge of the hill until you can snake your way back down into this zone of blocs.

**35. ○ Hippo Hoedown**\*\*\* v7 (Pads)
This unusual boulder features excellent compression climbing on a perfect refrigerator-width prow. Most climbers SDS with their feet in the hole and heel-hook their way out to a tricky lip encounter pulling onto the left face.
FA: S. Rothstein

**36. ○ White Elephant**\*\* v7 (Pads)
Yet another compression problem located on a separate tier right below Hippo Hoedown. Stand start and compress your way up the prow to a hard last move.
FA: N. Pearl

**37. ○ Stolen Rib**\*\* v2 (Pads)
This fun arête feature is located a little downstream from Hippo Hoedown on a separate tier just above the Cobra Bloc. Layback and heel-hook your way up the nice prow feature.
FA: D. Demyanek

### NARROWS BLOCS SECOND TIER

| | | PAGE |
|---|---|---|
| Q. | Sloper Mantle Proj | 143 |
| R. | Submarine Boulder | 143 |
| S. | Rainbow Boulder | 143 |
| T. | The Fable | 143 |
| U. | Tiger Boulder | 143 |

## SECOND TIER

The farthest reaches of the Narrows Blocs area is referred to as the Second Tier. This area is probably better described as the East side of Ice Canyon, but it's very high up on the hillside and is easily reached once you're at The Loft.

There are many large boulders here with excellent rock quality. Some of the landings are even flat compared to the rest of the Narrows Blocs. This is a brief overview of the major boulders in the zone, there are many more developed and undeveloped boulders not listed.

## GETTING THERE

GPS: 40°40'22.72"N 105°25'39.83"W

From The Loft (a.k.a. the very top of the hill that holds most of the Narrow Blocs), you will find a small meadow or plateau area. Walk south and a little west until some small boulders come into view. Keep walking until you can see down into Ice Canyon. The Submarine and Fable boulders are 20 yards downhill to the south/southwest from here.

Alternatively, take the Ice Canyon trail from the Cornershop Bloc and walk slightly uphill to reach the Second Tier.

SLOPER MANTLE PROJ
TO SUBMARINE / FABLE

## Q - SLOPER MANTLE PROJ

A funny little blunt egg-shaped boulder that just seems impossible to climb. It is mostly a good landmark for finding the Second Tier when walking from The Loft. When you find this boulder, walk to your right until the hill steepens, then back left to find the Submarine Boulder.

SUBMARINE

## R - SUBMARINE BOULDER

An obvious steep prow jutting out from the hillside. A good landmark to find the rest of the boulders at the Second Tier.

**38.** ○ **Submarine**\*\*\* **v9** (Pads)
Start on an incredible incut edge and perform a sweet move to a crazy sloper rail. Continue compressing to a final hard thrutch to a flat rail out right. More in-your-face climbing gets you to the top but it's not as hard as the first half.
FA: B. Scott

RAINBOW

## S - RAINBOW BOULDER

A nice face on a medium-sized boulder with good stone and a flat landing. Located about 10 yds right of the Submarine.

**39.** ○ **Rainbow Traverse**\*\* **v4** (Pads)
Start on a nice jug and traverse or angle all the way left on crimps and slopers.
FA: S. Rothstein

**40.** ○ **Over the Rainbow**\*\* **v6** (Pads)
Do Rainbow Traverse to the middle then dyno to the big jug up and right.
FA: K. Worobec

**41.** ○ **Rainbow Direct**\* **v3** (Pads)
Starts the same as the traverse, but climb straight up to a sinker mega jug at the lip.
FA: S. Rothstein

FABLE

## T - FABLE BOULDER

This massive boulder hosts excellent rock quality on some beautiful looking stone.

**42.** ○ **Open Book**\*\* **v5** (Pads)
Stand start on the gaston crimp rail, make tricky moves through sloper sidepulls, and then gun for the lip.
FA: Nick Perl

**43.** ○ **The Fable**\*\*\*\* **v3** (Pads)
A stunning line of holds out the multi-colored 18 foot tall face. Doesn't get much better than this.
FA: B. Hoffman, J. Atkinson

**44.** ○ **Aesop**\*\* **v9** (Pads)
A crimpy SDS variation to The Fable on small but positive edges and good stone.
FA: S. Rothstein

**45.** ○ **The Oracle**\*\*\* **v10** (Pads)
Big moves to a lot of crimpy holds with an exit up and right.
FA: S. Rothstein

## U - TIGER BOULDER

Down and right from the Fable is a great boulder with a tiered roof feature on its downhill side.

**46.** ○ **Tigris**\*\* **v7** (Pads)
SDS in a compression position and work your way up and right on increasingly better holds to a solid topout.
FA: N Perl, B. Hoffman

Connor Jeffress at the exciting final moves to the anchor on **Duke of Weselton*** **12d**  Photo: B. Scott

# ICE CANYON

**19.1 MILES** FROM TED'S PLACE

##

**TYPE(S): SPORT, TRAD & ICE CLIMBING**
**DIFFICULTY RANGE: 5.10 - 5.12C**
**APPROACH TIME: 30 - 45 MIN**
**SEASON: SPRING, FALL & WINTER**

*RIVER CROSSING REQUIRED*

## CLIMBING OVERVIEW

Ice Canyon (a.k.a. Poverty Gulch) is an amazing little off-shoot from the main Poudre Canyon. Although ravaged by the High Park Fire and associated flooding, the area is still serene and beautiful with its bubbling stream and towering walls.

*MOSTLY SHADE ALL DAY*

Ice Canyon was first documented as a climbing area in the original Ley/Allen guidebook. This small canyon was mostly mentioned as the access point to Coyote Head and their route, **The First Labor of Hercules**\*\*\* 5. But the guide also mentions people climbing on the small ice flows that form at the bottom during the winter. This is still probably the most popular use for the area. The small ice flows are easily seen from Hwy 14, and with the river frozen that time of year, it attracts lots of thirsty beginner ice climbers. In recent years, some single pitch sport climbing has also been developed. This area should be enjoyed for its adventurous spirit rather than a plethora of routes.

## GETTING THERE

GPS: 40°40'25.88"N 105°25'44.85"W

From Ted's Place, drive 19.1 miles to a sharp turn in the Narrows where Ice Canyon branches off to the south. You can park here, but the easiest crossings are downstream from the canyon, similar to those used for Narrows Blocs.

Once you cross the river, it is not simply a straight forward hike following the stream. If going to the ice flow, it is very obvious, but if you're going to the sport routes listed here, it can be tricky. A few months a year in late fall, you can scramble up the initial section where the ice flow forms. But a lot of the time, it is wet, slippery and not suggested. You have two alternatives:

1. Find a section of talus just before the mouth of the canyon and follow this uphill until you can traverse back left and down to the creek. (this route is marked above). There are a lot of 5th class sections and it should not be taken lightly.

2. BEST OPTION: Follow the directions for Narrows Blocs (page 135) and hike up to the Cornershop Bloc and locate an old mining trail that leads back west towards Ice Canyon. Follow this trail until it descends into Ice Canyon and deposits you at the base of Arendelle.

**ICE CANYON**

Garrett Bales getting crossed up on **Marshmallow**\*\*\* **12c** Photo: B. Scott

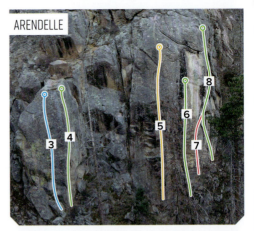

## ARENDELLE

This aesthetic looking wall is easily noticed from Hwy 14. Black and white streaked rock mixed with interesting angled rock makes the movement here quite fun. The rock quality is unusual too, featuring some semi-pocketed rock in places. Located at the upper end of the canyon before you get to Coyote Head.

### 3. ○ Jack Frost\*\* 11b (6 Bolts)
This excellent face climb on quality stone will keep you on your toes all the way to the anchor.
FA: C. Hofer

### 4. ○ Marshmallow\*\*\* 12c (6 Bolts)
This obvious arête is technical and deceptively hard. Getting off the mid-way rail and onto the arête again is the crux.
FA: B. Scott

### 5. ○ Olaf's Bulge\*\*\* 10a (4 Bolts + GEAR)
This route is fun from start to finish. Begin on an arête with an opposing seam past 4 bolts. Climb into a steep but juggy crack feature with lots of gear before a final slab crux right before the anchor.
FA: J. Tarry

### 6. ○ Duke of Weselton\*\*\* 12d (7 Bolts)
The stellar center line up the center of the wall is only marred by the fact that it stops short of the top. Start with a short dihedral feature until you can move out right onto some cool pocketed jugs. Continue up the subtle dihedral until a final pumpy highstep to reach the anchor.
FA: B. Scott

### 7. ○ Cryokinetic\*\* 13b (9 Bolts)
A vicious four move boulder problem on immaculate stone takes you into the rest of Bitchy Sister.
FA: B. Scott

### 8. ○ Bitchy Sister\*\* 12b (8 Bolts)
Start up a left leaning layback feature which holds the crux around Bolt 2. Move back right to another layback/flake feature which is tricky to exit. Big moves on edges up the slab gets you to the anchor.
FA: J. Tarry, B. Scott

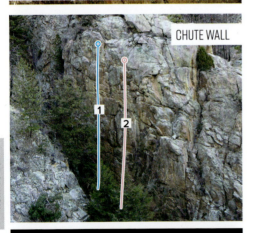

## CHUTE WALL

This interesting corridor has potential for many routes but it has largely been neglected. Good rock and excellent setting make this place low-hanging fruit for new development.

### 1. ○ Giving Tree\*\* 11a (10 Bolts)
Climb a nice series of edges and jugs out the long slightly overhanging wall.
FA: Noah Kaufman

### 2. ○ JTarrys Route (8 Bolts)
Another nice route up the long panel in the corridor. A route in progress that is partially bolted and cleaned.
Bolted By J. Tarry

## ICE CANYON

## COYOTE HEAD

This infamous pinnacle has been spotted by climbers for generations. The earliest name is documented in the Ley/Allen guidebook as the **First Labor of Hercules**. Fast forward 30 years to Matt Fanning's ascent of **Juwana Arête** where he referred to it as the "Poudre Horn." Strangely enough, I always heard it called Coyote Head, which was a name coined by Craig Leubben one day and it is listed as such here. A striking pinnacle of orange and grey rock that seems to hang over the entire canyon.

### 9. ○ The First Labor of Hercules*** 5 (GEAR)
Routes don't get more old-school or classic in the Poudre Canyon than this little mini-route. The easiest way up the pinnacle involves maybe a move or two of 5th class climbing but this route is mostly scrambling.
FA: S. Allen, S. Wakefield '72

### 10. ○ The Coyote**** 12a (9 Bolts)
Another incredible and aesthetic line from Mr. McCorkel. Start with a deceptively tricky boulder problem to reach Bolt 2. Continue up the golden face on incuts and hidden jugs to the glory romp up the spectacular arête. Do this climb.
FA: S. McCorkel, Matt Flach

### 11. ○ Juwana Arête** 12a (8 Bolts)
Start on the left side of the arête moving right until you can gain the right arête and transition onto the right face. Climb seams and the dueling arêtes to the anchor.
FA: Matthew Fanning

Jason Tarry cruising to the anchor on **The Coyote**** 12a**  Photo: B. Scott

POUDRE CANYON GUIDE - 3RD EDITION

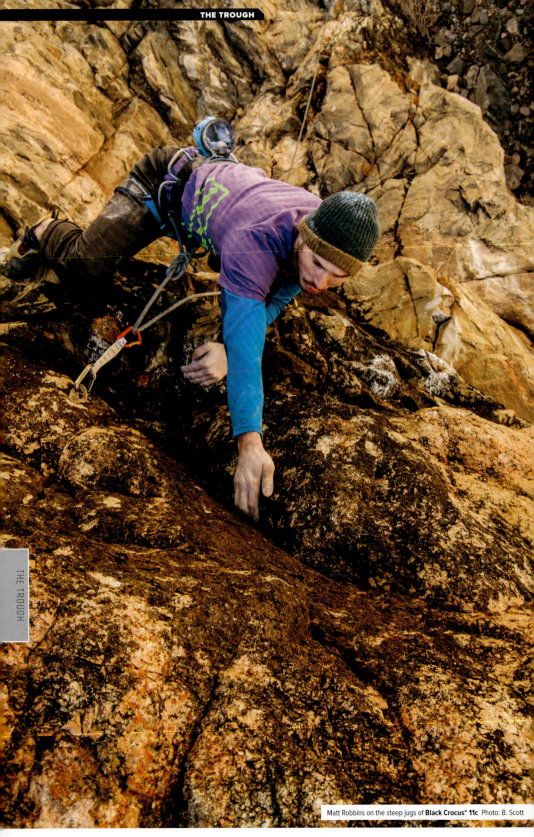

Matt Robbins on the steep jugs of **Black Crocus\* 11c**  Photo: B. Scott

**19.4 MILES** FROM TED'S PLACE

# THE TROUGH

TYPE(S): **SPORT**
DIFFICULTY RANGE: **5.10 - 5.12**
APPROACH TIME: **2 SEC**
SEASON: **YEAR ROUND**

## CLIMBING OVERVIEW

MOSTLY SHADE ALL DAY

The Trough is a hidden wall in the Upper Narrows that looks terrible and broken, but the rock is surprisingly solid and the crag offers a few fun routes with a two second approach from your car.

## GETTING THERE

GPS: 40°40'30.71"N 105°25'44.83"W

From Ted's Place drive approx. 19.4 miles and park in the pullout on the north side of the road (across from mile marker 103). The pullout is on a blind corner, so be careful when pulling into and out of the spot, especially on busy days.

**1.** ○ **High as I Wanna Be*** **12a** (6 Bolts)
This nice face climb is just right of the obvious crack feature. Crimp edges down low lead to a slightly overhung face that is higher quality than one might expect.
FA: C. Luebben et al.

**2.** ○ **Life in the Trough*** **10a** (6 Bolts)
Just uphill from My Name Is Mud, you will find this shallow arête. Horizontals down low lead to bigger holds on the broken arête feature.
FA: C. Luebben et al.

**3.** ○ **My Name Is Mud** **10d** (4 Bolts)
Start on the large refrigerator block, then follow wavy horizontals on the left side of the pegmatite band before moving left to a bolt on the arête and anchors of Dog Will Hunt.
FA: C. Luebben et al.

**4.** ○ **Dog Will Hunt** **11d** (5 Bolts)
Climb up the pegmatite face, over the bulge, then move left to join My Name Is Mud for the last bolt and anchors.
FA: C. Luebben

**5.** ○ **Black Crocus*** **11c** (5 Bolts)
Head up the black streak which is surprisingly steep on big holds with big moves.
FA: G. Hand

**6.** ○ **Wild Rose*** **11c** (6 Bolts)
This short route is a direct line to the top of Hyssop that begins about 20 feet uphill and climbs directly to the anchors.
FA: G. Hand, C. Heyliger

**7.** ○ **Hyssop*** **11b** (6 Bolts)
This route is the lowest route on the wall, beginning about 15 feet left of the road. Be careful to belay and keep your gear away from the road. From near the right arête of the Trough, climb up the pegmatite rock, trending left to avoid the rotten rock on the south face.
FA: G. Hand, C. Heyliger

***Climber Spotlight:*** Dr. Ken Duncan is the definition of "life-long climber." Ken has been climbing at a very high level since 1973 when he took a half-day climbing class in Tuolumne, CA. Climbers like Ken cut their teeth with Goldline Ropes and horribly stiff climbing shoes. Because of this, they always have the best climbing stories to tell. He shared this epic story with me out in the canyon one day:

"One summer during college I worked at a climbing school in Switzerland and stayed in a new hut high in the mountains. The guides that worked for the school loved to trundle and it just so happened that there was a bit of dynamite left over from the hut construction.

One evening after work, we decided to use up the remaining dynamite in the ultimate trundle. Not too far from the hut was a 100 meter long steep slab with some huge boulders sitting on top. Shortly after dark, a little carefully placed dynamite was touched off and a VW bus-sized boulder thundered down the slab in a tremendous shower of sparks and dust. Since then, while developing routes, I've trundled some refrigerator-sized blocks but nothing has come remotely close to the massive fireworks of the Swiss trundle."

Ken Duncan on the brilliant **Fish and Whistle**\*\*\*\* **11b**  Photo: B. Scott

# EDEN AREA

**19.5 MILES** FROM TED'S PLACE

GRADE DISTRIBUTION

**TYPE(S): SPORT & TRAD**
**DIFFICULTY RANGE: 5.9 - 5.12A**
**APPROACH TIME: 5 SEC**
**SEASON: YEAR ROUND**

## CLIMBING OVERVIEW

The Eden Area comprises some of the most popular and easily accessible climbing in the entire canyon. Most famous for the classic East Of Eden trad route, this area hosts a lot of other fantastic pitches. Excellent rock, no approach, what else could you ask for.

## GETTING THERE

**GPS: 40°40'37.58"N 105°25'47.13"W**
The Eden Area lies 19.5 miles from Ted's Place. Park in a pullout below a large, clean face with a prominent right-facing dihedral (East of Eden). Eve's Cave lies 30 yards upstream from this pullout. Nod is the upper right-hand portion of the Eden Wall.

## EDEN WALL

**1. ○ Forbidden Fruit**  12a** (11 Bolts)
Ballet and burl, Forbidden Fruit has some of the best steep slab climbing in the Poudre followed by a powerful roof. Fancy footwork is the key to the crux. Climb straight up the steepening face past the somewhat height-dependent crux, then turn the roof (5.11) at its apex. Move right to an easy arête leading to the anchors.
FA: Ken Duncan, Dede Humphrey

**2. ○ Garden of Eden** 11a** (10 Bolts)
Begin just left of the obvious black streak. Move past 10 bolts, then finish up a left leaning crack system that ends at cold shut anchors.
FA: Unknown

**3. ○ West of Eden** 10b R** (GEAR)
Climb the obvious crack on the face just left of East of Eden. The crack gets thinner, and the protection is trickier near the top of the pitch.
FA: M. Wilford

**4. ○ Fish and Whistle**** 11b** (12 Bolts)
Fish & Whistle climbs the dramatic arête to the left of East of Eden. Rumored to be the site of some old bolt-chopping, no signs of previous bolts or even climbing have been found. Even the origin of the name has been lost to history. Long story short, this spectacular climb sits right on the road and is one of the best sport climbs in the canyon. Giggle your way up awesome exposure on jugs and edges right up the arête.
FA: K. Duncan, D. Humphrey

POUDRE CANYON GUIDE - 3RD EDITION  **151**

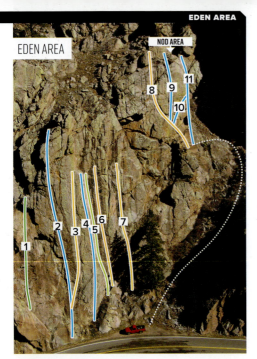

EDEN AREA

NOD AREA

## NOD

To reach the Nod area, scramble up the steep gulley just east of the Eden parking pullout, heading toward the sharp arête (Moment Of Clarity) high on the upper right-hand portion of the wall. Belay at the base of the arête, taking care not to knock rocks down the gulley.

### 8. La Royale* 10b (GEAR)
This left-angling crack feature is visible from the parking pullout and is an exciting endeavor with excellent position on the wall. From the MOC belay, carefully traverse left (you can clip Bolt 1 of MOC) and set up a belay below the short dihedral/bulge feature. Pull the bulge and follow the left leaning crack to the top.
FA: S. McCorkel, R. Green '97

### 9. With Cheese** 11a (GEAR)
Do the first part of La Royale, but head over the bulge and climb straight up the middle crack to the top. Protection can be a bit tricky.
FA: S. McCorkel, R. Green '97

### 10. Pulp Friction 11b (4 Bolts + GEAR)
Variation, move from La Royale into MOC at the first bulge.
FA: S. McCorkel, Roe Green '97

### 11. Moment of Clarity (MOC)** 11c (4 Bolts + GEAR)
From a belay directly below the sharp arête, carefully traverse left around the corner to clip a bolt. Continue up the arête, following bolts and placing an occasional piece of gear to reduce runouts. Bring small to medium cams.
FA: S. McCorkel, Tim Mannschreck

### 12. TM Crack** 10d (GEAR)
Climb the crack on the hidden east face of Nod. Short but splitter on quality rock.
FA: T. Mannschreck '97

### 5. East of Eden**** 9 (GEAR)
Another incredible and iconic Poudre gem. One of the most traveled pitches in the canyon since it is right off the road. You can belay out of your car if you want to. Origin of the name and who did the FA are all sadly lost to history. Excellent rock takes you on a journey from handjams to slippery laybacks on polished feet. A new anchor was installed in 2015 and a 70 meter rope is suggested.
FA: Unknown

### 6. Sin*** 10d (14 Bolts)
Sin is a long pitch of great climbing. Turn a roof at Bolt 1, then face climb to a mantle onto a ledge. At the second bolt above the ledge, move right out of the crack to stay on the best climbing and continue to the anchors.
K. Duncan, D. Humphrey

### 7. Tree of Knowledge*** 10b (15 Bolts)
Climb the slab to an engaging mantle at the break. Continue up the black streak/corner. This route can be seeping water in winter and early spring.
FA: J. Tarry, R. Nelson

## EVE'S CAVE

Approx. 30 yards upstream from East of Eden lies a small cave/overhang with a few old routes that are seldom climbed.

### 13. Over the Edge** 11b (5 Bolts + GEAR)
Exciting, devious and "balancy" moves just left of the arête that forms the edge of the cave.
FA: C. Luebben

### 14. The Adulteress 11b (2 Bolts + GEAR)
Most climbers will hate this overhanging rotten hand and finger crack, but it stays dry during rainstorms.
FA: C. Luebben

### 15. Original Sin*** 10c (8 Bolts)
Edge your way up this super-clean, thin slab. Pull the roof, and run it out to the higher bolt.
FA: C. Luebben

### 16. Temptation** 11c (5 Bolts + GEAR)
Squeak through the thin crux on this one. It's harder if you're short. At this time, this route doesn't have any hangers.
FA: C. Luebben

# TWILIGHT AREA

**19.5 MILES** FROM TED'S PLACE

**TYPE(S): SPORT, TRAD & BOULDERING**
**DIFFICULTY RANGE: 5.10 - 5.13C, V10-VII**
**APPROACH TIME: 5 - 30 MIN**
**SEASON: SPRING, FALL & WINTER**

RIVER CROSSING REQUIRED

## CLIMBING OVERVIEW

The Twilight Area comprises several smaller zones including: Twilight Wall, Sunnyvale, Upper Midlife Wall, Lemon Cave and Wild Wall. This area is known for its striking walls that seem to hang over the river. Mostly single-pitch sport climbs, this area is named after an infamous boulder problem that was one of the first developed rock climbs in the area.

## GETTING THERE

**GPS: 40°40'38.74"N 105°25'51.42"W**
The Twilight Area lies 19.5 miles up canyon from Ted's Place. There are several pullouts to choose from: Eden Area, Snake Eyes Wall and Supercollider pullouts are all the closest. Cross the river directly in front of the Twilight Wall. **BEWARE OF RIVER CONDITIONS.** This crossing is directly above the infamous rapid called "White Line" and you DO NOT want to get sucked into it. If the water level is any higher than 1.5 feet, do not cross. Most of the year though it is about mid-calf or frozen altogether in the winter.

The author trying a project at the right end of the Twilight Wall   Photo: A. Cross

POUDRE CANYON GUIDE - 3RD EDITION   153

# TWILIGHT WALL

MOSTLY SHADE ALL DAY

To reach the Twilight Wall, park at the Eden Area, walk upstream and carefully cross the river directly below the wall. This crossing should not be attempted if river levels are over 1.5 feet.

### 1. ⬤ Muffin Top*** 12b (6 Bolts)
The difficulties start right from the ground (stick-clip is a good call). Climb into a undercling/sidepull and continue on leaning edges to Bolt 2. From here, fire onto the "arête" feature and do a big move to a jug. Continue on jugs to a lip encounter with the "muffin" hold followed by a weird mantle sequence. A tricky lip traverse leads to the anchor.
FA: B. Scott

### 2. ⬤ Landing Strip*** 13b (7 Bolts)
Climb up through a tricky initial roof to gain a series of left-trending edges to Bolt 2. From here, a big, low-percentage move right leads to some awesome slopers before a big rest at Bolt 4. From here, move left and do the top-half of Muffin Top to the shared anchor.
FA: B. Scott

### 3. ⬤ Wihizzle Dihizzle*** 12c (10 Bolts)
Wihizzle Dihizzle is the obvious white dihedral. It is a steep and pumpy line with multiple cruxes that will make you say "it's off the hizzle for shizzle dih-izzle."
FA: D. Peavey

### 4. ⬤ ShoNuff** 12d (10 Bolts)
Who's the master?! ShoNuff! Start above the Twilight Boulder and step across onto the wall and Bolt 1. Continuous pumpy 5.12 climbing leads into a desperate sequence to reach the chains.
FA: D. Peavey

Simon Longacre on an early ascent of **Landing Strip*** 13b**  Photo: B. Scott

### 5. ⬤ Twilight*** v10 (Pads)
The namesake for the cliff is this testpiece of a boulder problem coming out a dark dirty cave. It seems like a lifetime ago that Clayton scratched his way out of this wretched cave. Back then it seemed like an obscure block but now its sees multiple repeats every season. If you like hard, fingery, power bouldering, this one is for you.
FA: Clayton Reagan

### 6. ⬤ Gypsies, Tramps, and Thieves** v11 (Pads)
Do the same start as Twilight, but move up and left through small edges/pinches. Finish on the same topout of Twilight.
FA: Andre Di Felice

# TWILIGHT AREA

Skyler Bol on the exposed moves of *The Scrilla*\*\*\* 12b   Photo: Tom Bol

### 7. Golden Man** 12d (12 Bolts)
Start with an awesome, technical dihedral directly out of the Twilight Cave. When the corner becomes a ramp, move left to a series of tricky 5.12 climbing. More steep, pumpy climbing leads through the blocky roof. After you've fully recovered on the ledge, launch into a strange sequence to clip the chains at the very top of the wall.
FA: B. Scott

### 8. The Scrilla*** 12b (12 Bolts)
This is a great extension to No Crisis. Place a long sling on the No Crisis anchor, and launch into some very steep terrain. A tricky move getting right is followed by steep, long moves all the way to the awesomely exposed anchor.
FA: D. Peavey

### 9. No Crisis** 11a (6 Bolts)
This is the second best warm-up at the Twilight Cave. Start with a tricky slab move to gain the steeper rock. Make a long reach right, then continue on a variety of holds and surprisingly pumpy movement to the chains.
FA: P. Heyliger

### 10. Sunset Years** 10b (8 Bolts)
This is the best warm-up route at the Twilight Cave. Begin with a short corner feature and continue on blocky/juggy terrain. It ends at the same anchor as No Crisis.
FA: P. Heyliger

### 11. Methuselah** 11c (8 Bolts)
Stick-clip Bolt 1, then climb the orange streak past a crux at Bolt 2. Continue up, then right at the roof to anchors shared with The Wizened. Long slings help protect the rope at the anchors.
FA: P. Heyliger

### 12. Money for Nothing** 12c (12 Bolts)
This is a bouldery extension to Methuselah. Instead of clipping anchors on Methuselah, continue up the steep prow feature on rad compression moves.
FA: D. Peavey

### 13. The Wizened** 12a (8 Bolts)
Stick-clip Bolt 1, then pop past the crux and follow the black streak through the apex of the roof. The anchors are shared with Methuselah.
FA: P. Heyliger

### 14. Render Unto Geezer 11d (8 Bolts)
Clip Bolt 1, then undercling up and right over a bulge to a roof. Turn the roof directly past the bolt to anchors shared with Antique Guns.
FA: P. Heyliger

### 15. Antique Guns 10d (8 Bolts)
Start off a big block turning the roof and passing a crux at Bolt 2. Climb carefully past some questionable flakes after Bolt 4. The anchors are shared with Render Unto Geezer.
FA: P. Heyliger

### 16. Unknown 11c (8 Bolts)
Climb past 3 bolts (taking care in the runout to Bolt 3). Pull the crux roof and finish at the anchors shared with Low-Hanging Fruit and Old Man River.
FA: P. Heyliger

### 17. Low-Hanging Fruit 11b (8 Bolts)
Climb past the crux roof, but hang in there as the pump continues to build. Be careful getting to the anchors shared with Old Man River.
FA: P. Heyliger

### 18. Old Man River 10c (8 Bolts)
Boulder over a low overhang, then climb an easy slab to cool moves over a bulge.
FA: P. Heyliger

**TWILIGHT AREA**

UPPER MIDLIFE WALL

LEMON CAVE

## UPPER MIDLIFE WALL

After crossing the river as for the Twilight Wall, veer left over the slab below the main wall, then climb the talus field to reach the hidden plateau and Upper Midlife Wall.

**19. ○ Teller* 11a** (4 Bolts)
Climb past the crux on cool plates at the top of the face. Shares chains with the two previous routes.
FA: P. Heyliger

**20. ○ Over the Hillary*** 10a** (5 Bolts)
The excellent arête. A #2 and #3 Camalot can be used to supplement runouts in the middle.
FA: P. Heyliger

**21. ○ Make a Wish** 11b** (9 Bolts)
Nice face climbing over a roof. A small cam is optional between Bolts 2 and 3.
FA: P. Heyliger

**22. ○ Creak Crack 7 R** (6 Bolts)
Climb the crack to a nice chimney at the top. Never totally cleaned, but could be worthy of a star if it got more traffic.
FA: P. Heyliger

**23. ○ Off the Rocker* 7** (6 Bolts)
Short but decent trad line, trend right to chains. Not shown in topo. Small to medium gear.
FA: P. Heyliger

## LEMON CAVE

This short and steep wall is situated in a beautiful setting right next to the water. Cross the river and head up past the Twilight Wall and the Upper Midlife Wall. When you reach the ridge, navigate down towards the river until you can locate the steep gulley that leads to the river and the Lemon Cave.

**24. ○ Random Darkness* 11c** (6 Bolts)
FA: B. Scott

**25. ○ Against the Grain** 12d** (6 Bolts)
FA: Adam Peters, D. Peavey

**26. ○ Suck a Lemon** 11d** (7 Bolts)
FA: B. Beavers, D. Peavey

## SUNNYVALE

Sunnyvale is a fantastic crag mostly developed by Bryan Beavers and Derek Peavey around 2012-2013. This crag is south-facing making it an excellent winter crag. The routes are deceptively hard in places but the rock and movement are awesome. To reach Sunnyvale, walk past the Upper Midlife Wall and follow the grassy ridge and faint cairned trail uphill to reach the crag.

**1. ○ Mustard Tiger** 11d** (6 Bolts)
A slap of slopers gives way to a hard stand up into a "tufa" like feature. Jugs lead to a final move to reach the chains.
FA: B. Beavers, D. Peavey

**2. ○ Dirty Burger** 11b** (9 Bolts)
More bubbly rock with slopey feet leads up and right to a crux at Bolt 4. Romp up the easy chimney to the chains.
FA: B. Beavers, D. Peavey

**3. ○ Bubbles** 12b** (10 Bolts)
Follow the right angling seam on slopers and crimps with aesthetic black and white streaked rock. A hard crux lies at Bolt 3 with a final spectacular finish on the steep arête.
FA: B. Beavers, D. Peavey

**4. ○ Trad Variation 10b** (GEAR)
This gear route starts up the crack left of Bubbles and crosses over to the angling crack above the slab section.
FA: B. Beavers

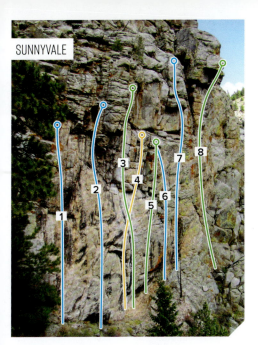

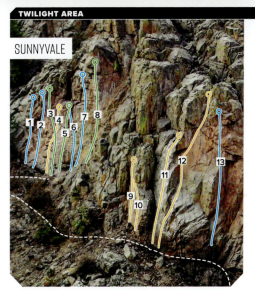

**5. The Way She Goes\*\* 12d** (6 Bolts)
Another bouldery climb on interesting slopey features on and around a seam feature. The upper dihedral is no gimmie and features very technical stemming.
FA: B. Beavers, D. Peavey

**6. Two Birds Stoned at Once 11d\*** (6 Bolts)
Climb up the right angling black crack with a hard crux down low. Finish on the easier right-facing corner.
FA: B. Beavers, D. Peavey

**7. The Green Bastard\*\* 11a** (6 Bolts)
Probably the best route to warm-up on at the crag. Start up a short, left-facing corner to a series of small ledges. The crux comes at the end when you must undercling out a bulge into a mantle with a high foot. Easy slab romp to the anchor.
FA: B. Beavers, D. Peavey

**8. The Swayze Express\*\*\* 12a** (6 Bolts)
This stunning face and roof climb is a must-do in the canyon. A 5th class scramble gets you to the base with a nice belay ledge. Start with some easy ledges to the crux of the climb moving up a reachy brown face section at Bolt 4. Fun moves on nice brown rock lead higher and higher to a stance below the final roof. The climbing from here to the anchor is as good as sport climbing gets at this grade.
FA: B. Beavers, D. Peavey

**9. Unnamed\*\* 10a** (6 Bolts)
Climb the discontinuous seam system to a tricky move at the small roof.
FA: B. Beavers, D. Peavey

**10. Unnamed\* 9** (6 Bolts)
A variation start that climbs the arête feature before meeting up with the previous route.
FA: B. Beavers, D. Peavey

**11. Hash Driveway\*\* 10a** (10 Bolts)
Climb the long, green slab on nice rock.
FA: B. Beavers, D. Peavey

**12. Back to Jail\*\* 10d** (6 Bolts + GEAR)
Climb the right angling crack and dihedral system to the top of this super exposed wall.
FA: B. Beavers, D. Peavey

**13. Starstruck\*\*\* 11b** (12 Bolts)
Scramble up to the obvious corner until the bolt line breaks out onto the steep face. Gain a ramp that leads to the amazing upper headwall.
FA: B. Beavers, D. Peavey

Bryan Beavers taking a lap on **Mustard Tiger\*\* 11d** Photo: B. Scott

# TWILIGHT AREA

**Climber Spotlight:** Jimmy Burckhard understands sacrifice and dedication more than a lot of people. After surviving a ground fall which should have taken his life, Jimmy fought through months of rehab to be able to walk and get out of bed again. Then, he worked even harder to send his first 5.14 and he continues to crush his projects to this day.

Jimmy Burckhard fighting icy temps on the spectacular **Rustic Wilderness**\*\*\*\* **13c**  Photo: B. Scott

TWILIGHT AREA

# WILD WALL

# WILD WALL

 MOSTLY SHADE ALL DAY

This jaw-dropping wall is easily one of the most aesthetic in the Narrows. Developed seemingly on a whim by Steve McCorkel, the routes on this wall are full value endurance fests on surreal looking granite. To reach the wall, follow directions for Upper Midlife Wall and continue uphill towards Sunnyvale. Just above the talus field is a subtle gulley on hikers right with a cairn at the top. 5th class up the gulley and follow the trail that wraps around to the base of the Wild Wall belay area.

**1. ○ Rustic Wilderness**\*\*\*\* **13c** (14 Bolts)
Spectacular line on a stunning wall with gut-busting exposure. Originally climbed in two pitches, this is now usually done as a 35 meter outing from the base of the wall. Start by scrambling up ledges to a grey slab that leads to the headwall. Excellent 5.12 climbing leads to the rest at the horizontal break. From here, launch into the headwall with an infamous shoulder busting move and a final crimpy finish. Traverse left from the last bolt and stay calm through the 20 foot runout to the anchor.
FA: B. Scott, Bolted by: S. McCorkel

**2. ○ Wildest Dreams**\*\*\*\* **13c** (14 Bolts)
This route was bolted as an additional variation or project to Rustic Wilderness, but it actually climbs the more direct part of the headwall with a topout directly to the anchor. Very similar to Rustic Wilderness but has a spicy right leaning traverse and a heart-breaking final crux.
FA: J. Burckhard, Bolted by: S. McCorkel

**3. ○ Wild and Scenic**\*\*\* **12d** (6 Bolts)
Another incredible line up the right side of the headwall. Start the same as Rustic Wilderness but move farther right on the slab to the left leaning jug rail that is a bit hollow. Easy but exposed moves get you to the horizontal break followed by a pumpy section out the iconic rail feature. From the end of the rail, move back left to a final punchy move to the anchor.
FA: S. McCorkel

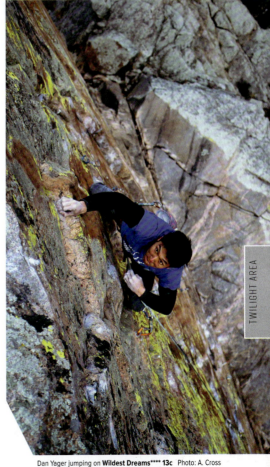

Dan Yager jumping on **Wildest Dreams**\*\*\*\* **13c**   Photo: A. Cross

Mark Wilford staring down the crux of the uber Luebben classic **Delicious Demon*** **11b**   Photo: B. Scott

**19.3 MILES** FROM TED'S PLACE

# SNAKE EYES WALLS

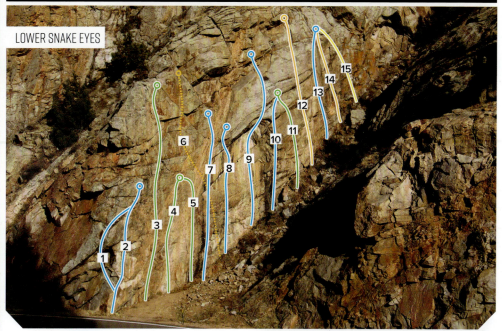

LOWER SNAKE EYES

GRADE DISTRIBUTION

AM SUN / PM SHADE

**TYPE(S): SPORT & TRAD**
**DIFFICULTY RANGE: 5.10 - 5.13C**
**APPROACH TIME: 5 SEC - 10 MIN**
**SEASON: YEAR ROUND**

## CLIMBING OVERVIEW

The Snake Eyes Walls are classic roadside areas that have been popular with climbers for decades. Initially developed by **Craig Luebben**, then later by **Paul Heyliger** and **Derek Peavey**. Excellent rock and a variety of grades and styles makes this a must see for any climber.

## GETTING THERE

**GPS: 40°40'40.02"N 05°25'49.97"W**

From Ted's Place, drive 19.3 miles up the canyon. You can park one car directly in front of the wall, or alternatively you can park at the Eden Area or Supercollider parking areas. If you can't find the Lower Snake Eyes Wall from the road, you need to get your eyes checked.

## LOWER SNAKE EYES WALL

**1.** ○ **Snake Trails 11b** (2 Bolts + GEAR)
Climb the left arête of Snake Eyes Wall, past two bolts and out a short roof to cold shuts. A hand-sized piece could be helpful to protect the runout to the anchors. Seldom done and may have been re-written/erased by Snakes on a Train.
FA: C. Luebben

**2.** ○ **Snakes on a Train**** 11d** (6 Bolts)
Short but nice rock and fun moves. Climb into an undercling flake before moving out right on techy feet to a big move over the final bulge.
FA: D. Peavey

**3.** ○ **Snake Eyes*** 12b** (8 Bolts)
A Luebben classic and the namesake for the wall. Awkward start leads to jugs followed by 3 bolts of hard 5.12 climbing. The bolts were updated in 2014 including a new anchor and an additional bolt for the scary runout to the anchors.
FA: C. Leubben

**4.** ○ **Cobra Kai**** 12d** (5 Bolts)
A brutal start in the shallow groove of pegmatite leads to jugs. Rest here because two more hard 5.12 cruxes on small holds await. The run to the anchor is also tricky and just a bit heady.
FA: D. Peavey

**5.** ○ **Box Cars**** 12c** (6 Bolts)
Tricky start leads to powerful moves on sidepulls with two enormous moves in a row. The rock is less than ideal up top but the holds you need are solid enough.
FA: D. Peavey, B. Beavers

Erin Robinson cruising up the fun edges of **Back On The Train** 11b  Photo: A. Cross

### 6. ○ Delicious Apple 10c (Bolts + GEAR)
A bit of a strange route that has been re-written/erased by more recent development. It combines portions of Delicious Demon and Back on the Train to end at its own ambiguous anchor location. Long slings are helpful.
**FA: B. Spiering**

### 7. ○ Back on the Train** 11b (8 Bolts)
Easy climbing leads to a hard match and underclinging move at Bolt 3. Big moves on angled rails lead to a final crimpy crux in the pegmatite band up high.
**FA: D. Peavey**

### 8. ○ Delicious Demon*** 11b (5 Bolts)
The other OG Luebben classic at the Lower Snake Eyes Wall climbs the black and white streaked wall to the obvious roof. Fun thought-provoking face climbing leads to the roof which involves a strange undercling to shoulder-press move.
**FA: C. Luebben**

### 9. ○ Fight Like a Brave** 11c (GEAR)
This bold trad line follows the left-facing corners and flakes before eventually moving out the right side of the main roof feature. Although this line isn't popular, it is a proud lead.
**FA: David Vartanian**

### 10. ○ The Wang Chung** 11c (5 Bolts + GEAR)
Layback up bulbous arête features to a right angling horizontal near the pegmatite pod. Move right to anchors of The Bum Lung. A #1 Camalot can be placed at the break to supplement the runout. Be wary of the large, potentially friable quartz blobs.
**FA: G. Hand, Tim O'Grady**

### 11. ○ The Bum Lung* 12b (5 Bolts)
Follow downsloping edges and rails to a blank bulge. Figure out how to get to the shallow horizontal crack and you're home free.
**FA: G. Hand**

### 12. ○ The Rung*** 10c (9 Bolts)
Probably the best warm-up on the wall. Climb flaky jugs to a large horn, then make fun moves through horizontals to a polished slab. One of the best moderates in the Narrows.
**FA: G. Hand**

### 13. ○ The Flung** 11d (6 Bolts)
Climb crumbly choss to Bolt 1, then head up the steep, clean face on spectacular stone, eventually reaching the fun, blunt arête. You can go either right or left to reach anchors. A stickclip may be handy for Bolt 1.
**FA: G. Hand**

### 14. ○ The Stung** 10b (6 Bolts)
This technical corner provides lots of nice moves in its short length. Named when Greg Hand was stung in the face by a wasp while cleaning before the first ascent, kicking off the "ung" theme.
**FA: G. Hand**

### 15. ○ The Dung 7 (3 Bolts)
A short and chossy endeavor up the far right side of the wall. Avoid pelting your belayer with crumbly rock by climbing in from the right at the start. The easiest but worst route on the wall. It could be better with some cleaning and traffic.
**FA: G. Hand**

## UPPER SNAKE EYES

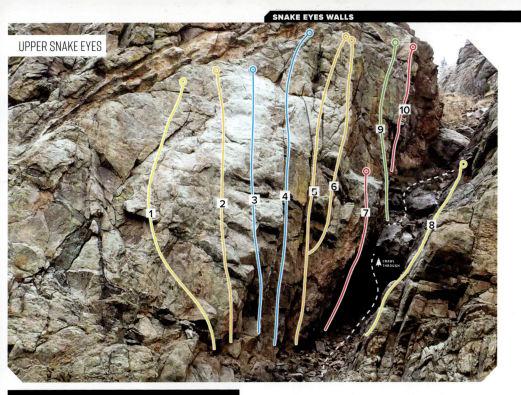

## UPPER SNAKE EYES WALL

GPS: 40°40'41.42"N 105°25'47.59"W
To reach Upper Snake Eyes Wall, hike uphill from Lower Snake Eyes Wall for 10min until it comes into view. You can either walk directly up the gulley (which can be loose) or climb up the slabs on the right side, then traverse back left to the Upper Snake Eyes Wall.

### 1. Off the Couch* 6 (GEAR)
This is a decent trad route on the left, which also provides access to the upper anchors for those interested in top-roping the other routes on the wall. The main pitch angles up and right (small-medium gear) up the crack with a tricky step right at the break past a loose-sounding flake.
FA: P. Heyliger and Friends

### 2. Luck of the Irish*** 10c (9 Bolts)
Start below broken rock and a small, right-facing corner with a bolt at the bottom, and follow the bolt line past a delicate crux up and left past the overlap. There are some amazing (lucky) holds on this route.
FA: P. Heyliger and Friends

### 3. Faith*** 11d (9 Bolts)
This fine route is powerful down low, very delicate up high, and requires faith in good, high-angle slab shoes. Take the arête just left of the corner, and crank some powerful moves that get a bit easier to a huge rest at a flake. Move up the groove (you can climb a bit right to clip the high bolt), then step left onto the steep, balding slab (crux).
FA: P. Heyliger and Friends

### 4. Home-School Ballerina*** 11c (8 Bolts)
One of the best routes on the wall climbs this unusual corner feature. Power will get you nowhere, and each move requires its own subtlety.
FA: P. Heyliger and Friends

### 5. Mr. Hand*** 10c (GEAR)
Mr. Hand is named in honor of one of the best climbing partners of all time. The obvious, hands to small hands splitter is pumpy down low (crux) to a hands-off rest, then it goes up progressively easier rock. It is one of the better trad routes in the canyon despite the choss down low.
FA: P. Heyliger and Friends

### 6. One Handicap*** 10c (1 Bolt + GEAR)
An in-obvious but very good trad line takes the crux of Mr. Hand and then breaks right (bolt) to the hanging flake to corners to the upper arête with a remarkable crack in it.
FA: P. Heyliger and Friends

### 7. Diamondback*** 13c (7 Bolts)
A short, powerful testpiece, reminiscent of routes at The Beach. Hard climbing right off the bat leads to a desperate four move crux on undercuts and crimps to a jug undercling.
FA: Noah Kaufman

### 8. Access Pitch 6 (2 Bolts)
To reach the upper tier of the wall you can tunnel through the chimney or climb this short route.
FA: P. Heyliger and Friends

**UPPER SNAKE EYES**

CRAWL THROUGH HOLE →

### 9. ○ Soul** 12b (5 Bolts)
Start up a right-facing corner, then move straight up (optional green/yellow Alien in slot) to the base of the right arête. Clip both bolts, then crank the crux to easier but still fun climbing.
FA: P. Heyliger and Friends

### 10. ○ Copperhead*** 13a (8 Bolts)
Once you reach the upper tier of the Upper Snake Eyes Wall there is one line that stands out. Copperhead climbs a striking arête feature on superb rock. Bring a full bag of technical tricks because this route throws it all at you. Gear can be used to take the sting out of the final runout to the anchor.
FA: N. Kaufman

### 11. ○ Sidewinder** 12b (8 Bolts)
Sidewinder is a nice variation pitch on excellent stone. Start on Where my Body Dies, and break left around Bolt 4 into the top half of Copperhead.
FA: N. Kaufman

### 12. ○ When My Body Dies** 12a (7 Bolts)
The gorgeous black/brown wall of the west face contains this excellent micro-route, with technical stemming up to and over the roof.
FA: P. Heyliger and Friends

### 13. ○ Poudre Kind of Groove* 10b (4 Bolts + GEAR)
Climb the obvious groove feature up a nice slab at the very uphill end of the wall/gulley.
FA: P. Heyliger and Friends

The author on the exquisite **Copperhead*** **13a**  Photo: Erin Robinson

# SUPERCOLLIDER / SOLAR PANEL

**19.4 MILES** FROM TED'S PLACE

TYPE(S): **SPORT**
DIFFICULTY RANGE: **5.10A - 5.11C**
APPROACH TIME: **5 SEC - 10 MIN**
SEASON: **YEAR ROUND**

## CLIMBING OVERVIEW

This is a recently developed zone comprising a roadside crag and a sunny cliff with a short walk up the hill. Great rock and fun moderates make this area a must-see for most climbers.

## GETTING THERE

GPS: 40°40'42.46"N 105°25'55.91"W

From Ted's Place, drive 19.4 miles up the canyon. Drive just past the Snake Eyes Wall to a large pullout on the north side of the road. Supercollider is directly above you, you can even belay from your car. Solar Panel is located a short five minutes walk up the gulley to the right of Supercollider.

## SUPERCOLLIDER

**1.** ○ **Winter's Edge**** 10a** (4 Bolts)
A tricky start leads to fun easy climbing on edges up to the anchors shared with Obtuse Dilemma.
FA: K. Duncan, D. Humphrey

**2.** ○ **Obtuse Dilemma**\*** 11d** (5 Bolts)
Obtuse Dilemma has challenging stemming up a flaring dihedral. It keeps your attention!
FA: K. Duncan, D. Humphrey

**3.** ○ **Black Serpent**** 11c** (9 Bolts)
Climb the triangular face past the snake to its apex and the large ledge (10a). It is best to belay here, as the crux is getting to the second bolt above the ledge. Figure out the techy boulder problem, then climb nice edges to another thin section getting to the last bolt.
FA: K. Duncan, D. Humphrey

Ken Duncan on his fantastic creation **Icarus**\*** 11b**  Photo: B. Scott

The always smiling Dede Humphrey romping up **Sunspot**\*\* **10d**   Photo: B. Scott

# SOLAR PANEL

## SOLAR PANEL

**GPS: 40°40'42.57"N 105°25'51.42"W**

The Solar Panel is a great sunny area with a collection of moderate sport climbs. Located just above the Supercollider wall, climb slabs on the right side of a gulley right above the parking area. Follow the cairned trail until the wall comes into view. **BE CAREFUL OF LOOSE ROCK AND KNOCKING ROCKS INTO THE ROAD.**

**1. Rising Sun\*\* 10a** (7 Bolts)
Scramble up to a nice belay ledge and move out left to Bolt 1 above a big ledge/chockstone. Fun face and slab climbing takes you the rest of the way. 70m rope is suggested.
FA: K. Duncan, D. Humphrey

**2. Sunkist\*\* 10c** (7 Bolts)
From the belay ledge, move up into the base of the big left leaning corner/overhang. Clip Bolt 1 and perform the crux of the climb getting established in the corner. From here, move around the bulge to a long section of great face climbing on golden rock.
FA: K. Duncan, D. Humphrey

**3. Sunspot\*\* 10d** (9 Bolts)
This climb starts in the center of the wall on a smaller initial panel with stellar stone. Tricky technical face climbing gets you to the big ledge. Excellent arête and face climbing leads you to the Sunkist anchor.
FA: K. Duncan, D. Humphrey

**4. Unnamed Crack\* 7** (GEAR)
A nice short gear route on the right side of the initial panel Sunspot climbs up.
FA: Unknown

**5. Icarus\*\*\* 11b** (5 Bolts)
Fantastic arête climbing on sidepulls and crimps, even if it is on the short side. Scramble around to the right side of the wall and a nice sunny belay area below the blunt arête.
FA: K. Duncan, D. Humphrey

**6. A Little Slice of Sunshine\*\* 10b** (5 Bolts)
The crag is completed with this face and slab climb on another undulating wall of fine Poudre granite. Shares anchors with Icarus and starts just to its right.
FA: K. Duncan, D. Humphrey

***Climber Spotlight:*** Ian Dory is one of the most accomplished climbers to ever come out of Fort Collins. A true Colorado native, Ian sent the testpiece **Circadian Rhythm**\*\*\* **v13** at the age of 16. A climber by profession, Ian has gone on to send some of the hardest problems in the world like Dai Koyamada's **Wheel of Life v16** in the Grampians and Daniel Wood's **Paint it Black v15** in RMNP. Ian's intuition and understanding of hard climbing is practically unparalleled in the Fort Collins climbing community.

Ian Dory sticking the crux move of **Chocolate Stout**\*\*\* **14a**   Photo: B. Scott

# THE BEACH

**19.5 MILES** FROM TED'S PLACE

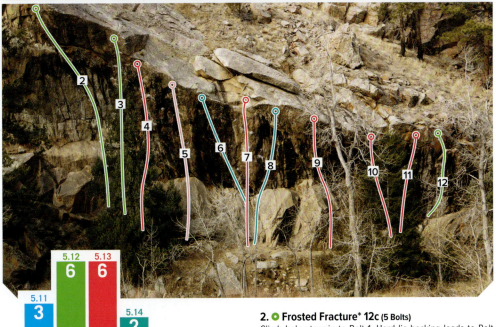

GRADE DISTRIBUTION

**TYPE(S): SPORT**
**DIFFICULTY RANGE: 5.11A – 5.14A**
**APPROACH TIME: 5 MIN**
**SEASON: SPRING, FALL & WINTER**

**RIVER CROSSING REQUIRED**

## CLIMBING OVERVIEW

The Beach has been looked at by just about every climber that has traveled up the canyon. An obviously short but viciously steep panel of rock that sits beckoning right next to the river. But for years it was called "too short" or "not worth the effort". That all changed over the winter of 2014 when the first routes were sent and the viability of The Beach became known. A short bouldery style similar to Rumney, NH, The Beach requires lots of finger strength and power. Most folks climb here in late fall through the winter.

## GETTING THERE

**GPS: 40°40'46.38"N 105°26'0.26"W**
The Beach lies 19.5 miles from Ted's Place. Park in a pullout on the right just past the Snake Eyes Wall but before The Beach. Cross the river directly in front of the wall.

**1.** ○ **Hard Cider*** **11b** (5 Bolts)
Located on the far left side of the main wall. This route climbs a left-facing corner to some fun face climbing before the anchor.
FA: R. D. Pascoe, Chris Hofer

**2.** ○ **Frosted Fracture*** **12c** (5 Bolts)
Climb ledgy terrain to Bolt 1. Hard lie-backing leads to Bolt 3. Continue on jugs to a jump/reach above Bolt 4. The crux comes in a sloper/lip traverse left with a mantle. There is a tricky/awkward final move to reach the chains.
FA: B. Scott

**3.** ○ **I.P.A.*** **12a** (5 Bolts)
A great route named after the best beer variety ever made. Climb up some ledges and launch into four bolts of awesome juggy holds, perfectly spaced apart. The classic "warm-up" for the harder climbing at this crag.
FA: J. Tarry, B. Scott

**4.** ○ **Harmonic Resonance*** **13c** (4 Bolts)
A stand-out route at a stacked wall. Easy setup moves lead to a subtle yet thuggy jump move past Bolt 3. After the jump, move back left into the redpoint crux deadpointing to a slopey but large edge.
FA: B. Scott

**5.** ○ **Open Beach Project** (3 Bolts)
Maybe something for the next generation. The holds are there but they're all small slopey things really far apart.
Bolted by B. Scott

**6.** ○ **Chocolate Stout*** **14a** (4 Bolts)
This route is the epitome of the style that The Beach haunts you with. Fingery, tensiony climbing leads to the powerful and massive crux move left into the matchbox hold. More small incuts and high feet lead to the sloping lip.
FA: Z. Lerner

# THE BEACH

### 7. ● Blonde Note*** 13a (5 Bolts)
A coveted benchmark for the bouldery style of The Beach. Climb the ramp to the steep wall and move up and right on decent holds and heel-hooks until you can reach the infamous tan rail. A trickey deadpoint move leads back left to an easy but super fun finish.
FA: B. Scott

### 8. ● Dirty Diet Coke** 14a (4 Bolts)
A seldom done testpiece of about ten moves in total. This route requires immense amounts of finger strength and deadly amounts of precision. A good belay is crucial to keep you safe on a few of the clips.
FA: S. Anderson

### 9. ● Hefeweizen** 13c (4 Bolts)
Another brutal one bolt boulder problem on small but decent edges that are all turned the wrong way.
FA: Sam Rothstein, Luis Serrano

### 10. ● Kona Blend** 13b (4 Bolts)
Climb up awkard but good holds with your feet on the ramp. For the crux, do an enormous move right to a slopey edge, or use small holds to stand into edges more directly. A big jump move gets you to the final holds.
FA: B. Scott

### 11. ● Samson Ale** 13b (4 Bolts)
Funny enough, this mini-route was the first bolted route on the wall. Even attempted as a boulder problem by Jason Kehl years ago. Start up the rail feature and perform an unusual kneebar move to do the enormous move up and left. Huge moves on big holds take you to the anchor.
FA: B. Scott

### 12. ● Duff* 12c (3 Bolts)
Easily the most absurd "route" at The Beach. Is it a route? Is it a boulder problem? Who knows, but it's nice to have the rope to keep you off the deck. For full points, climbers must start low on the flat white edge.
FA: B. Scott

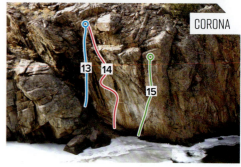

*The next three routes are located on the far right side of The Beach in a small corridor on the river's edge.*

### 13. ● Bartles & Jaymes** 11a (3 Bolts)
Start on the sloping shelf with the feet and the obvious hands, reach to slopers, then make the crux move to a high crimp. Juggy holds get you to a funny mantle onto the ledge.
FA: R.D. Pascoe, B. Scott

### 14. ● Corona** 13a (4 Bolts)
This route climbs the center of the nice tan panel of rock. An easy start sends you into a really strange and tedious boulder problem that climbs left, then up, then back right to a deadpoint. All in the span of only about six feet but requires eight hand moves. A great route if you enjoy the funny style of The Beach.
FA: Skyler Bol

### 15. ● Low Tide* 12a (3 Bolts)
Low Tide starts in the same gulley as Corona but instead traverses right and over the water. Step off the ground onto a diagonal seam feature. Move into underclings around Bolt 2 and a large jug out left to clip Bolt 3. From here, move right through pinches, slopers, and edges on a pretty face.
FA: S. Bol

LAST TURN CRAG

## LAST TURN CRAG

Last Turn Crag is located on the south side of The Beach. Walk along the shore until you can navigate up through some small talus to the ledgy base of the cliff. Not the best rock in the world, but the 5.12 routes are fun and aesthetic.

### 16. ○ Pale Corner 11d (5 Bolts)
They can't all be winners?! Climb some pretty rotten rock up a broken face until the rock gets better and you can move towards a small corner feature up and right.
**FA: B. Scott**

### 17. ○ The Benchmark*** 12c (5 Bolts)
Originally graded 11b in the Second Edition by the first ascentionist. A nod to his strict habit and love of sandbagging all his rock climbs. Climb some chunky rock to the horizontal break. An excellent sequence takes you up the edge of the block and up the cool face on incuts and seams.
**FA: C. Cross**

### 18. ○ Rock Wars* 12b (5 Bolts)
Start in the rotten dihedral before moving left to gain the prominent layback feature up the face. Technical terrain leads to a tricky crux reaching the large undercling feature at the top.
**FA: B. Scott**

THE BEACH

Spencer Anderson getting the F.A. of **Dirty Diet Coke** ** **14a**   Photo: B. Scott

Jason Tarry with his "try-hard" face on **Kona Blend** ** **13b**   Photo: B. Scott

Ryan Bogus eyeing the crux mixed section (December, 2013) of **Group Therapy**\*\*\*\* **Wi6, M5**  Photo: Michael Engelstad

## GROUP THERAPY

Michael Engelstad approaching the business in 2013   Photo: J. Levine

Author's Note: This description and history was compiled and written by local climber Michael Engelstad while he was a standing Board Member on the NCCC in 2014.

**1.** ⊙ **Group Therapy**\*\*\*\* **WI6, M5** (Ice Screws + GEAR)
Driving down the canyon in winter, you have likely narrowly avoided crashing into the river while gawking at this ice formation in the Narrows.

This route has a long yet inconsistent history. As lifelong Poudre Canyon climber Rodney Ley recalled, the route had been given top-rope attention in the late 80s by Ian Rich and Malcom Daly. In the late 90s, it was again top-roped by DJ Nechrony and Adam Dabcock.

In 1998, the climb formed exceptionally well and again drew the attention of the area's ice aficionados. Dave Sheldon upped the ante and climbed two separate lines (left of center, right of center) onsight, on lead, and claimed what was likely the first lead ascent. He called the route "Group Therapy" and suggested the rating in its state to be WI6, M5.

Rob Cordery Cotter also climbed the route that same year using leashed tools, plastic boots and a GORE-TEX onesie. He protected the route with pegs, nuts and screws. The route also became known as "Wrangler Dangler" around this time.
**FA: Dave Sheldon**

## GETTING THERE

GPS: 40°40'46.99"N 105°26'6.06"W
From Ted's Place, drive 19.6 miles up the canyon to the west end of the Narrows. There is a large pullout on the riverside of the road just past The Beach area. From this pullout, you can look directly at the climb across the river. Hopefully, the river is frozen or the climb is probably not in season. Cross the river and navigate the steep hillside to the base of the best ice climb in the canyon.

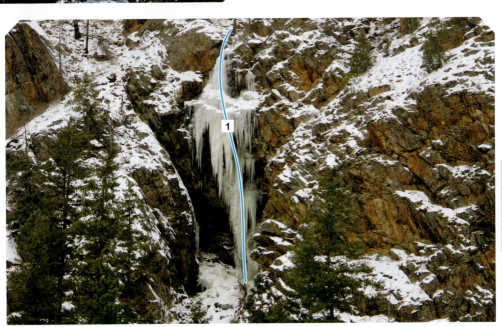

**23.0 MILES** FROM TED'S PLACE

# MOUNTAIN PARK BOULDER

**TYPE(S): BOULDERING**
**DIFFICULTY RANGE: V5-V9**
**APPROACH TIME: 5 SEC**
**SEASON: FALL, WINTER & SPRING**

## CLIMBING OVERVIEW

This incredible boulder sits alone on a random turn of the highway between the Narrows and Pingree Park Road. The rock quality is excellent and besides the road, the setting is quite nice. The obvious line directly up the center has become an infamous project, but it simply may not go or is contrived.

## GETTING THERE

GPS: 40°40'48.49"N 105°27'24.21"W
From Ted's Place, drive 23.0 miles up the canyon. Park in a pullout on the south side of the road about 20 yards downstream from the boulder. The boulder is tricky to see from the road, so if you get to the entrance to Mountain Park Campground you have gone too far and need to turn-around.

**1.** ◉ **Pinchy Sit**** v5** (Pads)
SDS on some cool mini-pinches and a heel-hook. A hard move gains the mid-way jugs followed by an easy topout left.
FA: Kevin Bohm

**2.** ◉ **Law of the Land*** v9** (Pads)
The best effort to date to try and climb the direct line. Start on the obvious starting hold and climb up the seam before doing a big move right to a crimp and eventually the arête which takes you to the top.
FA: C. Horvat

**3.** ◉ **Thin Ice**** v6** (Pads)
A fun line on crimps starting on the left face and moving up the arête and eventually onto the slab on the right face.
FA: K. Bohm

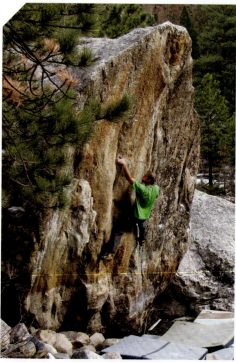

The author failing on an attempt at the direct line   Photo: C. Cross

174   POUDRE CANYON GUIDE - 3RD EDITION

**27.1 MILES** FROM TED'S PLACE

# ICELAND

ICELAND - RIGHT

**TYPE(S): BOULDERING**
**DIFFICULTY RANGE: V2-V10**
**APPROACH TIME: 5 SECONDS**
**SEASON: SPRING, FALL & WINTER**

## CLIMBING OVERVIEW

Iceland is hands down, one of the most unique bouldering settings in the state. The crag is an exposed cliff band of impeccable polished stone that sits directly in the Poudre River. Although the wall is partially submerged and unclimbable for much of the year, during extreme winter conditions, the entire river freezes and creates a perfect landing zone. Overhanging and featured for its entire length, Iceland provides an incredible concentration of high-quality problems that are a must-see. However, this area is not for the faint of heart or those who get cold easily. Be extremely careful on the ice.

MOSTLY SHADE ALL DAY

## GETTING THERE

**GPS: 40°41'25.20"N 105°30'21.58"W**
The parking area for Iceland is found just upstream from the Egger's fishing area, 27.6 miles from Ted's Place.

From the pullout, follow a faint fisherman's trail upstream 50 yards. The first routes begin just after leaving the gravel bar, where the ice starts and circulation stops.

**1. ◉ Ice 9\*\* v9** (Pads)
SDS on slopey polished edges. Make a big move to the arête pinch followed by the crux move to the slopey shelf.
**FA: Andre Di Felice**

**2. ◉ Seam\*\* v5** (Pads)
SDS on edges, right hand to pinch, then follow a seam to the lip of the boulder.
**FA: B. Scott**

**3. ◉ Pinchy Underclings\*\* v5** (Pads)
SDS and move into the obvious pinchy underclings to the break before the lip. A tricky lip encounter gets you to the top.
**FA: B. Scott**

**4. ◉ Round Room\* v4** (Pads)
SDS on a large undercling tongue. Move up and right, out the roof to a tricky reach.
**FA: B. Scott**

**5. ◉ Unnamed v3** (Pads)
Climb blocky jugs through a vague dihedral to an easy topout.
**FA: Unknown**

**6. ◉ Fire on Ice\*\*\* v9** (Pads)
Start on the slopey jug and move into the crucial sidepull. Use a heel-toe cam to move onto some horribly slopey edges before a deadpoint to the obvious hole. Another big power move gets you to the lip and easy topout.
**FA: C. Cross**

ICELAND

Paul Dusatko on the epic stone and icy setting of **Vanilla Ice*** **v7**  Photo: B. Scott

# ICELAND

ICELAND - LEFT

**7.** ◎ **Vanilla Ice**\*\*\* **v7** (Pads)
Start on the large block pinch and move up and left across the face. A hard move to a sloper followed by dynamic moves to the lip.
FA: Unknown

**8.** ◎ **Center Right**\*\* **v5** (Pads)
Start on the blocky jug and move right and up to an obvious incut edge before moving back left to the crack.
FA: Unknown

**9.** ◎ **Jason's Little Thingy**\*\* **v7** (Pads)
Start on a two finger undercling and do a big move to the break. Handjam underclings in the slot to move to the lip.
FA: J. Tarry

**10.** ◎ **Brown Jump**\*\* **v4** (Pads)
Climb the blocky corner with a big move, then layback out the seam to the lip.
FA: Unknown

**11.** ◎ **Tricky Dicky**\* **v6** (Pads)
SDS on the slopey jug, move into a small undercling to gain the sidepulls on the face or just lunge all the way to the break.
FA: Jeremy Bisher

**12.** ◎ **Unnamed v2** (Pads)
Climb the blocky short arête.
FA: Unknown

**13.** ◎ **Unnamed v2** (Pads)
Climb cool blocky edges to an easy mantle.
FA: Unknown

**14.** ◎ **Unnamed v3** (Pads)
Climb the short layback feature.
FA: Unknown

ICELAND - CENTER

Doug McKee warming up on **La-Z-Boy** ** 10a   Photo: B. Scott

**27.3 MILES** FROM TED'S PLACE

# GRANDPA'S BRIDGE

**TYPE(S): SPORT**
**DIFFICULTY RANGE: 5.10A - 5.13C**
**APPROACH TIME: 5 - 30 MIN**
**SEASON: YEAR ROUND**

## CLIMBING OVERVIEW

Grandpa's Bridge is another newly developed zone that has a nice variety of styles and routes with lots of potential for more routes. A prominent area from the road featuring granite spires and corridors. It is also home to the Amphitheater which boasts some of the steepest routes in the canyon.

## GETTING THERE

**GPS: 40°41'24.95"N 105°30'31.50"W**

From Ted's Place, drive 27.3 miles up the canyon. Park in a massive pullout/parking area on the north side of the road right before Hwy 14 crosses over the Poudre River at the aptly named Grandpa's Bridge. From here, follow the trail along the river to reach the crags. Alternatively if you are heading to the Amphitheater and the river is crossable, continue driving to another pullout at mile 27.8. Here, you can cross directly to the Amphitheater and save some hiking time.

## RIVERSIDE ZONE

This area comprises the routes closest to the river and the parking area. Fun climbs on good stone with relatively easy access. From the parking area on the east side of the bridge, follow a trail that parallels the river heading upstream. It ends at the river's edge, just past Grandpa's Cough Syrup. Wade or hop rocks along the shore until you can reach La-Z-Boy. Make sure to check the river levels because the rock hop/wading section can be impassible during the spring run-off.

**1. ○ Grandpa's Cough Syrup\*\* 11b** (5 Bolts)
This is a great route with surprisingly good rock. Climb up on a ledge to Bolt 1. Continue on easy face climbing to a jug below the roof. Traverse left here and then back right to a tricky bulge/mantle encounter to reach the chains.
**FA: D. McKee**

# GRANDPA'S BRIDGE

Jason Tarry at the crux of **Golden Pagoda**\*\*\* **13b**  Photo: Kyle Kamrath

## SLAB AREA

### 2. ○ La-Z-Boy** 10a (10 Bolts)
If you've driven past this section of the canyon, you've probably wondered if there is a route on this wall. It has an obvious position with surprisingly good rock. Start with some steep moves on big jugs to a quick mantle into the groove. A tricky move gains the ledge followed by easy but thought-provoking climbing to the anchor.
**FA:** D. McKee, J. Tarry, R.D. Pascoe, B. Scott

### 3. ○ Power Pagoda** 11c (8 Bolts)
Power Pagoda is a fun route that begs to be climbed when you see it from the road, and its rock quality is surprisingly good. Start with some easy terrain to a tricky crux at Bolt 3 moving to the lip of the halfway ledge. Another crux comes pulling off the ledge where you need to find holds around the left arête. A final punchy move gains a luxurious layback flake that takes you to the anchor.
**FA:** R.D. Pascoe, B. Scott

### 4. ○ Golden Pagoda*** 13b (8 Bolts)
This is a stunning line up the steepest, central section of the Pagoda Tower. The first crux is right off the ledge with slopers, crimps, and compression to reach a slopey hole. After the slopey hole, continuous and pumpy underclings lead to a final desperate stab to a cool pinchy jug at the lip.
**FA:** B. Scott

## SLAB AREA

This area has great potential for moderates, but only one route exists to date. From the Riverside zone walk 20 yards upstream until you can navigate up a series of ramps then back left to the wall.

### 5. ○ Sunday Stroll*** 8 (10 Bolts)
Start with some fun romping on small knobs and edges. A steep bulge is easily navigated on the right with a big, undercling tongue. More awesome chicken-heads and jugs lead up the final slab to the anchor.
**FA:** R.D. Pascoe

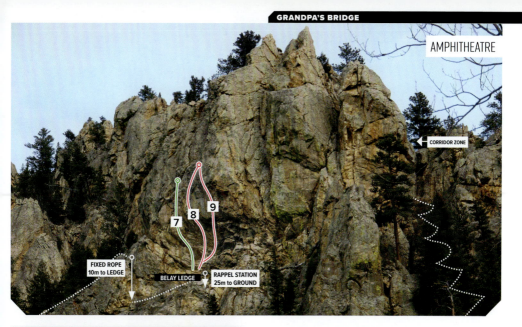

## PAPA'S BULGE AREA

This lone route is a nice warm-up for the difficulties at the Amphitheater. From the Riverside Zone, walk 100 yards upstream along the river until this short overhang comes into view 20 yards above the riverbank.

### 6. ○ Papa's Bulge** 12a (5 Bolts)
This is an excellent, short overhang. Start by following a left-leaning crack for 2 bolts to the base of the overhang. Continue out the short, steep wall on underclings, sidepulls, and slopers. A final pumpy mantle brings you to the chains.
FA: J. Tarry, B. Scott

## AMPHITHEATER

There are two ways to reach the Amphitheater. From the main area, continue walking along the river's edge past Papa's Bulge until the crag comes into view. Alternatively, you can park in the large pullout upstream from the bridge directly across from the Amphitheater. This is much faster but impossible if the river is high.

Once you're at the base of the hill below the Amphitheater, walk up the left side of the hill until you're even with the crag and perform a short 10m rappel on a fixed line to reach the spacious ledge. At the end of your climbing day, there is a convenient rappel station off the ledge. With a 25m rappel you will reach the ground and walk away.

### 7. ○ Gippeto** 12c (8 Bolts)
Start with a reachy move getting past a short, right-facing corner. Continue on big holds to the crux above the black chicken-head. A decent rest leads to a short traverse back right before the anchor.
FA: B. Scott

### 8. ○ Honest Jon*** 13c (9 Bolts)
Start with some less than desirable rock to reach Bolt 1 above the rap anchor. Layback up the dihedral feature until you can surf core-sucking kneebars to the capped roof. There is a brief rest at the lip of the overhang before engaging in technical, thin face climbing up the awesome headwall to the anchor.
FA: J. Tarry, B. Scott

### 9. ○ Monstro*** 13c (9 Bolts)
Monstro is the stunning line that attracted all the initial development of the area. Start with some big jugs to reach Bolt 3. Perform an amazing, right-trending traverse through a beautiful seam to a crappy kneebar rest. From here, launch into a series of underclings and sidepulls (crux) to gain the less overhanging headwall. A final 5.12 crux will test your redpoint determination.
FA: J. Tarry, B. Scott

## CORRIDOR ZONE

The Corridor Zone is basically the backside of the Amphitheater. From the base of Amphitheater hill, locate a subtle gulley on the right side of the formation that you can slowly slog up to the base. There are several other routes in progress or yet to be bolted in this zone.

### 10. ○ Grandpa's Challenge** 11b (9 Bolts)
Start with some techy slab climbing to reach the base of the overhang. Move out the overhang to a desperate stab to a giant chicken-head at the lip. Thought provoking slab leads to the anchor.
FA: R. D. Pascoe, J. Tarry, B. Scott

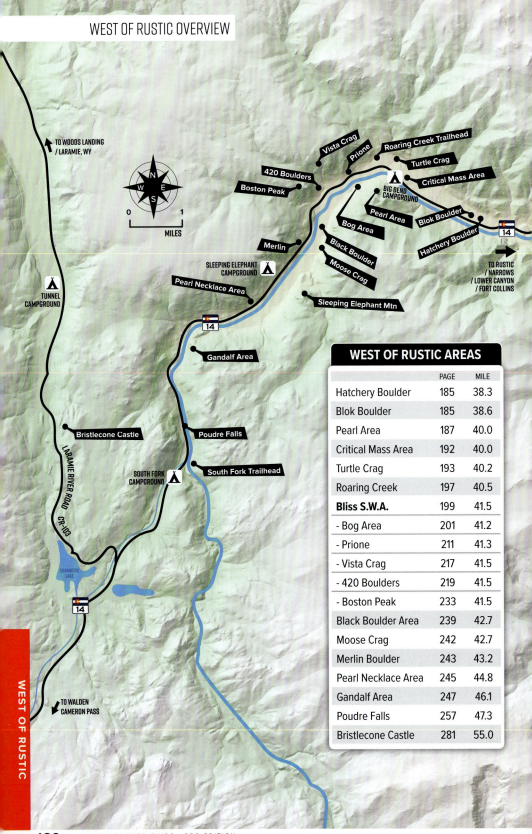

# WEST OF RUSTIC

**38.0 - 55.0 MILES** FROM TED'S PLACE

The majestic West of Rustic area looking towards Sleeping Elephant Mountain from the flanks of Boston Peak  Photo: B. Scott

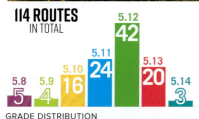

**114 ROUTES** IN TOTAL

GRADE DISTRIBUTION
- 5.8: 5
- 5.9: 4
- 5.10: 16
- 5.11: 24
- 5.12: 42
- 5.13: 20
- 5.14: 3

**308 BOULDER** PROBLEMS IN TOTAL
- v0-v2: 30
- v3-v4: 91
- v5-v6: 61
- v7-v8: 67
- v9-v10: 42
- v11-Above: 17

**TYPE(S): SPORT, TRAD, & BOULDERING**
**DIFFICULTY RANGE: 5.8 - 5.14C, V1-V13**
**APPROACH TIME: 2 SEC - 1 HOUR OR MORE**
**SEASON: YEAR ROUND**

## CLIMBING OVERVIEW

The climbing areas located West of Rustic comprise the best climbing the canyon has to offer...period. Stunning landscapes coupled with incredible stone in every shape and style imaginable make this every climber's dream. The canyon is wide and open here, dotted with black and white streaked cliffs which loom over fields of house-sized boulders.

The earliest record of climbing here is in **Bob Horan's** Fort Collins Area Guide from 1995. In it, he describes **Scott Blunk, John Shireman, Chris Vogues,** and **Mark Wilford** being active in the area, but no further details are given. I started climbing here on a tip from **Hank Jones** in 1999 who had parked his RV up there and developed some obvious low-hanging fruit. **Pat Goodman** and I stumbled upon the 420 Boulders one day and my eyes became open to all that the Upper Canyon has to offer. Those early days of bouldering development were done by guys like **Jeremy Bisher, Pat Goodman,** Ryan Anglemeyer, Tom Blackford, Francis Sanzaro, Will Lemaire, Mike Mangino, Mike Auldridge, Herm Feissner, Jay Shambo, and the author.

In 2002, the legendary **Chris Sharma** passed through town and established the classic testpieces Sharma Lunge*** v10 and Kingpin**** v12. **Dave Graham** also spent some time here in those early days snagging coveted first ascents like Black Boulder*** v9, Cloudwalker*** v10 and the world-renowned Circadian Rhythm*** v13. All of this hype brought an explosion of traffic to the canyon in those years following and with that excitement came motivation to find new amazing boulders. Climbers like **Brian Camp, Jason Nadeau, Colin Horvat, Paul Dusatko, Zach Lerner, Skyler Bol,** and **Sam Rothstein** have all contributed hundreds of additional problems since those early days.

Around 2008, a friend loaned me a hammer drill and I began exploring the cliffs above the boulders. These initial forays into bolting led to cliffs like Vista Crag and Turtle Crag. I quickly realized how incredible the potential for route climbing was West of Rustic. This surge of motivation eventually led to areas like Poudre Falls, Bristlecone Castle, and Moose Crag. Most of the bolting, cleaning and sending work was being done by **Jason Tarry, Chris Tirrell, Doug McKee, Ryan Nelson, R.D. Pascoe, Chris Hofer,** myself and **Steve McCorkel** at Boston Peak. New crags, routes and boulders continue to be found and developed to this day.

POUDRE CANYON GUIDE - 3RD EDITION

**Climber Spotlight:** Born in Telluride, Colorado, Paul Dusatko began climbing in 1989. Paul started his journey as a trad climber in Joshua Tree and Yosemite, followed by a stint of sport climbing, before finding his passion of bouldering and moving back to Colorado in 2008. Paul's influence was felt immediately in Northern Colorado through his management of Miramont's climbing wall where he gave it a much needed upgrade to a modern climbing facility. Devoted to stewardship, he spent time as a board member on the NCCC and has developed countless hard boulder problems in the area. Paul's dedication to the climbing community, the industry and the lifestyle we all love is unparalleled.

Paul Dusatko on the epic starting moves of **Blok Two**** v10** Photo: B. Scott

**38.3 MILES** FROM TED'S PLACE

# HATCHERY BOULDER AREA

## HATCHERY

## BLOK

**TYPE(S): BOULDERING**
**DIFFICULTY RANGE: V1 - V11**
**APPROACH TIME: 1 MIN**
**SEASON: YEAR ROUND**

## HATCHERY BOULDER

The Hatchery Boulder has been climbed on for generations and is a great warm-up block for the rest of the West of Rustic area. Lots of variations and contrivances exist. No names have ever stuck for any of these problems.

MOSTLY **SUNNY** ALL DAY

**GPS: 40°41'58.76"N 105°42'1.68"W**
From Ted's Place, drive 38.3 miles up Hwy 14. The boulder is located 20 yards off the highway on the north side of the road. There is a large pullout on the south side about 100 yards before the boulder. Park here and walk to the boulder.

**1. ◯ Unnamed* v3 (Pads)**
Stand start the left arête, then figure out the tricky topout.

**2. ◯ Unnamed v4 (Pads)**
This obvious line with a long reach to the lip climbs the middle of the face.

**3. ◯ Unnamed ** v1 (Pads)**
Make an awkward move to jugs.

**4. ◯ Unnamed* v3 (Pads)**
The most obvious line on the boulder climbs this great short arête. Start at a chest high slopey edge and move through big moves on nice holds. From the last jug, you can climb direct up the arête or traverse left to an easier topout.

**5. ◯ Unnamed* v3 (Pads)**
SDS on an edge, then move directly up the face.

**6. ◯ Unnamed v4 (Pads)**
SDS to the right of #5. Move up small edges to the lip.

## BLOK BOULDER

**GPS: 40°42'1.49"N 105°42'13.61"W**
From Ted's Place, drive 38.5 miles up Hwy 14. The parking is the next major pullout upstream from the Hatchery Boulder. Blok One is ten yards off the road on the north side of Hwy 14.

**7. ◯ Blok Two** v10 (Pads)**
The center line up the overhang throws an incredible amount of tedious and tricky movement at you in its short length. SDS on an undercling and move through a very sequential sequence with a final thrutch to another good undercling. Topout up the arête to the obvious ending jug.
**FA: Jeff Silcox**

**8. ◯ Blok One** v7 (Pads)**
Originally done years ago by Jay Shambo as a quality stand start at about v4. "Modern" climbers have since added a low SDS which consists of a powerful traverse on underclings and slopey edges.
**FA: Brian Camp**

**9. ◯ Blok of Aragon* v11 (Pads)**
Start on the far right side of the boulder and climb into Blok Two and finish with the left most topout. 17 moves of pure dirt-burglar brilliance from the king of dirt burglars himself.
**FA: Paul Dusatko**

POUDRE CANYON GUIDE - 3RD EDITION  **185**

PEARL AREA

Matt Tschohl (above) and Jason Tarry (right) on **Eye Of Samara\*\*\* v10**  Photo: B. Scott, Andy Mann

**40.0 MILES** FROM TED'S PLACE

# PEARL AREA

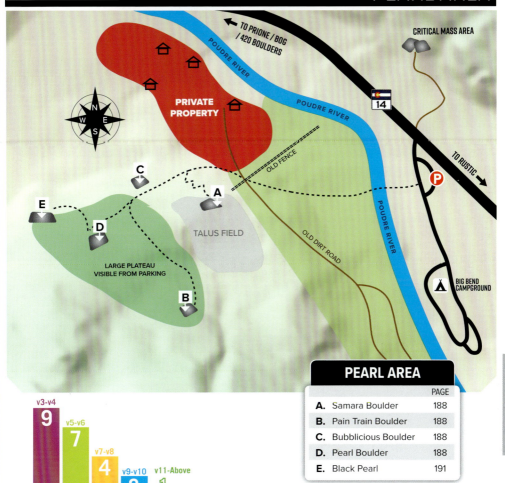

## PEARL AREA

| | | PAGE |
|---|---|---|
| A. | Samara Boulder | 188 |
| B. | Pain Train Boulder | 188 |
| C. | Bubblicious Boulder | 188 |
| D. Pearl Boulder | | 188 |
| E. | Black Pearl | 191 |

**GRADE DISTRIBUTION**
- v3-v4: 9
- v5-v6: 7
- v7-v8: 4
- v9-v10: 2
- v11-Above: 1

**TYPE(S): BOULDERING**
**DIFFICULTY RANGE: V0 - V10**
**APPROACH TIME: 20 - 30 MIN**
**SEASON: SPRING, FALL & WINTER**

RIVER CROSSING REQUIRED

## CLIMBING OVERVIEW

The Pearl Area is know for highballs. The blocks are tall, polished, impeccable granite that can be intimidating and committing. While the climbing is excellent at the Pearl Area, please be discreet as it borders private land.

This guide covers only a portion of the developed bouldering in this area. There is a large talus field above the Black Pearl boulder which has seen intermittent development over the years. Go check it out!

## GETTING THERE

**GPS: 40°42'30.71"N 105°44'4.83"W**

From Ted's Place, drive 40.0 miles up the canyon to the Big Bend Campground. Park in the "day use" pullout on the left before driving all the way in to the campground.

From the parking lot near the Big Bend Campground, head towards the river. Wade across the river, then move uphill and go west across a large meadow. Cross an old fence line and turn immediately uphill following a faint cairned path. When the trail crests the plateau, move west/southwest to find the Pearl Boulder.

The Pearl Area borders private property, so be discreet and careful not to wander onto private land. Also, wading across the Poudre River is required, so the Pearl Area is inaccessible during spring runoff, which generally extends from May through late July.

POUDRE CANYON GUIDE - 3RD EDITION  **187**

PEARL AREA

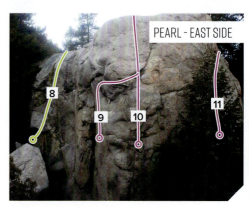

## A - SAMARA BOULDER

This lone problem is a proud tick on any hardman's list. There are a few other problems in this talus field, but you'll probably only visit this problem.

**1. ◯ Eye Of Samara*** v10 (4-5 Pads)
Start sitting pinching a large sidepull. Move through a pocket, slopers and edges to a final crux sequence to the lip. Initially done as a huge dyno, a compression method is more common now.
FA: B. Scott

## B - PAIN TRAIN BOULDER

This boulder is reached by turning left / south once you reach the plateau. The boulder lies on the edge of the plateau all by itself.

**2. ◯ Jump Start* v3 (Pads)
The right line on the north face. Jumpstart to a big sloper, then pull another large move to a jug.
FA: Travis Shipman

**3. ◯ Pain Train** v8 (Pads)
The center line on the north face. Start crouched on a fingerlock, move to a pinch, then a hard move to a sloper. Topout by following the crack/seam.
FA: T. Shipman

## C - BUBBLICIOUS BOULDER

On the way up to the Pearl Plateau, you will encounter this lovely gem right off the trail to hiker's right.

**4. ◯ Unnamed v4 (Pads)
Start with a right-hand edge above your head. Establish, then jump for the lip. Hard mantle.
FA: B. Scott

**5. ◯ Bubblicious** v5 (Pads)
Start in a subtle dihedral and move up and left to a small edge on the face. An awkward foot/hand match sets you up for the big move to the incredible bubble at the lip. Mantle the bubble and topout.
FA: B. Scott

**6. ◯ Shmamie's Slopers* v8 (Pads)
This heinous little SDS begins on obvious holds. Move to a bad edge before the lip, then hard slopers above the lip.
FA: Jamie Emerson

## D - PEARL BOULDER

This boulder provides some of the best rock and movement in the entire canyon. Almost every problem is tall and committing. Lots of pads are suggested. Because of the lack of a safe downclimb, a fixed rope may be found on the north face. Make sure to check the rope for wear before downclimbing.

**7. ◯ 40 Grit** v5 (4-5 Pads)
Start as for Fran's Problem but move left and up into the dihedral. A friction move entering the dihedral gives the route its name. Continue up the dihedral on easy climbing to a lip/tree encounter.
FA: B. Scott

**8. ◯ Fran's Problem* v5 (4-5 Pads)
Start on edges at head height under a small roof. Move right to a match in a vertical seam. Keep moving right to a slopey jug and a hard mantle. Rest up and follow the right angling seam through heady terrain to the topout.
FA: Francis Sanzaro

**9. ◯ Rucksack Showdown** v4 (4-5 Pads)
Start in the obvious layback corner left of Fran's Problem. From the top of the corner, grab underclings to traverse back right into the topout for Nutsack Hoedown. The direct finish is still un-climbed.
FA: B. Scott

**10. ◯ Nutsack Hoedown*** v4 (4-5 Pads)
Besides the name, this is the best moderate problem on the boulder. Pinches and edges lead to an undercling rest before the slab. From here, committing moves through an undercling and gaston get you on top.
FA: Matt Findley

**11. ◯ Will's Face/Arête* v4 (4-5 Pads)
Seldom climbed face and arête. Probably sandbagged.
FA: W. Lemaire

# PEARL - WEST SIDE

### 12. ⊙ Unnamed Slab v3 (4-5 Pads)
Climb the face to the left of the rope ladder. Easy but technical climbing will keep your attention until the lip.
FA: Ryan Anglemeyer

### 13. ⊙ Rope Ladder v3 (4-5 Pads)
This slab climb behind the rope ladder is fun and techy. Watch for descending climbers.
FA: R. Anglemeyer

### 14. ⊙ Daytripper Arête** v6 (4-5 Pads)
Start as for Rasta Drop but climb the arête directly. Hard moves gain a cresent sidepull. The last moves are climbed on the slab to the left.
FA: B. Scott

### 15. ⊙ Rasta Drop*** v7 (4-5 Pads)
Named after the dreadlocked first ascentionist who back splatted on the rocks below. Start on the left arête and move up and right towards the obvious jug halfway up Big Oyster. A hard stand-up on an undercling or a dyno will get you to the glory headwall.
FA: Jeremy Bisher

### 16. ⊙ Big Oyster*** v9 (4-5 Pads)
A technical dihedral masterpiece on perfect rock. Start on an obvious undercling and crux around the bulge to an edge. Move left to an obvious jug and topout straight up the headwall.
FA: Will Lemaire

### 17. ⊙ Moonbeam** v6 (4-5 Pads)
Starting in the Big Oyster dihedral, traverse right on bad underclings until you're able to move back left to the dihedral again. A big move left gets you into the same topout as Rasta Drop and Big Oyster.
FA: B. Scott

### 18. ⊙ Opal Arête*** v4 (4-5 Pads)
This seldom done arête climbs immaculate stone up a perfect round prow. Easy climbing leads to a stance with an undercling on the left and a sidepull on the right. A big move to a perfect hidden jug will gain access to the ledge and the top.
FA: B. Scott

### 19. ⊙ The Beckoning Silence*** v12 (4-5 Pads)
From two obvious edges, make a committing double catch to the arête and continue to the top. One of the most aesthetic arêtes in the canyon. Originally climbed with the aid of a net system to cover the landing area when you miss the dyno.
FA: C. Cross '08

Nick Flessner performing the upper crux on the immaculate **Small Axe**\*\*\*\* v8   Photo: Erik Page

## E - BLACK PEARL BOULDER

From the Pearl Boulder's west face, find a subtle gulley moving northwest around the steep slope. As the subtle gulley ends, move uphill to your left to find the Small Axe Boulder.

**20. Crossroads** v4** (4-5 Pads)
Start in a jug at the base of the roof on its far left side. Climb long, but easy moves around two roofs moving up and left to the base of a tall slab. Rest up, then launch into the upper slab sequence on techy edges and seams.
FA: B. Scott

**21. Hot Drinks** v6** (4-5 Pads)
Start on a large shelf over a log landing. Climb up and left into a hollow sidepull. Make increasingly committing moves out the overhang to an easy topout.
FA: B. Scott

**22. Black Pearl** v6** (4-5 Pads)
The first line completed on the boulder. Starting in a jug at the bottom of a black streak, strenuous climbing leads to a series of jugs before a final crux moving over the lip and a bad landing.
FA: Thomas Blackford

**23. Small Axe**** v8** (4-5 Pads)
Easily one of the best problems in the canyon; if you enjoy bouldering, this is a must-do problem. Starting on an obvious matched crimp. Climb large moves on edges through the amazing steep wall. Hard crux to the jug, then a technical sequence to get over the lip.
FA: Clayton Reagan

Mike Englestad with the font slapper, Uncle Andy Hanenberg miming moves, with Nick Flessner and Eric Palmer talking shop  Photo: E. Page

**40.0 MILES** FROM TED'S PLACE

# CRITICAL MASS AREA

**KINGFIN BOULDER**

TYPE(S): **BOULDERING**
DIFFICULTY RANGE: **V3 - V12**
APPROACH TIME: **1 MIN**
SEASON: **YEAR ROUND**

## GETTING THERE

GPS: 40°42'43.28"N 105°43'29.46"W

Directly across from the Big Bend Campground is the Critical Mass Area. A left turn sends you to Big Bend Campground, a right turn, at the seasonal mail-box post, takes you to King Fin and Critical Mass. Drive on the dirt road staying to the left at all turns. The road dead ends at a cul-de-sac with both the Critical Mass and King Fin Boulders visible from the car.

MOSTLY **SUNNY** ALL DAY

### 1. Critical Mass** v12 (Pads)
SDS at the far end of the cave. Bust out technical moves via crimps, slopers, toe-hooks, and heinous body tension. RMNP-style rock climbing.
FA: A. Di Felice

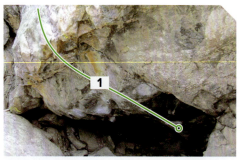

## KING FIN BOULDER

### 2. Fin King v3 (Pads)
Start on a large sloping ledge and head up the arête on edges and slopers.
FA: Jay Shambo, Herm Feissner

### 3. Scrimps v3 (Pads)
Bust three moves to the arête off a crimpy stand start.
FA: J. Shambo, H. Feissner

### 4. Face Down, Ass Up* v8 (Pads)
SDS in the Hanta Virus cave and traverse right into the far left side of King Fin, then head left onto the main headwall via Hank's Rig. Dyno to the sloping but good lip hold.
FA: Paul Dusatko

### 5. Gastoner* v7 (Pads)
Same start as Face Down, Ass Up then bust straight up where Hanks Rig heads back left. Topout just left of King Fin.
FA: Aaron Edwards

### 6. Ridin' Spinnaz* v5 (Pads)
Same start as Face Down, Ass Up and finish up King Fin.
FA: Beau Kahler

### 7. Hank's Rig* v6 (Pads)
Start as for King Fin, but finish via the left headwall.
FA: Hank Jones '99

### 8. King Fin*** v4 (Pads)
Climb the right arête up quality stone and unique holds. Classic Poudre Canyon roadside climbing.
FA: J. Shambo

**40.2 MILES** FROM TED'S PLACE

# TURTLE CRAG

**TYPE(S): SPORT, TRAD & BOULDERING**
**DIFFICULTY RANGE: 5.9 - 5.13; V0 - V5**
**APPROACH TIME: 20 MIN**
**SEASON: FEB - MAY; AUG - DEC**

## CLIMBING OVERVIEW

If bouldering on a rope is your thing, then Turtle Crag is another place to go. What Turtle Crag lacks in height, it makes up for in movement and difficulty. Turtle Crag is south-facing and a great option in the winter, when the rest of the upper canyon is coated in snow.

MOSTLY SUNNY ALL DAY

## GETTING THERE

**GPS: 40°42'58.57"N 105°43'49.37"W**
From Ted's Place, drive 40.2 miles up the canyon until just past the Big Bend Campground. Park in a pullout on the southside of Hwy 14 across from Turtle Crag itself.

From the pullout, cross the road and find a vague trail that switchbacks up a subtle gulley towards the main Turtle Crag dome. Upon reaching the buttress, go right to The Patio or traverse left to the Golden Arête Wall.

## PIGEON BOULDER

Just to the east of Turtle Crag lies the Pigeon Boulder. An obvious blunt prow is easily seen from the road. This prow has been top-roped but never sent with pads or solo. There is also a fun collection of boulder problems on the backside of the main boulder itself.

## BEAST WALL

This is the first little wall you come to after hiking up from the road. The routes are short and similar to The Beach, good rock but very bouldery.

**1.** ○ **Blue Streak* 12a (3 Bolts)**
Start on large jugs and angle up and right past Bolt 1. Continue up the right- leaning seam/flake to a crux at Bolt 3. Very hard for the grade, probably sandbagged.
**FA: B. Scott**

**2.** ○ **Black Beast** 13b (3 Bolts)**
A bolted boulder problem out a short roof feature on good rock. A crucial toe-hook in the steep bulge crux will help get you through to the anchor.
**FA: C. Cross, J. Tarry, B. Scott**

POUDRE CANYON GUIDE - 3RD EDITION    **193**

Jimmy Burckhard snagging his first, First Ascent with **Slow And Steady** ** **12b**  Photo: B. Scott

# TURTLE CRAG

## GOLDEN ARÊTE WALL

Doug McKee on the F.A. of **Consolation Prize* 9** Photo: B. Scott

## THE PATIO

From the Beast Wall, walk around to the right and uphill along the cliff until this ledge comes into view. The routes are also similar to The Beach, good rock but bouldery.

### 3. Opium Train Project (4 Bolts)
The obvious line on the left side of the patio. Climb excellent rock past two bolts, with the tricky crux between Bolts 2 and 3 up the crack/seam feature.
**Bolted by B. Scott**

### 4. Patio Face** 12a (4 Bolts)
Start with a tricky boulder problem right off the ground on nice white rock. Some continuous 5.11 terrain leads to the anchor.
**FA: B. Scott**

## GOLDEN ARÊTE WALL

From the Beast Wall, walk to the left along the main face for approx. 50 yards until the Golden Arête and Tan Panel come into view.

### 5. Escape From the Gnar 12d (6 Bolts)
This would be the best route at the crag if it were solid. All the bolts are in good rock, but almost all the holds up high are hollow and connected to each other. Dangerous.
**FA: B. Scott**

### 6. Golden Arête*** 12b (5 Bolts)
Amazing tiger striped granite covers this short little gem. Start as for the Tan Panel, but stay on the arête the whole way. Beware of the tricky clip at Bolt 3, which starts the crux compression boulder problem. Pre-placing draws is recommended after warming up on Tan Panel.
**FA: C. Tirrell, J. Tarry, B. Scott**

### 7. Tan Panel* 11b (5 Bolts)
Step off a large boulder near the arête. Move up to a large ledge at Bolt 2. Climb the crux to Bolt 3, then meander up the big flake to the anchors.
**FA: B. Scott**

### 8. Consolation Prize* 9 (2 Bolts + GEAR)
The obvious crack line looks much better than it climbs but is still a worthy outing.
**FA: Doug McKee**

### 9. Slow and Steady** 12b (6 Bolts)
A relatively easy start takes you up the corner feature. The crux forces you onto the arête proper, with techy footwork and a hard last move.
**FA: J. Burckhard**

### 10. Open Project (4 Bolts)
Between the Black Beast Wall and the Golden Arête Wall is another small panel of nice rock. A really hard crux section lies between Bolts 2 and 4. You figure it out!
**Bolted by B. Scott**

Brett Hoffman on the pumpy middle section of **Panty Line**\*\*\* v8  Photo: B. Scott

# ROARING CREEK BOULDER

**40.5 MILES** FROM TED'S PLACE

**TYPE(S): SPORT, BOULDERING**
**DIFFICULTY RANGE: 5.12A- 5.13C; V3 - V8**
**APPROACH TIME: 20 MINUTES**
**SEASON: YEAR ROUND**

## CLIMBING OVERVIEW

MOSTLY SUNNY ALL DAY

The Roaring Creek Trail is popular for hiking and backpacking, but also offers a few worthwhile climbs. From the parking lot, there is one large boulder that looms over the canyon. This boulder can be seen from many points in the canyon and offers great rock in a spectacular position.

## GETTING THERE

GPS: 40°42'59.73"N 105°44'6.71"W
From Ted's Place, drive 40.4 miles to the Roaring Creek Trailhead parking lot on the west side of Hwy 14.

## DINGO BOULDER

This is a nice boulder with some more moderate climbs to warm-up on. Located on the faint trail on the way to the Roaring Creek Boulder once you get off the main trail.

**1.** ○ **Dixie Dingo**** v3 (Pads)
SDS with a left-hand on the obvious sidepull and right-hand on the sloper. Make a move straight up to the crimps and then out left to slopers. Move up to the pinch and sloper, where the line transitions to a slab.
**FA: Fritz Mercer**

**2.** ○ **Full Frontal**** v4 (Pads)
SDS on two crimps that are located in the horizontal seam, and reach up to a left-hand crimp and right-hand crimp. Trend right, following the seam, using left incuts and right sidepulls. The stand start from the left and right crimps is about v2.
**FA: F. Mercer**

## ROARING CREEK BOULDER

This boulder can be seen to the north from the parking lot. Walk up the trail until it starts heading down a hill towards the creek. Find a faint trail heading uphill and traverse back right across the hillside towards the boulder.

**3.** ○ **Panty Line**\*\*\* v8 (Pads)
Start on underclings near the arête. Do a hard move to gain the prominent slot. Follow the seams up and left to the white jugs. Finish by traversing all the way left until the seams go over the lip on the far left side of the west face.
**FA: B. Scott**

**4.** ○ **Unnamed 12a** (4 Bolts)
Start up the seam/layback feature on nice rock. Hard moves on edges lead to the ledge and easy mantle.
**FA: Unknown**

**5.** ○ **Eyes of the World**\*\*\* 13c (3 Bolts)
Start on the right face using underclings and a pocket to gain the left arête. Continue on incredibly techy terrain with a hard 3rd clip and an even harder move to the lip.
**FA: B. Scott**

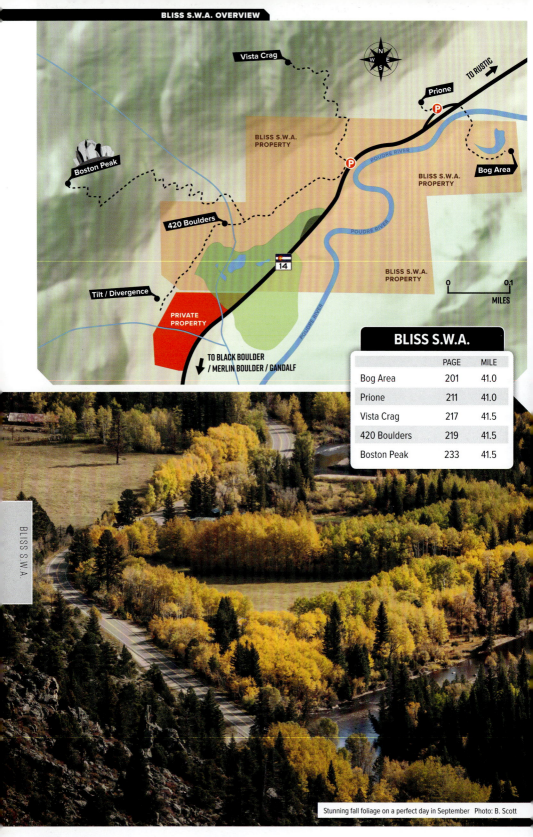

Stunning fall foliage on a perfect day in September   Photo: B. Scott

# 41.2-41.5 MILES FROM TED'S PLACE — BLISS STATE WILDLIFE AREA (S.W.A.)

The sublime walk into the 420 Boulder's on a perfect fall day   Photo: B. Scott

**TYPE(S): SPORT, TRAD & BOULDERING**
**DIFFICULTY RANGE: 5.8-5.14, V0 - V13**
**APPROACH TIME: 5 MIN - 1 HOUR**
**SEASON: YEAR ROUND**

## CLIMBING OVERVIEW

Bliss State Wildlife Area (S.W.A.) is an incredible section of the Poudre Canyon. Soaring cliffs and massive boulders are mixed with rushing streams, lush aspen trees and tons of wildlife. This state land is managed by the Colorado Department of Wildlife (DOW) instead of the usual US Forest Service management throughout the rest of the canyon.

Bliss S.W.A. holds several of the major climbing areas West of Rustic has to offer. The 420 Boulders, the Bog, Vista Crag and Boston Peak are all partially located on this property. As climbers visiting the area, extra care should be taken while visiting Bliss S.W.A. Be sensitive of all private property and be respectful of hunters that could be using the area too.

## GETTING THERE

From Ted's Place, drive 41.0 miles up the canyon and park at the dirt loop road for the Bog Area and Prione, or park at the pullouts for the 420 Boulders where you can also access Vista Crag and Boston Peak.

Jason Tarry making that face again on **Tangerine Sky**\*\*\* v4   Photo: B. Scott

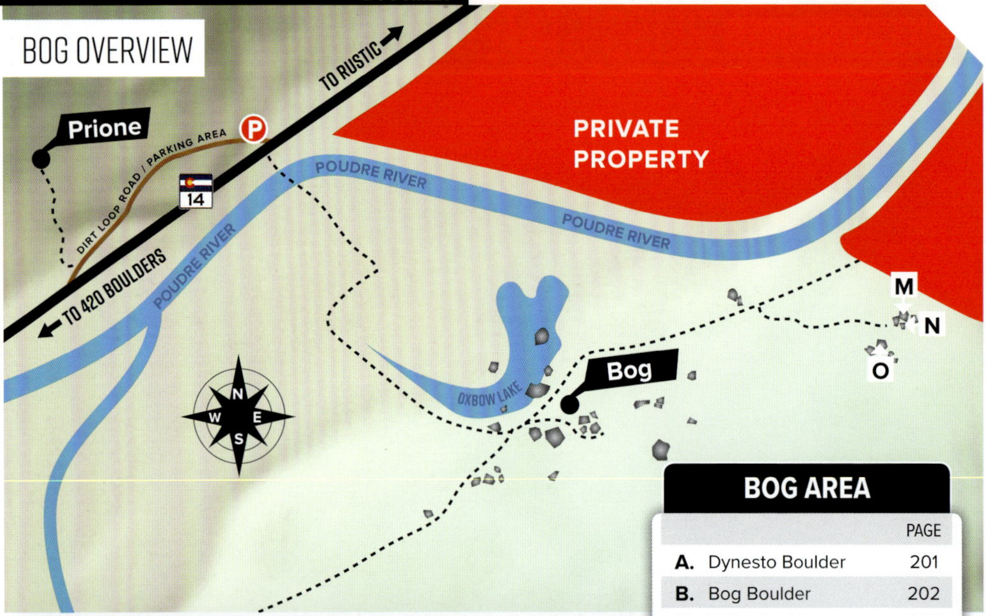

# BOG OVERVIEW

**BOG AREA**

TO RUSTIC
Prione
DIRT LOOP ROAD / PARKING AREA
14
TO 420 BOULDERS
POUDRE RIVER
PRIVATE PROPERTY
OXBOW LAKE
Bog
M
N
O

## BOG AREA

| | | PAGE |
|---|---|---|
| **A.** | Dynesto Boulder | 201 |
| **B.** | Bog Boulder | 202 |
| **C.** | Indian Ladder | 203 |
| **D.** | Saddle Up Boulder | 205 |
| **E.** | Root Canal Boulder | 206 |
| **F.** | Serpentine Boulder | 206 |
| **G.** | Simple Boulder | 206 |
| **H.** | Pats Arête Boulder | 207 |
| **I.** | Sparkle Boulder | 207 |
| **J.** | Perched Boulder | 207 |
| **K.** | Cookie Monster | 207 |
| **L.** | Squeeze Arête | 208 |
| **M.** | Castaway Boulder | 208 |
| **N.** | Pee Pants Boulder | 209 |
| **O.** | Mast Boulder | 209 |

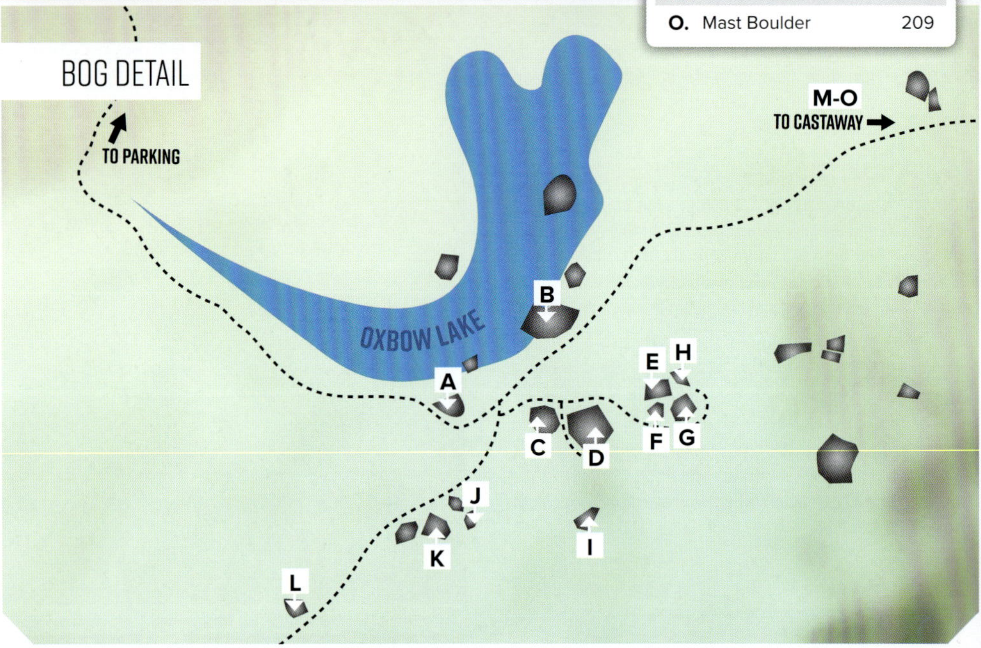

# BOG DETAIL

TO PARKING
M-O TO CASTAWAY
OXBOW LAKE

**41.2 MILES** FROM TED'S PLACE

# BOG AREA

GRADE DISTRIBUTION

**TYPE(S): BOULDERING**
**DIFFICULTY RANGE: V0 - VII**
**APPROACH TIME: 15 MIN**
**SEASON: YEAR ROUND**

RIVER CROSSING REQUIRED

## CLIMBING OVERVIEW

AM SHADE / PM SUN

The Bog is another unusual bouldering feature located in the canyon. This oxbow lake has been famous with fisherman for years around the Rustic community. It wasn't until **Ryan Anglemeyer** and **Thomas "Tam" Blackford** explored the area on a hunch, that The Bog was exposed to rock climbers. The Bog is great year round, with bouldering pads on ice in the winter and shallow water bouldering in the summer.

## GETTING THERE

**GPS: 40°42'31.75"N 105°44'38.06"W**
To get to The Bog drive 41.2 miles from Ted's Place to an obvious dirt loop road / pullout on the west side of the road.

From here, wade across the Poudre and follow the trail that leads along the south side of the oxbow lake to reach the Dynesto Boulder. **DO NOT TRY TO CROSS THE RIVER DURING HIGH WATER, FROM MAY THROUGH LATE JULY.**

DYNESTO

## A - DYNESTO BOULDER

This scenic boulder is the first one you come to off the trail. Nice warm-ups overlooking the oxbow lake.

**1. Dingus\*\*\* v4 (Pads)**
Start on a massive jug and do a huge move to an amazing slopey rail. Another big slap gains the slopey lip and mantle.
FA: Mike Mangino

**2. Traverse Variation\*\* v7 (Pads)**
Start on Dynesto and traverse into Dingus on small crimps.
FA: R. Anglemeyer

**3. Dynesto\*\*\* v6 (Pads)**
The infamous all points off/blind dyno. Start on the large jug and dyno up and left to the perfect jug at the lip.
FA: B. Scott

**4. Unnamed\* v2 (Pads)**
Start on the right side of the Dynesto starting jug and perform one big move to the lip and mantle.
FA: R. Anglemeyer

## B - BOG BOULDER

Excellent tight-grain granite in a scenic and relaxing location. This house-sized boulder sits half in and half out of the oxbow lake. The Bog Boulder is also an unusual block because you can shallow-water solo several excellent routes in the summer or climb them once the ice is frozen thick enough in the winter.

### 5. Mr. Smackmag*** v7 (Pads)
From two obvious sloper edges, jump to the amazing sloping jug and move left to a relatively easy topout. Excellent. It can also be done as a SDS from the low-foot rail (v8).
FA: Mike Auldridge

### 6. Beachside Face v4 (Pads)
On the north side of boulder lies a tall face just beyond the waters edge and to the right of Mr. Smackmag. Start on edges and climb up to hard moves high off the deck.
FA: R. Anglemeyer

### 7. Slopey Thrutch v5 (Pads)
Start on obvious crimps at chest height. Hard move over lip to sloper.
FA: R. Anglemeyer

### 8. Iron Helix*** v6 (Pads)
Same start as Ladies Way on a juggy sidepull on the right side of a dihedral. Do a big move to the sloper rail on the left side of the dihedral. From here, a hard sequence into a small undercling is followed by a big throw to the lip.
FA: B. Scott

### 9. Ladie's Way* v3 (Pads)
The easiest waterside problem on the boulder. Start on a juggy sidepull and move up and right to pinches and blocky jugs to the lip.
FA: R. Anglemeyer

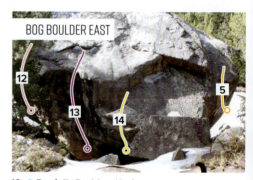

### 10. Daniel's Problem** v9 (Pads)
Start on an obvious jug. Use heel-hooks to grab two mini-pinches, then jump for the jug lip.
FA: Daniel Woods

### 11. Orange Arête v4 (Pads)
Start matched on an edge at head height. Pull into an undercling then move up and right to an awkward move to a jug.
FA: R. Anglemeyer

### 12. Shoreside Project (Pads)
To the left of the warm-ups. Follow a line of miserable crimps on a white wall over a slopey, sandy landing.
FA: Open Project

### 13. Warm-up II* v3 (Pads)
SDS in the hole with hands on two crimps. Use a high heel to make one hard move to a big sloping rail. Move into a right-hand layback through the scoop. Topout using an obvious undercut flake over the lip.
FA: R. Anglemeyer

### 14. Warm-up I* v2 (Pads)
The first of two moderates to the left of Mr. Smackmag. SDS on a slopey rail in a cave/hole. Try not to dab as you move through a cool second rail and a nice mantle.
FA: R. Anglemeyer

INDIAN LADDER

## C - INDIAN LADDER BOULDER

**15. High Noon** v7** (4-5 Pads)
Climb the blunt northwest arête. Difficult crux up high transitioning to the lip.
FA: B. Scott

**16. Dave's Dihedral* v5** (4-5 Pads)
Follow the obvious corner up and right into Center Indian.
FA: Dave Ludders

**17. Center Indian** v3** (4-5 Pads)
Begin on a small crimp in the shallow dihedral in the middle of the face. Move to a jug before eventually escaping on the ledge that cuts left.
FA: Ken Kenny

**18. Indian Ladder**** v5** (4-5 Pads)
One of the most classic lines at The Bog. Grab a droopy tufa like feature and perform a jump move to a sick slopey jug. Big moves on big holds take you to the casual topout. Named after the side profile of a Native American and his head dress in the middle of the problem (the jump move is to his mouth).
FA: J. Bisher

**19. Face Right of Indian Ladder v4** (Pads)
From a sidepull just to the right of Indian Ladder, move to a jug then up and right to topout. Hard crux right before the lip.
FA: J. Shambo

**20. Southwest Slab* v3** (Pads)
Start on obvious crimps just around the corner from Indian Ladder, then cruise up the fun face climb. Also can be done as an excellent dyno from the start holds all the way to the lip.
FA: J. Shambo

**21. Southeast Slab* v3** (Pads)
From a crimp in the pegmatite on the right side of the wall, stand into an undercling and go up.
FA: J. Shambo

Jason Tarry jumping to the mouth on **Indian Ladder**** v5**  Photo: B. Scott

Nick Perl winding up for a big move on the classic **Simple**\*\*\* **v6**  Photo: B. Scott

SADDLE UP - NORTH

## D - SADDLE UP BOULDER

**22. Unknown v2** (Pads)
Begin sitting on a blade on the boulder's northwest corner. Follow a faint seam to a jug and mossy topout.
FA: R. Anglemeyer

**23. Saddle Down*** v9** (Pads)
An often looked at wall but rarely attempted. Start with a hard move off the ground to get to the triangle hold. Big moves on small but decent edges gets you to the easy topout.
FA: B. Scott

**24. Saddle Up** v7** (4-5 Pads)
This excellent highball is not for the faint of heart. Scramble on top of the massive cheater stone and pull yourself onto the wall. Perform a terrifying highstep to reach a slopey left-hand crimp. Then gun it for the lip hold and try not to think about the consequences of failure.
FA: M. Auldridge

**25. Unnamed* v6** (Pads)
Start in an overhanging dihedral with an edge and a sloper. Pull-on and jump to the jug up and left. Continue over the black bulge to topout.
FA: R. Anglemeyer

**26. Ken's Roof** v9** (Pads)
Start sitting and move through a variety of awesome holds and steep position to the lip.
FA: K. Kenny

**27. Tall Face v3** (Pads)
Climb the tall face on the southwest side. Beware of choss.
FA: R. Anglemeyer

SADDLE UP - SOUTH

**28. Arête #19** v4** (Pads)
Start crouched on an obvious edge. Follow good incuts near the arête to the lip. There is a faint 19 that appears to be naturally etched in the rock.
FA: B. Scott

**29. Under the Gaydar* v10** (Pads)
SDS on the obvious rail feature. Do some hard laybacking and compression moves into the start of Arête #19.
FA: Brian Camp

**30. Green Monster*** v7** (Pads)
Stand start on a large undercling at head height. Make a big move to an awesome triangle-shaped pinch then exit out the groove up and a little right.
FA: B. Scott

## E - ROOT CANAL BOULDER

Located just up the hill from the Bog Boulder sitting right next to the massive Saddle Up Boulder.

### 31. ○ Root Canal** v6 (Pads)
Start at the obvious horizontal break and climb up onto the airy slab. Good holds are just a bit far apart and the feet are very precise. Excellent slab climbing.
FA: J. Tarry

## F - SERPENTINE BOULDER

This nice medium-sized boulder sits right next to Saddle Up Boulder and the Root Canal Boulder.

### 32. ○ Serpentine** v6 (Pads)
SDS on the obvious perfect starting hold. Perform a big and tricky reach to the arête. Continue up the nice angled arête to an easy topout.
FA: R. Anglemeyer

### 35. ○ Simple*** v6 (Pads)
This excellent climb is a must-do for anyone visiting the Bog. Located on the northeastern corner of the block, the problem starts on a left-hand sidepull and a thin right-hand undercling before making long dynamic moves to the top.
FA: B. Scott

## G - SIMPLE BOULDER

From the Saddle Up Boulder, walk northeast for 30 yards into a cluster of three large boulders. Simple is the boulder farthest east, closest to the talus field.

### 33. ○ Unnamed Face v3 (Pads)
Beginning in the depression, climb up and slightly right on thin crimps.
FA: R. Anglemeyer

### 34. ○ Unknown Face v3 (Pads)
Make moves up the middle of the face on good rock, but beware of the poor landing.
FA: R. Anglemeyer

### 36. ○ Bisher Arête** v8 (Pads)
Start on two crimps at chest height. Do a huge move to another awesome edge right on the arête. A few more tricky and commiting moves get you to the easy topout.
FA: J. Bisher

### 37. ○ Sue's Face*** v3 (Pads)
Follow a line of crimps up the black face to a jump to the lip or a big move from the arête. A SDS can also be done for a couple of extra moves.
FA: Susan Scott

### 38. ○ Slopey Arête v3 (Pads)
Climb the right-to-left angling arête from a SDS to the top.
FA: R. Anglemeyer

## H - PAT'S ARÊTE

**39.** ○ **Shambo Overhang\* v6** (Pads)
Start on an obvious jug in the center of the face. Climb underclings and edges up and left to an easy topout.
FA: J. Shambo

**40.** ○ **Another Pat's Arête\*\* v4** (Pads)
Climb the obvious right arête. A hard move guards the top holds and the mantle.
FA: P. Goodman

## J - PERCHED BOULDER

This nice medium-sized boulder sits right next to Saddle Up Boulder and the Root Canal Boulder.

**42.** ○ **Unnamed\*\* v5** (Pads)
Jumpstart to an sharp edge followed by easier moves up the slabby face.
FA: R. Anglemeyer

## I - SPARKLE BOULDER

Located just uphill from the Green Monster at the edge of the talus, several moderate slabs can be found on the south and east face of the Sparkle Boulder, although the landing zones leave something to be desired.

**41.** ○ **Sparkle\*\* v8** (Pads)
Start matched on a crystally sloper before slapping out right and continuing up the arête.
FA: J. Shambo

## K - COOKIE MONSTER BOULDER

From Indian Ladder, walk southwest down a faint trail to the boulder on hiker's left.

**43.** ○ **Cookie Monster\*\*\* v10** (Pads)
This infamous problem was originally done as a massive two handed dyno to the lip out this horizontal roof. Since then, holds have been broken or chipped off and its un-clear whether the problem has been repeated in its current form.
FA: M. Auldridge

**44.** ○ **Shoeless Trippin' in The Poudre\*\* v9** (Pads)
An excellent compression problem on good stone. From two opposing sidepulls, squeeze your way up the dueling arêtes on the boulder's southwest corner.
FA: J. Bisher

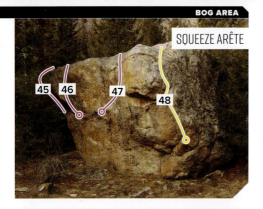

## L - SQUEEZE ARÊTE BOULDER

From Indian Ladder, walk southwest down a faint trail passing the Cookie Monster Boulder until you reach this last boulder of the field on hiker's right. A sunny south-facing bloc with several easier problems over flat landings.

#### 45. Squeeze Arête** v4 (Pads)
An often over looked problem on great rock with nice compression climbing. SDS on a big flat jug and heel-hook your way up the arête until you can grab the big hold out right and squeeze your way to the topout.
FA: R. Anglemeyer

#### 46. Center 1* v3 (Pads)
Stand start on some cool crystal edges. Move up and left before a big move to the lip straight above.
FA: S. Scott

#### 47. Center 2* v3 (Pads)
Another stand start on a sharp edge but move up and right this time on small edges and tenuous feet. Another big move at the top to a perfect jug.
FA: S. Scott

#### 48. Right Side* v2 (Pads)
SDS on a nice layback jug and angle up and left following the arête until you are able to mantle out right.
FA: R. Anglemeyer

## M - CASTAWAY BOULDER

GPS: 40°42'34.09"N 105°44'25.57"W
To reach the Castaway Boulder, walk northeast along the main trail passing through The Bog area until you walk under a small tree that has fallen across the trail (the branches have been trimmed to allow you to walk under it). Just after the tree, cut uphill (east), following a faint trail to the top of a small plateau. Castaway faces west and sits roughly in the middle of the cluster of boulders. Private property is found just to the north of the Castaway area, so be careful not to walk too far before veering uphill.

#### 49. Castaway** v11 (Pads)
If you like hard crimping, this is the problem for you. Start on a crimp sidepull, then crush your way through increasingly smaller holds and a hard finishing move.
FA: Theo Merrin

Herm Feissner trying **Castaway**\*\*\* **v11** as a project around 2001   Photo: B. Scott

Brett Hoffman snagging an ascent of **I Peed My Pants In Chalk**\*\*\* v6   Photo: B. Scott

## N - PEE PANTS BOULDER

Sitting right next to Castaway is an attractive looking boulder with an obvious dihedral and an arête.

### 50. I Peed My Pants in Chalk*** v6 (Pads)
This aesthetic arête was first climbed around 2001 and promptly lost to obscurity. SDS on the obvious flake jug and pinch your way up the amazing arête to a final deadpoint move to the lip that may soil your drawers.
FA: M. Auldridge, B. Scott

## O - MAST BOULDER

The Mast Boulder sits about 50 yards south or downstream of the Castaway Boulder. This massive bloc hosts a collection of taller problems on good stone.

### 51. Walk the Plank v8 (Pads)
Start in the cave hole and do the hardest moves right off the start. Juggy moves lead to a drop-off once your on the slab.
FA: S. Rothstein

### 52. Galleon** v6 (Pads)
Stand start on a big jug rail and launch into a sea of slopey edges and sidepulls into the committing finish.
FA: R. Nelson, Ben Jurenka

### 53. Full Mast*** v9 (4-5 Pads)
A very proud and aesthetic line that is not for the faint of heart. Do the crux of Walk the Plank but head directly up the wall into Half Mast.
FA: K. Worobec

### 54. Half-Mast** v6 (4-5 Pads)
An insane highball with little or no room for error. Start on jugs and climb into small edges all the way to the lip.
FA: K. Worobec

### 55. Crow's Nest*** v6 (Pads)
Another aesthetic line on a boulder with a bunch of them. Stand start and do a few compression moves to gain a jug. Launch into the heady but easier romp up the tall arête.
FA: B. Jurenka

Cam Shubb working the first section of **White Stripe**\*\*\* **v8**   Photo: B. Scott

# PRIONE

**41.3 MILES** FROM TED'S PLACE

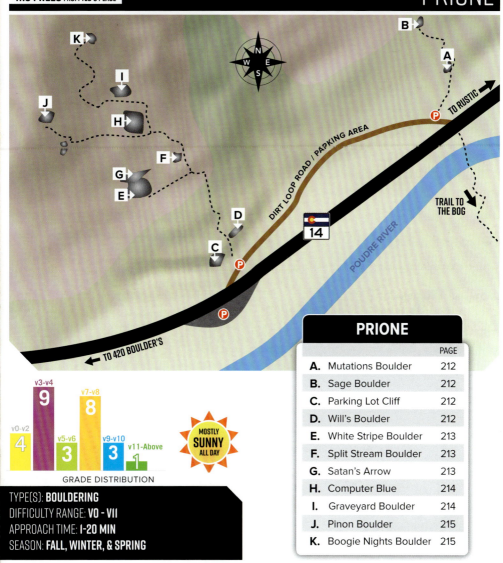

| | PRIONE | PAGE |
|---|---|---|
| A. | Mutations Boulder | 212 |
| B. | Sage Boulder | 212 |
| C. | Parking Lot Cliff | 212 |
| D. | Will's Boulder | 212 |
| E. | White Stripe Boulder | 213 |
| F. | Split Stream Boulder | 213 |
| G. | Satan's Arrow | 213 |
| H. | Computer Blue | 214 |
| I. | Graveyard Boulder | 214 |
| J. | Pinon Boulder | 215 |
| K. | Boogie Nights Boulder | 215 |

**TYPE(S): BOULDERING**
**DIFFICULTY RANGE: V0 - VII**
**APPROACH TIME: 1-20 MIN**
**SEASON: FALL, WINTER, & SPRING**

MOSTLY SUNNY ALL DAY

## CLIMBING OVERVIEW

Prione is a cluster of large boulders spilling out of a talus field. The rock quality is excellent for the most part with its compact dark black gneiss split by pegmatite and quartz veins. The area is remarkably close to the popular Bliss S.W.A. / 420 Boulders, and has been explored by lots of climbers over the years. **Colin Horvat**'s excellent problem Graveyard Machine was one of the first established problems whose history stuck. After that, **Brian Camp** and **Jason Nadeau** began a more serious phase of development where the majority of the problems like Computer Blue and the Pinon Boulder were cleaned and developed.

## GETTING THERE

**GPS: 40°42'37.51"N 105°44'56.57"W**

From Ted's Place, drive 41.3 miles up the canyon to a dirt loop road / pullout on the west side of Hwy 14. This is also the same pullout used for The Bog. Most of the climbing is found by using a faint trail at the south side of the loop road. The Parking Lot Cliff and Will's Boulder are the easiest landmarks to get you started.

POUDRE CANYON GUIDE - 3RD EDITION   **211**

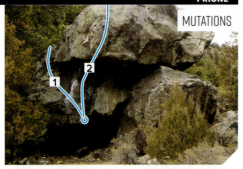

## A - MUTATIONS BOULDER

Located off on its own on the north side of the dirt loop road is this stellar block of black gneiss. Not much of a trail but it's about 50 yards from the road.

**1. ○ Last Past** v9 (Pads)
SDS under the roof on a flat undercling and do some thuggy moves to a sloper before engaging the hard mantle left.
FA: B. Camp

**2. ○ Mutations* v10** (Pads)
Start the same as Last Past, but from the sloper move right on edges and engage the tricky final bulge/roof.
FA: C. Horvat

## B - SAGE BOULDER

From the Mutations Boulder, walk uphill, vaguely following the edge of the talus field until you come to this large, dark grey boulder. Sage is on the upstream side (not pictured).

**3. ○ Sage*** v8** (Pads)
Another Horvat classic on immaculate stone. SDS on obvious holds near the arête. Slap and compress your way up the feature to a final big move to a slopey flat hold.
FA: C. Horvat

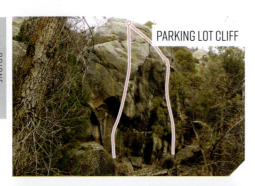

## C - PARKING LOT CLIFF

This obvious chunk of stellar rock sits right off the dirt loop road. A couple lines have been cleaned and attempted on a rope but none of the lines have ever successfully been sent. There is a bolted anchor on top for easy top-roping.

## D - WILL'S BOULDER

A classic boulder with perfect landings and amazing rock. Originally climbed on by Will Lemaire back in the early 2000s, this great moderate boulder has largely snuck under the radar. Located just up the hill from the Parking Lot Cliff.

**4. ○ Old Luke** v2** (Pads)
Super fun climbing near the arête with an easy but commiting top half. Start on a cool right-hand pinch.
FA: W. Lemaire

**5. ○ Left Variation* v3** (Pads)
A variation start to Old Frenchy with nice big edges that lead up and right into the same topout.
FA: W. Lemaire

**6. ○ Old Frenchy*** v3** (Pads)
Such a fun climb up the center of the boulder with a nice flat landing. Start on jugs and climb the groove/crack to a funny little mantle before an easy topout.
FA: W. Lemaire

**7. ○ Right Variation* v3** (Pads)
Start the same as Old Frenchy but move up and right on crimps to hard move off a sidepull, easy topout.
FA: W. Lemaire

**8. ○ Pinch Jump** v6** (Pads)
Start on another obvious jug and do a big move to a big sloping rail. Another huge move to a pinch followed by a really hard highstep gets you to the ledge and an easy mantle.
FA: W. Lemaire

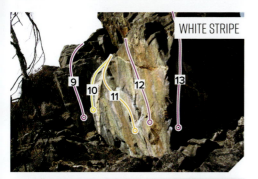

## E - WHITE STRIPE BOULDER

From Will's Boulder, walk up the cairned trail until you reach this massive buried boulder that looks more like a cliff. Identified by a large white pegmatite vein. A great sunny warm-up area with a nice variety of grades and styles.

**9. ○ Murky Waters*** v3 (Pads)
SDS and climb into some cool rail jugs. A big move up and left takes you to a long mellow ramble to the top.
FA: N. Perl

**10. ○ Black Arête* v1 (Pads)
Stand start and squeeze your way up to big jugs. You can traverse left into Murky Waters for an easy topout.
FA: C. Shubb

**11. ○ White Stripe*** v8 (Pads)
SDS at the base of the seam and climb up and left on an interesting series of sloper dishes and bighter crimps.
FA: B. Scott

**12. ○ Tangerine Sky*** v4 (Pads)
Start standing with an undercling and the right arête. Climb up the beautiful seam feature to a tricky crux moving left to a big jug and easy topout.
FA: B. Scott

**13. ○ Little Stripes** v3 (Pads)
SDS on the arête and climb excellent rock on slopers and pinches to a weird move at mid-height to gain more jugs and the long easy topout.
FA: C. Shubb

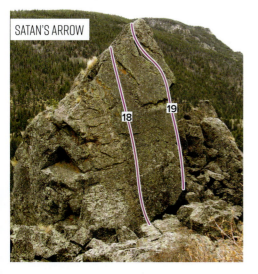

## F - SPLIT STREAM BOULDER

Located near the White Stripe Boulder. This overhanging boulder has nice stone and a couple nice problems.

**14. ○ Split Stream* v6 (4-5 Pads)
Start on a nice incut jug and move up the slopey rail until you can jump to the horn jug. Awkward tiered landing.
FA: B. Scott

**15. ○ Open Project** (Pads)
Underclings to a big move to horrendous slopers.
FA: Open Project

**16. ○ Undercling Arête* v3 (Pads)
Compress the arête and climb a few moves into some obvious underclings and a casual topout.
FA: B. Scott

*Just below the Split Stream Boulder is a small boulder with an obvious triangle-shaped roof.*

**17. ○ Triangle** v2 (Pads)
Start on jugs and do a hard move to the arête followed by a nice juggy topout.
FA: B. Scott

## G - SATAN'S ARROW

This huge spire like boulder sits just above the White Stripe Boulder. There is a bolted anchor on top if you want to inspect either of the huge highballs that are established on it.

**18. ○ The Dark Tower** v3 (4-5 Pads)
This boulder was cleaned, prepped, then F.A.'d by accident. Climb the intimidating green slab on edges for days.
FA: Aaron Ramras, Max Bradley

**19. ○ Shadow's Edge* v3 (4-5 Pads)
The arête is a nice warm-up for the more intimidating center line. Move up the arête until you can foot traverse across the angling crack to the topout. Spicy.
FA: R. Nelson

**20. ○ Bon Voyage** v2 (Pads)
Around the corner to the right of the main face is an interesting hole in the talus that contains this fun moderate.
FA: J. Tarry, R. Nelson

Michael Englestad focused on a big move on **Computer Blue*** v9   Photo: E. Page

COMPUTER BLUE

## H - COMPUTER BLUE BOULDER

The largest boulder in the talus field holds some really interesting conglomerate rock. Dark greyish-blue gneiss is spider webbed with quartz and pegmatite dikes.

### 21. ⊙ Computer Blue*** v9 (Pads)
SDS on a small right-hand pocket and a slopey edge. The first big move to a left-hand may be the hardest move. From here, head right around the roof and up the seam to a chunky ledge. The F.A. dropped off here but the full topout up the short finger crack is considered the full problem.
FA: J. Nadeau, Full Topout: J. Thompson, K. Worobec

### 22. ⊙ American Spirit** v7 (Pads)
SDS variation to Computer Blue on fun pinches and slopey holds to the same topout.
FA: J. Nadeau

### 23. ⊙ H.A.L.** v7 (Pads)
Heuristically programmed ALgorithmic computer. The evil little brother of Computer Blue. Start on an obvious jug edge and climb deceptively tricky moves though slopey edges over a scary knife blade boulder. Finish on the same finger-crack topout as for Computer Blue.
FA: B. Scott

GRAVEYARD

## I - GRAVEYARD BOULDER

This excellent boulder is located in the talus field just above the Computer Blue Boulder.

### 24. ⊙ Graveyard Machine*** v8 (Pads)
Stellar movement and excellent rock out this steep bulge. Start on an undercling feature and move up through slopey crimps and the awesome arête pinch. The move to the lip is the deceptively tricky crux.
FA: C. Horvat

## J - PINON BOULDER

To locate this boulder, start at the Computer Blue Boulder and walk across the talus field in the up-stream direction. It is hiding on the edge of the talus, about a five minute walk.

### 25. ○ Filth Pig* v6 (Pads)
SDS on an obvious edge and climb up through tricky slopers to a walk-off to the left.
FA: B. Camp, J. Nadeau

### 26. ○ Corn Sacker** v7 (Pads)
SDS on a rounded blob and move left to a sharp undercling. A hard move gains the lip and traverse back right for a classic mantle onto the slab.
FA: B. Camp, J. Nadeau

### 27. ○ Pinon** v8 (Pads)
SDS on a rounded blob and stand into underclings and perform a reachy move up and right to the lip.
FA: B. Camp, J. Nadeau

## K - BOOGIE NIGHTS BOULDER

This boulder can be tricky to locate. From Graveyard Boulder walk upstream towards Pinon Boulder, but after 50 yards turn and walk directly uphill. The boulder is hiding behind and above a large cedar tree.

### 28. ○ Boogie Nights*** v11 (Pads)
A long standing Brian Camp project that climbs a nice overhang with an infamous protruding black dike feature. Start low on white crimps and move to the pocket flake before engaging the black dike feature which ends with a perfect jug and easy mantle.
FA: S. Rothstein

### 29. ○ Disco Biscuit v7 (Pads)
Start on some quartz crystal underclings and squeeze your way out the compression feature.
FA: S. Rothstein

Nick Perl on the rad triangle pinch of **Graveyard Machine*** V8  Photo: B. Scott

Jason Tarry on the **Eukie Extension**\*\*\* **13a**  Photo: B. Scott

**41.5 MILES** FROM TED'S PLACE

# VISTA CRAG

**TYPE(S): SPORT & TRAD**
**DIFFICULTY RANGE: 5.11 - 5.14B**
**APPROACH TIME: 30 - 45 MIN**
**SEASON: SPRING, FALL & WINTER**

## CLIMBING OVERVIEW

Creamy white calcite covered granite and bright orange streaks make Vista Crag some of the prettiest rock in the canyon. However, climbing at Vista Crag tends to be very strenuous and hard for the grade. The drive is far, the hike is long and steep, but the rock quality and the views make it all worth it. If you like hard sport climbing on the best rock in the canyon, Vista Crag is waiting for you.

## GETTING THERE

GPS: 40°42'42.14"N 105°45'19.68"W

From Ted's Place, drive 41.5 miles up the canyon and park in a small pullout on either side of the road at a green gate with a DOW sign. **DO NOT PARK IN FRONT OF THE ACCESS GATE AND BE SURE TO PARK COMPLETELY OFF THE HIGHWAY.** If the parking lot is full, a larger pullout with ample space can be found about 0.2 miles farther up the road. A faint but cairned trail switchbacks up the hillside eventually traversing back across to Vista Crag itself.

### 1. ○ Streaky Open Project (4 Bolts)
This project is broken into two distinct sections by a ledge. The first half climbs a beautiful, technical slab on black and orange streaked rock. The second section climbs a steep, short overhang involving a huge move to a pinch flake.
**Bolted by B. Scott**

### 2. ○ Big Bad Beav** 11c (9 Bolts)
Originally done as a trad route, this climb was retro bolted (with the F.A.'s permission). Start with a tricky section on blocky rock involving handjams and tricky body positions. The second half of the route above the ledge climbs an incredible series of seams, pinches, and even a granite tufa to the anchor.
**FA: B. Beavers**

### 3. ○ Vista Cruiser*** 11b (7 Bolts)
The first established line at the crag. Climb the obvious left-facing white dihedral with a tricky mantle crux at Bolt 2 followed by continuous corner climbing to the anchor.
**FA: B. Scott**

Zach Lerner snagging the coveted F.A. of **Creme De La Poudre*** 14b   Photo: B. Scott

### 7. Eukie Extension*** 13a (14 Bolts)
From the chains of Easy Eukie, engage a tricky layback feature right off the ledge. At the end of the layback flake, do a big move left (crux) followed by more 5.12 climbing to the anchor at the top of the wall.
**FA: J. Tarry**

### 8. Eukie Arête** 13b (8 Bolts)
Eukie Arête is a slightly contrived line that starts on Easy Eukie. Climb Easy Eukie until you pass the mantle after the chain draw. From here, move right to a jug at the base of a short orange arête. Compression climbing leads to a deadpoint to the top of the arête.
**FA: J. Tarry**

### 9. Creme de la Poudre*** 14b (9 Bolts)
This is one of the most obvious and sought after lines at the cliff. The rock is reminiscent of Mt. Arapiles or the Grampians in Australia. Climb an easy intro section to the jugs at Bolt 3. From here, you're stuck with an incredibly slopey right-hand layback rail and a few miserable left-hand holds. It is still probably 5.13a through the last bolt or two after the crux.
**FA: Z. Lerner**

### 10. Slippery Slope*** 13c (12 Bolts)
Start on some tricky slab terrain to the horizontal break. A tricky bulge gets you to more jugs at the start of the crux. Slap your way up a compression feature to the horizontal seam. Do a big move to the chiseled slot followed by some incredibly technical and balancy dihedral work (crux). After resting on the ramp above the crux, get ready for the final "5.12 punch it move" to gain the top of the wall and the chains. There are two manufactured holds on this route.
**FA: B. Scott**

### 4. Vista Cruiser Extension*** 12c (13 Bolts)
Climb Vista Cruiser to the anchor and get a full rest. From here, climb into the base of the roof, and do a very tricky sequence to get up and around it. Continuous 5.12 climbing in a steep dihedral leads to the anchor.
**FA: B. Scott**

### 5. Straw Into Gold*** 13d (14 Bolts)
The first section of this route is a fantastic 5.12b in its own right. There is a bail biner at the end of this section. From the no-hands rest below the big roof, do a tricky move to gain the big horizontal. From here, continue on edges moving up then left then back up and right again to the incredible headwall.
**FA: B. Scott**

### 6. Easy Eukie*** 12a (8 Bolts)
Climb the incredible overhanging flakes to a crux mantle above the chain draw. Continue up the corner to a final crux before the ledge/anchors. The first section of this route to the chain draw is the preferred warm-up at the crag at 5.11c.
**FA: J. Tarry**

### 11. Schwagn Wagon* 11c (10 Bolts)
Climb easy terrain to Bolt 3. Move right up a short crack, then hand traverse back left to Bolt 4 (crux). Climb the obvious corner all the way to the ledge.
**FA: D. McKee, B. Scott**

### 12. Three Ring Circus* 12 (GEAR)
Start up a dirty crack or the first two bolts of Schwagn Wagon to gain a ledge, then delicately climb a short, broken section before pulling the crux and enjoying the steep, right-leaning crack to the top.
**FA: C. Cross**

### 13. Pocket Talk** 12c (10 Bolts)
Start by climbing a short moderate wall to the ramp/ledge. Once you reach the steep wall, engage the massive hueco feature, and climb up into the top of Three Ring Circus.
**FA: B. Scott, D. Yager**

**41.5 MILES** FROM TED'S PLACE

# 420 BOULDERS

Puffing Stone and the Balance Boulder   Photo: B. Scott

GRADE DISTRIBUTION

AM SUN / PM SHADE

**TYPE(S): BOULDERING**
**DIFFICULTY RANGE: V0 - V13**
**APPROACH TIME: 10-20 MIN**
**SEASON: YEAR ROUND**

## CLIMBING OVERVIEW

The 420 Boulders offer some of the best bouldering in the Poudre Canyon. The rock is impeccable granite and there is a high concentration of problems of all grades, including several of the hardest problems in the area. Although the area can be a bit buggy in the summer time, the 420s stay climbable nearly year round and are a must-see for any rock climber. The bouldering at the 420s falls within the boundary of the Bliss State Wildlife Area (S.W.A.) and is managed by the D.O.W.

The Tilt/Divergence section of the 420 Boulders is extremely close to private property. Please do not trespass on any private property or climb on the Kingpin Boulder. This has been the site of many confrontations between climbers and landowners. Please do not jeopardize future access and leave the Kingpin Boulder off your radar.

**RESTRICTIONS**
- No Camping
- No Fires
- Dogs must be leashed unless being used for hunting purposes
- Do not interfere with hunters or fisherman
- No Paintball

Matt Tschohl on the classic **Canopener**\*\*\* **v11**   Photo: G. Moser

## GETTING THERE

**GPS: 40°42'21.45"N 105°45'30.13"W**
The 420 Boulders are found along Hwy 14, about 41.5 miles from Ted's Place. A small pullout on either side of the road and a green gate with a DOW sign mark the entrance to the 420 Boulders. **DO NOT PARK IN FRONT OF THE ACCESS GATE AND BE SURE TO PARK COMPLETELY OFF THE HIGHWAY.** If the parking lot is full, a larger pullout with ample space can be found about 0.2 miles farther up the road. From the closed green DOW gate, walk up the old dirt road/trail approx. 0.5 miles to Hank's Boulder.

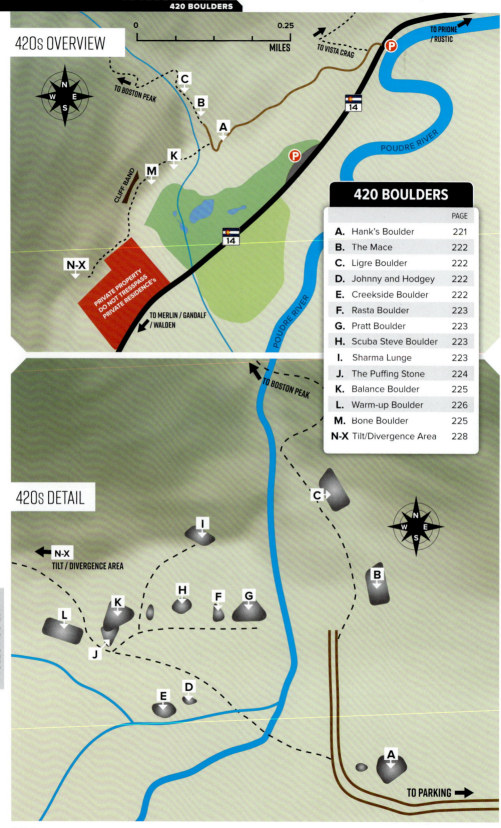

Hank's Boulder in January 2018

Hank's Boulder in May 2018

## A - HANK'S BOULDER

This was the first boulder you came to as you walked in from the road. It sat like a beacon in an aspen grove and signaled the beginning of the main 420s area.

On the morning of Wednesday May 16th, 2018, climbers Chris Neal and Chris Majerczyk were warming-up on Hank's Boulder. Visiting from South Carolina, these two guys enjoyed the last two sends ever of Hank's Arête before moving on to the Balance Boulder. Approx. 45min later, they came back to find Hank's Boulder lying on its face in the mud. A brush with death that most boulderers would never dream possible.

Several weeks of rain resulted in the base of the boulder being turned into a mud pool. Coupled with a flooding creek and the fact that the boulder was basically an upside down triangle, gravity finally sent the boulder flat on it's face. I have included the problems and descriptions for history's sake, even though these problems will never be climbed again.

**1. Auldridge Jump Problem\* v2** (Pads)
As seen in SoLuTiOnS: run and jump off the graffiti covered rock and launch for the lip of Hank's Boulder near the topout of One Ton Ho.
FA: M. Auldridge

**2. One Ton Ho\*\* v8** (Pads)
This excellent compression problem climbs the southeast arête of Hank's Boulder, moving slightly right at the top. Classic moves and great rock.
FA: J. Shambo

**3. Scarface\*\*\* v6** (Pads)
Begin on a flat edge and follow a series of crimps up and slightly left. A must-do and trademark Poudre climb.
FA: J. Shambo

**4. Public Property v11** (Pads)
Start on Scarface but move up and right to the top.
FA: Paul Robinson

Mike Auldridge on the dyno variation to **Sloper Jumpstart\*\*\* v1** circa: 2001
Photo: B. Scott

**5. Sloper Jumpstart\*\*\* v1** (Pads)
Jump to the obvious slopers in the middle of the face and topout. A fun warm-up. Can also be done as a massive dyno to the lip of the boulder as Mike Auldridge is demonstrating.
FA: H. Jones

**6. Hank's Arête\*\* v5** (Pads)
SDS on the boulder's north arête. Slap up the arête to a delicate topout.
FA: H. Jones

**7. Hank's Lunge\*\*\* v5** (Pads)
Grab a crimp sidepull and small sloper, then huck to a perfect lip jug. Technical and an absolute must-do. A SDS begins on the Unnamed Moderate, then traverses up and left into the regular problem.
FA: H. Jones

**8. Unnamed Moderate\* v3** (Pads)
Begin as for the SDS to Hank's Lunge, but head straight up. Take care not to impale yourself on the large nails sticking out of the pine tree.
FA: H. Jones

## B - THE MACE

Follow the faint dirt road uphill (50 yards+/-) from Hank's Boulder to reach The Mace and the Ligre Boulder. Both boulders have several classic lines that are well worth your time and skin.

**9.** ○ **Moderate on Left Face*** v2 (Pads)
Start on an obvious edge and move up and left onto the slab.
FA: R. Anglemeyer

**10.** ○ **The Mace**** v3 (Pads)
Stand start by standing on top of a boulder and grabbing obvious crimps before reaching straight up. A lower start (v8) begins by establishing on two micro crimps before moving into the stand start holds.
FA: P. Goodman, J. Shambo

**11.** ○ **Mr. Harry**** v4 (Pads)
The classic center line up the face. Stand start on the flat edge and move through a gaston to a rad slopey mantle.
FA: B. Scott

**12.** ○ **Poudre Arête**** v9 (Pads)
Grab sharp crimps and heel-hook through the crux, finishing straight up.
FA: A. Di Felice

## C - LIGRE BOULDER

To reach the Ligre Boulder, walk uphill from the Mace Boulder following the creek for approx. 50 yards.

**13.** ○ **The Ligre**** v7 (4-5 Pads)
Slap up the left arête before moving to a high crux on slopers at lip. Fantastic all the way.
FA: B. Scott

**14.** ○ **Will's Slab**** v10 (4-5 Pads)
Climb the delicate slab to the left of the tree. Highball and still unrepeated at time of writing.
FA: W. Lemaire

**15.** ○ **Hank's Other Arête**** v3 (Pads)
Layback up the knife-edge arête on the right side of the tree.
FA: H. Jones

## D - JOHNNY & HODGEY BOULDER

From Hank's Boulder, follow the well-beaten trail through the aspen trees, across the creek and into the woods. Johnny and Hodgey is the triangle-shaped boulder next to the trail.

**16.** ○ **Johnny & Hodgey**** v5 (Pads)
Establish on the slopey left arête before making a hard jump to the jug lip. You can SDS too for a couple extra points.
FA: B. Scott

**17.** ○ **Right Arête*** v0 (Pads)
Cruise up the right arête. A fun warmup.
FA: R. Anglemeyer

## E - CREEKSIDE BOULDER

Just behind Johnny and Hodgey is a nice boulder next to the stream that hosts many moderates. There are many variations and contrivances that provide a relaxing warm-up session.

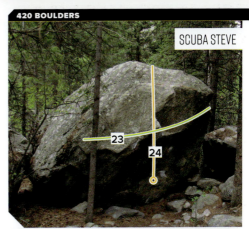

## F - RASTA BOULDER

To reach the Rasta and Pratt Boulders from Johnny and Hodgey, continue on the trail toward the main area for 20 yards, then turn right (east). The Rasta Boulder sits just before the Pratt Boulder, an obvious house-sized block visible through the trees.

**18.** ○ **Rasta Font Trainer**\*\* **v7** (Pads)
A classic lowball that begins on the left edge of the boulder before traversing right then up a shallow seam.
FA: H. Feissner

**19.** ○ **Grey Matter**\*\* **v9** (Pads)
Same start as Rasta Font Trainer, but continue traversing right across the lip to the right side of the boulder.
FA: B. Camp

## G - PRATT BOULDER

**20.** ○ **Unnamed**\* **v0** (Pads)
Begin left of the Flesh Eater arête. Climb up and left on jugs.
FA: R. Anglemeyer

**21.** ○ **Flesh Eater**\*\* **v5** (Pads)
This line ascends the blunt southeastern corner of the Pratt Boulder on flat crimps and pinches.
FA: P. Goodman

**22.** ○ **Chucky**\*\* **v5** (Pads)
Head straight up the middle of the face on this horrifying highball slab.
FA: P. Goodman

## H - SCUBA STEVE BOULDER

The Scuba Steve Boulder sits midway between the Rasta Boulder and the Balance Boulder. Scuba Steve is the most popular problem on the boulder and may be found on the west face.

**23.** ○ **Ben's Craptastic Traverse**\* **v5** (Pads)
Begin on a jug on the far left side of the boulder's west face. Traverse right, through Scuba Steve, before topping out on the right arête.
FA: B. Scott

**24.** ○ **Scuba Steve**\* **v7** (Pads)
Begin on two underclings and make a big move to a good edge or sidepull. Exponentially harder the shorter you are.
FA: Chris Way, J. Shambo

**25.** ○ **Unnamed**\* **v4** (Pads)
Start low on a left-hand crimp, right-hand pinch, then crank to better edges. Also good as a stand start.
FA: R. Anglemeyer

**26.** ○ **Unnamed**\* **v3** (Pads)
Crimp your way up the left part of the east face.
FA: R. Anglemeyer

## I - SHARMA LUNGE

From the Balance Boulder, walk 30 yards northeast on a faint path toward the hillside. The Sharma Lunge is found on a perfect granite block sitting by itself, next to a small pine tree.

**27.** ○ **What's Left of the Bottom of My Heart**\*\* **v12** (Pads)
SDS just left of Sharma Lunge and make hard moves left to the arête feature, with a tricky heel move to gain the lip of the boulder.
FA: Chris Schulte

**28.** ○ **Sharma Lunge**\*\*\* **v9** (Pads)
Established by Chris on the same day he would go on to do the F.A. of Kingpin\*\*\*\* v12. Grab the highest right-hand pinch and a left-hand sidepull, then huck to the perfect lip. One of the most stellar lines at the 420s.
FA: Chris Sharma

# 420 BOULDERS

PUFFING STONE

## J - THE PUFFING STONE

The Puffing Stone is an excellent small boulder that the Balance Boulder leans on. Named after the "rock pipe" that was drilled into the start of the problem F.A.S.T. Great rock and cool slopers are the norm here.

### 29. Easy Arête** v2 (Pads)
This super fun moderate ascends the left arête of the Puffing Stone with nice moves on excellent rock. One of the best for the grade.
FA: H. Jones

### 30. Puffing Stone*** v5 (Pads)
A must-do moderate classic. Begin on flat edges just to the left of the obvious rail system, then head up and left on fun, gymnastic moves.
FA: P. Goodman

### 31. F.A.S.T. ** v7 (Pads)
(a.k.a. Fun Ass Stoner Traverse)
Begin on the jug in the corridor between the Puffing Stone and the Balance Boulder (just past the rock pipe). Traverse left out the lip to the corner, then drop down into Puffing Stone to finish it off. An easier variation traverses the lip all the way to the top without dropping into Puffing Stone.
FA: B. Scott

### 32. Herm's Micro Mantle* v7 (Pads)
The Poudre's smallest and quite possibly most technical mantle problem. Begin laying down on the blunt prow opposite Short Chubby Demon, grab the left sidepull and begin pressing. Almost guaranteed to give you either better technique or a bruised knee and ego.
FA: H. Feissner

## K - BALANCE BOULDER

The Balance Boulder beckons to climbers from all over the world. This perfect diamond-shaped boulder hovers magically off the ground with support from its two adjacent neighbors. An aura looms around this boulder much like the forest it resides in. Incredible rock quality and an unbelievably diverse collection of problems make this one of the best boulders in the entire Poudre Canyon. This is the boulder that started it all for me; after Pat Goodman and I found this rock I knew I was committed to finding all the other awesome rocks and cliffs this canyon has to offer.

Sam Rothstein going to battle on **Circadian Rhythm** *** v13  Photo: V. Aspinall

# 420 BOULDERS

BALANCE - SOUTH

BALANCE - WEST

### 33. ○ Circadian Rhythm*** v13 (Pads)
Currently the hardest established problem in the Poudre, Circadian Rhythm follows powerful and tensiony moves that lead up a deceptively steep wall on the Balance Boulder's northeast face. The only diminishing part of the line is its close proximity to the Puffing Stone Boulder, otherwise it is a beautiful climb on perfect rock.
FA: Dave Graham

### 34. ○ Swiss Army** v13 (Pads)
Just to the right of Circadian Rhythm is a series of impossible looking slopers on the lip of a bulge. Originally done as a jumpstart by Johnny Goicoechea and given the name One Man Army v9, it has since been done by a lower/static start that increases the grade dramatically.
FA: Z. Lerner

### 35. ○ It's Ice** v4 (Pads)
Squeeze two pinches and start slapping your way to the top. Powerful and uber classic.
FA: P. Goodman

### 36. ○ Moderate* v4 (Pads)
Follow nicely cut edges between It's Ice and Hickman Over the Poudre Bridge. Excellent angled rail features on this one.
FA: R. Anglemeyer

### 37. ○ Hickman Over the Poudre Bridge* v8 (Pads)
Start as for Stickman Crossing the Brooklyn Bridge, but head left out the short bulge.
FA: P. Goodman

### 38. ○ Stickman Crossing the Brooklyn Bridge* v8 (Pads)
SDS at the bottom of the "V" on the right arête. Move up the right arête before stepping back left onto the face. Deceptively technical.
FA: H. Feissner

### 39. ○ Canopener*** v11 (Pads)
The epic center line on the back of the Balance Boulder. An open dihedral of perfect stone in an enchanting setting. SDS in the cave on a large edge and move into the dihedral for lots of technical body tension moves. Legendary.
FA: W. Lemaire

### 40. ○ Right-hand Man** v4 (Pads)
Jumpstart to the large jug near the end of Canopener. Do a large move right to the notch in the arête, match, then perform an excellent mantle right up the scoop.
FA: J. Bisher

### 41. ○ Unnamed* v8 (Pads)
Start right-hand on Short Chubby Demon crimp, but move straight up, finishing on Right-hand Man. Another seldom done problem but excellent and powerful in its own right.
FA: Chris Way

### 42. ○ Short Chubby Demon*** v6 (Pads)
Start with a left-hand crimp and a right-hand sidepull on the face. Slap to the arête and paddle your way to the top. Named after an unpopular roommate at the time.
FA: J. Bisher

## WARM-UP - WEST

## L - WARM-UP BOULDER

The Warm-up Boulder is found just past the Puffing Stone and Balance Boulder, next to a creek bed. It has a variety of excellent climbs of different grades, which makes it a great place for warming up or for groups with varying abilities.

**43. ○ Perch** v6** (Pads)
SDS from the jug on the northwest corner. Go up the left side of arête without using any of the jug holds to the right. Fun and worthwhile.
FA: J. Bisher

**44. ○ Warm Me*** v3** (Pads)
Same start as Perch, but stay right on good holds. Excellent for the grade.
FA: R. Anglemeyer

**45. ○ Middle Up** v2** (Pads)
Begin just to the right of the tree on two good crimps in the crack. Crank straight up.
FA: R. Anglemeyer

**46. ○ Moderate Straight Up* v1** (Pads)
Just to the right of Middle Up. Start in the crack and move up to obvious holds.
FA: R. Anglemeyer

**47. ○ Bisher Traverse*** v7** (Pads)
Follow the obvious seam from left to right, beginning on the start hold of Perch and finishing on the southwest arête. A classic for folks who like crimping, smearing, and going sideways for days.
FA: J. Bisher

**48. ○ Southwest Arête* v3** (Pads)
Squeeze your way up the arête. The SDS is hard and sharp, but the stand start is enjoyable and a good warm-up. A fun variation is to start on the south face and traverse into the arête via the slopey lip.
FA: R. Anglemeyer

**49. ○ South Face** v3** (Pads)
Grab a good edge in the middle of the face and reach to a sidepull on impeccable rock. Finish straight up without getting tangled in the tree.
FA: R. Anglemeyer

**50. ○ Angle Dangle** v3** (Pads)
This interesting roof problem can be quite devious and involves some good trickery. SDS on good holds at a lip, then go up and slightly right to finish. A number of variations exist, but the right finish is the best.
FA: R. Anglemeyer

**WARM-UP - EAST**

**51. ○ Unnamed* v2 (Pads)**
Begin on the obvious crimps just to the right of the downclimb. Edge your way straight up to the top of another great warm-up. This route also shares the same start holds as the Tsunami traverse.
FA: R. Anglemeyer

**52. ○ Tsunami Traverse** v8 (Pads)**
Start on the low, obvious edge for the previous route, then traverse right into Tsunami. Fun line.
FA: B. Scott

**53. ○ Tsunami** v6 (Pads)**
From two edges on the face, reach right and finish up the arête.
FA: B. Scott

## M - BONE BOULDER

From the main Balance Boulder area, walk along the trail leading south toward the Tilt/Divergence area. Directly after the trail passes through a section of deadfall logs, you will see a couple of slabby boulders on the left (east) side. Several fun slab climbs are on these boulders. Bone Boulder is just past the slabs on the right, and may be identified by the obvious t-bone feature that forms an arête facing the trail.

**54. ○ T-Bone** v8 (Pads)**
Start at the bottom of the t-bone with a left-hand on the sloper and right-hand on the arête feature. Go straight up.
FA: B. Scott

**55. ○ T-Bone Right** v4 (Pads)**
Start as for T-Bone, but go immediately right into the shallow dihedral feature, then up.
FA: J. Bisher

BONE

# TILT / DIVERGENCE AREA

## GETTING THERE

**GPS: 40°42'10.87"N 105°45'42.73"W**

From T-Bone, continue southwest along the access trail, passing a large cliff wall on your right. Directly after the cliff wall, you will see a short boulder with a cairn on top of it. This is a private property boundary. The trail once crossed into the landowner's property, but it has since been redirected to stay on public land.

## RESTRICTIONS & ACCESS

Stick to the trail and please be respectful when climbing in this area, as it closely borders private land and there have already been issues with trespassing and disrespectful use. The trail passes between two boulders, one of which has several nice climbs, before jogging to the right (west) and eventually leading to Tilt. Follow the cairns and avoid going east toward the cabins and private property. The Kingpin Boulder is fully on private property and completely closed to climbing at this time. The landowners have asked that climbers do NOT approach the boulder or the cabins in the area for any reason.

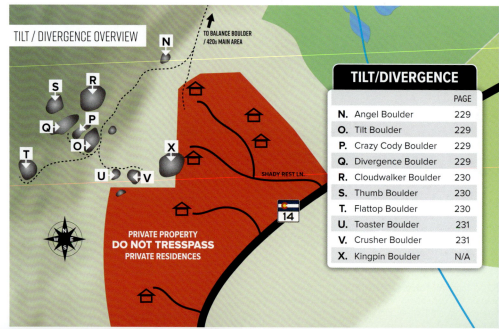

| TILT/DIVERGENCE | | |
|---|---|---|
| | | PAGE |
| N. | Angel Boulder | 229 |
| O. | Tilt Boulder | 229 |
| P. | Crazy Cody Boulder | 229 |
| Q. | Divergence Boulder | 229 |
| R. | Cloudwalker Boulder | 230 |
| S. | Thumb Boulder | 230 |
| T. | Flattop Boulder | 230 |
| U. | Toaster Boulder | 231 |
| V. | Crusher Boulder | 231 |
| X. | Kingpin Boulder | N/A |

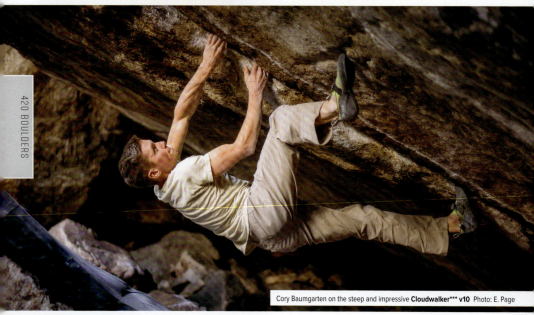

Cory Baumgarten on the steep and impressive **Cloudwalker*** v10  Photo: E. Page

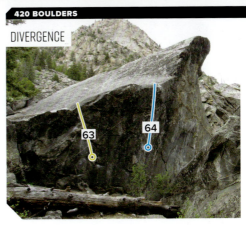

## N - KNIGHT BOULDER

This massive boulder lies right off the trail once you get in the vicinity of the houses.

### 56. ○ When Angels Dance*** v4 (4-5 Pads)
This beautiful triangle-shaped boulder was walked past for years before being climbed. Follow the obvious line of holds up the center of the face to a tricky move before the lip.
FA: R. Nelson

## O - TILT BOULDER

The keystone for this section of the Tilt / Divergence area. Good rock and a nice variety of boulder problems over relatively flat landings.

### 57. ○ Ben's Face v3 (Pads)
Climb the middle of the crimpy face. You can either mantle straight up, or trend a little to the right for a slightly easier finish.
FA: B. Scott

### 58. ○ Ben's Goofy Face** v4 (Pads)
SDS on the large jug near the right arête. Head straight up the crimpy face for a harder version of the previous route.
FA: B. Scott

### 59. ○ Jousting at Windmills** v9 (Pads)
SDS on the same jug as Ben's Goofy Face, then traverse right and finish Tilt. Long and crimpy with a redpoint crux right at the end.
FA: J. Shambo

### 60. ○ Tilt*** v7 (Pads)
Begin on two crimps just under the roof, then follow the shallow seam to the right. A classic and very popular line; one of the best v7s in the canyon.
FA: P. Goodman

### 61. ○ Fire Pit* v8 (Pads)
In the corridor, just around the corner from Tilt, you will find a sidepull just under a roof on the left wall. Begin here and climb up and right to exit in the middle of the face.
FA: W. Lemaire

## P - CRAZY CODY BOULDER

### 62. ○ Crazy Cody** v6 (Pads)
This excellent problem is just past Fire Pit, on the opposite side of the corridor. Begin on the obvious jug and squeeze your way up the arête to an exciting topout. The landing is a bit dodgy and requires a good spotter, but otherwise it is an excellent problem. The problem was named after a psycho cat that tormented the author.
FA: B. Scott

## Q - DIVERGENCE BOULDER

Walk around the Tilt Boulder to the west, then uphill to the Divergence Boulder.

### 63. ○ Moderate Warm-up* v2 (Pads)
Start on the obvious and slightly hollow jug on the wall's left (southwestern) end. Climb up and left for a nice warm up before sacrificing your tips to Divergence.
FA: R. Anglemeyer

### 64. ○ Divergence*** v9 (Pads)
Two types of climbers definitely diverge at this problem—those who can do it and those who can't...most fall into the latter category.
FA: B. Scott, P. Goodman

## R - CLOUDWALKER BOULDER

This gigantic boulder sits teetering almost on the edge of the talus. Amazing for its sheer size alone it only hosts two completed problems to date.

**65.** **Cloudwalker\*\*\* v10** (Pads)
Just around the corner from Divergence, you will find an obvious cave with a beautiful crack splitting it. Another legendary problem from Mr. Graham. A long pumpy sequence up the crack leads to an awkward heart breaker move rolling over the lip.
FA: D. Graham

**66.** **Centerfold\*\* v10** (Pads)
On the downhill side of the Cloudwalker Boulder is a short roof on lookers right. Flat undercling match start, then traverse left on pinches and crimps.
FA: P. Dusatko

## S - THUMB BOULDER

Almost directly west/uphill of Divergence, a large, thumb-like boulder juts out of the talus. Three climbs are found on its west face.

**67.** **Moderate in Hole v4** (Pads)
Crawl out of hole on northwest face of the Thumb Boulder. Awkward landing.
FA: J. Tarry

**68.** **The Thumb\* v6** (Pads)
Start with a right-hand sidepull in the pegmatite, then move up and left out the left arête of the roof. Wild move to a thumb gaston.
FA: W. Lemaire

**69.** **Green Thumb\* v1** (Pads)
Climb the bright green arête, start on the right side.
FA: W. Lemaire

## T - FLATTOP BOULDER

The Flattop Boulder is 40 yards west of Tilt at the end of a faint social trail that takes off from the west side of Tilt. Will's problem is the first problem you will come to.

**70.** **Wipe Out v9** (Pads)
A truly sharp and terrible testpiece. Start low on two tiny holds and crimp your way straight up on anything that works.
FA: A. Di Felice

**71.** **Pegmatite\* v4** (Pads)
Follow pegmatite crimps up and left.
FA: R. Anglemeyer

**72.** **Wave 2\* v5** (Pads)
Begin as for Wave 1, but go left and mantle into V-groove on good holds.
FA: R. Anglemeyer

**73.** **Wave 1\* v7** (Pads)
Start on an obvious jug at waist level, then follow edges up and slightly left before moving right to a difficult finishing sequence. A touch contrived, but fun nonetheless.
FA: R. Anglemeyer

**74.** **Thin 'N' Crispy\*\* v7** (Pads)
From a left-hand on a crimp in the pegmatite and right-hand sidepull, crank up thin edges to a faint arête feature.
FA: P. Goodman

Jeremy Bisher attempting **Deadmoo5**\*\* **V10** back around 2001 when it was still just a project   Photo: B. Scott

**75.** ◉ **Chossy Arête v3** (Pads)
Head up the chossy south arête, 15 feet left of Goldrusher. Not spectacular, but there.
FA: R. Anglemeyer

**76.** ◉ **Goldrusher**\*\* **v6** (Pads)
Begin between two trees on the north face of the Flattop Boulder. Grab two crimps and stand into a flat undercling before moving up and right to the arête/lip to finish.
FA: B. Scott

**77.** ◉ **Will's Problem**\*\* **v5** (Pads)
The first problem you come to if you walk from Divergence or Tilt. Grab two edges at chest height, then chuck to a slopey pinch on the northwest arête.
FA: W. Lemaire

## U - TOASTER BOULDER

This infamous little boulder sits about 50 yards downhill from the Flattop Boulder. This boulder is very close to private property. Be respectful and climb quietly.

**78.** ◉ **The Toaster**\*\*\* **v2** (Pads)
SDS on a cool blocky layback feature. Move into some more blocky laybacks to a couple quartz knobs at the topout.
FA: B. Scott

**79.** ◉ **Diamond Arête**\*\* **v1** (Pads)
On the backside of the Toaster is this incredible arête. So simple in nature but perfect to climb on.
FA: Unknown

**80.** ◉ **Toll Booth Willie**\*\* **v8** (Pads)
Another fun problem on great stone. A series of crimps that is probably easier to just campus.
FA: C. French

## V - CRUSHER BOULDER

The last boulder downhill from Tilt before the Kingpin Boulder. Nice stone and a protected from view uphill face make this worth a visit for any climber.

**81.** ◉ **Crusher**\*\*\* **v5** (Pads)
This little SDS climbs so well it's hard to believe. SDS on a layback block and move up and left to a tricky move gaining the slab. If you head right at the topout, it's slightly harder.
FA: J. Bisher

**82.** ◉ **Deadmoo5**\*\* **v10** (Pads)
Possibly the coolest sloper hold in the entire canyon? This short testpiece has excellent rock and deceptively hard tension/movement. Start crouched on a crimp for the left and a good hold for the right. Move through the friction-dependent sloper to the easy topout.
FA: P. Dusatko

**41.5 MILES** FROM TED'S PLACE

# BOSTON PEAK

GRADE DISTRIBUTION

**TYPE(S): SPORT, TRAD & BOULDERING**
**DIFFICULTY RANGE: 5.8 - 5.14, V0 - V10**
**APPROACH TIME: 45 MIN - 1 HOUR**
**SEASON: FALL, WINTER, & SPRING**

## CLIMBING OVERVIEW

Boston Peak is one of the most obvious and striking features in the Poudre Canyon. A steep, jagged mountain that seems to guard over this breath taking portion of the canyon. With an elevation of 9,363 ft, it is nearly an alpine climbing area. Some unknown local maintains an American Flag at the very summit that is easily visible from Hwy 14.

The earliest known climbing history comes from the adventures of **Steve McCorkel** who began climbing there circa 2010. After Steve established the testpiece **Foreplay/Longtime**\*\*\*\* **13a** he opened up the area to the rest of the climbing community and development continues to this day.

## GETTING THERE

**GPS: 40°42'22.69"N 105°45'54.92"W**
Drive approx. 41.5 miles up the canyon from Ted's Place to the 420 Boulders parking. Follow directions to the Ligre Boulder but continue walking uphill following cairns. Cross the stream on a log bridge and start the slow uphill slog. After about 30min, the cairned trail will traverse back left across the hillside before heading directly uphill again for the final push to the base of the Orange Wall.

Jason Tarry on the stunning **Foreplay/Longtime**\*\*\*\***13a** Photo: B. Scott

# BOSTON PEAK

## ORANGE WALL

## A - ORANGE WALL

Follow directions from the 420 Boulders (page 219) to locate the Ligre Boulder and the start of the Boston Peak trail. Hike up the Boston Peak trail for approx. 45min to one hour to reach the base of the Orange Wall.

### 1. O Callan's Crack**** 12a (5 Bolts + GEAR to #3)
Callan's Crack is a stand-out pitch of incredible face and crack climbing on creamy orange and white granite. Climb some less-than-desirable rock past two bolts to an excellent, left-facing corner. Continue on fun face climbing before the crux traverse moving up and right to the base of the obvious splitter crack straight out of Yosemite.
FA: D. McKee

### 2. O Tea Party*** 13a (10 Bolts)
Does face climbing get much better? Start with a tricky move to gain the ledge above Bolt 1. Continue on punchy 5.12 climbing through the grey stone to reach another ledgy zone. From here, perfect white stone leads into the crux dyno move. Excellent, reachy face climbing above the dyno leads to the anchor.
FA: B. Scott

### 3. O Paul Revere**** 13d (18 Bolts)
Paul Revere is a 42 meter outing on fantastic shapes and colors of really unusual granite. From the Tea Party anchor, move up and right to an angled rail. Perform the crux compression/jump move to a brown jug. Easier climbing leads into the final crux of Cradle of Liberty.
FA: Ethan Pringle

### 4. O Hayden House** 10b (8 Bolts)
The name comes from the famous Boston stop on the Underground Railroad. Start with a nice section of crack climbing on finger-locks and jams. Continue past some ledgy terrain to a short, left-facing corner. Stem your way up, and reach for a just out-of-sight jug.
FA: B. Scott

### 5. O Cradle of Liberty**** 13c (18 Bolts)
Start by climbing Hayden House. From the anchor traverse right to the cruxy undercling flake. Three different cruxes broken up by 5.12 climbing gets you to the anchor. The double-pocket feature could be the best single hold in the canyon.
FA: B. Scott

### 6. O J.F.K.** 12a (12 Bolts)
JFK is an excellent face climb, similar to Departed but less slabby. Climb some ledgy terrain to a hard crux section at Bolt 6. Fun but thought provoking moves gets you to the anchor on the big ledge.
FA: J. Tarry, B. Scott

### 7. O Departed** 12a (12 Bolts)
Departed is another fantastic face and slab climb that will test your fingers and toes. Start with some easy ledgy terrain until the wall starts to steepen. Fun 5.11 climbing leads to a rest near the crack out right. A tricky clip and traverse left leads to a crux move off gastons and bad feet.
FA: E. Pringle, R.D. Pascoe

### 8. O Unknown Crack Route (GEAR)
Climb some ledgy and bushy terrain to the obvious crack ending at a tree. Possibly the oldest route at Boston Peak?
FA: Unknown

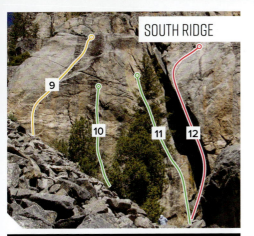

## B - SOUTH RIDGE

Follow directions from the 420 Boulders (page 219) to locate the Ligre Boulder and the start of the Boston Peak trail. Hike up the Boston Peak trail for approx. 45min to one hour to reach the Orange Wall. Continue past the Orange Wall for 10min to reach the South Ridge.

### 9. Freedom Trail** 10b (7 Bolts)
Named after the famous tourist sightseeing walk around Boston, this climb is also for everyone. An initial (V3/4) boulder problem can be skipped by pulling past Bolt 1 to better holds. After the A0 start, continue on big hand holds with slopey feet at times up the obvious rail feature. A final slopey stand up guards the chains.
FA: B. Scott, D. McKee, J. Tarry, P. Hurtgen

### 10. Marky Mark*** 12d (6 Bolts)
Marky Mark is a shorter, power-endurance based route that has a bunch of really technical climbing on rad edges, sidepulls and underclings. Start with big moves on good holds to reach the crux at Bolt 3. A techy highstep leads to a cool sloper and a foot intensive move to a good undercling. A few more strenuous 5.11 moves get you to the anchor.
FA: B. Scott

### 11. How Bout Dem Apples** 12c (7 Bolts)
This is a fun outing on nice rock with lots of edges and some tricky foot work. The hardest move is probably right before Bolt 3, moving off an angled rail to a nice flat edge. Above the ledge, the climbing is slabby but engaging.
FA: B. Scott

### 12. Jolly Jane**** 13a (11 Bolts)
This awesome pillar feature is named after the infamous Massachusetts serial killer who claimed to have killed 33 people. Excellent 5.12 arête climbing leads to a hard crux right before the angle change. Enjoy a nice stance on the vertical wall before launching into the long final slab. This is one of the best slab climbs in the canyon.
FA: B. Scott

### 13. Donnie loves Jenny** 10d (6 Bolts)
This ascends a great little panel of rock that works as an excellent warm-up for the routes near it. Start with good edges to reach the arête feature on the left. A cruxy stand-up move at Bolt 4 leads to easier terrain and the anchor.
FA: R.D. Pascoe, C. Martin

### 14. Poopoo Plater*** 12a (Bolts + GEAR)
P1: Start up broken terrain until you reach a slabby left-facing corner behind a tree.
P2: From the bolted anchor, climb up the left-facing dihedral until you can move onto the face and continue up the bolts.
FA: S. McCorkel

### 15. Pura Aventura*** 11 (GEAR)
This is the famous multi-pitch route up the longest feature on Boston Peak. It involves about five pitches of corner and crack climbing to reach the summit. It is likely un-repeated and details of the individual pitches are unknown.
FA: S. McCorkel

### 16. Sons of Liberty*** 10c (GEAR)
Start on the first pitch of Pura Aventura then climb out the steep and exposed hand and fist crack.
FA: R. Nelson

### 17. Scorsese**** 14c (12 Bolts + GEAR)
Scorsese is a jaw-dropping line on a cliff with a sea of them. It is hard to believe there are actually perfectly sculpted holds up this amazing, overhanging prow of orange, green, and white granite. Start by climbing the first pitch of Pura Aventura. Small gear can be used here on the left crack. From the ledge, climb into an arching finger crack before moving back right to the arête. Launch into the compression crux followed immediately by pumpy 5.13 climbing. Rest up at the final jug before performing the crux dyno to the chains.
FA: E. Pringle

## BOSTON PEAK

***Climber Spotlight:*** Any pre-conceived notion about professional rock climbers you may have had is immediately thrown out the window when you meet Ethan Pringle. Compassionate, caring, and genuinely psyched, climbing with Ethan is always a treat. Ethan came for a visit in the fall of 2017 and fell head first into the bounty of projects waiting at Boston Peak. On his third day of effort, he sent Scorsese**** 14c second go and still had enough energy to get the first ascent of Paul Revere*** 13d that same day.

Ethan Pringle working towards the F.A. of **Scorcese**\*\*\*\* **14c**  Photo: A. Cross

### HALL OF FAME

**18.** ◉ **Tattered Glory\*\*\* 11a** (GEAR)
Located just to the right of the 1st pitch of Pura Aventura. Start below the main ledge with a quick right traverse to gain the short left-facing corner. Above the main ledge the start of the crack is the crux. After the crux the amazing Yosemite style crack leads up the corner and over the bulge to the anchor.
FA: J. Tarry

## C - HALL OF FAME

The quintessential area at Boston Peak is loaded with good rock, striking lines and an incredible setting. Follow directions from the 420 Boulders (page 219) to locate the Ligre Boulder and the start of the Boston Peak trail. Hike up the Boston Peak trail for approx. 45min to one hour to reach the Orange Wall. Continue following the cairned trail for 20min until you have hiked past and above the South Ridge to reach the Hall of Fame. Approx. 1 hour and 15min hiking time.

**19.** ◉ **84 Beacon Street\*\*\* 10b** (2 Bolts + GEAR)
This is named after the address for the iconic Boston bar. Ramble up the slabby/ledgy corner past two bolts until you can step left and up to the foot-ledge at the base of the splitter zig-zag crack. From here, follow the golden crack past finger-locks, edges, and jugs with ample gear placements and a great, exposed finish.
FA: C. Hofer, D. Brown

**20.** ◉ **Mr. Brownstone 10** (GEAR)
Climb the obvious left-facing tan corner to the right of 84 Beacon Street. May or may not have a bolted anchor.
FA: S. McCorkel

**21.** ◉ **Heartbreaker\*\*\* 12** (12 Bolts)
A slab testpiece from McCorkel to the right of the black streak. Start by angling up and right until the slab steepens. A hard 5.12 crux leads to more 5.11 climbing. One hanger up high has been damaged from rockfall.
FA: S. McCorkel

**22.** ◉ **Foreplay/Longtime\*\*\*\* 13a** (14 Bolts)
THE area testpiece for any obsessed sport climber. An easy start leads to a devious crux on the low-angle slab/arête before gaining a no-hands stance. Launch into another 60 ft of crimps and sidepulls on impeccable rock up the striking arête feature.
FA: S. McCorkel

**23.** ◉ **It's Only Rock 10** (GEAR)
Climb the wide corner following seams with ample face holds. There is no fixed anchor at time of writing and a walk-off is required.
FA: S. McCorkel

**24.** ◉ **Bunker Hill\*\* 12b** (6 Bolts)
Start by stemming up between the rock and a tree until you reach a nice stance on the tree to clip Bolt 1. Make a lurch move to gain a jug rail, followed by another big lurch to a sloping rail. A devious technical crux on small feets gets you past Bolt 3 before engaging in awesome 5.11 terrain to the short anchor.
FA: B. Scott

**25.** ◉ **Southie Boyz\*\*\* 13b** (9 Bolts)
It takes an army to build a castle in the sky. This route climbs a stunning pillar feature right in the heart of the Hall of Fame. The difficulties start right from the ground on cool pinches and edges. A tricky crux revolving around a hard move to the "golfball" hold at Bolt 3. Get it all back at Bolt 5 before launching into the incredibly technical and tedious crux traversing to the left arête. Although probably only 5.11, the final few bolts are not to be taken lightly.
FA: B. Scott

**26.** ◉ **Sidewalk Sam\*\*\* 8** (5 Bolts)
Named after the beloved Boston sidewalk chalk artist, this climb follows an excellent panel of rock with a nice touch of exposure. Climb some hollow flakes at the start to a fun romp up crimps and knobs to the chains.
FA: B. Scott

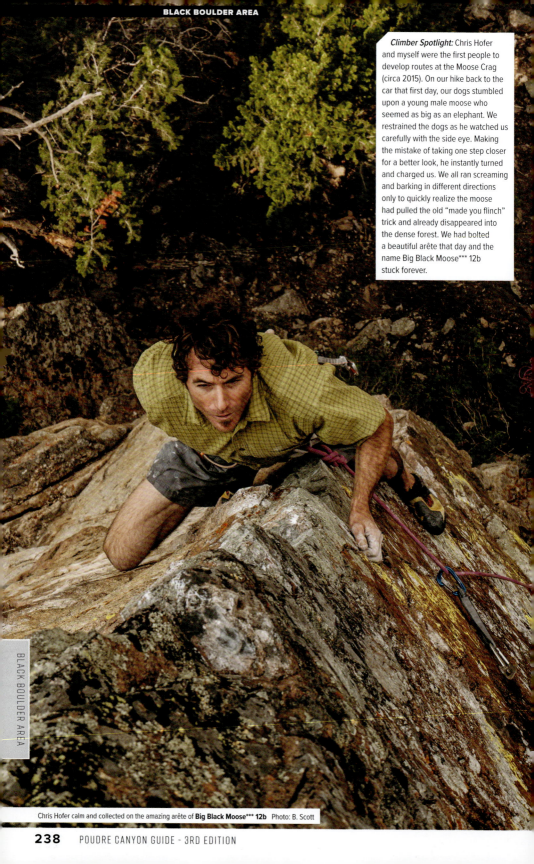

**Climber Spotlight:** Chris Hofer and myself were the first people to develop routes at the Moose Crag (circa 2015). On our hike back to the car that first day, our dogs stumbled upon a young male moose who seemed as big as an elephant. We restrained the dogs as he watched us carefully with the side eye. Making the mistake of taking one step closer for a better look, he instantly turned and charged us. We all ran screaming and barking in different directions only to quickly realize the moose had pulled the old "made you flinch" trick and already disappeared into the dense forest. We had bolted a beautiful arête that day and the name **Big Black Moose*** 12b** stuck forever.

Chris Hofer calm and collected on the amazing arête of **Big Black Moose*** 12b** Photo: B. Scott

**42.7 MILES** FROM TED'S PLACE

# BLACK BOULDER AREA

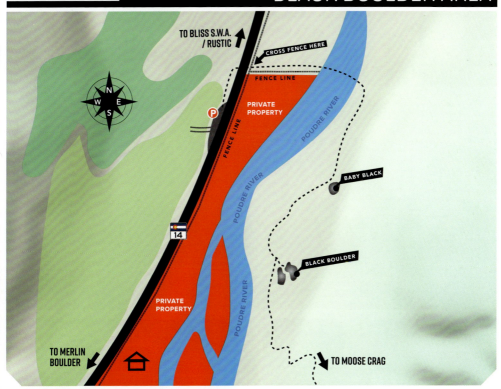

**TYPE(S): BOULDERING & SPORT**
**DIFFICULTY RANGE: V3-V9, 5.12B-5.13B**
**APPROACH TIME: 20 - 30 MIN**
**SEASON: SPRING, FALL & WINTER**

**RIVER CROSSING REQUIRED**

## GETTING THERE

**GPS: 40°41'36.52"N 105°45'33.75"W**

From Ted's Place drive, 42.7 miles up the canyon until you come to large meadow on the west side of the road. Look for a large pullout near a small grove of aspen trees and park there. Walk back downstream and cross the fence-line at the "No Hunting" sign. Follow the fence-line to the river and cross. Find a faint trail and walk back upstream along the river to the Black Boulder.

To reach Moose Crag, walk a little past the Black Boulder upstream until you can find a faint cairned trail that leads up and right, through a forest and across a talus field to the wall. 45min - 1 hour in total hiking time.

## CLIMBING OVERVIEW

The Black Boulder Area is a small zone revolving around a few quality boulders and a small sport crag. It has long been rumored that this area is on private property, but this is not the case. The majority of the climbing is on Colorado state land and US National Forest property. It is confusing because you do cross a fence-line with a "No Hunting" sign, but this property is public.

**PLEASE BE RESPECTFUL TO LAND OWNERS AND THEIR PROPERTY SO YOU DO NOT JEOPARDIZE FUTURE ACCESS.**

The bouldering at the Black Boulder is on compact granite with nice landings. The namesake of the area is an old Dave Graham problem from circa 2001 or so.

Moose Crag is a new sport climbing area first developed in 2015. It hosts a collection of really nice 5.12 climbing in a quiet and scenic setting.

Ryan Nelson on the start of **Big Black Moose*** **12b**   Photo: B. Scott

POUDRE CANYON GUIDE - 3RD EDITION   **239**

BLACK BOULDER AREA

# BLACK BOULDER AREA

## BLACK BOULDER

The Black Boulder is actually two large boulders sitting right next to each other. Excellent rock and a quiet setting next to the river make this a must-see for any climber. **Please be respectful of adjacent private property, keep your power screams to yourself and make sure your dogs are staying near by.**

### 1. ○ Baby Black* v5 (Pads)
After you cross the river and start walking upstream, you will come across this small boulder right off the trail. The backside has a decent crimp problem from a SDS.
FA: Unknown

### 2. ○ Sloper Gold** v6 (Pads)
Once you reach the Black Boulder, you will walk right to this short blunt arête. Nice rock and holds that are deceptively difficult to move through.
FA: Unknown

### 3. ○ Occam's Razor*** v9 (Pads)
A brutal SDS to the Classic Warm-up. Revolving off a long pull on a sharp edge (hence the name).
FA: E. Paige

### 4. ○ Classic Warm-up*** v3 (Pads)
An excellent problem on quality stone. Pulling off the ground and doing the first move is the hardest bit.
FA: Unknown

### 5. ○ Long Time Gone** v5 (Pads)
Another great problem that will get your fingers ready for the Black Problem. Start on good edges and do a big move to a sloping jug, back left to a gaston and a committing topout.
FA: Unknown

### 6. ○ Don't Tell Mom** v3 (Pads)
A recent addition named after a certain climber's decision to climb a highball a few months after recovering from a ground fall in a climbing gym. Obvious start to a techy slab.
FA: Andy Abeleria, M. Bradley, R. Nelson

# BLACK BOULDER AREA

Cory Baumgarten slapping **The Black Problem**\*\*\* v9  Photo: E. Page

## BLACK BOULDER - NORTH FACE

## BLACK BOULDER - SOUTH FACE

**7.** ○ **Rocket Man**\*\* v8 (Pads)
A classic from the way-back machine. So old the holds are now covered in lichen again. Perform a really difficult jumpstart followed by some campusing to the topout. The SDS is a quality project still awaiting an ascent.
FA: F. Sanzaro

**8.** ○ **Angry Black Man**\*\* v7 (Pads)
The consolation prize to an ascent of the Black Problem, this boulder is surprisingly fun and tricky. Start on the obvious Swiss-style sloper rail and do a really hard move to the lip.
FA: Unknown

**9.** ○ **Black Problem**\*\*\* v9 (Pads)
Years ago, I found this boulder problem one day and started scrubbing away. DG was up in the canyon wandering around and found my truck. He tracked me down and proceeded to stomp this new problem in a handful of tries. Dave was so excited and kept rambling about the rock quality and how much he loved the Poudre. SDS on a left-hand slopey edge and a brutal small undercling for the right. Proceed to slap and compress your way to the lip on perfect Swiss-style granite, one of the best of the grade in the canyon.
FA: Dave Graham

**10.** ○ **Take a Knee**\* v6 (Pads)
SDS and move up and right to a tricky topout.
FA: Ken Klein, M. Englestad, Ethan Saffer

Francis Sanzaro on his F.A. of **Rocket Man**\*\* v8, Circa: 2001  Photo: B. Scott

# MOOSE CRAG

Peter Hurtgen on the F.A. of **Bullwinkle**\*\*\* 12c  Photo: B. Scott

## MOOSE CRAG

**GPS: 40°41'20.39"N 105°45'30.38"W**

Moose Crag is a great cliff with generally good rock and excellent movement. Follow directions to the Black Boulder, then find a faint cairned trail that leads up and right, through a forest and across a talus field to the wall. 30-45min in total hiking time.

### 1. ⊙ Smoke Trail** 12d (14 Bolts)
This route climbs the center of the grey tower feature. Ramble up some choss to Bolt 1. Continue on techy 5.11 terrain to the big ledge. From here, it is a long series of 5.12 climbing that has no specific crux, but it never really gives up until the chains. Beware of some less-than-perfect rock right off the ledge, but the rest is good stone.
FA: B. Scott, C. Hofer

### 2. ⊙ Bullwinkle** 12c (12 Bolts)
This route is the obvious line to the right of Smoke Trail. The route begins with around 50 feet of wandering 5.10 terrain and ends with a short, bouldery, compression crux that takes you to the chains. The 5.10 terrain will clean up with traffic, and the crux climbs on bullet-hard rock.
FA: P. Hurtgen

### 3. ⊙ Tonka*** 12b (9 Bolts)
Tonka was named in honor of beloved friend and crag dog, Tonka Tarry. RIP. This route has really good edge and face climbing that is diverse and technical. It is equally as good as its neighbor Big Black Moose but requires a different skill set altogether. Do this route!
FA: J. Tarry, B. Scott

### 4. ⊙ Big Black Moose*** 12b (9 Bolts)
This route is probably the main reason you hiked up to the Moose Crag. A stellar arête climb with sustained climbing the whole way. Start near a right-facing corner, and angle up and right on techy face climbing to the arête. Compression climbing up the arête, on a variety of holds and features, and with fantastic position all the way to the anchor.
FA: B. Scott, C. Hofer

### 5. ⊙ Miguel*** 13b (6 Bolts)
This was named after the infamous street dog Miguel (a.k.a. Mickey). Start with some unfortunate climbing up a big, chossy ramp until you can mantle onto a big start ledge. From the ledge, climb a short corner feature to the first crux moving through the white face. After the rest, move right and over a small roof to gain the headwall. Angle back left on sidepulls and gastons to a pumpy finish right at the anchor.
FA: B. Scott

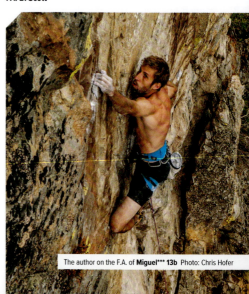

The author on the F.A. of **Miguel**\*\*\* 13b  Photo: Chris Hofer

**43.2 MILES** FROM TED'S PLACE

# MERLIN BOULDER

**TYPE(S): BOULDERING**
**DIFFICULTY RANGE: V1 - V7**
**APPROACH TIME: 2 SEC**
**SEASON: YEAR ROUND**

## CLIMBING OVERVIEW

The Merlin Boulder is a large, trailer-sized block hiding right off the road. It boasts perfect rock, great landings, and an ultra-classic boulder problem a stone's throw from your car.

## GETTING THERE

GPS: 40°41'20.95"N 105°46'0.09"W
From Ted's Place, drive 43.2 miles up Hwy 14. The boulder is located 20 yards off the road on the west side. Park off the road on the west side and walk to the boulder.

**1.** ○ **Edge Project (Pads)**
An obvious problem on an obvious boulder. Crimp climbing at its finest and hardest, attempted by many strong climbers.
FA: Open Project

**2.** ○ **Merlin*** v7 (Pads)**
SDS on an obvious incut sidepull. Move though a slopey layback to a sharp edge on the left face, jump to the large incut angled jug. Originally done as a jumpstart by Mark Wilford and John Sherman.
FA: H. Jones

**3.** ○ **Slopey Mantle v2 (Pads)**
To the right of Merlin behind the tree is a slopey hold at chest height. Mantle and continue up the slab.
FA: R. Anglemeyer

**4.** ○ **Downclimb v1 (Pads)**
On the west side, there is an obvious slab with an edge/layback system. Climb this to the top. This is also the downclimb off the boulder.
FA: R. Anglemeyer

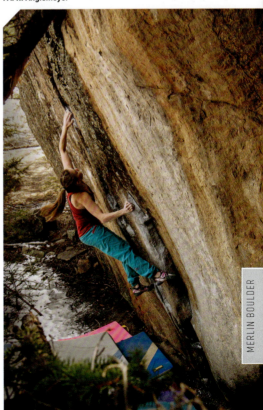

Emily Dusatko sticking the crux of **Merlin*** v7   Photo: B. Scott

POUDRE CANYON GUIDE - 3RD EDITION

**44.8 MILES** FROM TED'S PLACE

# PEARL NECKLACE AREA

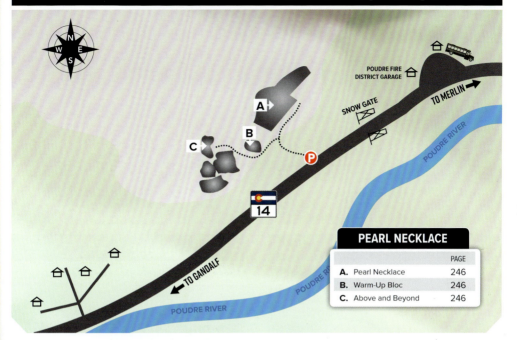

### PEARL NECKLACE

| | | PAGE |
|---|---|---|
| A. | Pearl Necklace | 246 |
| B. | Warm-Up Bloc | 246 |
| C. | Above and Beyond | 246 |

**TYPE(S): BOULDERING**
**DIFFICULTY RANGE: V0 - VII**
**APPROACH TIME: 1 MIN**
**SEASON: YEAR ROUND**

## CLIMBING OVERVIEW

The Pearl Necklace area is a more recently developed zone of nice granite blocs in a hidden talus field right off the road. The area testpiece Pearl Necklace is one of the best of its grade in the Poudre Canyon.

MOSTLY SUNNY ALL DAY

## GETTING THERE

**GPS: 40°40'22.34"N 105°47'19.46"W**

From Ted's Place, drive 44.8 miles up Hwy 14. After you pass the Sleeping Elephant Campground and the Trading Post, look for a Poudre Canyon Fire District sign on a small garage on the west side of the road. There is also a house in the large pullout/parking area and an old bus someone lives in from time to time. Just past the fire district sign is a snow gate, and just beyond that are the boulders hiding just off the west side of the road in an aspen grove.

Skyler Bol warming up on *Freaky Friday*** v3  Photo: T. Bol

POUDRE CANYON GUIDE - 3RD EDITION   **245**

## A - PEARL NECKLACE BOULDER

The namesake of the area for a reason. This boulder is more of a cliffband than an actual free standing boulder. The boulder is on the north end of the small talus field. A couple faint trails lead to it from the road.

### 1. Pearl Necklace**** v10 (Pads)
This epic problem is shrouded in mystery. Anonymous climbers cleaned and glued this problem at some point in time but never told anyone about it. Zach gets credited with the F.A. but he did not name or reinforce any of the holds with glue. The origin of the name is still shrouded in mystery. Start low on two sloper jugs and fire up the jutting prow on underclings and incut crimps. Most climbers mantle the final jug and jump off, but the full topout is described as a 5.9 solo.
FA: Z. Lerner

### 2. Flex Industry*** v11 (Pads)
A lower start that adds more big moves on slopey holds before performing the crux of Pearl Necklace.
FA: R. Quanstrom

### 3. Open Project (Pads)
Start the same as Flex Industry but climb through the obvious seam feature.
FA: Open Project

## B - WARM-UP ROOF

Located in the middle of the area on the edge of the talus field but closer to the aspen trees.

### 4. Warm-up Roof* v3 (Pads)
SDS and climb nice steep jugs out the short overhang.
FA: R. Nelson

## C - ABOVE AND BEYOND BOULDER

Located on the south side of the talus field, this massive boulder holds two nice highballs. Rock quality is very good and the landings are quite manageable.

### 5. Second Thoughts*** v4 (4-5 Pads)
Climb the obvious angling flake/seam feature. A big move near the top leads to an engaging topout
FA: R. Nelson

### 6. Above and Beyond*** v8 (4-5 Pads)
Start the same as for Second Thoughts but climb direct through nice crimps to a huge committing throw to the lip.
FA: Luis Bellido

### 7. Down and Below** v5 (4-5 Pads)
Climb the nice black and white streaked wall.
FA: Sam Hoffecker

**46.1 MILES FROM TED'S PLACE**

# GANDALF AREA

## GANDALF AREA

| | | PAGE |
|---|---|---|
| A. | Warm-up Wall | 248 |
| B. | Against Humanity | 248 |
| C. | Lone Highway | 248 |
| D. | Gandalf Boulder | 249 |
| E. | Corkscrew Boulder | 251 |
| F. | Sunny Boulder | 251 |
| G. | Maybe Baby | 251 |
| H. | Olafs Bulge | 251 |
| I. | Sea Boulder | 252 |
| J. | Pats Crack | 252 |
| K. | Tractor Beam | 253 |
| L. | Shapes and Sizes | 253 |
| M. | Renee Boulder | 254 |
| N. | Green Slab | 254 |
| O. | Sluice Box | 254 |
| P. | Blitzcrieg | 254 |
| Q. | Redline | 255 |
| R. | Polychrome | 255 |
| S. | Neon Boulder | 255 |
| T. | Paper Tiger Boulder | 255 |

**GRADE DISTRIBUTION**

**TYPE(S): BOULDERING**
**DIFFICULTY RANGE: V0 - V12**
**APPROACH TIME: 1 - 20 MIN**
**SEASON: SPRING, FALL & WINTER**

**RIVER CROSSING REQUIRED**

## CLIMBING OVERVIEW

Gandalf is another one of the major bouldering areas West of Rustic. A massive talus field of house-sized blocs that spills down onto the river's edge. Similar in nature to a lot of the talus bouldering at RMNP and Mt. Evans. Some of the best rock and movement in the canyon can be found here.

## GETTING THERE

**GPS: 40°39'57.25"N 105°48'28.79"W**

From Ted's Place, drive 46.1 miles up Hwy 14. Turn left into the Tunnel Picnic Area and continue to the small parking lot. The bouldering is found directly across the river in the obvious boulderfield. The river crossing is completely impassable during spring runoff, May-July.

# GANDALF AREA

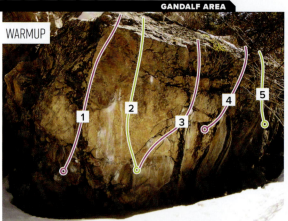

WARMUP

AGAINST HUMANITY

## A - WARM-UP WALL

The Warm-up Wall is found directly across the river from the Tunnel Picnic Area parking lot.

**1. ○ Left Arête** v4 (Pads)
SDS on a couple of blocky holds. Move up into an obvious layback. Slap the arête and jump for a jug at the top of the arête.
FA: R. Anglemeyer

**2. ○ Squeeze Problem** v6 (Pads)
This excellent problem begins on a left-hand sidepull and the same right-hand undercling as the Pinch Problem before eventually slapping out left to the long, sloping crescent feature and moving to the top for an exciting finish.
FA: P. Goodman

**3. ○ Pinch Problem** v4 (Pads)
Start low on the incut undercling at the bottom of a right-trending seam. Move through positive crimps to an obvious deck-of-cards pinch then figure out how to get to the glory jug and casual topout.
FA: C. Way, J. Shambo

**4. ○ Unnamed Corner** v3 (Pads)
Start on an obvious slopey jug at head height. Climb up and right through a small corner to an easy topout.
FA: R. Anglemeyer

**5. ○ Unnamed** v5 (Pads)
Grab two opposing sidepulls and head left up the blunt bulge on small crimps. Good moves on great rock. A variation begins in the same place, but heads up and right into Warm-up Crack.
FA: R. Anglemeyer

**6. ○ Warm-up Crack** v1 (Pads)
SDS on a jug and climb the obvious crack just left of Moss Fest. A fun classic with a slightly bushy finish.
FA: R. Anglemeyer

**7. ○ Moss Fest** v2 (Pads)
Scratch your way to the top of the far right side of the Warm-up Wall without getting completely covered in moss. Might be a nice moderate climb if it ever cleans up.
FA: R. Anglemeyer

## B - AGAINST HUMANITY BOULDER

**8. ○ Crime** v8 (Pads)
An infamous problem from Mr. Feissner. Start on Against Humanity and move into some bicep busting underclings. A big move to a sidepull leads to the techy slab.
FA: H. Feissner

**9. ○ Against Humanity** v6 (Pads)
One of the finest problems in the Poudre and an absolute must-do. From the large sidepull/undercling feature, move up and right to good holds, then keep it together for a big finishing move. A slightly more difficult start begins nearly laying down on good underclings and moves into the regular problem, also first done by Mr. Lemaire.
FA: W. Lemaire

**10. ○ Dump Truck** v10 (Pads)
SDS in the back of the cave on underclings. Do a big move out right to an incut edge, then traverse left finishing on Crime.
FA: P. Dusatko

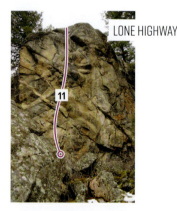

LONE HIGHWAY

## C - LONE HIGHWAY BOULDER

**11. ○ Lone Highway** v3 (Pads)
Seldom done but a very fun tall line. Nice edges and jugs lead all the way up the aesthetic face.
FA: B. Scott

GANDALF AREA

## D - GANDALF BOULDER

From Against Humanity Boulder, walk 20 yards downstream until you can find a trail that leads directly up the hill 20 yards to the infamous Gandalf Boulder.

### 12. ○ Black Swan** v12 (4-5 Pads)
SDS matched on a crystally sloper, then follow the obvious pegmatite dike up and right, with a big jump into the start of Gandalf.
FA: Blake Rutherford

### 13. ○ Gandalf**** v6 (4-5 Pads)
An ultra classic highball. From a triangle-shaped pinch at head level, move through small crimps and a bad foot to a large sidepull/gaston. Then figure out how to make the long, intimidating dyno before topping out slightly to the right.
FA: W. Lemaire

### 14. ○ Orbital Resonance** v10 (4-5 Pads)
Begin on the start jug of Flow Futuristic, and make a big move left to a hold and use a back-hand to transition left into the rest of Gandalf from there.
FA: Jason Kehl

### 15. ○ Flow Futuristic** v8 (4-5 Pads)
From the large jug just left of the arête, move into underclings and make a big cross to a crimp sidepull followed by a jump to the amazing jug hole. Finish on the Gandalf topout.
FA: J. Kehl

### 16. ○ Face* v4 (4-5 Pads)
Located just around the west face from Flow Futuristic. Reach as high as you can to good holds in the seam just right of the arête, then move onto the west face for an exciting highball.
FA: B. Scott

### 17. ○ Courting Doom** v9 (Pads)
Begin on an obvious rail feature, move left onto some sidepulls and finish on a tricky arête feature.
FA: C. Reagan

### 18. ○ Harder They Come*** v9 (Pads)
SDS on the massive undercling flake. Do a big first move to edges and proceed on powerful moves to the lip.
FA: J. Shambo

### 19. ○ One Arm Scissor** v10 (Pads)
Originally called "Don't Name This Problem" due to Mr. Shambo's opinion that it was just a "choss" pile. Nowadays, its considered a beloved Gandalf classic that has been renamed. Start the same as Harder They Come but move right out the overhang.
FA: J. Shambo

### 20. ○ Big Flake v1 (Pads)
On the southeast corner there is an obvious flake/crack running up and right. A fun laybacking moderate adventure, but falling is probably not a good idea.
FA: R. Anglemeyer

POUDRE CANYON GUIDE - 3RD EDITION

Eric Palmer with a send on the new-school classic **Flight Syndrome**\*\*\* v9  Photo: E. Page

## E - CORKSCREW BOULDER

Located above Gandalf is a steep boulder coming out of a talus hole. Originally named for an unusual log that looked like a corkscrew at its base.

### 21. ○ Corkscrew** v6 (Pads)
Start matched on an obvious crimp edge and perform a hard move to the big edge at the lip. Traverse right into Flight Syndrome to topout. A lower start has been done that adds a few moves called "Float Syndrome v9".
FA: B. Scott

### 22. ○ Flight Syndrome*** v9 (Pads)
Start on a nice edge on the right side of the wall and climb excellent moves on edges to the obvious topout.
FA: S. Rothstein

## G - MAYBE BABY BOULDER

From Gandalf, walk up and left along the edge of the talus field and the forest. Walk past the Sunny Boulder 30 yards to this overhanging boulder just uphill.

### 24. ○ Beau Dirt** v3 (Pads)
Stand start on two sidepulls and layback your way up the nice rail feature.
FA: B. Kehler

### 25. ○ Maybe Baby** v10 (Pads)
SDS on a slopey crimp edge with a high foot. Do a really hard move to the angled lip feature then move left into Beau Dirt.
FA: J. Glassberg

### 26. ○ Longmont Rimjob* v6 (Pads)
Stand start on an obvious slopey edge and perform a tricky reach move before the easy slab to the top.
FA: C. Griffin

### 27. ○ Natural Selection** v10 (Pads)
Located on the far right side of the Maybe Baby Boulder. Stand start on an undercling and a crimp, hard move into another undercling. Landing is really bad unless filled with snow in the winter/early spring.
FA: S. Rothstein

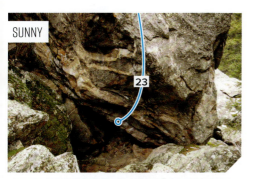

## F - SUNNY BOULDER

From Gandalf, walk up and left along the edge of the talus field and the forest. After about five minutes, this cave will come into view on hikers right.

### 23. ○ Sunny*** v10 (Pads)
SDS in the back of a cave and climb on strenuous crimps and edges to an easy topout. Impeccable rock quality on this boulder problem.
FA: S. Bol

## H - OLAF'S BULGE BOULDER

This boulder sits just above and behind the Maybe Baby Boulder if approaching from the north side of the field.

### 28. ○ Olaf's Bulge*** v9 (Pads)
Start on the two obvious start holds, grab a bad crimp around right followed by a hard move to a slopey angled crimp.
FA: J. Glassberg

# GANDALF AREA

Sheldon Deeny with the rarely seen "eyes closed ascent" of **Harder They Come**\*\*\* v9  Photo: E. Page

SEA

## I - SEA BOULDER

Located just to the south from the Maybe Baby Boulder, approx. 25 yards away on a steep black face.

### 29. ◐ Sea of Simulation\*\*\* v12 (Pads)
Start with a desperate stab to a rail sidepull on perfect rock. Another powerful move on bad feet gets you to the mantle.
FA: J. Glassberg

## J - PAT'S CRACK BOULDER

This large house-sized boulder sits about 50 yards uphill east from the Gandalf Boulder. A large right-angling gash splits the boulder's right side, inside of which you will find Pat's Crack and Mike's Arête.

### 30. ◐ Mike's Arête\*\* v9 (Pads)
This variation to Pat's Crack climbs the more accessible left arête instead of the tips seam. Compress your way up the arête until you can mantle into the top of Pat's Crack.
FA: M. Auldridge

PAT'S CRACK

### 31. ◐ Pat's Crack\*\*\* v9 (Pads)
This testpiece will test your finger crack technique and mental fortitude. This massive boulder is split by a large gash on its south side. Pat's Crack climbs a tiny splitter seam that just fits tips.
FA: Geoff Sluyter

### 32. ◐ Johnny Karate\*\* v8 (Pads)
On the uphill side of the boulder is a small cave/overhang. Start on obvious edges and climb out the bulge to the left.
FA: S. Rothstein

### 33. ◐ Mouserat\*\* v10 (Pads)
Same start as Johnny Karate but move right out the roof.
FA: J. Glassberg

TRACTOR BEAM

GANDALF AREA

SHAPES AND SIZES

## K - TRACTOR BEAM BOULDER

**34.** **Tractor Beam**** v7 (Pads)
A crack splits the right side of this hanging boulder. Begin on the slopey sidepull and climb straight up. Two projects have been attempted to the left, but nothing has been completed as of yet.
FA: B. Camp

## L - SHAPES & SIZES BOULDER

From Tractor Beam, pick your way about 50 yards south through the talus towards another huge block. The two difficult lines climb the overhangs on the east face.

**35.** **Dihedral with an Undercling**\*** v12 (Pads)
A striking line with nice rock coming out of a hole. Climb through edges to a series of underclings taking you up and left to the finish.
FA: B. Rutherford

**36.** **Shapes and Sizes**\*** v11 (Pads)
Start on an obvious jug in the back of the cave. Climb big holds to an incut at the lip. Do a big move to the jug rail or climb the right arête on crimps. Be wary of back-slap potential on the rock behind you.
FA: Carlo Traversi

Eric Page cranking on some classic Poudre stone with an ascent of **Sunny**\*** v10  Photo: E. Page

POUDRE CANYON GUIDE - 3RD EDITION    253

## M - RENEE BOULDER

A precarious looking overhanging prow with a decent landing. Located in the middle of the talus field directly behind the Green Slab Boulder.

**37. ○ Geriatrics\*\* v8** (Pads)
An easier variation to Renee starting on the obvious stand start jug. Do a big move left to a flat edge before climbing up to good holds and moving back right for the same topout as Renee.
FA: B. Scott, J. Tarry

**38. ○ Renee\*\* v10** (Pads)
Start inverted on an angled incut and move to a big jug. Move around the bulge to a slopey right-hand followed by a big move left to a quarter-pad edge. Easy topout but not a giveaway either.
FA: Z. Lerner

## N - GREEN SLAB BOULDER

An enormous boulder in the middle of the field with an obvious lichen covered slab that may or may not have been climbed before. However, the backside has several nice moderates on good stone.

**39. ○ Unknown 1\* v2** (Pads)
SDS on a nice sidepull and climb up and right though nice edges and an easy topout.
FA: Unknown

**40. ○ Unknown 2\* v4** (Pads)
Climb the beautiful gold panel on nice opposing edges to a chill little mantle.
FA: Unknown

## O - SLUICE BOX BOULDER

Located towards the south end of the talus field in a hidden cave. Approx. 50 yards south of the Green Slab Boulder.

**41. ○ Sluice Box\*\* v10** (Pads)
SDS in the back of a cave on an angling crack. Perform three hard and thuggy compression moves in a row on really nice rock. Surprisingly steep and powerful.
FA: J. Glassberg

## P - BLITZKRIEG BOULDER

Located in the southern portion of the talus field right above the Redline Boulder.

**42. ○ Blitzkrieg\*\* v4** (Pads)
An ancient problem from yester-year that rarely gets climbed. Stand start up the steep prow on lots of edges.
FA: Damon Smoko

## GANDALF AREA

## Q - REDLINE BOULDER

The Redline Boulder is a hidden cave made of several boulders leaning together. At the southern end of the talus field approx. 50 yards from the Green Slab Boulder.

**43.** O **Redline\*\* v8** (Pads)
This short, but excellent problem is worth looking for. Begin on two crimps, slap to a slopey rail and head slightly right to finish.
FA: B. Scott

## R - POLYCHROME BOULDER

This giant boulder sits at the very south end of the talus field. Set apart from the rest of the talus, at the top of a small scree field. If you walk out of the talus you have gone too far.

**44.** O **Polychrome\*\* v9** (Pads)
Start on a bad undercling and a sharp incut crimp. Move up and left through solid edges and pinches to a hard last move to the lip.
FA: S. Rothstein

## S - NEON BOULDER

Located about 20 yards uphill from the Polychrome Boulder hiding in a small grove of trees.

**45.** O **Railin' Bars\*\* v6** (Pads)
SDS compressed at the bottom of the slopey rail. Squeeze up the short prow using heel-hooks and kneebars.
FA: N. Perl

**46.** O **Neon Demon\*\* v9** (Pads)
SDS on the crimp rail at the back of the cave. Power out the overhang using pinches, slopers and crimps.
FA: N. Perl

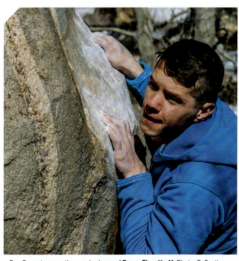

Roy Quanstrom on the gnarly sloper of **Paper Tiger\*\* v11** Photo: B. Scott

## T - PAPER TIGER BOULDER

This boulder is actually not at the Gandalf Area at all. From Gandalf, drive approx. 0.5 miles upstream to the first right-hand bend. Park in a shallow pullout here and cross the road. The Paper Tiger lies just off Hwy 14 on the river's edge.

**47.** O **Paper Tiger\*\* v11** (Pads)
Start on two horrible slopers and compress your way up the small egg-shaped boulder.
FA: Will Anglin

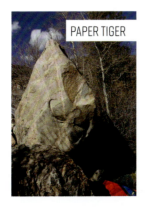

**Climber Spotlight:** Jason Tarry is my oldest friend. We started climbing together back at Whipps Ledges, Hinkley, Ohio in 1996. I was super green when Jason showed me the world of bouldering and sport climbing. He took me on my first road trips to the New River Gorge in his trusty old Jeep Wrangler with the doors off. To this day, Jason is absolutely my go-to climbing partner. We still climb together just about every week and we have worked as a team to develop countless front range climbing areas for which he humbly lets me take most of the credit.

We share a deep passion for developing aesthetically pleasing lines on new boulders and cliffs. This photo is an example of why Jason is the best climbing partner in the world. Giggling with psyche for the possibilities that lie in front of him. Covered in dirt and lichen from head to toe, he is re-born with every new climb from the perils of modern adult life to that happy 19 year old kid who needs nothing but rocks, chalk and endless sunny days.

Jason Tarry giggling over the river and the new route he is about to bolt....**Water Rights**\*\*\*\* **12b**   Photo: B. Scott

**46.7 MILES** FROM TED'S PLACE

# POUDRE FALLS

Poudre Falls churning with spring run-off   Photo: B. Scott

GRADE DISTRIBUTION

**TYPE(S): SPORT, TRAD, & BOULDERING**
**DIFFICULTY RANGE: 5.8 - 5.14A, V1-V10**
**APPROACH TIME: EAST SIDE, 10 MIN; WEST SIDE, 20 MIN**
**SEASON: SPRING, SUMMER & FALL**

## CLIMBING OVERVIEW

Development of the Poudre Falls area began in the late summer of 2012. A nice collection of shorter cliffs and crags visible from Hwy 14 that had been un-developed by the Fort Collins climbing community in the past.

The White Wall was one of the first sectors to see development. After quickly realizing how difficult the climbing is on the White Wall, developers soon began bolting easier lines to use as warm-ups and training for the major challenges on the White Wall.

The variety of climbing styles is incredible at Poudre Falls. Slabs, overhangs, arêtes, endurance routes, powerful bouldery routes, climbing over the river, climbing high up on the sides of the canyon, all while being nestled in a perfect alpine forest with aspens, moss, and tons of little critters running around.

**EAST SIDE:** This is a great morning sector. The cliffs stay generally shady until about 1:00pm. The belay areas are shaded in the afternoon but the climbing can be hot without cloud cover.

**WEST SIDE:** This is an excellent afternoon/evening sector. Shade hits most of the cliffs by 1:00pm during the summer, but mornings can be very hot.

Poudre Falls is generally a summer/fall area. Usually the snow is melting by May but a lot of the cliffs are prone to seeping until June or so. July and August can be a little hot, but it's still very climbable and the camping is perfect.

## GETTING THERE

**GPS: 40°38'49.79"N 105°48'35.34"W**

From Ted's Place, drive 46.7 miles up the canyon (1 hour 15 min). The West Side parking lot is on the west side of Hwy 14 before a bridge. It is past the Gandalf Bouldering area but before the Big South Trailhead as you are heading west toward Cameron Pass. East Side parking areas are just 0.25 miles farther. Look at the overview map on page 258 for a better understanding of the parking areas.

Ethan Pringle snagging the F.A. of **Coach Myles**\*\*\* **13d**  Photo: J. Levine

More than 65 routes have been developed covering grades from 5.8-5.14. The climbing is generally bouldery and technical in nature. Most routes are on the shorter side, but there are a few 30 meter monsters awaiting the endurance focused climber. During the summer of 2015, the East Side of Poudre Falls began being developed. This is a great morning crag with lots of quality routes in the 5.11 and 5.12 grade range.

## CAMPING & LODGING

Camping at Poudre Falls is easy and relatively convenient. Car camping is not suggested as it may impact access in the future. If you do camp, please walk-in 100 yards to the obvious meadow where the West Side main trail heads uphill. There are two fire pits and room for 10-20 tents in the meadow. Please clean up after yourself and pack out your trash to help maintain the area for future visitors.

Alternatively, there are many pay campgrounds scattered throughout the canyon that require a reservation with Sleeping Elephant Campground and Big South Campground being the closest. The Laramie River Road and Chambers Lake vicinity have a lot of unregulated camping options as well.

There are also several locations to rent cabins. Trading Post Resort and Sportsman's Lodge are the closest to Poudre Falls:

tradingpostresort.com

sportsmanslodgecolorado.com

poudreriverresort.com

Mike Botkin on **First In Time**\*\* **11b**  Photo: Micah Wright

## EAST SIDE BOULDERING

There are several significant boulders worth visiting on the East side of the canyon at Poudre Falls. This guide only covers a small portion of the developed bouldering.

RUDE BEAUTY

## RUDE BEAUTY BOULDER

To reach this boulder, park in the large pullout on the east side of the road, right across from the entrance to the West Side parking (see Poudre Falls overview map, pg. 258). Hike about 2min down towards the river to find this massive boulder.

**1. ○ Rude Beauty**** v8** (Pads)
Sitting in a tranquil location next to the bubbling river is this excellent problem. Start on a flat edge and move up and right into the compression feature. Nice rock and good movement make this a new school classic.
FA: R. Nelson

**2. ○ Quilling Me Softly** v5** (Pads)
Dogs and porcupines don't mix. Start right of Rude Beauty and climb a techy edge sequence into a topout just right of Rude Beauty.
FA: M. Englestad

**3. ○ Warm-up* v2** (Pads)
Located on the south side of the boulder, SDS and traverse up and right into the jug rail.
FA: Unknown

**4. ○ Unnamed Arête** v4** (Pads)
Squat start on two sidepulls and throw to the large sloping lip. Match and mantle.
FA: R. Nelson

**5. ○ Soggy Doggy** v2** (Pads)
Soggy Doggy starts on the smooth rock pedestal near the water on the south side of the boulder. Climb up the slab and topout with delicate movement on polished river stone.
FA: O. Murphy, R. Nelson

RIVER BOULDER

## RIVER BOULDER

To reach this boulder, park on the west side of the road right after you cross the bridge. If you reach the Jungle Wall parking you have gone too far. Cross an old barbed wire fence and follow a trail through a meadow to reach the river and the boulder. The landing is usually dry from September - March.

**6. ○ Stone Record*** v3** (Pads)
Climb edges and sidepulls on or near the arête feature but mostly left of it.
FA: J. Bisher

**7. ○ Center Perfection*** v4** (Pads)
Start on a perfect jug feature and climb techy terrain through slimpers and edges to the top over perfect sand...or water.
FA: R. Anglemeyer

**8. ○ Treading Water*** v8** (Pads)
Another perfect starting edge leads into a very subtle, yet long move to an impossible sloper.
FA: R. Anglemeyer

ROADSIDE

## ROADSIDE BOULDER

Located on the east side of the road right across from the Jungle Wall Parking. Excellent rock and lots of friendly holds makes this a nice warm-up before you head up the hill.

## TELEGRAPH BOULDER

From the Roadside Boulder, head directly up the hill behind it. After less than 5min the Telegraph Boulder should come into view.

### 9. ◯ Tomahawk Chop*** v4 (Pads)
SDS on a big jug/flake sticking out of the base of the boulder. Fun moves on excellent stone take you up and left to the top.
FA: R. Nelson

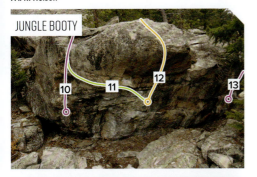

## JUNGLE BOOTY BOULDER

To reach this boulder, hike up the Jungle Wall Trail. When you reach the top of the slabs on the hike, you will be staring at this boulder.

### 10. ◯ Hello* v3 (Pads)
Climb nice crimps to a semi-detached jug at the lip.
FA: R. Anglemeyer

### 11. ◯ Au Revoir** v5 (Pads)
SDS at the same start as Wave Goodbye. Climb big holds until you can move left into Hello on crimps.
FA: R. Anglemeyer

### 12. ◯ Wave Goodbye*** v7 (Pads)
SDS on obvious holds. Climb big edges to a couple small crimps and perform an awesome jump move to a nice sloper at the lip. Move up and left to topout.
FA: B. Scott

### 13. ◯ Right Arête** v3 (Pads)
A nice starting jug leads to a bit of compression before the lip.
FA: R. Anglemeyer

# POUDRE FALLS

Jason Nadeau trying moves on **Tiger Milk*** v11   Photo: B. Scott

## WEST SIDE BOULDERING

There is also a bit of scattered bouldering on the West Side of Poudre Falls. Most notably, the Pin Stripe Boulder but the talus field below the South Wall also has several established problems not covered in this guide.

## PIN STRIPE BOULDER

Another example of the astounding rock quality that lies hidden in the forests West of Rustic. Something out of Magic Wood in Switzerland, this bloc has incredible striped granite with interesting holds and movement. From the West side parking, follow the lower trail towards the River Wall. Walk past the camping area, past the old trash dump and cross a small stream. Locate a faint trail going uphill before the talus.

### 14. ◯ Spidey Arête** v7 (Pads)
SDS and compress your way up the sweet arête.
FA: B. Scott

### 15. ◯ Gutterball** v8 (Pads)
Stand start into a tricky jump move out left on cool pinches.
FA: S. Rothstein

### 16. ◯ Tiger Milk*** v11 (Pads)
SDS on the obvious start holds and move up into cool sidepulls and pinches on amazing rock.
FA: Ryan Silven

### 17. ◯ Knees for Life** v6 (Pads)
Stand start on the right arête and climb into a knee-bar to move towards the lip.
FA: B. Scott

Chris Hofer surfing an ocean of rock on **Black Hole**\*\*\* **11c**  Photo: B. Scott

# ASTRONOMY WALL

**GPS: 40°38'47.17"N 105°48'28.73"W**

To access Astronomy Wall, drive upstream past the West Side parking, past the big pullout for Jungle Wall, and past a section of road cut to a subtle pullout on the east side of Hwy 14. From here, follow a cairned trail directly up a line of trees between the obvious talus slopes (5-10min hike from the car). Astronomy Wall can be seen uphill from the parking.

### 1. ○ Meteor Mining** 10c (5 Bolts)
Climb the open corner feature to some tricky climbing to reach the anchor.
FA: M. Wright, M. Botkin

### 2. ○ Black Hole*** 11c (8 Bolts)
Start on the left side of a big hole/cave feature. Climb big holds through the initial bulge/overhang. Techy, slabby cruxes keep coming after the bulge. The final two bolts are an easy layback corner/groove.
FA: B. Scott

### 3. ○ Wormhole*** 11a (9 Bolts)
Begin on the right side of the cave feature until you can stem the entire cave at Bolt 2. Continue through the overhang on underclings and laybacks. The upper slab follows a continuous flake/seam feature with friendly edges to the chains.
FA: B. Scott

### 4. ○ Nova*** 11b (12 Bolts)
Start by climbing the arch feature with lots of stemming and big holds. Continue over the bulge with sustained 5.11 climbing for three bolts. The upper slab has lots of fun continuous 5.10 slab climbing.
FA: J. Tarry, C. Hofer, B. Scott

### 5. ○ Oh' Ryan*** 11b (10 Bolts)
Climb onto a short pillar feature. Move up on edges and laybacks to a tricky crux at Bolt 3. Continue on fun slabby terrain with lots of friendly edges and jugs to the anchor.
FA: R. Nelson

### 6. ○ Andromeda Galaxy*** 10b (11 Bolts)
An easy start leads to an early crux moving left off the shelf at Bolt 3. Continue past hand-cracks and edges to a second crux moving right to underclings and then over a bulge. Easy but thought provoking climbing leads to the chains.
FA: J. Tarry, C. Hofer, B. Scott

### 7. ○ Farthest Planet** 11b (10 Bolts)
Starting right of a little tree, climb ledgy terrain to Bolt 3. From here, use underclings to gain edges below the small roof. A big reach over the roof gains a technical headwall (crux) and doesn't let up until you mantle onto the ledge.
FA: R.D. Pascoe, J. Tarry

ASTRONOMY

ASTRONOMY

**Climber Spotlight:**
Dan Yager is everyone's favorite Ninja Warrior. Dan is easily one of the most committed and compassionate climbers I've ever met. A small business owner and stay-at-home Dad for two kids, it is unreal the amount of hard routes Dan has been able to accomplish. You can frequently find Dan climbing in the canyon mid-winter in sub 32° weather with his "hot rocks" and a big smile on his face.

Dan Yager on **Journey To Pluto**\*\*\* **13b**  Photo: A. Cross

### 8. ○ Intergalactic*** 12c (9 Bolts)
Climb broken terrain to a move right onto the ledge. Move right off the ledge into a long boulder problem ending at an undercling around Bolt 7. Move up into another blocky undercling to get through the final steep section. Excellent techy slab and seam climbing leads to the anchor.
**FA: R. Nelson, C. Hofer**

### 9. ○ Groove Project (8 Bolts)
Start on Intergalactic to gain the ledge. From here, some 5.12 terrain leads into an extremely technical crux that requires lots of patience and hard body positions.
**Bolted by B. Scott**

### 10. ○ Journey to Pluto*** 13b (7 Bolts)
This semi-infamous route is an excellent test of finger strength and technical footwork. Start by rambling up the ledges past the first three bolts. Launch into the short but beautiful headwall on nice stone. The crux involves moving through some miserably slopey crimps to reach a heart-breaker crux right before the chains.
**FA: B. Scott**

### 11. ○ Milky Way** 10a (7 Bolts)
The crux lies within the first few moves off the ground with some techy footwork. After you romp up the ledge, enjoy nice jugs up a corner feature to a tricky chimney move to the anchor.
**FA: B. Scott**

Ryan Nelson cruxing out on the slab of **Black Hole**\*\*\* **11c**  Photo: B. Scott

## JUNGLE WALL

**GPS: 40°38'54.35"N 105°48'30.12"W**

To access Jungle Wall, you can park at the large pullout on the west side near the Poudre Falls sign. From this pullout, cross Hwy 14 and find the trail on the left side of a road-cut slab. The cairned trail heads up over glacial slabs to reach the cliff base from the south end. Approx. 10min hiking time.

### 12. ○ Toucan** 11b (6 Bolts)
Climb up to the ledge before gaining the steep wall. Sidepulls and laybacks on nice rock takes you to the anchor.
**FA: R.D. Pascoe**

### 13. ○ Zebra*** 12a (6 Bolts)
Climb up a small broken tower and clip Bolt 1. Move up onto a large hanging flake before gaining the steep headwall. The crux involves a long reach on small edges at Bolt 4.
**FA: J.Tarry, B. Scott, R.D. Pascoe**

### 14. ○ Vulture*** 11b (7 Bolts)
The first route bolted at the East Side of Poudre Falls. Layback and stem a dihedral feature past 3 bolts. Continue following cracks and jugs until the crack becomes a seam at the crux. Tricky footwork on the upper slab leads to an insecure mantle before the chains.
**FA: J. Tarry**

### 15. ○ Dragonfly** 11c (6 Bolts)
A surprisingly nasty boulder problem guards the moves off the ground. After that, an easy romp on handjams and jugs takes you to the top.
**FA: C. Hofer**

### 16. ○ Butterfly*** 11d (6 Bolts)
A tricky start up a seam leads directly into the crux at Bolt 2. A big move at Bolt 3 gains a series of jugs but lots of technical terrain remains to the anchor. The butterfly that seems to be etched in the rock is left of Bolt 4.
**FA: J. Tarry, B. Scott, R.D. Pascoe, C. Hofer**

### 17. ○ Chimpanzee** 12b (4 Bolts)
Climb off a ledge on cool sidepulls and edges to a big jump move at Bolt 3 to gain the lip of the steep wall.
**FA: B. Scott**

### 18. ○ Open Project (3 Bolts)
This painfully short route is also deceptively difficult. Start about 10 feet to the left of Snake on a small ledge. Climb from underclings directly into a short steep bulge.
**Bolted by B. Scott**

### 19. ○ Snake** 12a (5 Bolts)
Start with a short roof to get onto the arête (crux). Compression climbing leads to a final crux gaining the slab.
**FA: J. Tarry, B. Scott, RD Pascoe**

### 20. ○ Gorilla** 12c (4 Bolts)
A tricky boulder problem (crux) right off the ground. Centering around a hard deadpoint getting over the bulge. Easier but technical 5.10 climbing leads to the anchor.
**FA: B. Scott, D. McKee**

### 21. ○ Rhino** 13a (6 Bolts)
Tricky moves right off the ground leads to easy climbing before the hard and powerful crux at the final bulge.
**FA: B. Scott, C. Hofer**

POUDRE FALLS

JUNGLE

JUNGLE

Chris Hofer on the fun arête moves of **Snake**\*\* **12b**  Photo: B. Scott

Jungle

POUDRE CANYON GUIDE - 3RD EDITION **267**

The author flailing up **Sloth**\*\*\* 13b   Photo: A. Cross

### 22. ◐ Puma*** 10b (6 Bolts)
Climb some nice bulgy slabs to a ledge at half height. Continue up a steep corner feature on jugs to a hard move at Bolt 5 before the balancey traverse back right to the anchor.
FA: Myles Pascoe

### 23. ◐ Pale Face Project (4 Bolts)
The stunning and impossible looking grey face. HARD and THIN but definitely not impossible for the mutants.
Bolted by B. Scott

### 24. ◐ Sloth*** 13b (4 Bolts)
Start with fun edge climbing to the base of the roof. A desperate thuggy boulder problem leads around the bulge to the anchor. Exquisite rock and compression climbing.
FA: J. Tarry

### 25. ◐ Orangutan** 12c (3 Bolts)
Don't let its short stature deter you. Quality rock and unusual movement make this a fun little exercise.
FA: B. Scott

### 26. ◐ Rumble in the Jungle** 13a (5 Bolts)
Another shorty route that will not give up without a fight. Climb the steep roof on pinches and crimps.
FA: D. Yager

R.D. Pascoe on the crux move of the **Zebra**\*\* 12a   Photo: B. Scott

# POUDRE FALLS - WEST SIDE OVERVIEW

## WEST SIDE

| | | PAGE |
|---|---|---|
| **A.** | White Wall | 270 |
| **B.** | Mega Bloks Wall | 270 |
| **C.** | Horizon Wall | 271 |
| **D.** | South Wall | 272 |
| **E.** | Little Wave Wall | 275 |
| **F.** | Myopia Wall | 275 |
| **G.** | Gold Wall | 276 |
| **H.** | Cove Wall | 277 |
| **I.** | River Wall | 279 |

## WEST SIDE ROUTES OVERVIEW

The West Side of Poudre Falls is the largest concentration of climbing in the area. It hosts an impressive variety of climbing from steep overhangs to slabby tech-fests. You can enjoy quiet nooks like the Gold Wall or get your photograph taken by the tourists on the River Wall.

## GETTING THERE

**GPS: 40°38'49.79"N 105°48'41.50"W**
From the West Side parking lot, walk upstream following a trail along the river. After a short walk uphill, you will come to a large meadow (a.k.a the camping area). The main climber trail begins at the start of this meadow and heads immediately uphill. If you are heading to the River Wall, continue walking straight through the meadow and follow the cairned trail that traverses the top of the cliff.

Doug Mckee on **Hyperopia**** **11b**   Photo: B. Scott

POUDRE FALLS

WHITE WALL

MEGA-BLOKS

## A - WHITE WALL

From the parking lot, walk 100yards upstream on the trail next to the river. When you reach the meadow, locate a cairned trail on your right. Follow this trail as it diagonals uphill to the south until you reach the White Wall. 10-15min.

### 27. Dihedron** 11a (8 Bolts)
Awkward moves off the ground lead to a stance left of a grey corner. Move back right with low feet and continue up the corner to easier terrain.
FA: J. Tarry, B. Scott

### 28. Saint Lupe Arête** 12d (6 Bolts)
Bouldery off the deck with the hardest moves around Bolt 3. A lot of holds broke after the original F.A. (8/2013) and the climb or moves have not been repeated since.
FA: B. Scott

### 29. Black Crack Project (8 Bolts)
The remaining project on the epic White Wall. Described as two v12 boulder problems back-to-back. Start just left of Albatross and climb up two bolts before angling left to a series of cracks and seams. The difficulty eases up significantly after Bolt 6.
Bolted by B. Scott, J. Tarry

### 30. The Albatross**** 14a (7 Bolts)
The route that started it all at Poudre Falls, creamy steep white granite with just enough holds. Start with a taxing opening sequence angling up and left to reach underclings at Bolt 3. The crux involves a sharp gaston and a bad sidepull to reach the break at Bolt 5. The upper headwall is a continuous series of 5.13 climbing to the anchor.
FA: B. Scott

### 31. Coach Myles*** 13d (6 Bolts)
Climb the right arching crack feature on underclings and sidepulls. Excellent rock and sustained movement make it a runner-up prize on the White Wall.
FA: E. Pringle

### 32. Bad Monkey** 12b (7 Bolts)
Located on a small separate wall between White Wall and Mega Bloks Wall. Climb ledgy terrain to Bolt 1. The crux comes at Bolt 2 getting to the lip of the roof. Over the roof, nice laybacks and flakes lead to an upper headwall. A diagonal crack with incuts followed by a short slab leads to the chains.
FA: B. Scott

## B - MEGA-BLOKS WALL

From the White Wall, Continue walking south/downstream along the West Side Main Trail. Routes are on climber's right directly off the trail just past Bad Monkey.

### 33. Whiskey Dickin** 10c (4 Bolts)
Most people start with a short hop to reach the first hold, followed by a hard reach off poor feet. More big reaches to good holds takes you to the anchor.
FA: R. Nelson

### 34. Mega Bloks*** 8 (6 Bolts)
The most popular moderate route at Poudre Falls. Nice juggy climbing with a crux in a shallow corner mid-way up the wall.
FA: R. Nelson

### 35. Green Monster** 9 (5 Bolts)
Start near a seap spot oozing green slime that never seems to dry. Easy terrain leads to a tricky stand-up near Bolt 3.
FA: B. Scott

## C - HORIZON WALL

From the White Wall, continue walking south/upstream along the main trail, passsing the Mega-Bloks wall. Horizon Wall is 20 yards farther south on the main trail.

### 36. Time Lost** 12d (7 Bolts)
Start with easy terrain to a tricky crux at Bolt 2 using a sidepull/undercling and a blind reach back left. Gymnastic terrain leads to a compression crux above Bolt 4.
FA: B. Scott

### 37. Chainsaw Massacre** 12b (6 Bolts)
A short arête that packs a punch. Pumpy climbing leads to the crux above Bolt 3. Easier 5.10 climbing up the slab to the anchor.
FA: B. Scott

### 38. Porter Slab** 8 (6 Bolts)
Climb the smooth, black slab on nice edges and techy high-steps to the anchor. Bolted ground-up on lead.
FA: C. Tirrell, B. Scott

### 39. Crazy Will** 10b (6 Bolts)
Climb the vertical face just left of Horizon Arête. Easy climbing on edges leads to a tricky move gaining a right-hand layback.
FA: B. Scott

### 40. Horizon Arête** 11a (7 Bolts)
This route has changed so many times since its initial first ascent, it's almost a different route. Continuous climbing up the prominent arête on edges. From the last bolt stay right of bolt line and mantle onto a shelf feature. From here, traverse back left to a long reach before the anchor. Very hard for the grade.
FA: J. Tarry

### 41. Puzzlebook** 10c (6 Bolts)
Start in a left-facing corner and climb past 3 bolts to a bulge with twin cracks. Climb the left crack and arête before stepping back right to the chains. Hard for the grade.
FA: B. Scott

Jessi Pinnock on **Chainsaw Massacre** ** 12b  Photo: B. Scott

# D - SOUTH WALL

From the White Wall, continue walking south/upstream along the West Side Main Trail. Pass the Horizon Wall and cross over a steep gulley. Continue South/upstream on the West Side Main Trail until Alpha Omega comes into view on climbers right.

### 42. ○ Red Dawn** 12c (6 Bolts)
Climb moderate terrain near the corner to an obvious crux traversing the steep wall back left to the arête.
FA: B. Scott

### 43. ○ Mellow Yellow** 11b (8 Bolts)
Juggy face climbing terrain leads to a crux move reaching a flake system at the top of the wall. Followed by a big move back left to Bolt 8 before a long easy slab to the anchor.
FA: B. Scott

### 44. ○ Silver Salute*** 11c (10 Bolts)
Climb chossy rock past the first two bolts. Enter a short left-facing corner to reach the sweet silver panel. Move back left at the end of the crux seam and climb fun easier terrain to the top.
FA: B. Scott

### 45. ○○ Mirror Mirror*** 9/12a (13 Bolts)
**P1:** Climb some edges to a shallow chimney covered in jugs. Stem your way to the anchor (5.9).
**P2:** Move up and right from the P1 anchor to a wave of incredible rock. Nice sustained 5.12 climbing leads out the bulge. Continue following a right-facing corner to a tricky move right before the anchor and the top of the South Wall. This is meant as an extension of P1 and can be done with a 70m rope (5.12a).
FA: B. Scott, J. Tarry

### 46. ○ Fog of War*** 13a (7 Bolts)
Climb an easy slab to a low crux at Bolt 4. Continue to a ledge rest and engage a final crux getting onto the arête followed by a desperate jump move to the anchor.
FA: B. Scott

### 47. ○ Boat Drinks*** 12b (4 Bolts + GEAR)
A mixed route with good trad gear in the upper half of the route. There are 4 bolts to start, the rest is all trad gear.
FA: J. Tarry

### 48. ○ Anunnaki**** 13b (12 Bolts)
The best endurance oriented route at the West Side of Poudre Falls. This line tackles an improbable series of overhangs on good rock and unusual holds. Hard for the grade, this route will test your resolve at the redpoint jump to mantle/undercling crux at the last big roof.
FA: B. Scott

### 49. ○ Shear Stress** 11b (GEAR)
Start with a steep handcrack that ends in a tricky sequence moving out left. Continue on easy terrain to an obvious ledge/break. Follow a left-facing tan colored corner to the chains.
FA: J. Tarry

### 50. ○ Alpha Omega*** 13b (7 Bolts)
This infamous power oriented route sits right at the beginning of the South Wall when approached from the Horizon Wall. A testy move past Bolt 1 gets you on the sloping ledge. Fun moves lead to a hard and desperate boulder problem over the small roof. Excellent 5.12 climbing up the beautiful upper panel leads to the chains.
FA: B. Scott, M. Tschol

Skyler Bol on the classic **Alpha Omega*** **13b**  Photo: B. Scott

## E - LITTLE WAVE WALL

This short but steep wall features powerful climbing on good stone. Even with its relatively close proximity to the Mega Bloks and Horizon Wall, the Little Wave Wall is seldom visited. There are two ways to reach the Little Wave Wall.

1. From the White Wall, walk south/upstream until just before you reach Mega Bloks Wall. Locate a downhill trail that will take you to the base of the Little Wave Wall.

2. From the parking lot, walk through the meadow and continue following a trail that parallels the river. Before the trail reaches the steep gulley where Aquatron lies, it will turn uphill and take you right to Little Wave Wall.

### 51. ◯ The Apprentice** 11b (6 Bolts)
The long vertical face on the southside of the Little Wave Wall. Start with a short right-facing corner followed by a techy traverse right to Bolt 3. More edges lead to easier climbing before a tricky crux to reach the anchor.
FA: B. Scott

### 52. ◯ Tombstone* 12b (3 Bolts)
Climb an obvious compression feature to Bolt 2. The crux involves moving off the Tombstone and over the lip to the anchor. A cam can be placed to protect the moves to Bolt 1.
FA: B. Scott

### 53. ◯ First Blood** 12b (4 Bolts)
Grab a ledgy feature and continue to a sidepull/undercut jug at Bolt 2. The first crux involves a long reach to a slopey edge followed by a dropknee move to reach the tufa/flake past Bolt 3. Jugs at Bolt 4 are followed by a slam-dunk move to the lip and a mantle.
FA: B. Scott

## F - MYOPIA WALL

The Myopia Wall is an excellent secluded wall with fantastic rock and an amazing belay area. This wall is worth a visit for any climber looking to explore something outside the main areas at Poudre Falls. From the White Wall, continue walking south/upstream along the main trail. Pass the Horizon Wall and cross over a steep gulley. After crossing the steep gulley, look for a cairned trail switchbacking directly uphill. Continue following the cairns as they angle up and left across the hillside and up some 5th class terrain.

### 54. ◯ Big Retina** 8 (5 Bolts)
A nice moderate to get the body warmed up. Jugs and laybacks follow the crack feature on the left side of the wall on excellent stone.
FA: M. Pascoe

### 55. ◯ Visine** 12a (5 Bolts)
Climb laybacks and jugs to a no-hands stance. Technical slab climbing leads to the anchor.
FA: R. Nelson

### 56. ◯ Myopia*** 11b (6 Bolts)
Use horizontal rails and small edges to work your way up into the delicate and powerful crux. Finish on the easier finger crack above.
FA: R. Nelson

### 57. ◯ Hyperopia*** 11b (4 Bolts)
Start with a tricky move to a jug at Bolt 1 and the bottom of the black streak. Continue climbing on a variety of holds and movement to a reachy crux around Bolt 3.
FA: J. Tarry, B. Scott

The author on **Golden Boy**\*\*\* **12c**  Photo: J. Levine

GOLD WALL

## G - GOLD WALL

The Gold Wall is another secluded wall that features nice rock, great views and potential for more climbing. From the White Wall, continue walking south/upstream along the West Side Main Trail. Pass the Horizon Wall and cross over a steep gulley. After crossing the steep gulley, look for a cairned trail heading directly uphill. Continue following the cairns as they angle up and left across the hillside and up some 5th class terrain. Pass the Myopia Wall and look for another 5th class section heading up and left to the Gold Wall.

### 58. Coffin Crack\*\*\*\* 9 (4 Bolts + GEAR)
Climb some broken rock to reach Bolt 1. Continue on edges and sidepulls past three more bolts to a ledge and the coffin. Continue on awesome laybacks and crack features. Standard rack to a #3.5 Camalot.
FA: J. Tarry

### 59. Golden Boy\*\*\* 12c (6 Bolts)
Scramble to a large ledge and follow jugs to Bolt 1. Continue on technical terrain to an obvious crux at Bolt 4 using seams and compression.
FA: B. Scott

### 60. Tantrum\*\*\* 12b (7 Bolts)
From the ledge, climb a broken flake past two bolts until you can move up and left through the overhang. The crux involves a long right-hand reach at the end of the overhang. Sustained 5.11 climbing to the top.
FA: B. Scott, J. Tarry

COVE WALL

## H - COVE WALL

This short but fun wall features the same setting as the River Wall, but without the committing rappels to the belay zone. From the parking lot, walk 100 yards upstream on the trail next to the river. Walk through a small meadow (camping) and continue following a trail that parallels the river. Look for a faint trail to a 5th class gulley that heads down to the water's edge on your left.

### 61. Over Appropriation** 11a/b (7 Bolts)
A fun bouldery start leads to a right-facing corner.
FA: M. Wright, E. Wright

### 62. First in Appropriation** 10b (7 Bolts)
Climb the first three bolts of First in Time, then walk left across the ledge and finish on Over Appropriation.
FA: M. Wright, E. Wright

### 63. First in Time*** 11b (9 Bolts)
Great edge climbing up the black streak.
FA: M. Wright, M. Botkin

### 64. First in Right*** 11b/c (7 Bolts)
Climb the first three bolts of First In Appropriation, then do an easy traverse to a ledge on the right. Technical face climbing brings you to the chains.
FA: M. Wright, E. Wright

POUDRE FALLS

RD Pascoe on **The Spectacle*** 11b  Photo: B. Scott

**Author's Note:** Jesse Levine and I thought up this photo one day after climbing at Poudre Falls. We just had to find the right kayaker. I've known Evan Stafford since 1998 and we both agreed he was the man for the job. Ever the professional, Evan proceeded to pull lap after lap of this rapid while Jesse snapped away. Evan is a legend and a treasured human to the local and national boating community. We are all lucky to have guys like Evan roaming the waters of Northern Colorado.

**73.** ⭕ **Water Rights**\*\*\* **12b (8 Bolts)**
An amazing sustained series of 5.12 climbing on perfect rock in a spectacular position.
**FA:** B. Scott, J. Tarry

The author on **Water Rights**\*\*\* **12b** with Evan Stafford manning the kayak and J. Levine behind the camera. Photo: J. Levine

# POUDRE FALLS

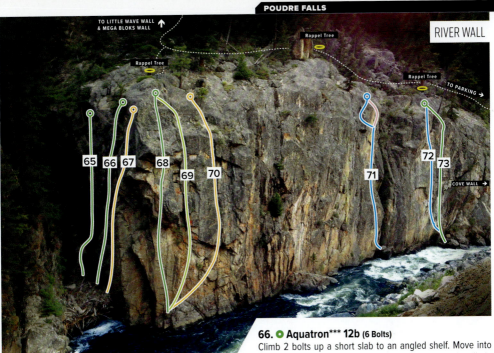

## I - RIVER WALL

From the parking lot, walk 100 yards upstream on the trail next to the river. Walk through a small meadow (camping) and continue following a trail that parallels the river. From the West Side Main Trail, the descent trail to the River Wall and Little Wave Wall is located between the Mega Bloks Wall and the route Bad Monkey.

**WARNING: The climbing at the River Wall is VERY COMMITTING in nature compared to most single-pitch climbing. All of the routes involve rappelling into a belay stance at the rivers edge which means you MUST ASCEND in order to get out.**

Here are a few helpful tips for climbing at the River Wall:
1. Check the river conditions first and make sure your belay platform is dry. High water is usually May-July.
2. Rappel off a tree if you don't feel comfortable downclimbing from the trail to the anchor.
3. Bring a jug and an etrier to escape in an emergency.
4. If you are unsure whether you can free climb back out, set a fixed line before you descend as a back up.
5. Routes have been bolted/developed assuming they will be inspected on rappel and that draws will be pre-placed on rappel.
6. Communication with your partner is essential. Be on the same plan about everything. Verbal communication is really hard or impossible due to the noise of the raging river.

### 65. Orion Skies** 12b (4 Bolts)
Chimney between a boulder to gain a sloping ledge. Use sidepulls and underclings to reach the jug and Bolt 1. Move through crimps, jugs and underclings to the crux at Bolt 3. Excellent stone throughout.
FA: B. Scott

### 66. Aquatron*** 12b (6 Bolts)
Climb 2 bolts up a short slab to an angled shelf. Move into a subtle scoop below the crux bulge. Left-hand sidepulls in a seam/crack, crimps and tricky footwork get you to Bolt 6.
FA: J. Tarry

### 67. Waterway** 10a (8 Bolts)
A nice moderate on blocky holds with fantastic position.
FA: R.D. Pascoe

### 68. Vide Noir*** 12b (8 Bolts)
"Black Void" pour les incultes. Start with a technical slab on perfect rock. Get a rest in the alcove perch before busting out the bulge roof.
FA: R. Nelson, B. Scott

### 69. Barrel Rider* 9 (8 Bolts)
Traverse right off the Vide Noir belay passing a bolt before heading up the crack.
FA: R. Nelson

### 70. Crack Route* 10c (1 Bolt + gear)
Step right from the Vide Noir belay and climb the broken crack to the top.
FA: R. Nelson

### 71. The Spectacle*** 11b (9 Bolts)
A tricky boulder problem getting to Bolt 2. Easy climbing to a steep crux at Bolt 6. From Bolt 7, traverse left and around to reach the anchor. The direct finish is an Open Project that is approx. 5.12d in difficulty.
FA: B. Scott, J. Tarry

### 72. Into the Drink*** 11d (9 Bolts)
Clip Bolt 1 on Water Rights and traverse left. Continue on laybacks and slopey jugs to a tricky face climbing section after the bulge. Just as good as Water Rights.
FA: J. Tarry

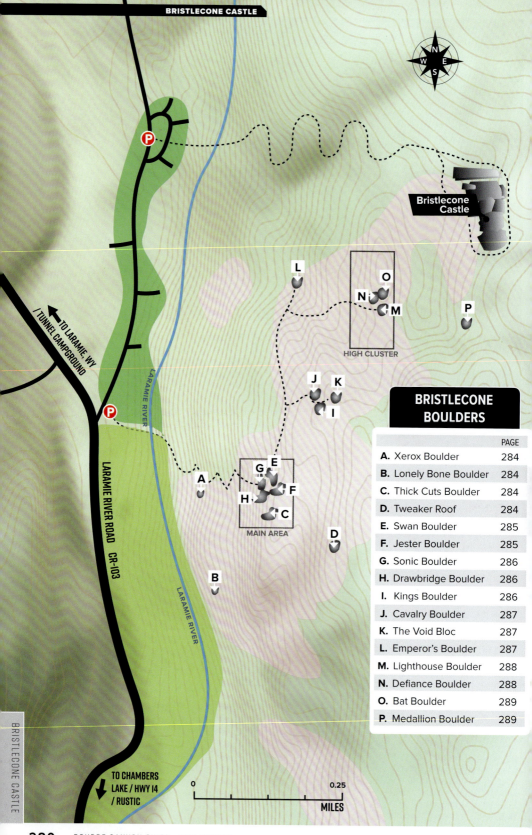

**55.0 MILES** FROM TED'S PLACE

# BRISTLECONE CASTLE

Towering cliffs over fields of boulders, this is the Bristlecone Castle   Photo: B. Scott

GRADE DISTRIBUTION

**TYPE(S): SPORT, TRAD, & BOULDERING**
**DIFFICULTY RANGE: 5.8 - 5.13D, V1-V10**
**APPROACH TIME: 15 MIN - 1 HOUR**
**SEASON: JUNE-NOV, SEASONAL ROAD CLOSURE**

## CLIMBING OVERVIEW

Bristlecone Castle is not technically in the Poudre Canyon, it is located in the Laramie River Valley which runs north towards Wyoming. First developed over the summer of 2011 by **Doug McKee, Chris Tirrell, Jason Tarry** and **the author**. The talus field of boulders below the cliff had been explored by climbers previously but nobody really sunk their teeth in until **Sam Rothstein, Jake Atkinson, Levi Van Weddingen, Cam Shubb** and others did over the summer of 2017.

This area is primarily a summer climbing area do to its alpine nature. In fact, the Laramie River Road is only open from June-September so the window for climbing here is relatively short. Good rock and incredible scenery make this a worthy adventure for any climber.

## GETTING THERE

GPS: 40°38'56.45"N 105°51'8.30"W

**HIKING DIRECTIONS TO THE BOULDERING:**
From Ted's Place, head west on Hwy 14 for 51 miles. Turn north on Laramie River Rd/CO 103 for four miles. Park at the obvious gated fork at the north end of a meadow for the bouldering or continue driving down the right fork to a large cul-de-sac camping area for the roped climbing. The cliff can be seen from this parking area.

**HIKING DIRECTIONS TO THE ROPED ROCK CLIMBING:**
From the camping area, head west and cross the Laramie River/Creek. From here, the forest becomes very dense and covered with deadfall. You need to try and locate a very subtle gulley leading uphill and east. If you can't find this gulley, then just pick the path of least resistance and start heading up the steep hillside. After about 30-40min of steep slogging, you should be able to make out the top of the Bristlecone Castle. Don't traverse directly to it; continue moving uphill, but angle slightly right towards the tower.

We usually have dogs with us and this makes the talus field at the base virtually impassable. So, we have always continued up and around the east flank of the tower, eventually finding a notch and moving back around to the north to the base of the climbs. If you don't have dogs or a reason to avoid going through the talus, then don't. It will save you 15min to walk through the talus instead of going up and around the back of the cliff.

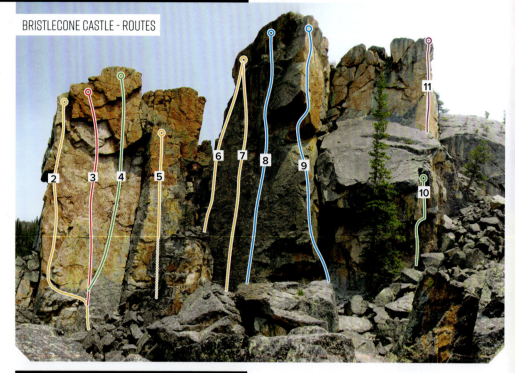

# BRISTLECONE CASTLE - ROUTES

### 1. ○ Path of Least Resistance 8 (GEAR)
Located on the north face of the north tower and easily seen on the approach trail. This short left-facing corner was the original approach route to the top of this tower. Beware of loose blocks near the top of the pitch.
FA: J. Tarry, D. McKee

### 2. ○ Golden Arête*** 10c (12 Bolts)
Gain a ledge and move left to Bolt 1. Move up a short left facing corner/flake until you can move back left. From here, follow a series of edges and overlaps to some mantles before the chains.
FA: J. Tarry, D. McKee, B. Scott

### 3. ○ Red Dragon** 13b (12 Bolts)
The initial section is about 5.12 to the first short roof. Long pulls on solid micro-edges lead over the roof to a bad rest. A big move up and right starts the crux and leads straight into a series of techy sidepulls and high feet to a rest before the last little roof. Its about 5.11 to the top from here but definitely no gimmie.
FA: B. Scott

### 4. ○ Guillotine*** 12a (GEAR)
An amazing crack and face line protected with natural gear. Climb a right leaning crack to the top of a short pillar. Continue up the crack to the base of the large roof. The crux climbs over and out this roof to the right with sidepulls and bad feet. A small cam protects the crux. Continue on varied 5.10 terrain with just enough gear to get you to the anchor.
FA: D. McKee

### 5. ○ Trout Whistle** 10a (GEAR)
Established ground up on trad gear, this great face climb hosts a ton of holds that are hard to see from the ground.
FA: D. McKee

### 6. ○ Keyhole Cousins 10b (2 Bolts + GEAR)
Start up twin parallel cracks. At the small overhang, transition right onto the face near the arête. Pull 5.10 moves past two close bolts. Then move right delicately and plug bomber cams before pulling the final 5.9 move to the top.
FA: Z. Lesch-Huie, R.D. Pascoe

### 7. ○ Frickin' Lawyers* 10b (TOP-ROPE)
Use Keyhole Cousins anchor to top-rope this route. It's a fun 5.9 techy slab to a ledge, then a hard 5.10 crux into the finish of Keyhole Cousins.
FA: Z. Lesch-Huie, R.D. Pascoe

### 8. ○ Green Dragon*** 11c (12 Bolts)
Start up a short bulge to gain the long edge covered face. Continue up the face to the base of the large roof. Move left to a seepy sidepull before moving back right through the crux and up the rest of the glorious headwall.
FA: B. Scott, D. McKee

## BRISTLECONE CASTLE

> **Climber Spotlight:** Doug McKee and I have been having adventures together since 1998. Back then, Doug was an east coast punk gym climber who had been doing comps for years. Nowadays, Doug has become an expert big-wall climber and sandstone tower first ascentionist. Being a Steamboat area resident, Doug happily makes the two-hour drive down to the Poudre on a regular basis. He and I have developed countless routes and walls in the Upper Canyon together. Bristlecone Castle was one such adventure Doug and I started. Initially walking up the hill to develop some bouldering, we stumbled upon the amazing tower and cliff features. We only hauled ropes and gear up the hill after that.

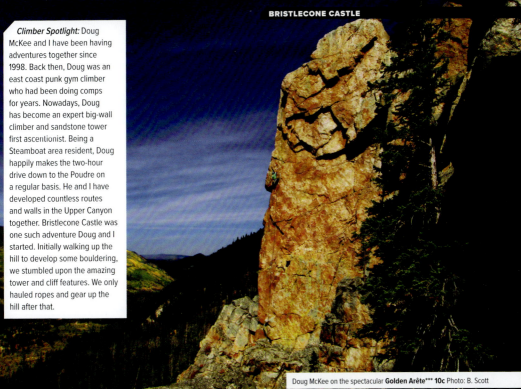

Doug McKee on the spectacular **Golden Arête**\*\*\* **10c** Photo: B. Scott

**9.** ○ **Iron Maiden**\*\*\* **11c** (12 Bolts)
Begin with a techy slab traverse out of the right-facing corner. Continue up the arête/face to the base of the big roof. Do a cruxy sequence up and right out the roof to a stance. Pull the balancy crux and enjoy fantastic climbing right on the exposed arête to the anchor.
FA: B. Scott, C. Tirrell, D. McKee

**10.** ○ **Short Stack**\* **12b** (6 Bolts)
This short route tackles an imposing short roof and a steep corner. Getting around the lip of the roof is definitely the crux.
FA: B. Scott

**11.** ○ **The Golden Shower**\*\*\* **8** (2 Bolts + GEAR)
Climb the crack to a pedestal then the arête to the chains. If you miss a crucial hold at the top, it will feel harder. If this was at The Palace, it would be one of the most popular climbs there. It has great photo opportunities!
FA: K. Duncan, D. Humphrey

**12.** ○ **Tech Savvy**\*\* **11b** (6 Bolts)
Located on the far right side of the cliff on a nice grey slab near a tree. Excellent technical face climbing on quality stone.
FA: K. Duncan, D. Humphrey

Dave Ludders finishing the crux of **Iron Maiden**\*\*\* **11c** Photo: B. Scott

# BRISTLECONE CASTLE - BOULDERING

The bouldering at "BCone," as it's been coined, is extensive to say the least. This guide covers only a small portion of the developed bouldering. There are plenty of boulders left to clean so head out there when you need a break from the RMNP chaos over the summer. The photos and descriptions for this section were provided by **Nick Perle, Jake Atkinson** and **Sam Rothstein.**

## A - XEROX BOULDER

One of the closest boulders to the road. It is located in the small talus below the main cluster.

**1.** ⭕ **Xerox\* v8** (Pads)
Stand start on a left-hand crimp and a right-hand sidepull on the arête. Move out right, get a very extended toe-hook, and work through a few more tough moves to gain the lip.
FA: S. Rothstein

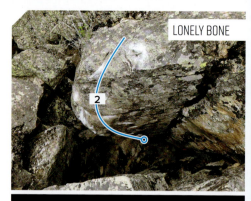

## B - LONELY BONE BOULDER

Hike to the main area, then continue past it into the next small talus field. 100 yards up from the river at the bottom of the second talus zone is a cluster of a few big blocs that look small but are actually quite big.

**2.** ⭕ **Lonely Bone\*\*\* v10** (Pads)
Stand start on a right-hand crimp, a left-hand tooth and make a hard first move out left. Continue through hard compression movement, set a bad heel, and throw for the Bone hold.
FA: S. Rothstein

**3.** ⭕ **Room with No View\*\* v8** (Pads)
Located on the opposite side from Lonely Bone. SDS on the large jug and traverse up and right to a techy mantle. This is RMNP style climbing.
FA: K. Worobec

## C - THICK CUTS BOULDER

Located on the southern edge of the main area. A very geometric looking boulder with an obvious arête.

**4.** ⭕ **Thick Cuts\*\* v5** (Pads)
Stand start compressed on the two arêtes, and climb straight up the golden prow feature.
FA: B. Hoffman

## D - TWEAKER ROOF

Located directly up from the Lonely Bone Boulder at the top of the second talus field.

**5.** ⭕ **Tweaker Roof\*\* v8** (Pads)
Start on the left side of the roof on good incuts, and move right and out of the cave into big incuts out the lip.
FA: S. Rothstein

**BRISTLECONE CASTLE**

SWAN

SWAN

## E - SWAN BOULDER

This is one of the first boulders encountered in the main cluster, 10-15min uphill and right after crossing the stream near the road.

### 6. ○ Branch Action* v3 (Pads)
SDS on a small left-hand and some big right-hand edges. Climb through perfect crimps and pinches until you get to the lip, then head right to jugs.
**FA: C. Shubb**

### 7. ○ Cygnus** v7 (Pads)
SDS on the arête and climb straight up the short prow using compression tactics.
**FA: Lance Carerra**

### 8. ○ Treedigger** v6 (Pads)
Stand start on the jug rail, climb up the arête, then head back right via hard moves at the lip and a tough mantle.
**FA: L. Van Weddingen**

### 9. ○ Ugly Duck* v1 (Pads)
Climb the middle of the face up good edges.
**FA: S. Rothstein**

### 10. ○ Ducks in a Row** v3 (Pads)
Start as for Swan, but after making the first left-hand move, transition straight to the slab and topout that way.
**FA: J. Atkinson**

### 11. ○ Swan*** v6 (Pads)
A tricky start move from the left end of the big rail feature gives way to some awesome, horizontal, compression moves and an engaging topout section.
**FA: S. Rothstein**

### 12. ○ Grey Goose*** v10 (Pads)
This climbs the right end of the big rail in the roof, five feet right of Swan. Start with a left-hand pinch and a right-hand edge. Make hard intro moves to the right, and fire straight out the roof on good stone.
**FA: S. Rothstein**

## F - JESTER BOULDER

### 13. ○ Jester*** v8 (Pads)
SDS with a right-hand sidepull and a left-hand sloper. Climb awesome small holds and tricky feet all the way. The stand start is a bit easier. (not pictured)
**FA: S. Rothstein**

**BRISTLECONE CASTLE**

Tristan Conway on **Sonic Alchemist**\*\*\* v9  Photo: Sam Rothstein

## I - KING'S BOULDER

To date this is the best boulder in the area with five amazing lines and more still to come. It has a beautiful orange face that is slightly overhanging with some divine edges, pinches, and slopers. Bring your finger strength and a decent head if you wish to join the King's ranks.

**19.** ○ **Duchess**\*\*\* v4 (Pads)
Start low on a nice left-facing, sidepull rail. Crank up through a sweet pinch and solid edges to a topout out left. It is a good warm-up for the other lines on the boulder.
FA: N. Perl

**20.** ○ **Squire**\*\*\* v4 (Pads)
Start as for Duchess, but move right using the awesome, protruding flake and topout as for We Three Kings.
FA: J. Atkinson

**21.** ○ **The Last King**\*\*\*\* v8 (Pads)
Start on the tombstone and climb straight up, then trend left and topout We Three Kings.
FA: N. Perl

**22.** ○ **We Three Kings**\*\*\* v8 (Pads)
Depending on how you do it, it's around 15 moves of goodness to reach the top. SDS matched on the tombstone flake and make the hard, crimpy traverse left topping out on the awesome moves up and protruding jug.
FA: J. Atkinson

**23.** ○ **Charlemagne**\*\*\*\* v9 (Pads)
Charlemagne is another climb fit for royalty. SDS on the tombstone flake, work up through some amazing edges until you can trend left and relax on the large horn. From there, make easier but scarier moves to the right.
FA: S. Rothstein

**24.** ○ **Chivalry**\*\*\* v8 (Pads)
Start on the sweet left-facing jug a few feet right of the prow. Make hard moves straight up before traversing left and then back right as for Charlemagne.
FA: S. Rothstein

**25.** ○ **Start Something**\*\* v0 (Pads)
Start from the huge undercling and bop up the slab.
FA: J. Atkinson

## G - SONIC BOULDER

**14.** ○ **Sonic Boom**\*\* v7 (Pads)
Start on two small crimps with a low left foot, then fire to the full pad crimp jug. Dyno over the pit to a decent edge and topout via sloper jugs.
FA: T. Conway

**15.** ○ **Sonic Alchemist**\*\*\* v9 (Pads)
Stand start on a jug above your head, and climb left and around the arête using hard tension and slopey crimps. The obvious stand start goes at about v5.
FA: L. Carerra, S. Rothstein

## H - DRAWBRIDGE BOULDER

**16.** ○ **Cut with a Sword**\* v4 (Pads)
Pull on the crimp and poor undercling. Smear your feet and hop to the lip. Traverse right through the laser cut crimp rail to topout.
FA: S. Rothstein

**17.** ○ **Drawbridge**\*\* v5 (Pads)
SDS on underclings. Paste your feet in smears, then make a hard move to a big edge. Continue left to the top.
FA: S. Rothstein

**18.** ○ **Coat of Arms**\* v7 (Pads)
Stand start on the low part of the landing using a left-hand undercling and small right-hand crimp. Pull on, make a few hard moves on perfect holds, and then topout straight up.
FA: Unknown

BRISTLECONE CASTLE

## K - THE VOID BLOC

The Void Bloc is close to the King's Boulder, just trend to hikers left and slightly uphill back into the talus.

### 29. ◯ Empty of Thought, Full of Mind*** v7 (Pads)
Start right-hand on the beautiful rail, left-hand undercling, and make a series of amazing moves up and left. Let it flow.
FA: N. Perl

### 30. ◯ The Void Bop* v3 (Pads)
This problem is super morpho...start either spanning really wide or with your left-hand on a small crimp in the face. Work up to the topout right of the pinnacle.
FA: N. Perl

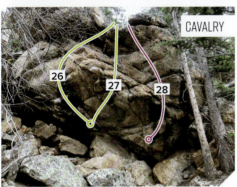

## J - CAVALRY BOULDER

Located behind the King's Boulder. The climbs at the Cavalry Boulder are moderate and the holds can provide a nice warm-up before you tackle the King's Boulder.

### 26. ◯ All the King's Horses** v6 (Pads)
Starting on the same juggy rail as All the King's Men, go left to an awesome pinch, and fire up through the crux. Topout to the right.
FA: S. Rothstein

### 27. ◯ All the King's Men** v5 (Pads)
Start on the nice juggy rail in the middle of the boulder, and move straight up using some cool holds and funky movement.
FA: S. Rothstein

### 28. ◯ Cavalry** v3 (Pads)
Starting on the right end of the big rail, move up to a sweet edge. Take the big holds to the top.
FA: J. Atkinson

## L - EMPEROR'S BOULDER

From the main area, traverse along the screefield as if you were heading to the bolted routes at the top. The boulder is 100 yards below Bristlecone Castle at the start of where the big talus begins again.

### 31. ◯ Emperor's New Clothes* v7 (Pads)
Start as low as possible on a good left-hand crimp and a right-hand sidepull. Pull on, and make a few hard moves to gain a jug. Then continue up on small holds before escaping out right to the arête.
FA: S. Rothstein

Levi Van Weddingen on the beautiful stone of **The Lighthouse**\*\*\* **v5**   Photo: S. Rothstein

## M - LIGHTHOUSE BOULDER

This wall is home to some good climbs with excellent landings on pristine Bristlecone rock. The Lighthouse Boulder can be spotted easily from the road by the round orange boulder that sits on top of it....way the heck up the hill. Located in the upper cluster of boulders referred to as the "High Cluster."

### 32. ◯ The Lighthouse*** v5 (Pads)
Stand start on good edges on the left side of the face and climb up and right through technical moves with slippery feet.
FA: L. Van Weddingen

### 33. ◯ Maritime** v2 (Pads)
Stand start on the jug undercling, and climb up and right through friendly holds to an easy topout.
FA: L. Van Weddingen, S. Rothstein

## N - DEFIANCE BOULDER

This huge boulder sits just behind the Lighthouse Boulder, and its brightly colored uphill face is easily recognizable.

### 34. ◯ Defiance** v6 (Pads)
Climb up the fine grained face on crimp teet, and finish on better crimps up to a techy finish.
FA: T. Conway

## O - BAT BOULDER

This is a humongous boulder in the biggest section of the upper talus, next to the Defiance and Lighthouse Boulders.

### 35. Bat Outta Hell** v5 (Pads)
SDS on the jug on the left side of the wall and climb through tricky layback moves down low until you can reach the crack system and airy topout.
FA: B. Hoffman

### 36. Dracula** v4 (Pads)
Stand start on the small edges in the middle of the face, make techy moves straight up, then head back left to gain the crack and tall finish.
FA: T. Conway

## P - MEDALLION BOULDER

Located at the very top of the talus field, almost at the cliffs but a bit farther south in a jumble of massive boulders.

### 37. Medallion*** v8 (Pads)
Start low on good edges at the bottom of the arête and climb up and left through large holds into small crimps just before the lip. Traverse left to topout and walk off.
FA: S. Rothstein

Sam Rothstein on the steep finish of **Medallion*** v8  Photo: S. Rothstein

Chris Hofer on the footwork intensive crux of **Marky Mark**\*\*\* **12c**  Photo: A. Cross

# INDEX

## Symbols

13th Step, The* 10a .................................. 73
40 Grit** v5 ............................................. 188
84 Beacon Street*** 10b ........................ 237
420 Boulders .......................................... 219

## A

Abbey Ale 10b ......................................... 57
Above and Beyond Boulder .................. 246
Above and Beyond*** v8 ...................... 246
Access Pitch 6 ....................................... 163
A Desperate Man* 10c .......................... 107
A Double-Edged Sword*** v2 ................. 92
Adulteress, The 11b .............................. 152
Adults Only Picnic** 9 ............................. 33
Aesop** v9 ............................................ 143
A-Frame Roof** 11d ................................ 42
Against Humanity Boulder ................... 248
Against Humanity**** v6 ...................... 248
Against the Grain** 12d ....................... 156
Ajna Sanctuary 10b ................................ 95
A-Lady* 11a ............................................ 81
Albatross, The**** 14a ......................... 270
A Little Slice Of Sunshine** 10b ............ 167
All In A Daze Work** 11c/d ..................... 80
All Roads Lead to Capuchin 10a ........... 128
All the King's Horses** v6 ..................... 287
All the King's Men** v5 ........................ 287
Alpha Omega*** 13b ........................... 272
Alvin* 6 .................................................. 44
Always Almonds 12a ............................ 119
American Spirit** v7 ............................. 214
Amphitheatre ....................................... 181
Anahata 12a ........................................... 94
Anchor Thief* 11c .................................. 56
Andromeda Galaxy*** 10b ................... 263
Angle Dangle** v3 ............................... 226
Angry Black Man** v7 .......................... 241
Another Pat's Arête** v4 ...................... 207
Antique Guns 10d ................................. 155
Anunnaki**** 13b ................................ 272
Apprentice, The** 11b ......................... 275
Aquatron*** 12b .................................. 279
Arda** 10b ............................................. 81
Arête #19** v4 ..................................... 205
Arête-o-matic* v3 ................................ 133
Are You Experienced?** 10b .................. 98
Aries Arête** 11b ................................. 118
Armor Plated* 11c .................................. 75
Around The World** v3 ......................... 89
Astronomy Wall ................................... 263
Atlas Shrugged Project .......................... 95
Auldridge Jump Problem* v2 ............... 221
Au Revoir** v5 ..................................... 261

## B

Baadlands* 10a ..................................... 111
Baby Black* v5 ..................................... 240
Backburner* v9 .................................... 138
Back in the Saddle* 10b ....................... 118
Back On Black** 12a .............................. 77
Back On Black Wall ................................ 77
Back on the Train** 11b ....................... 162
Back to Jail** 10d ................................. 157
Bad Monkey** 12b ............................... 270
B.A.H. 9 .................................................. 71
Balaam* 11c ........................................... 65
Balance Boulder ................................... 224
Balcony Direct Project ........................... 41
Balcony Railbumper** 12c ..................... 41
Ballet Of The Bulge*** 11b .................... 67
Bananarête** 9 ...................................... 64
Bandito's Bat Roost 8 ............................ 57
Barfy's Favorite** 7 ............................... 45
Bartles & Jaymes** 11a ........................ 170
Bat Boulder ......................................... 289
Bat Outta Hell** v5 .............................. 289
Battle Axe* 9 .......................................... 79
B.B.T. Wall .............................................. 73
Beachside Face v4 ............................... 202
Bean Boulder ......................................... 92
Beast Wall ............................................ 193
Beau Dirt** v3 ...................................... 251
Beckoning Silence, The*** v12 ............ 189
Behold My Creation* 10a ..................... 127
Benchmark, The** 12c ......................... 171
Be Not Afraid* 12c ............................... 123
Ben's Craptastic Traverse* v5 .............. 223
Ben's Face* v2 ..................................... 130
Ben's Face  v3 ...................................... 229
Ben's Goofy Face** v4 ......................... 229
Berlin Airlift 10a .................................. 123
Bert* 10b ............................................... 58
Better Call Maynard* 10c .................... 129
Better Than the Internet** 11b ............. 66
Better Than Watching
         Television*** 11c .................... 65
Between the Sheeps*** 10d ................ 117
Big As A House 10b ................................ 72
Big Bad Beav** 11c ............................... 217
Big Black Moose*** 12b ...................... 242
Big Flake v1 ......................................... 249
Bighorns* 11a ...................................... 113
Big Mac*** 12c ...................................... 76
Big Oyster*** v9 .................................. 189
Big Retina** 8 ...................................... 275
Bisecting Fist Crack** 10b ..................... 42
Bisher Arête** v8 ................................. 206
Bisher Boulder ..................................... 140
Bisher Traverse*** v7 .......................... 226
Bitchy Sister** 12b .............................. 146
Bit Of A Dandy** 9 ............................... 103
Bitter Clinger* 11c ............................... 109
Black Arête* v1 .................................... 213
Black Beard's Traverse** v7 ................... 37
Black Beast** 13b ................................ 193

Black Boulder ....................................... 240
Black Boulder Area ............................... 239
Black Crocus* 11c ................................ 149
Black Dog* 8 .......................................... 45
Black Eye In Overtime** 12b ................. 59
Black Eye In The Sky** 11d .................... 59
Black Hole*** 11c ................................ 263
Black Pearl Boulder ............................. 191
Black Pearl** v6 ................................... 191
Black Problem*** v9 ........................... 241
Black Seam Boulder ............................ 137
Black Serpent** 5.11c ......................... 165
Black Slab Boulder .............................. 136
Black Swan** v12 ................................ 249
BlackWave** 12c ................................... 64
Black Widow* v7 ................................... 89
Blake's Dyno** v8 .................................. 90
Blast a Blessing* 10b .......................... 129
Bliss State Wildlife Area (S.W.A.) ........ 199
Blitzkrieg Boulder ................................ 254
Blitzkrieg** v4 ..................................... 254
Blocky Arête* v2 .................................... 48
Blok Boulder ........................................ 185
Blok of Aragon* v11 ............................ 185
Blok One** v7 ...................................... 185
Blok Two** v10 .................................... 185
Blonde Note*** 13a ............................ 170
Blood of the Lamb** 11b .................... 117
Blood Runs Frozen** 10c .................... 123
Blue Collar Baby** 11b .......................... 59
Blue Feather*** v6 .............................. 140
Blue-Footed Boobie* 8 ........................ 120
Blue Steel* 12a ...................................... 77
Blue Streak* 12a ................................. 193
Boat Drinks*** 12b ............................. 272
Bodies Like Sheep 10c .......................... 73
Bog Area .............................................. 201
Bog Boulder ......................................... 202
Bolt Dependence* 11b .......................... 64
Bone Book* 10b ................................... 128
Bone Boulder ....................................... 227
Bone Tomahawk** v10 .......................... 90
Boogie Nights Boulder ........................ 215
Boogie Nights*** v11 .......................... 215
Book of Sheep** 7 ............................... 115
Booty Prize* 12a .................................... 57
Booze Tube** 10b .................................. 41
Bosch Hog 11d ....................................... 67
Bostock From Little Bird*** 11b .......... 116
Boston Peak ......................................... 233
Bouldering Traverse* v2 ....................... 42
Box Cars** 12c ..................................... 161
Boys Are Back In Town** 12a ................ 77
Branch Action* v3 ................................ 285
Breakin' Trail 10c ................................... 73
Bridge Engineer* 11c ........................... 123
Brinks Corner* 10 .................................. 52
Brink's Rock ........................................... 51
Bristlecone Castle ............................... 281
Bristlecone Castle - Bouldering ........... 284
Britney's Spear** 11c ............................ 67
Brown Chossum Special, The 10d ........ 75

## C

| Entry | Page |
|---|---|
| Brown Jump** v4 | 177 |
| Bubbles** 12b | 156 |
| Bubblicious Boulder | 188 |
| Bubblicious** v5 | 188 |
| Bullwinkle** 12c | 242 |
| Bum Lung, The* 12b | 162 |
| Bunker Hill** 12b | 237 |
| Burro, The** 12a | 110 |
| Butt Dragger Traverse* v4 | 49 |
| Butterfly*** 11d | 266 |
| Cab Ride** 10c | 39 |
| Cacao 11c | 119 |
| Cactus Garden | 83 |
| Callan's Crack**** 12a | 234 |
| Cal Trop 9 | 71 |
| Candyland | 119 |
| Cannon Ball** 12c | 75 |
| Canopener*** v11 | 225 |
| Cappuccino** 12c | 119 |
| Captain Awesome* 10c | 113 |
| Captain Galapagos* 8 | 120 |
| Car Bomb* 11b | 41 |
| Castaway Boulder | 208 |
| Castaway** v11 | 208 |
| Castle Magic*** 12b | 98 |
| Cavalry Boulder | 287 |
| Cavalry** v3 | 287 |
| Center 1* v3 | 208 |
| Center 2* v3 | 208 |
| Centerfold** v10 | 230 |
| Center Indian** v3 | 203 |
| Center Perfection*** v4 | 260 |
| Center Right** v5 | 177 |
| Chainsaw Massacre** 12b | 271 |
| Chamber, The | 75 |
| Change the Wind to Silence** 9 / 10c | 123 |
| Charlemagne**** v9 | 286 |
| Charlie Chaplin* v4 | 138 |
| Checkpoint Charlie* 9 | 123 |
| Check Your Head*** 10c | 71 |
| Check Your Six** 11b | 71 |
| Cheerleaders Gone Hippie* 9 | 71 |
| Chess Boulder | 91 |
| Chess** v2 | 91 |
| Chimney Sweep Wall | 58 |
| Chimpanzee** 12b | 266 |
| Chips and Beer** 9 | 33 |
| Chivalry*** v8 | 286 |
| Chocolate Stout*** 14a | 169 |
| Choss Dodger 11b | 57 |
| Chossy Arête v3 | 231 |
| Chromosphere** v8 | 49 |
| Chucky** v5 | 223 |
| Churchill Rejects*** 9 | 76 |
| Chute Wall | 146 |
| Circadian Rhythm*** v13 | 225 |
| Cirque Du Poudre*** 12c | 81 |
| Citadel** 11b | 80 |
| Citadel, The | 80 |
| Clams Boulder | 132 |
| Clams Casino*** v7 | 132 |
| Classic Warm-up*** v3 | 240 |
| Cleaning Day 11 | 124 |
| Clean-Up On Aisle 9** 9 | 66 |
| Cloudwalker Boulder | 230 |
| Cloudwalker*** v10 | 230 |
| Coach Myles*** 13d | 270 |
| Coat of Arms* v7 | 286 |
| Cobra Bloc | 141 |
| Cobra Kai** 12d | 161 |
| Coffin Crack**** 9 | 276 |
| Colors Crag | 97 |
| Comped at the Omni* 8 | 120 |
| Computer Blue Boulder | 214 |
| Computer Blue*** v9 | 214 |
| Conclave, The 7 | 110 |
| Consolation Prize* 9 | 195 |
| Cookie Monster Boulder | 207 |
| Cookie Monster*** v10 | 207 |
| Copperhead** 13a | 164 |
| Corkscrew Boulder | 251 |
| Corkscrew** v6 | 251 |
| Cornershop Boulder | 136 |
| Corn Sacker** v7 | 215 |
| Corona** 13a | 170 |
| Corridor Wall | 52 |
| Corridor Zone | 181 |
| Cosmic Trigger 9 | 94 |
| County Line*** 8 | 67 |
| Courting Doom** v9 | 249 |
| Cove Wall | 277 |
| Coyote, The**** 12a | 147 |
| Crack Dihedral* 6 | 82 |
| Cracker Jack 10b | 119 |
| Crack in a Ship** v2 | 36 |
| Crack of Lamb** 11a | 116 |
| Crack Route* 10c | 279 |
| Cracks Boulder | 139 |
| Cradle of Liberty**** 13c | 234 |
| Crazy Cody Boulder | 229 |
| Crazy Cody** v6 | 229 |
| Crazy Will** 10b | 271 |
| Creak Crack 7 R | 156 |
| Creekside Boulder | 222 |
| Creepy* 10b | 71 |
| Creme de la Poudre*** 14b | 218 |
| Crescent Boulder | 139 |
| Crescent, The*** v9 | 139 |
| Crime** v8 | 248 |
| Crimson Stain** 12b | 119 |
| Critical Mass Area | 192 |
| Critical Mass** v12 | 192 |
| Crossbow 10b | 71 |
| Crossing Over*** 12b | 102 |
| Cross Mojonation! 11a | 73 |
| Crossroads** v4 | 191 |
| Crosstown** 12a | 98 |
| Crown Boulder | 133 |
| Crown Low** v9 | 133 |
| Crown, The*** v7 | 133 |
| Crows Nest*** v6 | 209 |
| Cruiser 9 | 75 |
| Crunchy Boulder | 132 |
| Crunchy Grooves*** v7 | 132 |
| Crusher Boulder | 231 |
| Crusher*** v5 | 231 |
| Cryokinetic** 13b | 146 |
| Crypt, The | 128 |
| Crystal Method* 11+ R | 65 |
| Crystal Wall | 63 |
| Cut With A Sword* v4 | 286 |
| Cyberpunk Project | 95 |
| Cygnus** v7 | 285 |
| Cynic, The* 10c | 126 |

## D

| Entry | Page |
|---|---|
| Daniel's Problem** v9 | 202 |
| Dark Horse Project*** | 61 |
| Dark Pony*** 13b | 61 |
| Dark Tower**, The v3 | 213 |
| Dash to Freedom* 11b | 123 |
| Das Leben der Anderen* 12c | 123 |
| Date Night** 11c | 100 |
| Dave's Dihedral* v5 | 203 |
| Daylight Buttress | 124 |
| Daylight Donuts 6 | 124 |
| Days Between Us** 11c | 110 |
| Daytripper Arête** v6 | 189 |
| DC Corner 6 X | 79 |
| Dead Hand*** v9 | 140 |
| Deadmoo5** v10 | 231 |
| Dear Slabby*** 11b | 79 |
| Death and Disfiguration* 11c | 75 |
| Debt, The* 11b | 129 |
| De Dios 11a | 124 |
| Defiance Boulder | 288 |
| Defiance** v6 | 288 |
| Delicious Apple 10c | 162 |
| Delicious Demon*** 11b | 162 |
| Departed** 12a | 234 |
| Detachment Disorder** 11a | 83 |
| Devil Wears Lace* v8 | 89 |
| Devo** 10b | 116 |
| Diamond Arête* v1 | 231 |
| Diamondback*** 13c | 163 |
| Diamond Boulder | 49 |
| Diamond in the Rough** v11 | 49 |
| Dihedral Project | 136 |
| Dihedrals Wall | 115 |
| Dihedral With An Underclimg*** v12 | 253 |
| Dihedron** 11a | 270 |
| Dingleberry Boulder | 89 |
| Dingleberry Traverse* v5 | 89 |
| Dingleberry* v1 | 89 |
| Dingo Boulder | 197 |
| Dingus**** v4 | 201 |
| Dirty Burger** 11b | 156 |
| Dirty Diet Coke** 14a | 170 |
| Dirty Work** 11c | 109 |
| Disco Biscuit v7 | 215 |
| Dittos* 9 | 118 |

## INDEX

Divergence Boulder ........................ 229
Divergence*** v9 .......................... 229
Dixie Dingo** v3 ........................... 197
D-Man** 11c .................................. 81
Dog Face* 10a ................................ 44
Dog Will Hunt 11d .......................... 149
Donnie loves Jenny** 10d ............... 235
Don't Damn It* 7 ............................. 47
Don't Doubt Me* 11a ..................... 126
Don't Tell Mom** v3 ....................... 240
Down and Below** v5 ..................... 246
Downclimb v1 ............................... 243
Down On The Pharm** 8 .................. 64
Dracula** v4 ................................. 289
Drawbridge Boulder ....................... 286
Drawbridge** v5 ........................... 286
Drawn & Quartered 11a ................... 75
Dream Of Poudre**** 13a ................. 61
Dr. Food** 10b ................................ 66
Dr. Kelman I Presume* 9 ................ 107
Duchess*** v4 ............................... 286
Ducks in a Row** v3 ....................... 285
Dudley Boulder .............................. 130
Dudley's Arête* v2 ......................... 130
Duff* 12c ...................................... 170
Duke of Weselton*** 12d ................ 146
Dumping K* 11a ............................ 116
Dump Truck** v10 ......................... 248
Dung, The 7 .................................. 162
Dynesto Boulder ............................ 201
Dynesto*** v6 ............................... 201

## E

East Of Eden**** 9 ......................... 152
Easy Arête** v2 ............................. 224
Easy Eukie*** 12a ......................... 218
Easy Sit* v2 .................................... 49
Eden Area ..................................... 151
Edge of Daylight 11a ...................... 124
Edge Project ................................. 243
Electric Ocean ................................. 93
Elijah** 12b .................................... 58
Eluebbenator* 11b, The ................... 39
Emerald Isle*** 12b ......................... 99
Emperor's Boulder ......................... 287
Emperor's New Clothes* v7 ............ 287
Empire of Crumbs 10b ................... 123
Empty of Thought, Full
    of Mind*** v7 ........................... 287
Entropy*** 11a .............................. 116
Escalera 8 ....................................... 81
Escape From The Gnar 12d ............ 195
Eukie Arête** 13b .......................... 218
Eukie Extension*** 13a .................. 218
Even the Sheep are Bored 9 ........... 113
Ever After* 12a .............................. 121
Eve's Cave ................................... 152
Ewe Man Group* 10b ..................... 113
Eye In The Sky*** 12d ..................... 67
Eyes of the World*** 13c ............... 197

## F

Fable Boulder ............................... 143
Fable, The**** v3 .......................... 143
Face Down, Ass Up* v8 .................. 192
Face Right Of Indian Ladder v4 ...... 203
Face the Change*** 11d ................ 116
Face* v4 ....................................... 249
Fahrenheit 5.11** 10b / 12b ............. 64
Fairy Godmother 5 ........................ 121
Faith*** 11d ................................. 163
Fake News** 12a ............................ 52
Fang* v6 ........................................ 89
Fantastic Planet** 9 / 11c ................. 64
Farthest Planet** 11b .................... 263
F.A.S.T. ** v7 ................................ 224
Fat Ram 9 .................................... 119
Fear No Evil ** 11d ........................ 115
Feather Boulder ............................ 140
Feather Tree** 12c .......................... 52
Feed My Sheep* 11c ..................... 118
Fertile Crescent** 10b ..................... 98
Fight Like  A Brave** 11c ............... 162
Filth Pig* v6 .................................. 215
Fin King v3 ................................... 192
Fire On Ice*** v9 ........................... 175
Fire on the Mountain*** v11 ............ 92
Fire Pit* v8 ................................... 229
Fire-Proof Boulder .......................... 92
Fire-Proof*** v10 ............................ 92
Firewoman Project .......................... 94
First Blood** 12b .......................... 275
First in Appropriation** 10b ........... 277
First Labor of Hercules, The** 5 ..... 147
Fish and Whistle**** 11b ............... 151
Fist, The ........................................ 57
Flail* 11a ....................................... 71
Flattop Boulder ............................. 230
Flesh Eater** v5 ............................ 223
Flesh is Weak, The* 10b ................ 128
Flex Industry*** v11 ...................... 246
Flight Syndrome*** v9 .................. 251
Flow Futuristic** v8 ...................... 249
Flue, The** 10c .............................. 58
Flung, The** 11d .......................... 162
Fog of War*** 13a ........................ 272
Folsom Flute*** 13c ....................... 61
Forbidden Fruit** 12a .................... 151
Foreplay/Longtime**** 13a ............ 237
Forest Fire 11b ............................... 73
For Shore* 9 .................................. 95
Forward Never Straight** 9 ............. 45
Fourth Floor Walk-up 12a .............. 129
Fractured Memories* 10b .............. 115
Fran's Problem* v5 ........................ 188
Freedom Trail** 10b ...................... 235
Freeze the Moon at Dawn* 12b ..... 125
French Arête .................................. 35
French Arête / Mike's Roof .............. 35
French Arête** v7 ........................... 35
French Press Boulder ...................... 91
French Press v4 .............................. 91

Frickin' Lawyers* 10b .................... 282
Frogs* 9 ........................................ 93
Frosted Fracture* 12c .................... 169
Frozen Echo** 12c .......................... 57
Full Frontal** v4 ........................... 197
Full Mast*** v9 ............................. 209

## G

Gaga at the Go-Go* 11b ................ 110
Galleon** v6 ................................. 209
Gandalf Area ................................ 247
Gandalf Boulder ............................ 249
Gandalf**** v6 ............................. 249
Gangsta Man In A Cadillac* 11a ...... 73
Garden of Eden** 11a .................... 151
Gastoner* v7 ................................ 192
Gates Of Crystal** 8 ....................... 66
General Lee, The** 12b .................. 67
Geriatrics** v8 ............................. 254
Ghost in the Machine** 12d .......... 118
Ghost Of Cedar Creek** 11a ............ 81
Ghost Train Boulder ...................... 131
Ghost Train**** v6 ....................... 131
Gippeto** 12c ............................... 181
Girl Problems* 9 ............................ 61
Git Wood* 11c ................................ 58
Giving Tree** 11a ......................... 146
Glaeken** 12c .............................. 100
Go Ahead Punk 11c ....................... 124
Goats That Haunt Me, The* 11c .... 126
Going Green* 9 .............................. 41
Goin' Streakin'** 11d ..................... 59
Golden Arête*** 10c ..................... 282
Golden Arête*** 12b ..................... 195
Golden Boy*** 12c ....................... 276
Golden Harvest**** 11c .................. 72
Golden Man** 12d ........................ 155
Golden Pagoda*** 13b .................. 180
Golden Shower, The*** 8 .............. 283
Goldrusher** v6 ............................ 231
Gold Wall .................................... 276
Golgotha* 12a .............................. 128
Good Ol' Boys* 12b ........................ 67
Good to the Last Dip* 10c ............. 113
Gorilla** 12c ................................ 266
Go Spuds Go*** 12a ....................... 44
Gossip Column 11a ........................ 79
Got the Horse Right Here** 10a .... 118
Grandpa's Bridge .......................... 179
Grandpa's Challenge** 11b ........... 181
Grandpa's Cough Syrup** 11b ...... 179
Graveyard Boulder ........................ 214
Graveyard Machine*** v8 ............. 214
Greatest Route at
    Greyrock, The*** 8 ..................... 45
Green Bastard, The** 11a .............. 157
Green Dragon*** 11c .................... 282
Green Lantern** 11d ...................... 76
Green Monster** 9 ....................... 270
Green Monster*** v7 .................... 205
Green Pastures* 10a ..................... 109

# INDEX

| Entry | Page |
|---|---|
| Green Slab Boulder | 254 |
| Green Thumb* v1 | 230 |
| Grey Goose*** v10 | 285 |
| Grey Matter** v9 | 223 |
| Greyrock | 43 |
| Ground Up Arête** v2 | 131 |
| Group Therapy**** WI6, M5 | 173 |
| Guard Your Dingy** 11a | 56 |
| Guillotine*** 12a | 282 |
| Gulf Stream** 13b | 60 |
| Gutterball** v8 | 261 |
| Gypsies, Tramps, & Thieves** v11 | 154 |

## H

| Entry | Page |
|---|---|
| Haggis* 10a | 111 |
| Half Life* 11b | 107 |
| Half-Mast*** 12b | 56 |
| Half-Mast** v6 | 209 |
| Hall of Fame | 237 |
| H.A.L.** v7 | 214 |
| Hangover 9 | 41 |
| Hank's Arête** v5 | 221 |
| Hank's Boulder | 221 |
| Hank's Lunge*** v5 | 221 |
| Hank's Other Arête** v3 | 222 |
| Hank's Rig* v6 | 192 |
| Hantavirus 10d | 78 |
| Happy Hour Crag | 39 |
| Hard Cider* 11b | 169 |
| Harder They Come*** v9 | 249 |
| Harmonic Resonance** 13c | 169 |
| Harvest Moon*** 11d | 72 |
| Harvest of Sorrow** 11c | 123 |
| Hash Driveway** 10a | 157 |
| Hatchery Boulder | 185 |
| Hatchery Boulder Area | 185 |
| Hayden House** 10b | 234 |
| Heartbreaker*** 12 | 237 |
| Hefeweizen** 13c | 170 |
| Hello* v3 | 261 |
| Herm's Micro Mantle* v7 | 224 |
| Hickman Over the Poudre Bridge* v8 | 225 |
| High As I Wanna Be* 12a | 149 |
| High Noon** v7 | 203 |
| High Speed Digger* 11c | 81 |
| Hippie Jump** v7 | 140 |
| Hippie Mafia*** v5 | 140 |
| Hippo Hoedown*** v7 | 142 |
| Hollow Flake Face 7 | 82 |
| Home-School Ballerina** 11c | 163 |
| Honest Jon*** 13c | 181 |
| Hoof in the Grave** 10d | 116 |
| Horizon Arête*** 11a | 271 |
| Horizon Wall | 271 |
| Hot Drinks** v6 | 191 |
| Hot Fire Boulder | 138 |
| Hot Fire*** v8 | 138 |
| How Bout Dem Apples** 12c | 235 |
| H.R. Puf 'N Stuff* 9 | 77 |
| Hydrology* v2 | 48 |
| Hyperopia*** 11b | 275 |
| Hyssop* 11b | 149 |

## I

| Entry | Page |
|---|---|
| I Am Your Father* 9 | 109 |
| I Can't Look Away** 12a | 127 |
| Icarus*** 11b | 167 |
| Ice 9** v9 | 175 |
| Ice Canyon | 145 |
| Iceland | 175 |
| If 6 was 9 Project | 98 |
| If Not for the Pigeons** 10a | 41 |
| I Have No Crook 10c | 124 |
| Illusions** 11c | 93 |
| Iluminatia, The** 10b | 93 |
| I'm the One** 11a | 127 |
| In Between The Sheets 11b | 75 |
| Indian Ladder Boulder | 203 |
| Indian Ladder**** v5 | 203 |
| Infernal Medicine * 10a | 115 |
| Inner Light, The* 11d | 113 |
| Inner Mounting Flame, The** 11c | 45 |
| Inside The Outside Whole 10d | 94 |
| Intergalactic*** 12c/d | 265 |
| Into the Drink*** 11c/d | 279 |
| Inyerbuttkwa** 10c | 67 |
| I.P.A.*** 12a | 169 |
| I Peed My Pants in Chalk*** v6 | 209 |
| Iron Curtain | 123 |
| Iron Helix*** v6 | 202 |
| Iron Lady* 10d | 123 |
| Iron Maiden*** 11c | 283 |
| I Shall Not Want* 11b | 109 |
| Is the Rope Long Enough?* 8 | 126 |
| I Still Can't Sleep* 12b | 113 |
| It Is What It Is* 11a | 75 |
| I Told You So* 10d | 126 |
| It's Ice** v4 | 225 |
| Its Only Rock 10 | 237 |
| Izabella** 10c | 98 |

## J

| Entry | Page |
|---|---|
| Jack Frost** 11b | 146 |
| Jame-O-Slab*** 10c | 41 |
| Jason's Little Thingy** v7 | 177 |
| Jersey Snake Bite* 12a | 52 |
| Jester*** 10b | 75 |
| Jester Boulder | 285 |
| Jester*** v8 | 285 |
| Jetstream Deluxe** 9 | 45 |
| J.F.K.** 12a | 234 |
| Jibbin' 9 | 94 |
| Johnny and Hodgey Boulder | 222 |
| Johnny & Hodgey** v5 | 222 |
| Johnny Karate** v8 | 252 |
| Jolly Jane**** 13a | 235 |
| Journey to Pluto** 13a/b | 265 |
| Jousting At Windmills** v9 | 229 |
| JTarrys Route | 146 |
| Jump Start* v3 | 188 |
| Jungle Booty Boulder | 261 |
| Jungle Wall | 266 |
| Just Another Day 10b | 124 |
| Juwana Arête** 12a | 147 |

## K

| Entry | Page |
|---|---|
| Keelhaul*** 12c | 56 |
| Keep, The | 99 |
| Keep The River Free** 10a | 45 |
| Ken's Roof** v9 | 205 |
| Keyhole Cousins 10b | 282 |
| King Fin Boulder | 192 |
| King Fin*** v4 | 192 |
| Kings Boulder | 286 |
| Klein Roof | 49 |
| Knees for Life** v6 | 261 |
| Knight Boulder | 229 |
| Knochenmann* 12b | 128 |
| Kona Blend** 13b | 170 |

## L

| Entry | Page |
|---|---|
| Laconia ** 12b | 116 |
| Ladies Way* v3 | 202 |
| Landing Strip*** 13b | 154 |
| Landscaper, The** v5 | 36 |
| La Royale** 10b | 152 |
| Last Day on Earth* v9 | 132 |
| Last In Show 11b | 75 |
| Last King, The**** v8 | 286 |
| Last Past** v9 | 212 |
| Last Turn Crag | 171 |
| Laugh and Play 7 | 124 |
| Law of the Land*** v9 | 174 |
| Layback Variation** v6 | 136 |
| La-Z-Boy** 10a | 180 |
| Ledge-o-matic* v3 | 133 |
| Le Don Boulder | 91 |
| Le Don*** v8 | 91 |
| Left Arête** v4 | 248 |
| Left Unnamed 10c | 107 |
| Left Variation* v3 | 212 |
| Legos 11 | 57 |
| Lemon Cave | 156 |
| Lenora*** 11c | 77 |
| Less Lichen, More Lovin'** 10a | 33 |
| Let Down Your Hair** 10b | 80 |
| Lichenback 11b | 60 |
| Lichen It** 12a | 73 |
| Life In The Trough* 10a | 149 |
| Life of Pie*** v8 | 141 |
| Lighthouse Boulder | 288 |
| Lighthouse, The*** v5 | 288 |
| Ligre Boulder | 222 |
| Ligre, The*** v7 | 222 |
| Liquor Jugs** 10a | 39 |
| Little Lamb 2 | 119 |
| Little Stripes** v3 | 213 |
| Little Things* 11a | 121 |
| Little Wave Wall | 275 |
| Lock and Key** V8 | 140 |
| Loft, The | 142 |
| Log Raft Boulder | 141 |
| Lone Highway Boulder | 248 |

# INDEX

| Entry | Page |
|---|---|
| Lone Highway** v3 | 248 |
| Lonely Bone Boulder | 284 |
| Lonely Bone*** v10 | 284 |
| Longmont Rimjob* v6 | 251 |
| Long Time Gone** v5 | 240 |
| Love It Or Hate It* 11b | 75 |
| LOWER CANYON | 31 |
| Lower Snake Eyes Wall | 161 |
| Low-Hanging Fruit 11b | 155 |
| Low Tide* 12a | 170 |
| Low Water Arête | 48 |
| Low Water Arête** v8 | 48 |
| Loyalist 9 | 72 |
| Luck of the Irish*** 10c | 163 |
| Luke* 11a | 109 |
| Lunch Bucket Crack** 8 | 66 |

## M

| Entry | Page |
|---|---|
| Mace**, The v3 | 222 |
| Machine Gun* 11c | 98 |
| Made You Look! CLOSED | 102 |
| Mad Hatter 9 | 121 |
| Magic Machine** 12b | 98 |
| Magneto* 11 | 57 |
| Make A Wish** 11b | 156 |
| Make My Day 12a | 124 |
| Man Dime Boulder | 130 |
| Mantle Mussel* v6 | 132 |
| Maritime** v2 | 288 |
| Marky Mark*** 12d | 235 |
| Marshmallow*** 12c | 146 |
| Mary 10b | 124 |
| Mass Appeal** 12b | 60 |
| Mast Boulder | 209 |
| Maundy Thursday* 10b | 118 |
| Maybe Baby Boulder | 251 |
| Maybe Baby** v10 | 251 |
| Medallion Boulder | 289 |
| Medallion*** v8 | 289 |
| Mega Bloks*** 8 | 270 |
| Mega-Bloks Wall | 270 |
| Megadittos* 12b | 118 |
| Melkor* 10d | 81 |
| Mellow Yellow** 11b | 272 |
| Merlin Boulder | 243 |
| Merlin*** v7 | 243 |
| Meteor Mining** 10c | 263 |
| Methuselah** 11c | 155 |
| Middle Class Cracker** 10b | 60 |
| Middle Class Wall | 59 |
| Middle Management** 10c | 59 |
| Middle Up** v2 | 226 |
| Miguel*** 13b | 242 |
| Mike's Arête** v9 | 252 |
| Mike's Roof | 36 |
| Mike's Roof*** v5 | 37 |
| Mineshaft Wall | 75 |
| Mirror Mirror*** 9/12a | 272 |
| Mirrors* 12a | 127 |
| Mish Mast 11d | 56 |
| Miss Rose** v8 | 137 |
| Moderate In Hole v4 | 230 |
| Moderate On Left Face* v2 | 222 |
| Moderate Straight Up* v1 | 226 |
| Moderate* v4 | 225 |
| Moderate Warm-up* v2 | 229 |
| Moment Of Clarity** 11c | 152 |
| Money for Nothing** 12c | 155 |
| Monstro*** 13c | 181 |
| Monstrosity*** 10b | 75 |
| Mood For A Day 10a / 11a | 64 |
| Moonbeam** v6 | 189 |
| Moonrise** v6 | 139 |
| Moose Crag | 242 |
| Moose Knuckles*** 12b | 60 |
| Moss Fest v2 | 248 |
| Moss King v4 | 89 |
| Mother Hibiscus Discordia 5.11 A1 | 93 |
| Mother Russia* 12a | 123 |
| Mountain Park Boulder | 174 |
| Mountain Standard* 10a | 107 |
| Mouserat** v10 | 252 |
| Mr. Brownstone 10 | 237 |
| Mr. Gone*** 10a | 45 |
| Mr. Hand*** 10c | 163 |
| Mr. Harry*** v4 | 222 |
| Mr. Smackmag*** v7 | 202 |
| Mr. Squigglie 10d | 93 |
| Muffin Top*** 12b | 154 |
| Murky Waters*** v3 | 213 |
| Mushroom, The* v4 | 90 |
| Mustard Tiger** 11d | 156 |
| Mutations Boulder | 212 |
| Mutations* v10 | 212 |
| My Day Off 10c | 124 |
| My Name Is Mud 10d | 149 |
| Myopia*** 11b | 275 |
| Myopia Wall | 275 |

## N

| Entry | Page |
|---|---|
| Nancy 8 | 66 |
| Nanny State* 10b | 117 |
| Narcissists Wall | 127 |
| Narrow Control*** v9 | 138 |
| NARROWS | 85 |
| Narrows Blocs | 135 |
| Natty's 3.2 Light Slab 9 | 77 |
| Natural Selection** V10 | 251 |
| Neon Boulder | 255 |
| Neon Demon** v9 | 255 |
| Never Forgotten** 10a | 117 |
| Never Troubles the Wolf* 10b | 110 |
| No Crisis** 11a | 155 |
| Nod | 152 |
| No Respect** 11d | 77 |
| Not Dead Yet* 12a | 128 |
| Not Enough** 9+ | 81 |
| Not My Day* 9 | 125 |
| Nova*** 11b | 263 |
| Nutsack Hoedown*** v4 | 188 |

## O

| Entry | Page |
|---|---|
| Obituary** 13a | 79 |
| Oboe, The** 7 | 129 |
| Obtuse Dilemma*** 11d | 165 |
| Ocatillo*** 10c | 83 |
| Occam's Razor*** v9 | 240 |
| O.D.K.**** 12a | 61 |
| Odyssey, The*** 12b | 47 |
| Odyssey Wall | 47 |
| O-Face, The** 11d | 64 |
| Off the Couch* 6 | 163 |
| Off The Rocker* 7 | 156 |
| Off With Their Heads 9 | 121 |
| Ogre* 10a | 79 |
| Oh'Ryan*** 11b | 263 |
| Oh the Ewemanity!* 7 | 113 |
| Olaf's Bulge*** 10a | 146 |
| Olaf's Bulge Boulder | 251 |
| Olaf's Bulge*** v9 | 251 |
| Old Frenchy*** v3 | 212 |
| Old Luke** v2 | 212 |
| Old Man River 10c | 155 |
| Old Project | 47 |
| Omega, The 9 | 113 |
| Once Upon a Time | 120 |
| Once Upon a Time* 10d | 121 |
| One Arm Scissor** v10 | 249 |
| One Handicap*** 10c | 163 |
| One Night Stand** 11b | 94 |
| One of These Days* 12a | 113 |
| One Ton Ho** v8 | 221 |
| Opal Arête*** v4 | 189 |
| Open Beach Project | 169 |
| Open Book** v5 | 143 |
| Opium Train Project | 195 |
| Oracle, The*** v10 | 143 |
| Orange Arête v4 | 202 |
| Orange Crimpsicle** 12d | 64 |
| Orange-Faced Devil*** v6 | 141 |
| Orange Wall | 234 |
| Orange You Glad 7 | 72 |
| Orangutan** 12c | 268 |
| Orbital Resonance** v10 | 249 |
| Original Sin*** 10c | 152 |
| Orion Skies** 12b | 279 |
| Over the Edge** 11b | 152 |
| Over The Hillary*** 10a | 156 |
| Over the Rainbow v6 | 143 |
| Over The Ramparts 11c | 76 |
| Overtime** 12b | 59 |

## P

| Entry | Page |
|---|---|
| Pain Train Boulder | 188 |
| Pain Train** v8 | 188 |
| Palace | 69 |
| Palace Guard 10b | 71 |
| Pale Corner 11d | 171 |
| Palm Sunday*10b | 128 |
| Palo Verde** 11a | 83 |
| Panty Line*** v8 | 197 |
| Papa's Bulge** 12a | 181 |

# INDEX

| Entry | Page |
|---|---|
| Papa's Bulge Area | 181 |
| Paper Tiger Boulder | 255 |
| Paper Tiger** v11 | 255 |
| Pardon Boulder | 91 |
| Pardon My French v6 | 91 |
| Party in the Back*** v2 | 133 |
| Party Mixer 10c | 80 |
| Paschal Lamb* 10b | 119 |
| Path of Least Resistance 8 | 282 |
| Patio Face** 12a | 195 |
| Patio, The | 195 |
| Pat's Arête | 207 |
| Pat's Crack Boulder | 252 |
| Pat's Crack*** v9 | 252 |
| Paul Revere**** 13d | 234 |
| Pearl Area | 187 |
| Pearl Boulder | 188 |
| Pearl Necklace Area | 245 |
| Pearl Necklace Boulder | 246 |
| Pearl Necklace**** v10 | 246 |
| Pee Pants Boulder | 209 |
| Peeps* 9 | 79 |
| Pee-wee Erect, The** 11a | 102 |
| Pee-wee's Big Stem CLOSED | 102 |
| Pee-wee's Playhouse | 102 |
| Pee-wee's Pretty Pumped!*** 11d | 102 |
| Pegmatite Crack* 7 | 82 |
| Pegmatite* v4 | 230 |
| Perched Boulder | 207 |
| Perch** v6 | 226 |
| Perfect Day 12a | 124 |
| Pet Cemetary 11c | 66 |
| Phantom Menace**** v9 | 131 |
| Phoenix Boulder | 137 |
| Phoenix*** v7 | 137 |
| Picnic Blank It** 10b | 33 |
| Pigeon Boulder | 193 |
| Pigeon Hole Bouncer** 11b | 41 |
| Pigeon** v2 | 137 |
| Pinch Jump** v6 | 212 |
| Pinch Problem** v4 | 248 |
| Pinchy Sit** v5 | 174 |
| Pinchy Underclings** v5 | 175 |
| Pine Vu Area | 47 |
| Pinklebear, The** 12c | 61 |
| Pinklepile 11b | 60 |
| Pink Panther* v9 | 90 |
| Pinon Boulder | 215 |
| Pinon** v8 | 215 |
| Pin Stripe Boulder | 261 |
| Pi** v6 | 141 |
| Place of the Skull* 8 | 128 |
| Plate Tectonics 11a | 56 |
| Pocket Arête Boulder | 49 |
| Pocket Arête*** v6 | 49 |
| Pocket Slab** v5 | 136 |
| Pocket Talk** 12c | 218 |
| Point Break boulder | 90 |
| Point Break* v6 | 90 |
| Polychrome Boulder | 255 |
| Polychrome** v9 | 255 |
| Pony, The** 10a | 110 |
| Poopoo Plater*** 12a | 235 |
| Porter Slab** 8 | 271 |
| Poudre Face | 71 |
| Poudre Falls | 257 |
| Poudre Kind of Groove* 10b | 164 |
| Poudre Pie** 12a | 76 |
| Poudre Practice Rock | 42 |
| Powder Her Face* 11a | 116 |
| Power Pagoda** 11c | 180 |
| Powerpoint 10d | 75 |
| Priceless** 11a | 109 |
| Prickly Pair Left** 11a | 83 |
| Prickly Pair Right** 11a | 83 |
| Prione | 211 |
| Project Man Dime*** v3 | 130 |
| Prometheus Boulder | 133 |
| Prometheus Dabbing** v4 | 133 |
| Prometheus Rising**** 13b | 93 |
| Promised Lands Boulder | 136 |
| Promised Lands* v10 | 136 |
| Public Property v11 | 221 |
| Puffing Stone, The | 224 |
| Puffing Stone*** v5 | 224 |
| Pug's Den** 11c | 72 |
| Pulp Friction 11b | 152 |
| Puma*** 10b | 268 |
| Pumpin' Puff Muffins* 10 | 66 |
| Pura Aventura** 11 | 235 |
| Pura Vida*** 11b | 53 |
| Puzzlebook** 10c | 271 |

## Q

| Entry | Page |
|---|---|
| Quantum Leap Boulder | 92 |
| Quantum Leap** v6 | 92 |
| Quilling Me Softly** v5 | 260 |

## R

| Entry | Page |
|---|---|
| Ra's Buttress Area | 101 |
| Rabble Rouser* 10b | 72 |
| Rack of Lamb* 10a | 116 |
| Rack, The* 10d | 75 |
| Radu** 12a | 100 |
| Rage Against The Machine 9 | 94 |
| Railin' Bars** v6 | 255 |
| Rainbow Boulder | 143 |
| Rainbow Direct v3 | 143 |
| Rainbow Traverse v4 | 143 |
| Rambo Peep*** 11b | 110 |
| Ram Strong* 11d | 113 |
| Random Darkness* 11c | 156 |
| Rapid Fire** 12d | 75 |
| Rapture Boulder | 132 |
| Rapture, The*** v4 | 132 |
| Rapunzel, Rapunzel** 10a | 80 |
| Rasta Boulder | 223 |
| Rasta Drop*** v7 | 189 |
| Rasta Font Trainer** v7 | 223 |
| Reckoning*** 12d | 100 |
| Red Dawn** 12c | 272 |
| Red Dragon** 13b | 282 |
| Red Hot Space Suit*** 12b | 77 |
| Redline Boulder | 255 |
| Redline** v8 | 255 |
| Red Planet** 12a | 77 |
| Red Queen* 11c | 121 |
| Red Rocket*** 13b | 52 |
| Red Wall | 77 |
| Render Unto Geezer 11d | 155 |
| Renee Boulder | 254 |
| Renee** v10 | 254 |
| Rhino** 13a | 266 |
| Ridin' Spinnaz** v5 | 192 |
| Right Arête* v0 | 222 |
| Right Arête** v3 | 261 |
| Right-hand Man** v4 | 225 |
| Right Side* v2 | 208 |
| Right Unnamed 10c | 107 |
| Right Variation** v3 | 212 |
| Rising Sun** 10a | 167 |
| Rites of Passage* 8 | 45 |
| River Boulder | 260 |
| River Mechanics Boulder | 48 |
| River Mechanics** v4 | 48 |
| River Rats 7 | 72 |
| Riverside Zone | 179 |
| River Wall | 279 |
| River Why, The*** 10a | 103 |
| Roadside Boulder | 260 |
| Road To Redemption*** 11b | 75 |
| Roaring Creek Boulder | 197 |
| Rocket Man** v8 | 241 |
| Rocks For Jocks 8 R | 71 |
| Rock Wars* 12b | 171 |
| Roll The Bonez* 12b | 80 |
| Roll the Stone Away** 10b | 115 |
| Room With No View** v8 | 284 |
| Root Canal Boulder | 206 |
| Root Canal** v6 | 206 |
| Rope Ladder* v3 | 189 |
| Round Room* v4 | 175 |
| Route With A View** 10b | 80 |
| Rucksack Showdown** v4 | 188 |
| Rude Beauty Boulder | 260 |
| Rude Beauty**** v8 | 260 |
| Rumble in the Poudre** 11a | 115 |
| Rung, The*** 10c | 162 |
| Rustic Wilderness**** 13c | 159 |
| Rusty Chains & Yellow Tat* 6 | 47 |
| Rusty Shackleford 11b | 76 |

## S

| Entry | Page |
|---|---|
| Saddle Down*** v9 | 205 |
| Saddle Up Boulder | 205 |
| Saddle Up** v7 | 205 |
| Sage Boulder | 212 |
| Sage*** v8 | 212 |
| Sail, The | 56 |
| Saint Lupe Arête** 12d | 270 |
| Saline Lock** 9 | 66 |
| Samara Boulder | 188 |
| Samson Ale** 13b | 170 |
| Samurai Boulder | 90 |
| Samurai** v12 | 90 |
| Sanctus* 10d | 75 |

## INDEX

Satan's Arrow ............................... 213
Scalp Collector** v10 ................... 137
Scarbanzo** v7 ............................... 92
Scarface*** v6 ............................... 221
Scepter, The*** 10a ....................... 78
Schwagn Wagon** 11c ................. 218
Scorpion and the Bobcat, The** v6 .. 36
Scorsese**** 14c ........................... 235
Scrapin' & Scrubbin' 10a .............. 72
Scrilla, The*** 12b ........................ 155
Scrimps v3 .................................... 192
Scuba Steve Boulder ................... 223
Scuba Steve* v7 ........................... 223
Sea Boulder ................................. 252
Seam** v5 ..................................... 175
Sea Of Lichen 8 ............................. 66
Sea of Simulation*** v12 ............. 252
Second Thoughts*** v4 ............... 246
Second Tier ................................... 142
Serpentine Boulder ..................... 206
Serpentine** v6 ............................ 206
Shadows Edge* v3 ....................... 213
Shambo Overhang* v6 ................ 207
Shapes and Sizes*** v11 .............. 253
Shapes & Sizes Boulder ............... 253
Sharma Lunge ............................. 223
Sharma Lunge*** v9 .................... 223
Shearing, The** 12a .................... 110
Shear Stress** 11b ....................... 272
Sheepdog* 11a ............................ 115
Sheep Mountain - Main Area ...... 109
She's A Daisy* 9 ............................ 67
Shireman Problem** v4 ................ 49
Shit, Piss, Spit Up & Drool** 12b .... 72
Shmamie's Slopers* v8 ............... 188
Shoeless Trippin'In
    The Poudre** v9 .................... 207
Shofar Away* 9 ............................ 129
Shofar So Good* 9 ....................... 129
ShoNuff** 12d .............................. 154
Shore Enough* 10a ....................... 95
Shore Footed** 10b/c .................. 95
Shoreside Project ........................ 202
Short Chubby Demon** v6 .......... 225
Short Shank 9 .............................. 124
Short Stack* 12b .......................... 283
Shoulda Coulda* 11a .................... 61
Side Show** 11c ............................ 81
Sidewalk Sam*** 8 ...................... 237
Sidewinder** 12b ........................ 164
Silver Girl** 10c ............................. 65
Silver Leaner** 12c ...................... 100
Silver Salute*** 11c ..................... 272
Simon** 8 ....................................... 44
Simple Boulder ............................ 206
Simple*** v6 ................................ 206
Sin*** 10d .................................... 152
Sin of Man*** 13b ....................... 137
Sit Among the Ashes 9 ............... 121
Six Seconds to Live* 11a ............. 107
Skeptic, The ................................. 126
Skeptic, The** 11c ....................... 126
Skin Deep* 11b ............................ 121

Skinny Dipping* 10d ..................... 33
Skyline Boulders .......................... 130
Slab Area ...................................... 180
Slice and Dice* v7 ......................... 89
Slip and Slide** v3 ....................... 131
Slippery Slope** 13c ................... 218
Slither*** v2 ................................. 141
Sloper Gold** v6 .......................... 240
Sloper Jumpstart*** v1 ............... 221
Sloper Mantle Proj ...................... 143
Slopey Arête v3 ........................... 206
Slopey Mantle v2 ........................ 243
Slopey Thrutch v5 ....................... 202
Slow and Steady** 12b ............... 195
Sluice Box Boulder ...................... 254
Sluice Box** v10 .......................... 254
Small Axe**** v8 ......................... 191
Small Fry*** 12a/b ........................ 76
Smashing Young Ram* 12a ........ 111
Smoke Dragon*** v7 ................... 132
Smoke Trail** 12d ....................... 242
Snake** 12a ................................. 266
Snake Eyes*** 12b ...................... 161
Snake Eyes Walls ......................... 161
Snakepit Boulder .......................... 35
Snakepit** v7 ................................ 35
Snakeskin** v8 .............................. 35
Snakes on a Train** 11d ............. 161
Snake Trails 11b .......................... 161
Snub Nose* 6 .............................. 109
Soggy Doggy** v2 ....................... 260
Solar Panel ................................... 167
So Long Self** 12a ...................... 127
Someday Never Comes*** 12b .. 102
Sonic Alchemist*** v9 ................. 286
Sonic Boom** v7 ......................... 286
Sonic Boulder ............................. 286
Sons of Liberty*** 10c ................ 235
Soot** 12a ..................................... 58
Soul** 12b ................................... 164
Sousa* 9 ...................................... 103
Southeast Face ............................. 44
Southeast Slab* v3 ..................... 203
South Face** v3 .......................... 226
Southie Boyz*** 13b ................... 237
South Ridge ................................ 235
South Wall ................................... 272
Southwest Arête* v3 .................. 226
Southwest Slab* v3 .................... 203
Sparkle Boulder .......................... 207
Sparkle** v8 ................................ 207
Speak Easy 10b ............................. 81
Spectacle, The*** 11b ................. 279
Spidey Arête** v7 ....................... 261
Spirit is Willing, The* 10c ........... 128
Split Stream Boulder .................. 213
Split Stream* v6 .......................... 213
Splitter Finger Crack 7 ................. 82
Spoon Woman 11a ....................... 94
Sport Bloc .................................... 137
Sporting Green*** 12a ................. 79
Spot Of Bother 10d ...................... 80
Squeeze Arête Boulder .............. 208

Squeeze Arête** v4 .................... 208
Squeeze Box Boulder ................... 89
Squeeze Box, The** v6 ................ 89
Squeeze Problem** v6 ............... 248
Squire*** v4 ................................ 286
Stanley's Steamer 11c .................. 72
Starstruck*** 11b ........................ 157
Start Something** v0 ................. 286
Steamliner** 11b .......................... 52
Steel Wool** 10b ........................ 109
Steep & Cheap** 11d ................... 73
Stickman Crossing the
    Brooklyn Bridge* v8 ............. 225
Stolen Rib** v2 ............................ 142
Stone Cold*** v8 ......................... 138
Stone Record*** v3 .................... 260
Stove Prairie Cracks ..................... 82
Straw Into Gold*** 13d .............. 218
Streaky Open Project ................. 217
Streaky Stylee*** 11d ................... 59
Strictly Business** 10c ................. 75
Strike** v6 .................................... 141
Stung, The** 10b ........................ 162
Submarine Boulder .................... 143
Submarine*** v9 ........................ 143
Suck a Lemon** 11d ................... 156
Sue's Face*** v3 ......................... 206
Sunday Buttress ........................... 72
Sunday Paper* 9 ........................... 79
Sunday's Child*** 12c .................. 72
Sunday Stroll*** 8 ...................... 180
Sun Deck Specials 7** .................. 39
Sunkist** 10c ............................... 167
Sunny Boulder ............................ 251
Sunny*** v10 .............................. 251
Sunnyvale .................................... 156
Sunset Years** 10b .................... 155
Sunspot** 10d ............................. 167
Super Chrome*** v10 .................. 49
Supercollider .............................. 165
Supercollider / Solar Panel ........ 165
Sure to Go 6 ................................ 124
Swan Boulder .............................. 285
Swan*** v6 .................................. 285
Swayze Express, The*** 12a ...... 157
Sweet Tooth 10c ......................... 119
Swiss Army** v13 ....................... 225

## T

Taco Bell*** 13a .......................... 129
Taco Wall ..................................... 129
Tailspin***** 12b .......................... 61
Take a Knee* v6 .......................... 241
Taker* 11b ................................... 100
Tall Face v3 ................................. 205
Tamed Donkeys** 11d ................. 60
Tangerine Project ......................... 93
Tangerine Sky*** v4 ................... 213
Tanked** 10b ................................ 41
Tan Panel** 11b .......................... 195
Tan Panel** 11c ............................ 42
Tantrum*** 12b .......................... 276

# INDEX

| Entry | Page |
|---|---|
| Tattered Glory*** 11a | 237 |
| T-Bone Right** v4 | 227 |
| T-Bone** v8 | 227 |
| Tea Party*** 13a | 234 |
| Tear Down This Wall* 12a | 123 |
| Tearing at All Their Dreams** 11c | 115 |
| Tear in the Curtain* 11d | 123 |
| Tech Savvy** 11b | 283 |
| Telegraph Boulder | 261 |
| Teller* 11a | 156 |
| Temple Of The Dog Project | 93 |
| Temptation** 11c | 152 |
| Tequila Worm 11a | 41 |
| Theodore** 6 | 44 |
| They All Losers* 10a | 120 |
| They Call Me Mr. Stumpy* 10c | 118 |
| Thick Cuts Boulder | 284 |
| Thick Cuts** v5 | 284 |
| Thin Ice** v6 | 174 |
| Thin N' Crispy** v7 | 230 |
| Three Bags Full** 10a | 111 |
| Three Flakes To The Wind** 8 | 39 |
| Three Ring Circus* 12 | 218 |
| Throne Boulder | 90 |
| Throne, The*** v3 | 90 |
| Thumb Boulder | 230 |
| Thumb, The* v6 | 230 |
| Thursday Afternoon Hooky 10b R | 64 |
| Ticking Clock 12a | 107 |
| Tier 2 / Left Side | 118 |
| Tier 2 / Right Side | 118 |
| Tiered Boulder | 48 |
| Tiger Boulder | 143 |
| Tiger Milk*** v11 | 261 |
| Till We Have Faces ** 12a | 116 |
| Tilt Boulder | 229 |
| Tilt/Divergence Area | 228 |
| Tilt*** v7 | 229 |
| Time Lost** 12d | 271 |
| TM Crack** 10d | 152 |
| Toaster Boulder | 231 |
| Toaster, The*** v2 | 231 |
| Toffee 11d | 119 |
| Toll Booth Willie** v8 | 231 |
| Tomahawk Chop*** v4 | 261 |
| Tombstone** 12b | 275 |
| Tonka*** 12b | 242 |
| Tool Man** 11c | 65 |
| Toplob* 11a | 118 |
| To the Slaughter** 11d | 115 |
| Tour De Poudre**** 10b / 12b | 65 |
| Tractor Beam Boulder | 253 |
| Tractor Beam** v7 | 253 |
| Trad Variation 10b | 156 |
| Traverse Variation** v7 | 201 |
| Treading Water*** v8 | 260 |
| Treebeard* v2 | 141 |
| Treedigger** v6 | 285 |
| Triangle** v2 | 213 |
| Tricky Dicky* v6 | 177 |
| Triple Tier Areas | 55 |
| Trough, The | 149 |
| Trout Whistle** 10a | 282 |
| Tsunami Traverse** v8 | 227 |
| Tsunami ** v6 | 227 |
| Turtle Crag | 193 |
| Turtle Head 7 | 72 |
| Twilight Area | 153 |
| Twilight*** v10 | 154 |
| Twilight Wall | 154 |
| Twinkletoes*** 13a | 60 |
| Two Birds Stoned at Once 11d | 157 |
| Two Minutes Hate 10b | 107 |
| Two Minute Wall | 107 |
| Two Righteous Hands* 10d | 126 |

## U

| Entry | Page |
|---|---|
| Ugly Duck* v1 | 285 |
| Undertall* 10a | 57 |
| Undertall Wall | 57 |
| Under The Gaydar* v10 | 205 |
| Uneedaluebben** 11a | 77 |
| Unfinished* 12a | 125 |
| Uninvited Guest* 9 | 33 |
| Unwilling*** v6 | 49 |
| Upper Echelon | 60 |
| Upper Snake Eyes Wall | 163 |
| Upseizing, The* 10c | 116 |

## V

| Entry | Page |
|---|---|
| Vanilla Ice*** v7 | 177 |
| Velvet Brown** 10c | 56 |
| Velvet Tan 10c | 57 |
| Vide Noir*** 12b | 279 |
| Vindicated** 9 | 117 |
| Vishokkuxxud-pokkuxxda*** 12a | 94 |
| Visine** 12a | 275 |
| Visiting Privileges* 11c | 129 |
| Vista Crag | 217 |
| Vista Cruiser*** 11b | 217 |
| Vista Cruiser Extension*** 12c | 218 |
| Void Bloc, The | 287 |
| Void Bop, The* v3 | 287 |
| Vulture** 11b | 266 |

## W

| Entry | Page |
|---|---|
| Waiting in Wool 10a | 118 |
| Wake Of The Red Witch** 12c | 80 |
| Walk Softly and Carry a Big Horn* 10c | 129 |
| Walk the Plank v8 | 209 |
| Wall with a View | 80 |
| Wang Chung, The** 11c | 162 |
| Warm Me*** v3 | 226 |
| Warm-up Boulder | 226 |
| Warm-up Crack** v1 | 248 |
| Warm-up II* v3 | 202 |
| Warm-up I* v2 | 202 |
| Warm-up Roof | 246 |
| Warm-Up Roof* v3 | 246 |
| Warm-Up* v2 | 260 |
| Warmup Wall | 248 |
| Watchtower*** 11a | 98 |
| Water Rights*** 12b | 278 |
| Wave 1* v7 | 230 |
| Wave 2* v5 | 230 |
| Wave Goodbye*** v7 | 261 |
| Way She Goes, The** 12d | 157 |
| Way to Dusty Death, The* 12a | 128 |
| We are the Wooled * 11a | 116 |
| We'll Always Have Broomfield* 10c | 120 |
| Werks Ewe Up** 10d | 115 |
| West of Eden** 10b R | 151 |
| WEST OF RUSTIC | 183 |
| We Three Kings*** v8 | 286 |
| What's Left Of The Bottom Of My Heart** v12 | 223 |
| When Angels Dance*** v4 | 229 |
| When My Body Dies** 12a | 164 |
| Where's The Beef?*** 12c | 71 |
| Whiskey Dickin** 10c | 270 |
| White as Snow*** 12a | 119 |
| White as Snow Wall | 119 |
| White Elephant** v7 | 142 |
| White Panel** 11c | 42 |
| White Stripe Boulder | 213 |
| White Stripe*** v8 | 213 |
| White Wall | 270 |
| Widowmaker Boulder | 92 |
| Widowmakers/Electric Ocean | 87 |
| Widowmaker, The*** 13a | 92 |
| Wihizzle Dihizzle*** 12c | 154 |
| Wild and Scenic*** 12d | 159 |
| Wildest Dreams**** 13c | 159 |
| Wild Rose** 11c | 149 |
| Wild Wall | 159 |
| Wills Boulder | 212 |
| Will's Face/Arête* v4 | 188 |
| Will's Problem** v5 | 231 |
| Will's Slab** v10 | 222 |
| Winter's Edge** 5.10a | 165 |
| Wipe Out v9 | 230 |
| With Cheese** 11a | 152 |
| Wizened, The** 12a | 155 |
| Wolf in Sheep's Clothing** 11b | 118 |
| Wolverine** 11 | 57 |
| Wonderful Wonderful Me* 11a | 127 |
| Woolite** 9 | 111 |
| Wooly Bully* 9 | 111 |
| Wooly Mammoth* 10a/12b | 111 |
| Working the Corner*** v4 | 136 |
| Work That Lovetron, Moses* 10b | 115 |
| Wormhole*** 11a | 263 |

## X

| Entry | Page |
|---|---|
| Xerox Boulder | 284 |
| Xerox* v8 | 284 |

## Y

| Entry | Page |
|---|---|
| Yankee Doodle* 8 | 103 |
| Yet Another 9 | 41 |
| You Call This PayDay? 12a | 124 |
| You're Not That Charming 8 | 121 |

## Z

# INDEX BY GRADE

## 5.0 - 5.7

| Route | Grade | Page |
|---|---|---|
| Little Lamb | 2 | 119 |
| Fairy Godmother | 5 | 121 |
| First Labor of Hercules, The*** | 5 | 147 |
| Access Pitch | 6 | 163 |
| Alvin* | 6 | 44 |
| Crack Dihedral* | 6 | 82 |
| Daylight Donuts | 6 | 124 |
| DC Corner | 6 | 79 |
| Off the Couch* | 6 | 163 |
| Rusty Chains & Yellow Tat* | 6 | 47 |
| Snub Nose* | 6 | 109 |
| Sure to Go | 6 | 124 |
| Theodore** | 6 | 44 |
| Barfy's Favorite** | 7 | 45 |
| Book of Sheep** | 7 | 115 |
| Conclave, The | 7 | 110 |
| Creak Crack | 7 | 156 |
| Don't Damn It* | 7 | 47 |
| Dung, The | 7 | 162 |
| Hollow Flake Face | 7 | 82 |
| Laugh and Play | 7 | 124 |
| Oboe, The** | 7 | 129 |
| Off The Rocker* | 7 | 156 |
| Oh the Ewemanity!* | 7 | 113 |
| Orange You Glad | 7 | 72 |
| Pegmatite Crack* | 7 | 82 |
| River Rats | 7 | 72 |
| Splitter Finger Crack | 7 | 82 |
| Sun Deck Specials** | 7 | 39 |
| Turtle Head | 7 | 72 |

## 5.8

| Route | Grade | Page |
|---|---|---|
| Bandito's Bat Roost | 8 | 57 |
| Big Retina** | 8 | 275 |
| Black Dog* | 8 | 45 |
| Blue-Footed Boobie* | 8 | 120 |
| Captain Galapagos* | 8 | 120 |
| Comped at the Omni* | 8 | 120 |
| County Line*** | 8 | 67 |
| Down On The Pharm** | 8 | 64 |
| Escalera | 8 | 81 |
| Gates Of Crystal** | 8 | 66 |
| Golden Shower, The*** | 8 | 283 |
| Greatest Route At Greyrock, The*** | 8 | 45 |
| Is the Rope Long Enough?* | 8 | 126 |
| Lunch Bucket Crack** | 8 | 66 |
| Mega Bloks*** | 8 | 270 |
| Nancy | 8 | 66 |
| Path of Least Resistance | 8 | 282 |
| Place of the Skull* | 8 | 128 |
| Porter Slab** | 8 | 271 |
| Rites of Passage* | 8 | 45 |
| Rocks For Jocks | 8 | 71 |
| Sea Of Lichen | 8 | 66 |
| Sidewalk Sam*** | 8 | 237 |
| Simon** | 8 | 44 |
| Sunday Stroll*** | 8 | 180 |
| Three Flakes To The Wind** | 8 | 39 |
| Yankee Doodle* | 8 | 103 |
| You're Not That Charming | 8 | 121 |

## 5.9

| Route | Grade | Page |
|---|---|---|
| Adults Only Picnic** | 9 | 33 |
| B.A.H. | 9 | 71 |
| Bananarête** | 9 | 64 |
| Battle Axe* | 9 | 79 |
| Bit Of A Dandy** | 9 | 103 |
| Cal Trop | 9 | 71 |
| Checkpoint Charlie* | 9 | 123 |
| Cheerleaders Gone Hippie* | 9 | 71 |
| Chips and Beer** | 9 | 33 |
| Churchill Rejects*** | 9 | 76 |
| Clean-Up On Aisle 9** | 9 | 66 |
| Coffin Crack**** | 9 | 276 |
| Consolation Prize* | 9 | 195 |
| Cosmic Trigger | 9 | 94 |
| Cruiser | 9 | 75 |
| Dittos* | 9 | 118 |
| Dr. Kelman I Presume* | 9 | 107 |
| East Of Eden**** | 9 | 152 |
| Even the Sheep are Bored | 9 | 113 |
| Fantastic Planet** | 9 | 64 |
| Fat Ram | 9 | 119 |
| For Shore* | 9 | 95 |
| Forward Never Straight** | 9 | 45 |
| Frogs* | 9 | 93 |
| Girl Problems* | 9 | 61 |
| Going Green* | 9 | 41 |
| Green Monster** | 9 | 270 |
| H.R. Puf 'N Stuff* | 9 | 77 |
| Hangover | 9 | 41 |
| I Am Your Father* | 9 | 109 |
| Jetstream Deluxe** | 9 | 45 |
| Jibbin' | 9 | 94 |
| Loyalist | 9 | 72 |
| Mad Hatter | 9 | 121 |
| Natty's 3.2 Light Slab | 9 | 77 |
| Not Enough** | 9 | 81 |
| Not My Day* | 9 | 125 |
| Off With Their Heads | 9 | 121 |
| Omega, The | 9 | 113 |
| Peeps* | 9 | 79 |
| Rage Against The Machine | 9 | 94 |
| Saline Lock** | 9 | 66 |
| She's A Daisy* | 9 | 67 |
| Shofar Away* | 9 | 129 |
| Shofar So Good* | 9 | 129 |
| Short Shank | 9 | 124 |
| Sit Among the Ashes | 9 | 121 |
| Sousa* | 9 | 103 |
| Sunday Paper* | 9 | 79 |
| Uninvited Guest* | 9 | 33 |
| Vindicated** | 9 | 117 |
| Woolite** | 9 | 111 |
| Wooly Bully* | 9 | 111 |
| Yet Another | 9 | 41 |

## 5.10

| Route | Grade | Page |
|---|---|---|
| 13th Step, The* | 10a | 73 |
| All Roads Lead to Capuchin | 10a | 128 |
| Baadlands* | 10a | 111 |
| Behold My Creation* | 10a | 127 |
| Berlin Airlift | 10a | 123 |
| Brinks Corner* | 10a | 52 |
| Dog Face* | 10a | 44 |
| Got the Horse Right Here** | 10a | 118 |
| Green Pastures* | 10a | 109 |
| Haggis* | 10a | 111 |
| Hash Driveway** | 10a | 157 |
| If Not for the Pigeons** | 10a | 41 |
| Infernal Medicine * | 10a | 115 |
| Its Only Rock | 10a | 237 |
| Keep The River Free** | 10a | 45 |
| La-Z-Boy** | 10a | 180 |
| Less Lichen, More Lovin'** | 10a | 33 |
| Life In The Trough* | 10a | 149 |
| Liquor Jugs** | 10a | 39 |
| Mood For A Day | 10a | 64 |
| Mountain Standard* | 10a | 107 |
| Mr. Brownstone | 10a | 237 |
| Mr. Gone*** | 10a | 45 |
| Never Forgotten** | 10a | 117 |
| Ogre* | 10a | 79 |
| Olaf's Bulge*** | 10a | 146 |
| Over The Hillary*** | 10a | 156 |
| Pony, The** | 10a | 110 |
| Pumpin' Puff Muffins* | 10a | 66 |
| Rack of Lamb* | 10a | 116 |
| Rapunzel, Rapunzel** | 10a | 80 |
| Rising Sun** | 10a | 167 |
| River Why, The*** | 10a | 103 |
| Scepter, The*** | 10a | 78 |
| Scrapin' & Scrubbin' | 10a | 72 |
| Shore Enough* | 10a | 95 |
| They All Losers* | 10a | 120 |
| Three Bags Full** | 10a | 111 |
| Trout Whistle** | 10a | 282 |
| Undertall* | 10a | 57 |
| Waiting in Wool | 10a | 118 |
| Winter's Edge** | 10a | 165 |
| Wooly Mammoth* | 10a | 111 |
| 84 Beacon Street*** | 10b | 237 |
| A Little Slice Of Sunshine** | 10b | 167 |
| Abbey Ale | 10b | 57 |
| Ajna Sanctuary | 10b | 95 |
| Andromeda Galaxy*** | 10b | 263 |
| Arda** | 10b | 81 |
| Are You Experienced?** | 10b | 98 |
| Back in the Saddle* | 10b | 118 |
| Bert* | 10b | 58 |
| Big As A House | 10b | 72 |
| Bisecting Fist Crack** | 10b | 42 |
| Blast a Blessing* | 10b | 129 |
| Bone Book* | 10b | 128 |
| Booze Tube** | 10b | 41 |
| Cracker Jack | 10b | 119 |
| Crazy Will** | 10b | 271 |
| Creepy* | 10b | 71 |
| Crossbow | 10b | 71 |
| Devo** | 10b | 116 |
| Dr. Food** | 10b | 66 |
| Empire of Crumbs | 10b | 123 |
| Ewe Man Group* | 10b | 113 |
| Fahrenheit 5.11** | 10b | 64 |
| Fertile Crescent** | 10b | 98 |
| First in Appropriation** | 10b | 277 |
| Flesh is Weak, The* | 10b | 128 |
| Fractured Memories* | 10b | 115 |

# INDEX

| Route | Grade | Page |
|---|---|---|
| Freedom Trail** | 10b | 235 |
| Frickn Lawyers* | 10b | 282 |
| Hayden House** | 10b | 234 |
| Iluminatia, The** | 10b | 93 |
| Jester*** | 10b | 75 |
| Just Another Day | 10b | 124 |
| Keyhole Cousins | 10b | 282 |
| La Royale* | 10b | 152 |
| Let Down Your Hair** | 10b | 80 |
| Mary | 10b | 124 |
| Maundy Thursday* | 10b | 118 |
| Meteor Mining** | 10b | 263 |
| Middle Class Cracker** | 10b | 60 |
| Monstrosity*** | 10b | 75 |
| Nanny State* | 10b | 117 |
| Never Troubles the Wolf* | 10b | 110 |
| Palace Guard | 10b | 71 |
| Palm Sunday* | 10b | 128 |
| Paschal Lamb* | 10b | 119 |
| Picnic Blank It** | 10b | 33 |
| Poudre Kind of Groove* | 10b | 164 |
| Puma*** | 10b | 268 |
| Rabble Rouser* | 10b | 72 |
| Roll the Stone Away** | 10b | 115 |
| Route With A View** | 10b | 80 |
| Shore Footed** | 10b | 95 |
| Speak Easy | 10b | 81 |
| Steel Wool** | 10b | 109 |
| Stung, The** | 10b | 162 |
| Sunset Years** | 10b | 155 |
| Tanked** | 10b | 41 |
| Thursday Afternoon Hooky | 10b | 64 |
| Tour De Poudre**** | 10b | 65 |
| Trad Variation | 10b | 156 |
| Two Minutes Hate | 10b | 107 |
| Unnamed** | 10b | 107 |
| West of Eden** | 10b | 151 |
| Work That Lovetron, Moses* | 10b | 115 |
| A Desperate Man* | 10c | 107 |
| Better Call Maynard* | 10c | 129 |
| Blood Runs Frozen** | 10c | 123 |
| Bodies Like Sheep | 10c | 73 |
| Breakin' Trail | 10c | 73 |
| Cab Ride** | 10c | 39 |
| Captain Awesome* | 10c | 113 |
| Change the Wind to Silence** | 10c | 123 |
| Check Your Head*** | 10c | 71 |
| Crack Route* | 10c | 279 |
| Cynic, The* | 10c | 126 |
| Delicious Apple | 10c | 162 |
| Dear Unnamed | 10c | 58 |
| Flue, The** | 10c | 58 |
| Golden Arête*** | 10c | 282 |
| Good to the Last Dip* | 10c | 113 |
| I Have No Crook | 10c | 124 |
| Inyerbuttkwa** | 10c | 67 |
| Izabella** | 10c | 98 |
| Jame-O-Slab*** | 10c | 41 |
| Left Unnamed | 10c | 107 |
| Luck of the Irish*** | 10c | 163 |
| Meteor Mining** | 10c | 263 |
| Middle Management** | 10c | 59 |
| Mr. Hand*** | 10c | 163 |
| My Day Off | 10c | 124 |
| Ocatillo*** | 10c | 83 |
| Old Man River | 10c | 155 |
| One Handicap*** | 10c | 163 |
| Original Sin*** | 10c | 152 |
| Party Mixer | 10c | 80 |
| Puzzlebook** | 10c | 271 |
| Right Unnamed | 10c | 107 |
| Rung, The** | 10c | 162 |
| Silver Girl** | 10c | 65 |
| Sons of Liberty*** | 10c | 235 |
| Spirit is Willing, The* | 10c | 128 |
| Strictly Business** | 10c | 75 |
| Sunkist** | 10c | 167 |
| Sweet Tooth | 10c | 119 |
| They Call Me Mr. Stumpy* | 10c | 118 |
| Upseizing, The* | 10c | 116 |
| Velvet Brown** | 10c | 56 |
| Velvet Tan | 10c | 57 |
| Walk Softly and Carry a Big Horn* | 10c | 129 |
| We'll Always Have Broomfield* | 10c | 120 |
| Whiskey Dickin** | 10c | 270 |
| Antique Guns | 10d | 155 |
| Back to Jail** | 10d | 157 |
| Between the Sheeps*** | 10d | 117 |
| Brown Chossum Special, The | 10d | 75 |
| Donni loves Jenny** | 10d | 235 |
| Hantavirus | 10d | 78 |
| Hoof in the Grave* | 10d | 116 |
| I Told You So* | 10d | 126 |
| Inside The Outside Whole | 10d | 94 |
| Iron Lady* | 10d | 123 |
| Melkor* | 10d | 81 |
| Mr. Squiggle | 10d | 93 |
| My Name Is Mud | 10d | 149 |
| Once Upon a Time | 10d | 121 |
| Powerpoint | 10d | 75 |
| Rack, The* | 10d | 75 |
| Sanctus* | 10d | 75 |
| Sin*** | 10d | 152 |
| Skinny Dipping* | 10d | 33 |
| Spot Of Bother | 10d | 80 |
| Sunspot** | 10d | 167 |
| TM Crack** | 10d | 152 |
| Two Righteous Hands* | 10d | 126 |
| Werks Ewe Up* | 10d | 115 |

## 5.11

| Route | Grade | Page |
|---|---|---|
| A-Lady* | 11a | 81 |
| Bartles & Jaymes** | 11a | 170 |
| Better than the Internet** | 11a | 66 |
| Bighorns* | 11a | 113 |
| Cleaning Day | 11a | 124 |
| Crack of Lamb** | 11a | 116 |
| Cross Mojonation! | 11a | 73 |
| De Dios | 11a | 124 |
| Detachment Disorder** | 11a | 83 |
| Dihedron** | 11a | 270 |
| Don't Doubt Me* | 11a | 126 |
| Drawn & Quartered | 11a | 75 |
| Dumping K* | 11a | 116 |
| Edge of Daylight | 11a | 124 |
| Entropy*** | 11a | 116 |
| Flail* | 11a | 71 |
| Gangsta Man In A Cadillac* | 11a | 73 |
| Garden of Eden** | 11a | 151 |
| Ghost Of Cedar Creek** | 11a | 81 |
| Giving Tree** | 11a | 146 |
| Gossip Column | 11a | 79 |
| Green Bastard, The** | 11a | 157 |
| Guard Your Dingy** | 11a | 56 |
| Horizon Arete*** | 11a | 271 |
| I'm the One* | 11a | 127 |
| It Is What It Is* | 11a | 75 |
| Legos | 11a | 57 |
| Little Things* | 11a | 121 |
| Luke* | 11a | 109 |
| Magneto* | 11a | 57 |
| Mother Hibiscus Discordia | 11a | 93 |
| No Crisis** | 11a | 155 |
| Palo Verde** | 11a | 83 |
| Pee-wee Erect, The** | 11a | 102 |
| Plate Tectonics | 11a | 56 |
| Powder Her Face** | 11a | 116 |
| Priceless** | 11a | 109 |
| Prickly Pair Left** | 11a | 83 |
| Prickly Pair Right** | 11a | 83 |
| Pura Aventura*** | 11a | 235 |
| Rumble in the Poudre* | 11a | 115 |
| Sheepdog* | 11a | 115 |
| Shoulda Coulda* | 11a | 61 |
| Six Seconds to Live* | 11a | 107 |
| Spoon Woman | 11a | 94 |
| Tattered Glory*** | 11a | 237 |
| Teller* | 11a | 156 |
| Tequila Worm | 11a | 41 |
| Toplob* | 11a | 118 |
| Uneedaluebben** | 11a | 77 |
| Watchtower*** | 11a | 98 |
| We are the Wooled* | 11a | 116 |
| With Cheese** | 11a | 152 |
| Wolverine** | 11a | 57 |
| Wonderful Wonderful Me* | 11a | 127 |
| Wormhole*** | 11a | 263 |
| Adulteress, The | 11b | 152 |
| Apprentice, The** | 11b | 275 |
| Aries Arête* | 11b | 118 |
| Back on the Train** | 11b | 162 |
| Ballet Of The Bulge*** | 11b | 67 |
| Blood of the Lamb** | 11b | 117 |
| Blue Collar Baby** | 11b | 59 |
| Bolt Dependence* | 11b | 64 |
| Bostock From Little Bird*** | 11b | 116 |
| Car Bomb* | 11b | 41 |
| Check Your Six** | 11b | 71 |
| Choss Dodger | 11b | 57 |
| Citadel** | 11b | 80 |
| Dash to Freedom* | 11b | 123 |
| Dear Slabby*** | 11b | 79 |
| Debt, The* | 11b | 129 |
| Delicious Demon*** | 11b | 162 |
| Dirty Burger** | 11b | 156 |
| Eluebbenator, The* | 11b | 39 |
| Farthest Planet** | 11b | 263 |
| Fish and Whistle**** | 11b | 151 |
| Forest Fire | 11b | 73 |
| Gaga at the Go-Go* | 11b | 110 |
| Grandpa's Challenge** | 11b | 181 |
| Grandpa's Cough Syrup** | 11b | 179 |
| Half Life* | 11b | 107 |
| Hard Cider* | 11b | 169 |
| Hyperopia*** | 11b | 275 |
| Hyssop* | 11b | 149 |
| I Shall Not Want* | 11b | 109 |
| Icarus*** | 11b | 167 |
| In Between The Sheets | 11b | 75 |

# INDEX

| | Route | Grade | Page |
|---|---|---|---|
| | Jack Frost** | 11b | 146 |
| | Last In Show | 11b | 75 |
| | Lichenback | 11b | 60 |
| | Love It Or Hate It* | 11b | 75 |
| | Low-Hanging Fruit | 11b | 155 |
| | Make A Wish** | 11b | 156 |
| | Mellow Yellow** | 11b | 272 |
| | Myopia*** | 11b | 275 |
| | Nova*** | 11b | 263 |
| | Oh'Ryan*** | 11b | 263 |
| | One Night Stand** | 11b | 94 |
| | Over the Edge** | 11b | 152 |
| | Pigeon Hole Bouncer** | 11b | 41 |
| | Pinklepile | 11b | 60 |
| | Pulp Friction | 11b | 152 |
| | Pura Vida*** | 11b | 53 |
| | Rambo Peep*** | 11b | 110 |
| | Road To Redemption*** | 11b | 75 |
| | Rusty Shackleford | 11b | 76 |
| | Shear Stress** | 11b | 272 |
| | Skin Deep* | 11b | 121 |
| | Snake Trails | 11b | 161 |
| | Spectacle, The*** | 11b | 279 |
| | Starstruck** | 11b | 157 |
| | Steamliner** | 11b | 52 |
| | Taker* | 11b | 100 |
| | Tan Panel* | 11b | 195 |
| | Tech Savvy** | 11b | 283 |
| | Vista Cruiser*** | 11b | 217 |
| | Vulture*** | 11b | 266 |
| | Wolf in Sheep's Clothing* | 11b | 118 |
| | All In A Daze Work** | 11c | 80 |
| | Anchor Thief* | 11c | 56 |
| | Armor Plated* | 11c | 75 |
| | Balaam* | 11c | 65 |
| | Better Than Watching Television** | 11c | 65 |
| | Big Bad Beav** | 11c | 217 |
| | Bitter Clinger* | 11c | 109 |
| | Black Crocus* | 11c | 149 |
| | Black Hole*** | 11c | 263 |
| | Black Serpent** | 11c | 165 |
| | Bridge Engineer* | 11c | 123 |
| | Britney's Spear** | 11c | 67 |
| | Cacao | 11c | 119 |
| | D-Man** | 11c | 81 |
| | Date Night** | 11c | 100 |
| | Days Between Us** | 11c | 110 |
| | Death and Disfiguration* | 11c | 75 |
| | Dirty Work* | 11c | 109 |
| | Feed My Sheep* | 11c | 118 |
| | Fight Like A Brave** | 11c | 162 |
| | Git Wood* | 11c | 58 |
| | Go Ahead Punk | 11c | 124 |
| | Goats That Haunt Me, The* | 11c | 126 |
| | Golden Harvest**** | 11c | 72 |
| | Green Dragon*** | 11c | 282 |
| | Harvest of Sorrow* | 11c | 123 |
| | High Speed Digger* | 11c | 81 |
| | Home-School Ballerina*** | 11c | 163 |
| | Illusions** | 11c | 93 |
| | Inner Mounting Flame, The** | 11c | 45 |
| | Into the Drink*** | 11c | 279 |
| | Iron Maiden** | 11c | 283 |
| | Lenora* | 11c | 77 |
| | Machine Gun* | 11c | 98 |
| | Methuselah** | 11c | 155 |
| | Moment Of Clarity** | 11c | 152 |
| | Over The Ramparts | 11c | 76 |
| | Pet Cemetary | 11c | 66 |
| | Power Pagoda** | 11c | 180 |
| | Pug's Den* | 11c | 72 |
| | Random Darkness* | 11c | 156 |
| | Red Queen* | 11c | 121 |
| | Schwagn Wagon* | 11c | 218 |
| | Side Show** | 11c | 81 |
| | Silver Salute*** | 11c | 272 |
| | Skeptic, The | 11c | 126 |
| | Stanley's Steamer | 11c | 72 |
| | Tan Panel* | 11c | 42 |
| | Tearing at All Their Dreams** | 11c | 115 |
| | Temptation** | 11c | 152 |
| | Tool Man** | 11c | 65 |
| | Visiting Privileges* | 11c | 129 |
| | Wang Chung, The** | 11c | 162 |
| | White Panel** | 11c | 42 |
| | Wild Rose* | 11c | 149 |
| | A-Frame Roof** | 11d | 42 |
| | Black Eye In The Sky** | 11d | 59 |
| | Bosch Hog | 11d | 67 |
| | Butterfly*** | 11d | 266 |
| | Crystal Method* | 11d | 65 |
| | Dog Will Hunt | 11d | 149 |
| | Face the Change*** | 11d | 116 |
| | Faith*** | 11d | 163 |
| | Fear No Evil ** | 11d | 115 |
| | Flung, The** | 11d | 162 |
| | Goin' Streakin'** | 11d | 59 |
| | Green Lantern* | 11d | 76 |
| | Harvest Moon*** | 11d | 72 |
| | Inner Light, The* | 11d | 113 |
| | Mish Mast | 11d | 56 |
| | Mustard Tiger* | 11d | 156 |
| | No Respect** | 11d | 77 |
| | O-Face, The** | 11d | 64 |
| | Obtuse Dilemma*** | 11d | 165 |
| | Pale Corner | 11d | 171 |
| | Pee-wee's Pretty Pumped!*** | 11d | 102 |
| | Ram Strong* | 11d | 113 |
| | Render Unto Geezer | 11d | 155 |
| | Snakes on a Train** | 11d | 161 |
| | Steep & Cheap** | 11d | 73 |
| | Streaky Stylee*** | 11d | 59 |
| | Suck a lemon** | 11d | 156 |
| | Tamed Donkeys** | 11d | 60 |
| | Tear in the Curtain* | 11d | 123 |
| | To the Slaughter* | 11d | 115 |
| | Toffee | 11d | 119 |
| | Two Birds Stoned at Once | 11d | 157 |

## 5.12

| | Route | Grade | Page |
|---|---|---|---|
| | Always Almonds | 12a | 119 |
| | Anahata | 12a | 94 |
| | Back On Black** | 12a | 77 |
| | Blue Steel* | 12a | 77 |
| | Blue Streak* | 12a | 193 |
| | Booty Prize* | 12a | 57 |
| | Boys Are Back In Town** | 12a | 77 |
| | Burro, The* | 12a | 110 |
| | Callan's Crack**** | 12a | 234 |
| | Coyote, The**** | 12a | 147 |
| | Crosstown** | 12a | 98 |
| | Departed** | 12a | 234 |
| | Easy Eukie*** | 12a | 218 |
| | Ever After* | 12a | 121 |
| | Fake News** | 12a | 52 |
| | Forbidden Fruit** | 12a | 151 |
| | Fourth Floor Walk-up | 12a | 129 |
| | Go Spuds Go*** | 12a | 44 |
| | Golgotha* | 12a | 128 |
| | Guillotine*** | 12a | 282 |
| | Heartbreaker*** | 12a | 237 |
| | High As I Wanna Be* | 12a | 149 |
| | I Can't Look Away** | 12a | 127 |
| | I.P.A.*** | 12a | 169 |
| | J.F.K.** | 12a | 234 |
| | Jersey Snake Bite* | 12a | 52 |
| | Juwana Arête** | 12a | 147 |
| | Lichen It** | 12a | 73 |
| | Low Tide** | 12a | 170 |
| | Make My Day | 12a | 124 |
| | Mirror Mirror*** | 12a | 272 |
| | Mirrors* | 12a | 127 |
| | Mother Russia* | 12a | 123 |
| | Not Dead Yet* | 12a | 128 |
| | O.D.K.**** | 12a | 61 |
| | One of These Days* | 12a | 113 |
| | Papa's Bulge** | 12a | 181 |
| | Patio Face** | 12a | 195 |
| | Perfect Day | 12a | 124 |
| | Poopoo Plater*** | 12a | 235 |
| | Poudre Pie** | 12a | 76 |
| | Radu** | 12a | 100 |
| | Red Planet** | 12a | 77 |
| | Shearing, The** | 12a | 110 |
| | Small Fry*** | 12a | 76 |
| | Smashing Young Ram* | 12a | 111 |
| | Snake** | 12a | 266 |
| | So Long Self** | 12a | 127 |
| | Soot** | 12a | 58 |
| | Sporting Green*** | 12a | 79 |
| | Swayze Express, The*** | 12a | 157 |
| | Tear Down This Wall* | 12a | 123 |
| | Three Ring Circus* | 12a | 218 |
| | Ticking Clock | 12a | 107 |
| | Till We Have Faces ** | 12a | 116 |
| | Vishokkuxxud-pokkuxxda*** | 12a | 94 |
| | Visine** | 12a | 275 |
| | Way to Dusty Death, The* | 12a | 128 |
| | When My Body Dies** | 12a | 164 |
| | White as Snow*** | 12a | 119 |
| | Wizened, The** | 12a | 155 |
| | You Call This PayDay? | 12a | 124 |
| | Zebra*** | 12a | 266 |
| | Aquatron*** | 12b | 279 |
| | Bad Monkey*** | 12b | 270 |
| | Big Black Moose**** | 12b | 242 |
| | Bitchy Sister** | 12b | 146 |
| | Black Eye In Overtime** | 12b | 59 |
| | Boat Drinks*** | 12b | 272 |
| | Bubbles** | 12b | 156 |
| | Bum Lung, The* | 12b | 162 |
| | Bunker Hill** | 12b | 237 |
| | Castle Magic*** | 12b | 98 |
| | Chainsaw Massacre** | 12b | 271 |
| | Chimpanzee** | 12b | 266 |
| | Crimson Stain** | 12b | 119 |
| | Crossing Over*** | 12b | 102 |
| | Elijah** | 12b | 58 |
| | Emerald Eisle*** | 12b | 99 |
| | First Blood** | 12b | 275 |
| | Freeze the Moon at Dawn* | 12b | 125 |

## INDEX

|  |  |  |
|---|---|---|
| General Lee, The** | 12b | 67 |
| Golden Arête** | 12b | 195 |
| Good Ol' Boys* | 12b | 67 |
| Half-Mast*** | 12b | 56 |
| I Still Can't Sleep* | 12b | 113 |
| Knochenmann* | 12b | 128 |
| Laconia** | 12b | 116 |
| Magic Machine** | 12b | 98 |
| Mass Appeal** | 12b | 60 |
| Megadittos* | 12b | 118 |
| Moose Knuckles*** | 12b | 60 |
| Muffin Top*** | 12b | 154 |
| Odyssey, The*** | 12b | 47 |
| Orion Skies** | 12b | 279 |
| Overtime** | 12b | 59 |
| Red Hot Space Suit*** | 12b | 77 |
| Rock Wars* | 12b | 171 |
| Roll The Bonez* | 12b | 80 |
| Scrilla, The*** | 12b | 155 |
| Shit, Piss, Spit Up & Drool** | 12b | 72 |
| Short Stack* | 12b | 283 |
| Sidewinder** | 12b | 164 |
| Slow and Steady** | 12b | 195 |
| Snake Eyes*** | 12b | 161 |
| Someday Never Comes*** | 12b | 102 |
| Soul** | 12b | 164 |
| Tailspin**** | 12b | 61 |
| Tantrum*** | 12b | 276 |
| Tombstone* | 12b | 275 |
| Tonka*** | 12b | 242 |
| Vide Noir*** | 12b | 279 |
| Water Rights*** | 12b | 278 |
| Balcony Railbumper** | 12c | 41 |
| Be Not Afraid* | 12c | 123 |
| Benchmark, The*** | 12c | 171 |
| Big Mac*** | 12c | 76 |
| BlackWave** | 12c | 64 |
| Box Cars** | 12c | 161 |
| Bullwinkle** | 12c | 242 |
| Cannon Ball** | 12c | 75 |
| Cappuccino** | 12c | 119 |
| Cirque Du Poudre*** | 12c | 81 |
| Das Leben der Anderen* | 12c | 123 |
| Duff* | 12c | 170 |
| Feather Tree** | 12c | 52 |
| Frosted Fracture* | 12c | 169 |
| Frozen Echo** | 12c | 57 |
| Gippeto** | 12c | 181 |
| Glaeken** | 12c | 100 |
| Golden Boy*** | 12c | 276 |
| Gorilla** | 12c | 266 |
| How Bout Dem Apples** | 12c | 235 |
| Intergalactic*** | 12c | 265 |
| Keelhaul*** | 12c | 56 |
| Marshmallow*** | 12c | 146 |
| Money for Nothing** | 12c | 155 |
| Orangutan** | 12c | 268 |
| Pinklebear, The** | 12c | 61 |
| Pocket Talk** | 12c | 218 |
| Red Dawn** | 12c | 272 |
| Silver Leaner** | 12c | 100 |
| Sunday's Child*** | 12c | 72 |
| Vista Cruiser Extension*** | 12c | 218 |
| Wake Of The Red Witch** | 12c | 80 |
| Where's The Beef?*** | 12c | 71 |
| Wihizzle Dihizzle*** | 12c | 154 |
| Against the grain** | 12d | 156 |
| Cobra Kai** | 12d | 161 |
| Duke of Weselton** | 12d | 146 |
| Escape From The Gnar | 12d | 195 |
| Eye In The Sky*** | 12d | 67 |
| Ghost in the Machine*** | 12d | 118 |
| Golden Man** | 12d | 155 |
| Marky Mark*** | 12d | 235 |
| Orange Crimpsicle** | 12d | 64 |
| Rapid Fire** | 12d | 75 |
| Reckoning*** | 12d | 100 |
| Saint Lupe Arete** | 12d | 270 |
| ShoNuff** | 12d | 154 |
| Smoke Trail** | 12d | 242 |
| Time Lost** | 12d | 271 |
| Way She Goes, The** | 12d | 157 |
| Wild and Scenic*** | 12d | 159 |

## 5.13

|  |  |  |
|---|---|---|
| Blonde Note*** | 13a | 170 |
| Copperhead** | 13a | 164 |
| Corona** | 13a | 170 |
| Dream Of Poudre**** | 13a | 61 |
| Eukie Extension*** | 13a | 218 |
| Fog of War** | 13a | 272 |
| Foreplay/Longtime**** | 13a | 237 |
| Jolly Jane**** | 13a | 235 |
| Obituary** | 13a | 79 |
| Rhino** | 13a | 266 |
| Taco Bell*** | 13a | 129 |
| Tea Party** | 13a | 234 |
| Twinkletoes*** | 13a | 60 |
| Widowmaker, The*** | 13a | 92 |
| Alpha Omega*** | 13b | 272 |
| Anunnaki**** | 13b | 777 |
| Black Beast** | 13b | 193 |
| Cryokinetic** | 13b | 146 |
| Dark Pony** | 13b | 61 |
| Eukie Arête** | 13b | 218 |
| Golden Pagoda*** | 13b | 180 |
| Gulf Stream** | 13b | 60 |
| Journey to Pluto** | 13b | 265 |
| Kona Blend** | 13b | 170 |
| Landing Strip*** | 13b | 154 |
| Miguel*** | 13b | 242 |
| Prometheus Rising**** | 13b | 93 |
| Red Dragon** | 13b | 282 |
| Red Rocket*** | 13b | 52 |
| Samson Ale** | 13b | 170 |
| Sin of Man*** | 13b | 137 |
| Southie Boyz*** | 13b | 237 |
| Cradle of Liberty**** | 13c | 234 |
| Diamondback*** | 13c | 163 |
| Eyes of the World*** | 13c | 197 |
| Folsom Flute*** | 13c | 61 |
| Harmonic Resonance*** | 13c | 169 |
| Hefeweizen** | 13c | 170 |
| Honest Jon*** | 13c | 181 |
| Monstro*** | 13c | 181 |
| Rustic Wilderness**** | 13c | 159 |
| Slippery Slope*** | 13c | 218 |
| Wildest Dreams**** | 13c | 159 |
| Coach Myles*** | 13d | 270 |
| Paul Revere**** | 13d | 234 |
| Straw Into Gold*** | 13d | 218 |

## 5.14

|  |  |  |
|---|---|---|
| Albatross, The**** | 14a | 270 |
| Chocolate Stout*** | 14a | 169 |
| Dirty Diet Coke** | 14a | 170 |
| Creme de la Poudre*** | 14b | 218 |
| Scorsese**** | 14c | 235 |

## v0 - v2

|  |  |  |
|---|---|---|
| Right Arête* | v0 | 222 |
| Start Something** | v0 | 286 |
| Green Thumb* | v1 | 230 |
| Big Flake | v1 | 249 |
| Black Arête* | v1 | 213 |
| Diamond Arête** | v1 | 231 |
| Dingleberry* | v1 | 89 |
| Downclimb | v1 | 243 |
| Moderate Straight Up* | v1 | 226 |
| Sloper Jumpstart*** | v1 | 221 |
| Ugly Duck** | v1 | 285 |
| Unknown Slab 2 | v1 | 35 |
| Warmup Crack** | v1 | 248 |
| Unknown Slab 1 | v1 | 35 |
| v1 | v1 | 185 |
| Warmup Crack | v1 | 248 |
| A Double Edged Sword*** | v2 | 92 |
| Auldridge Jump Problem* | v2 | 221 |
| Ben's Face* | v2 | 130 |
| Blocky Arête* | v2 | 48 |
| Bouldering Traverse* | v2 | 42 |
| Chess** | v2 | 91 |
| Crack in a Ship** | v2 | 36 |
| Dudley's Arête* | v2 | 130 |
| Easy Arête** | v2 | 224 |
| Easy Sit* | v2 | 49 |
| Ground Up Arête** | v2 | 131 |
| Hydrology* | v2 | 48 |
| Maritime** | v2 | 288 |
| Middle Up** | v2 | 226 |
| Moderate On Left Face* | v2 | 222 |
| Moderate Warmup* | v2 | 229 |
| Moss Fest | v2 | 248 |
| Old Luke** | v2 | 212 |
| Party in the Back*** | v2 | 133 |
| Pigeon* | v2 | 137 |
| Right Side* | v2 | 208 |
| Slither*** | v2 | 141 |
| Slopey Mantel | v2 | 243 |
| Soggy Doggy** | v2 | 260 |
| Stolen Rib** | v2 | 142 |
| Toaster, The*** | v2 | 231 |
| Treebeard* | v2 | 141 |
| Triangle** | v2 | 213 |

## v3 - v4

|  |  |  |
|---|---|---|
| Angle Dangle** | v3 | 226 |
| Arête-o-matic* | v3 | 133 |
| Around The World** | v3 | 89 |
| Beau Dirt** | v3 | 251 |
| Ben's Face** | v3 | 229 |
| Branch Action* | v3 | 285 |
| Cavalry** | v3 | 287 |
| Center 1* | v3 | 208 |
| Center 2* | v3 | 208 |
| Center Indian* | v3 | 203 |
| Chossy Arête | v3 | 231 |

# INDEX

| Route | Grade | Page |
|---|---|---|
| Classic Warmup*** | v3 | 240 |
| Dark Tower, The** | v3 | 213 |
| Dixie Dingo** | v3 | 197 |
| Don't Tell Mom** | v3 | 240 |
| Ducks in a Row** | v3 | 285 |
| Fable, The**** | v3 | 143 |
| Fin King | v3 | 192 |
| Hank's Other Arête** | v3 | 222 |
| Hello* | v3 | 261 |
| Jump Start* | v3 | 188 |
| Ladies Way* | v3 | 202 |
| Ledge-o-matic* | v3 | 133 |
| Left Variation* | v3 | 212 |
| Little Stripes** | v3 | 213 |
| Lone Highway** | v3 | 248 |
| Mace, The** | v3 | 222 |
| Murky Waters*** | v3 | 213 |
| Old Frenchy*** | v3 | 212 |
| Project Man Dime*** | v3 | 130 |
| Rainbow Direct | v3 | 143 |
| Right Arête* | v3 | 261 |
| Right Variation* | v3 | 212 |
| Rope Ladder | v3 | 189 |
| Scrimps | v3 | 192 |
| Shadows Edge* | v3 | 213 |
| Slip and Slide** | v3 | 131 |
| Slopey Arête | v3 | 206 |
| South Face** | v3 | 226 |
| Southeast Slab* | v3 | 203 |
| Southwest Arête** | v3 | 226 |
| Southwest Slab* | v3 | 203 |
| Stone Record*** | v3 | 260 |
| Sue's Face*** | v3 | 206 |
| Tall Face | v3 | 205 |
| Throne, The*** | v3 | 90 |
| Void Bop, The* | v3 | 287 |
| Warm Me*** | v3 | 226 |
| Warm-Up Roof | v3 | 246 |
| Warmup II* | v3 | 202 |
| Another Pat's Arête** | v4 | 207 |
| Arête #19** | v4 | 205 |
| Beachside Face | v4 | 202 |
| Ben's Goofy Face** | v4 | 229 |
| Blitzcrieg** | v4 | 254 |
| Brown Jump** | v4 | 177 |
| Butt Dragger Traverse* | v4 | 49 |
| Center Perfection*** | v4 | 260 |
| Charlie Chaplin* | v4 | 138 |
| Crossroads** | v4 | 191 |
| Cut With A Sword* | v4 | 286 |
| Dingus*** | v4 | 201 |
| Dracula** | v4 | 289 |
| Duchess*** | v4 | 286 |
| Face Right Of Indian Ladder | v4 | 203 |
| Face* | v4 | 249 |
| French Press | v4 | 91 |
| Full Frontal** | v4 | 197 |
| It's Ice** | v4 | 225 |
| King Fin*** | v4 | 192 |
| Left Arête** | v4 | 248 |
| Moderate In Hole | v4 | 230 |
| Moderate* | v4 | 225 |
| Moss King | v4 | 89 |
| Mr. Harry*** | v4 | 222 |
| Mushroom, The* | v4 | 90 |
| Nutsack Hoedown*** | v4 | 188 |
| Opal Arête*** | v4 | 189 |
| Orange Arête | v4 | 202 |
| Pegmatite* | v4 | 230 |
| Pinch Problem** | v4 | 248 |
| Prometheus Dabbing** | v4 | 133 |
| Rainbow Traverse | v4 | 143 |
| Rapture, The*** | v4 | 132 |
| Right Hand Man** | v4 | 225 |
| River Mechanics** | v4 | 48 |
| Round Room* | v4 | 175 |
| Rucksack Showdown** | v4 | 188 |
| Second Thoughts*** | v4 | 246 |
| Shireman Problem** | v4 | 49 |
| Squeeze Arête** | v4 | 208 |
| Squire*** | v4 | 286 |
| T-Bone Right** | v4 | 227 |
| Tangerine Sky*** | v4 | 213 |
| Tomahawk Chop*** | v4 | 261 |
| When Angels Dance*** | v4 | 229 |
| Will's Face/Arête** | v4 | 188 |
| Working the Corner*** | v4 | 136 |

## v5 - v6

| Route | Grade | Page |
|---|---|---|
| 40 Grit** | v5 | 188 |
| All the King's Men** | v5 | 287 |
| Au Revoir** | v5 | 261 |
| Baby Black* | v5 | 240 |
| Bat Outta Hell** | v5 | 289 |
| Ben's Craptastic Traverse* | v5 | 223 |
| Bubblicious** | v5 | 188 |
| Center Right** | v5 | 177 |
| Chucky** | v5 | 223 |
| Crusher*** | v5 | 231 |
| Dave's Dihedral* | v5 | 203 |
| Dingleberry Traverse* | v5 | 89 |
| Down and Below** | v5 | 246 |
| Drawbridge** | v5 | 286 |
| Flesh Eater** | v5 | 223 |
| Fran's Problem* | v5 | 188 |
| Hank's Arête** | v5 | 221 |
| Hank's Lunge*** | v5 | 221 |
| Hippie Mafia** | v5 | 140 |
| Indian Ladder**** | v5 | 203 |
| Johnny & Hodgey** | v5 | 222 |
| Landscaper, The** | v5 | 36 |
| Lighthouse, The*** | v5 | 288 |
| Long Time Gone** | v5 | 240 |
| Mike's Roof | v5 | 37 |
| Open Book** | v5 | 143 |
| Pinchy Sit** | v5 | 174 |
| Pinchy Underclings** | v5 | 175 |
| Pocket Slab*** | v5 | 136 |
| Puffing Stone*** | v5 | 224 |
| Quilling Me Softly** | v5 | 260 |
| Ridin' Spinnaz* | v5 | 192 |
| Seam** | v5 | 175 |
| Slopey Thrutch | v5 | 202 |
| Thick Cuts** | v5 | 284 |
| Wave 2* | v5 | 230 |
| Will's Problem** | v5 | 231 |
| Against Humanity**** | v6 | 248 |
| All the King's Horses** | v6 | 287 |
| Black Pearl** | v6 | 191 |
| Blue Feather*** | v6 | 140 |
| Corkscrew** | v6 | 251 |
| Crazy Cody** | v6 | 229 |
| Crows Nest*** | v6 | 209 |
| Daytripper Arête** | v6 | 189 |
| Defiance** | v6 | 288 |
| Dynesto** | v6 | 201 |
| Fang* | v6 | 89 |
| Filth Pig* | v6 | 215 |
| Galleon** | v6 | 209 |
| Gandalf**** | v6 | 249 |
| Ghost Train**** | v6 | 131 |
| Goldrusher** | v6 | 231 |
| Half Mast** | v6 | 209 |
| Hank's Rig** | v6 | 192 |
| Hot Drinks** | v6 | 191 |
| I Peed My Pants in Chalk*** | v6 | 209 |
| Iron Helix*** | v6 | 202 |
| Knees for Life** | v6 | 261 |
| Layback Variation** | v6 | 136 |
| Longmont Rimjob* | v6 | 251 |
| Mantel Mussel** | v6 | 132 |
| Moonbeam** | v6 | 189 |
| Moonrise** | v6 | 139 |
| Orange-Faced Devil*** | v6 | 141 |
| Over the Rainbow | v6 | 143 |
| Pardon My French | v6 | 91 |
| Perch** | v6 | 226 |
| Pi** | v6 | 141 |
| Pinch Jump** | v6 | 212 |
| Pocket Arête*** | v6 | 49 |
| Point Break* | v6 | 90 |
| Quantum Leap** | v6 | 92 |
| Railin Bars** | v6 | 255 |
| Root Canal** | v6 | 206 |
| Scarface*** | v6 | 221 |
| Scorpion and the Bobcat, The** | v6 | 36 |
| Serpentine** | v6 | 206 |
| Shambo Overhang* | v6 | 207 |
| Short Chubby Demon*** | v6 | 225 |
| Simple*** | v6 | 206 |
| Sloper Gold** | v6 | 240 |
| Split Stream* | v6 | 213 |
| Squeeze Box, The** | v6 | 89 |
| Squeeze Problem** | v6 | 248 |
| Strike** | v6 | 141 |
| Swan*** | v6 | 285 |
| Take a Knee* | v6 | 241 |
| Thin Ice** | v6 | 174 |
| Thumb, The* | v6 | 230 |
| Treedigger** | v6 | 285 |
| Tricky Dicky* | v6 | 177 |
| Tsunami ** | v6 | 227 |
| Unwilling*** | v6 | 49 |

## v7 - v8

| Route | Grade | Page |
|---|---|---|
| American Spirit** | v7 | 214 |
| Angry Black Man** | v7 | 241 |
| Bisher Traverse*** | v7 | 226 |
| Black Beard's Traverse** | v7 | 37 |
| Black Widow* | v7 | 89 |
| Blok One** | v7 | 185 |
| Clams Casino*** | v7 | 132 |
| Coat of Arms* | v7 | 286 |
| Corn Sacker** | v7 | 215 |
| Crown, The*** | v7 | 133 |
| Crunchy Grooves*** | v7 | 132 |
| Cygnus** | v7 | 285 |
| Disco Biscuit | v7 | 215 |
| Emperor's New Clothes** | v7 | 287 |
| Empty of Thought, Full of Mind*** | v7 | 287 |
| F.A.S.T. ** | v7 | 224 |
| French Arête | v7 | 35 |
| Gastoner** | v7 | 192 |
| Green Monster** | v7 | 205 |
| H.A.L.** | v7 | 214 |
| Herm's Micro Mantel* | v7 | 224 |
| High Noon** | v7 | 203 |
| Hippie Jump** | v7 | 140 |

## INDEX

|  |  |  |
|---|---|---|
| Hippo Hoedown*** | v7 | 142 |
| Jason's Little Thingy** | v7 | 177 |
| Ligre, The*** | v7 | 222 |
| Merlin*** | v7 | 243 |
| Mr. Smackmag*** | v7 | 202 |
| Phoenix*** | v7 | 137 |
| Rasta Drop*** | v7 | 189 |
| Rasta Font Trainer** | v7 | 223 |
| Saddle Up** | v7 | 205 |
| Scarbanzo** | v7 | 92 |
| Scuba Steve* | v7 | 223 |
| Slice and Dice* | v7 | 89 |
| Smoke Dragon*** | v7 | 132 |
| Snakepit** | v7 | 35 |
| Sonic Boom** | v7 | 286 |
| Spidey Arête** | v7 | 261 |
| Thin N' Crispy** | v7 | 230 |
| Tilt*** | v7 | 229 |
| Tractor Beam** | v7 | 253 |
| Traverse Variation** | v7 | 201 |
| Vanilla Ice*** | v7 | 177 |
| Wave 1* | v7 | 230 |
| Wave Goodbye*** | v7 | 261 |
| White Elephant** | v7 | 142 |
| Above and Beyond*** | v8 | 246 |
| Bisher Arête** | v8 | 206 |
| Blake's Dyno** | v8 | 90 |
| Chivalry*** | v8 | 286 |
| Chromosphere** | v8 | 49 |
| Crime** | v8 | 248 |
| Devil Wears Lace* | v8 | 89 |
| Face Down, Ass Up* | v8 | 192 |
| Fire Pit* | v8 | 229 |
| Flow Futuristic** | v8 | 249 |
| Geriatrics** | v8 | 254 |
| Graveyard Machine*** | v8 | 214 |
| Gutterball** | v8 | 261 |
| Hickman Over the Poudre Bridge* | v8 | 225 |
| Hot Fire*** | v8 | 138 |
| Jester*** | v8 | 285 |
| Johnny Karate** | v8 | 252 |
| Last King, The**** | v8 | 286 |
| Le Don*** | v8 | 91 |
| Life of Pie*** | v8 | 141 |
| Lock and Key** | v8 | 140 |
| Low Water Arête | v8 | 48 |
| Medallion*** | v8 | 289 |
| Miss Rose** | v8 | 137 |
| One Ton Ho** | v8 | 221 |
| Pain Train** | v8 | 188 |
| Panty Line*** | v8 | 197 |
| Pinon** | v8 | 215 |
| Redline** | v8 | 255 |
| Rocket Man** | v8 | 241 |
| Room With No View** | v8 | 284 |
| Rude Beauty**** | v8 | 260 |
| Sage*** | v8 | 212 |
| Shmamie's Slopers* | v8 | 188 |
| Small Axe**** | v8 | 191 |
| Snakeskin** | v8 | 35 |
| Sparkle** | v8 | 207 |
| Stickman Crossing the Brooklyn Bridge* | v8 | 225 |
| Stone Cold*** | v8 | 138 |
| T-Bone** | v8 | 227 |
| Toll Booth Willie** | v8 | 231 |
| Treading Water*** | v8 | 260 |
| Tsunami Traverse** | v8 | 227 |
| Walk the Plank | v8 | 209 |
| We Three Kings*** | v8 | 286 |
| White Stripe*** | v8 | 213 |
| Xerox* | v8 | 284 |

### v9 - v10

|  |  |  |
|---|---|---|
| Aesop** | v9 | 143 |
| Backburner* | v9 | 138 |
| Big Oyster*** | v9 | 189 |
| Black Problem*** | v9 | 241 |
| Charlemagne**** | v9 | 286 |
| Computer Blue** | v9 | 214 |
| Courting Doom** | v9 | 249 |
| Crescent, The*** | v9 | 139 |
| Crown Low** | v9 | 133 |
| Daniel's Problem** | v9 | 202 |
| Dead Hand*** | v9 | 140 |
| Divergence*** | v9 | 229 |
| Fire On Ice*** | v9 | 175 |
| Flight Syndrome*** | v9 | 251 |
| Full Mast*** | v9 | 209 |
| Grey Matter** | v9 | 223 |
| Harder They Come*** | v9 | 249 |
| Ice 9** | v9 | 175 |
| Jousting At Windmills** | v9 | 229 |
| Ken's Roof** | v9 | 205 |
| Last Day on Earth* | v9 | 132 |
| Last Past** | v9 | 212 |
| Law of the Land*** | v9 | 174 |
| Mike's Arête** | v9 | 252 |
| Narrow Control*** | v9 | 138 |
| Neon Demon** | v9 | 255 |
| Occam's Razor*** | v9 | 240 |
| Olaf's Bulge*** | v9 | 251 |
| Pat's Crack | v9 | 252 |
| Phantom Menace**** | v9 | 131 |
| Pink Panther* | v9 | 90 |
| Polychrome** | v9 | 255 |
| Saddle Down*** | v9 | 205 |
| Sharma Lunge | v9 | 223 |
| Shoeless Trippin'In The Poudre** | v9 | 207 |
| Sonic Alchemist*** | v9 | 286 |
| Submarine*** | v9 | 143 |
| Wipe Out | v9 | 230 |
| Blok Two** | v10 | 185 |
| Bone Tomahawk** | v10 | 90 |
| Centerfold** | v10 | 230 |
| Cloudwalker*** | v10 | 230 |
| Cookie Monster*** | v10 | 207 |
| Deadmoo5** | v10 | 231 |
| Dump Truck** | v10 | 248 |
| Fire Proof*** | v10 | 92 |
| Grey Goose*** | v10 | 285 |
| Lonely Bone*** | v10 | 284 |
| Maybe Baby** | v10 | 251 |
| Mouserat** | v10 | 252 |
| Mutations* | v10 | 212 |
| Natural Selection** | v10 | 251 |
| One Arm Scissor** | v10 | 249 |
| Oracle, The*** | v10 | 143 |
| Orbital Resonance** | v10 | 249 |
| Pearl Necklace**** | v10 | 246 |
| Promised Lands* | v10 | 136 |
| Renee** | v10 | 254 |
| Scalp Collector** | v10 | 137 |
| Sluice Box** | v10 | 254 |
| Sunny*** | v10 | 251 |
| Super Chrome*** | v10 | 49 |
| Twilight*** | v10 | 154 |
| Under The Gaydar* | v10 | 205 |
| Will's Slab** | v10 | 222 |

### v11 - Above

|  |  |  |
|---|---|---|
| Blok of Aragon* | v11 | 185 |
| Boogie Nights*** | v11 | 215 |
| Canopener*** | v11 | 225 |
| Castaway** | v11 | 208 |
| Diamond in the Rough** | v11 | 49 |
| Fire on the Mountain*** | v11 | 92 |
| Flex Industry*** | v11 | 246 |
| Gypsies, Tramps, & Thieves** | v11 | 154 |
| Paper Tiger** | v11 | 255 |
| Public Property | v11 | 221 |
| Shapes and Sizes*** | v11 | 253 |
| Tiger Milk*** | v11 | 261 |
| Beckoning Silence, The*** | v12 | 189 |
| Black Swan** | v12 | 249 |
| Critical Mass** | v12 | 192 |
| Dihedral With An Undercling*** | v12 | 253 |
| Samurai** | v12 | 90 |
| Sea of Simulation*** | v12 | 252 |
| What's Left Of The Bottom Of My Heart** | v12 | 223 |
| Circadian Rhythm*** | v13 | 225 |
| Swiss Army** | v13 | 225 |